Vanished Civilizations

PUBLISHED BY
THE READER'S DIGEST ASSOCIATION LIMITED
LONDON · NEW YORK · SYDNEY · MONTREAL

Contents

Timelines across history

BC	Europe	Middle East
Before 7000	*c.*10,000 As ice sheets retreat, hunter-gatherers move north and colonize northern Britain, northern Germany, and Scandinavia; more land becomes available around the Alps. Dogs are domesticated.	*c.*11,000 Dogs are domesticated. *c.*9000 Earliest agriculture in the Levant in the eastern Mediterranean. *c.*7500 Sheep and goats are first herded in mountains of western Iran.
7000	*c.*6500 Earliest agriculture and pottery in Greece and the Balkans.	*c.*7000 First stone ramparts built at Jericho. Farming communities become widespread. The earliest fired pottery is made at Ganj Dareh. Neolithic settlement begins at Çatal Hüyük. *c.*6500 Copper smelting begins at Çatal Hüyük. Cattle are domesticated.
6000	*c.*6000 First agricultural settlements in southern Central Europe.	6000–5000 First Neolithic settlements at Ugarit in Syria and Nineveh in Iraq. *c.*5500 First irrigated agriculture at Choga Mami in Iraq. Settlements appear in southern Mesopotamia, later to become cities of Eridu, Ur, and Al-ubaid.
5000	*c.*5000 Farming communities established in western Europe. Metalworking in copper and gold begins in the Balkans. 4500–3500 Earliest agriculture in Britain and northern Europe. First megalithic tombs constructed in western Europe.	4500 Ubaid culture of southern Mesopotamia spreads throughout northern Mesopotamia and adjacent areas.
4000	*c.*3500 Copperworking spreads across southern and eastern Europe.	*c.*4000 Foundation of Susa in Elam. *c.*3600 The Mesopotamian city of Uruk emerges. Copper casting begins in many areas, including Nahal Mishmar in Palestine. *c.*3300 Invention of writing in Sumer. Wheeled vehicles and potter's wheel developed in Mesopotamia.
3000	*c.*3000 Beginning of Bronze Age in Greece and Crete. 2500 Horses, wheeled vehicles, and the plough now widespread in Europe. Copperworking spreads to Britain.	*c.*3000 Bronze Age begins in Asia Minor. 2600–2100 Royal tombs of Ur constructed. *c.*2350 Semitic kingdom of Akkad established in southern Mesopotamia. Destruction of Mari, which is rebuilt within Sargon of Akkad's realm. 2113–2004 Ur reaches a peak under its 3rd dynasty. Ziggurats are built.
2000	*c.*2000 First palaces built in Crete at Knossos, Phaestos, and Mallia. Fortified settlements appear in eastern and central Europe – sites include Barca and Spissky Stvrtok in the Carpathians.	1900–1700 Emergence in Asia Minor of a Hittite kingdom that becomes centre of Hittite Empire. *c.*1900 Beginning of ironworking in Asia Minor.
1800	*c.*1700 Earthquakes destroy first palaces in Crete; they are rebuilt. *c.*1650 Linear A script first used by the Minoans at Knossos on Crete.	*c.*1800 Peak of Mari civilization. Shamshi-Adad founds empire in Assyria. 1792–1750 Hammurabi extends Babylonian empire into southern Mesopotamia. 1759 Hammurabi destroys Mari after defeating its ruler, Zimri-Lim. *c.*1700 First alphabetic script devised by Canaanites working in Sinai.
1600	*c.*1600 Achaeans found kingdom at Mycenae. Peak of Minoan civilization, the influence of which spreads throughout the Aegean world.	*c.*1596 Hittite king Mursilis I takes Babylon, ending the Hammurabi dynasty. Kassite barbarians take over Babylonia.
1400	*c.*1400 Linear B script first used at Knossos. End of Minoan civilization. Mycenaeans settle in Crete and trade throughout the eastern and central Mediterranean.	1380–1346 Reign of Hittite ruler Suppiluliumas; he conquers Syria and takes the Hittite Empire to its peak, with Hattusas as its capital. 1366–1330 Under Ashur-Uballit I, Assyria becomes independent of Babylonia. 1350–1250 Peak of Ugarit civilization. Use of Ugaritic alphabetic cuneiform script. In Asia Minor, period VII of Troy – thought to have been the Troy of Homer's *Iliad*.
1300	1250–1150 Destruction of Mycenaean towns in Greece. Disappearance of Mycenaean civilization.	13th century Battle of Kadesh between the Hittites under Muwatallis II and the Egyptians under Rameses II. 1300–1100 Union of kingdoms of Susa and Anshan under the Anzanites. Kingdom of Elam extends its dominion to Babylonia.
1000	*c.*1000 Ironworking spreads through Europe. *c.*900 End of Dark Age in Greece. 850–750 The Greek poet Homer composes the *Iliad* and the *Odyssey*.	*c.*1000 Hebrew kingdom of Saul and David established. Beginning of Phoenician expansion throughout the Mediterranean. 878 Assyrian King Assurnasirpal II makes Kalhu (present-day Nimrud) his capital.
800	*c.*800 Foundation of Etruscan city of Tarquinia. 776 Traditional date of first Olympic Games in Olympia, Greece. 753 Traditional date of founding of Rome. 668 Foundation of Byzantium in Turkey as a Greek colony.	713 Sargon II founds Dur-Sharrukin (present-day Khorsabad) as Assyrian capital. 704–681 Reign of Sennacherib in Assyria. His capital is founded at Nineveh, and the empire reaches its peak. 646 Assyrians sack Susa.
600	*c.*600 Greeks establish trading colony at Massilia (modern Marseille). 509 Republic established in Rome. 490-479 Greece and Persia at war. 478 Formation of Delian League, initially around Greek island of Delos.	539 Cyrus, king of the Persians, takes Babylon. 522 Darius I ascends the Persian throne; begins to reorganize and extend his large empire, making Persepolis the new capital. 486 Xerxes becomes Persian king and continues the building of Persepolis.

Africa	Asia	The Americas
		BC
*c.*8500 Hunter-gatherer communities in the Sahara create earliest rock art in the form of engravings on stone.	*c.*11,000 World's first pottery made in Japan. **From 10,000** Jomon period of hunter-gatherers and fishers begins – the earliest major culture in Japan.	**By 10,000** Humans reach the Americas from Siberia. **By 9000** Colonizing communities reach southern tip of South America. Dogs are domesticated.
*c.*7000 Pottery appears in the Sahara. *c.*6500 Cattle herded in the Sahara.	*c.*7000–6500 First farmers at Mehrgarh in Pakistan. *c.*6500–6000 First farmers in China grow millet in the Huang He (Yellow River) valley and rice in the Chang Jiang (Yangtze) valley.	**Around 6500** Beginning of plant cultivation in parts of the Andes.
*c.*6000 First farming communities in the Nile Valley in Egypt.	**Before 5000** Pottery made at Mehrgarh in Pakistan.	*c.*5600 Wild squashes, avocados, and other plants gathered in Central America.
*c.*4500 Agriculture established in Egypt. First settlements emerge in Fayum on the Upper Nile.	*c.*4500 Water conservation methods developed for farming, encouraging growth of settlements in Indo-Iranian borderlands.	*c.*5000 Wild maize harvested in Mexico.
*c.*4000 Beginning of agriculture in sub-Saharan Africa. Extension of Egyptian influence southwards. Corpses are naturally mummified by burial in dry sand. **3300** First walled towns appear in Egypt.	*c.*4000 In China, jade traded as a luxury commodity; first painted ceramics made by the Yangshao culture. **4000–3500** Farming communities spread into Indus valley; found settlement at Harappa by 3300.	*c.*4000 Domestication of llamas and guinea pigs in Andean region. **4000–3600** Pottery made in Amazonia and Colombia. *c.*3800 Fishing communities in coastal Peru weave mats from wild fibres and begin cultivation.
*c.*3000 Hieroglyphics are developed. *c.*3100 Unification of Upper and Lower Egypt. *c.*2700 Foundation of Egyptian Old Kingdom. **2600–2500** Great pyramids built at Giza. *c.*2100 Foundation of Egyptian Middle Kingdom.	*c.*3000 First copper working in China. **2700** First silk weaving in China. *c.*2700–2600 Harappa in Indus Valley becomes a city; the Harappans develop a written language.	*c.*3000 Seaworthy rafts used by Andean cultures. *c.*2500 Potatoes cultivated in Andes; large temple complexes constructed. *c.*2350 Appearance of crude pottery in Mexico.
2000–1500 Egyptian control extends through Nubia, the region along the Nile, south of Egypt.	**2000** Bronze in use in Indus Valley.	*c.*2000 Advance in loom weaving occurs in Peru with use of heddles – rods which separate warp threads to allow passage of shuttle.
*c.*1786 Middle Kingdom ends after invasion of the Hyksos, immigrants from Palestine or Syria.	*c.*1800 Complex bronze vessels cast in China. Decline of Indus civilization at cities of Harappa and Mohenjo-Daro. *c.*1700 Foundation of Shang dynasty in China – first dynasty for which there is documentary evidence.	*c.*1800 Cultivation of sunflower and other local plants in south-east North America.
*c.*1570 The kings of Thebes – Kamose and Ahmose – drive out the Hyksos and rebuild the Egyptian empire; New Kingdom begins.	*c.*1600 The earliest known Chinese writing is inscribed on oracle bones in the form of questions addressed to the gods, which were answered using divination techniques.	*c.*1500 Metalworking develops in Peru.
1379–1362 Reign of Akhenaten; foundation of the city of Amarna. *c.*1360 Tutankhamun succeeds Smenkhkare as pharaoh of Egypt.	**14th century** In China, Anyang becomes the capital of the Shang.	*c.*1400 Maize-growing spreads to coastal regions of Peru.
1198–1166 Reign of Pharaoh Rameses III; he inflicts several defeats on marauders from the Mycenaean world known as the Sea Peoples.	*c.*1122 Foundation of Western Zhou dynasty. *c.*1027 Western Zhou dynasty overthrows Shang dynasty.	*c.*1200 Birth of the earliest complex culture in Central America, the Olmecs of the southern coast of the Gulf of Mexico, and the earliest in Peru, the Chavín. Olmec ceremonial centre built at San Lorenzo.
*c.*920 Foundation of a Nubian dynasty which conquers Egypt. **814** Foundation of Carthage.	**1000–800** Farming villages established in Ganges Valley. Iron working becomes widespread in India.	*c.*1000 Copper smelting begins in the Andes.
671 Assyrians conquer Egypt.	*c.*770 Eastern Zhou dynasty sets up its capital at Luoyang.	*c.*800 Temple complex constructed at Chavín de Huantar in Peru. Early Maya settle in villages at Tikal (in present-day Guatemala). La Venta on the gulf coast of Mexico becomes main Olmec ceremonial centre.
525 Cambyses II, king of Persia and son of Cyrus the Great, conquers Egypt. *c.*500 Fine terracotta sculptures produced by the flourishing Nok civilization in Nigeria.	*c.*500 Founding of Pataliputra, capital of the Mauryan dynasty, which controls most of India by 320 BC. *c.*450–400 Tombs of nomadic horsemen built at Pazyryk in Siberia's Altai Mountains.	*c.*500 Peak of the Olmec civilization in Central America. Construction of city of Monte Albán, centre of Zapotec and Mixtec culture, in Oaxaca Valley, Mexico.

	Europe	Middle East
400	**336–323** Reign of Alexander the Great; he conquers Egypt and subjugates most of western Asia. **219** Carthaginian general Hannibal marches on Italy.	**4th century** The Nabataeans settle in Petra. **331** Alexander the Great burns Persepolis. **c.248–214** Reign of Iranian king Tiridates I; he establishes the Parthian kingdom.
200	**200–100** Peak of economic power of Delos. **196** Romans take Greek colony of Byzantium. **146** Destruction of Corinth; Greece integrated into Roman Empire. **88** Delos sacked by Asian king Mithridates. **58–50** Julius Caesar conquers Gaul.	**c.150** The Essenes, dissident Jews, settle in Qumran. **1st century** Reign of Antiochus I, king of Commagene. His shrine is built at Nimrud Dagh.
AD	**43** Romans invade Britain. **79** Vesuvius erupts, burying Herculaneum and Pompeii.	**68–70** Destruction of Jerusalem by the Roman armies. Dead Sea scrolls concealed at Qumran. **100–240** Zenith of city of Hatra. **106** Trajan annexes Petra to the Roman Empire.
100		
200	**293** Roman emperor Diocletian reorganizes his empire and founds the tetrarchy: two Augustuses and two Caesars share the government of the provinces.	**226** Ardashir defeats the Parthians in Iran; founds Sassanian dynasty of Persia. **240** Hatra taken by the Sassanian king Shapur I.
300	**313** An edict of Constantine I makes Christianity a legal religion throughout the Roman world. **393** Roman emperor Theodosius I suppresses Olympic Games. **395** Death of Theodosius: Roman Empire divided into Western and Eastern empires.	**330** Constantine I founds a second capital on the site of Byzantium, at the heart of what is to become Rome's Eastern Empire. He names the city Constantinople.
400	**410** Rome taken by Alaric, king of the Visigoths. **486** Clovis founds a great Frankish kingdom in Gaul. **492** Ostrogoths, led by Theodoric, conquer Italy.	**408** Death of Arcadius, first emperor of Rome's Eastern Empire.
500	**533–55** Eastern Roman Empire reconquers much of the West, led by Roman general Belisarius.	**527** Justinian succeeds Justin I in Constantinople. **541–6** Persia invades the Eastern Roman Empire.
600	**7th century** Barbarian kingdoms established in Europe; conversion of some groups to Christianity.	**632** Death of Muhammad, founder of Islam. **642** Islamic conquest of the Sassanian Empire.
700	**711** Arabs invade Spain. **732** Charles Martel, the Frankish chieftain, stops the Arab invasion between Poitiers and Tours, turning the tide of Arab conquest in Europe.	**750** The Omayyad caliphs of Damascus are overthrown by the Abbassids, who found Baghdad.
800	**800** Charlemagne, grandson of Charles Martel and king of the Franks, is crowned Emperor of the Romans.	**809** Death of great Abbassid caliph, Harun ar-Rashid, sparks civil war within the empire.
900	**900** Break-up of Carolingian Empire – the territories of the second Frankish ruling dynasty. **962** German king Otto I is crowned Holy Roman Emperor.	**10th century** Abbassid caliphate weakens in face of local dynasties.
1000	**1031** Beginning of reconquest of Spain from the Arabs. **1095** Pope Urban II encourages the first Crusade.	**1055** Seljuk Turks take Baghdad and begin to control Abbassid caliphate. **1071** The Turks defeat the Byzantines of the Eastern Roman Empire at Manzikert. They invade Anatolia.
1100	**1153** Frederick I Barbarossa is crowned Holy Roman Emperor. **1194** Accession of Frederick II as last great Holy Roman Emperor.	**1100–18** Baldwin I reigns as the first Frankish king of Jerusalem.
1200	**1208–29** Crusade against the Albigensians – Christian heretics based in southern France. **1236** Mongols begin conquest of Russia.	**1204** The fourth Crusade takes Constantinople and sets up an Eastern Latin Empire.
1300	**1338** Beginning of the Hundred Years War between France and England.	**1356** The Ottoman Turks – now masters of Asia Minor – establish a foothold in Europe at Gallipoli.
1400	**1429–30** Joan of Arc intervenes in the Hundred Years War. **1480** Ivan III frees Russia from Mongol rule.	**1453** The Turks, under Sultan Mehmed II, take Constantinople.
1500	**1509–47** Reign of Henry VIII in England.	**1520–56** Reign of Suleiman the Magnificent; peak of the Ottoman Empire.

Africa	Asia	The Americas
202 Carthaginian general Hannibal defeated at Zama in North Africa by Roman general Scipio Africanus.	*c.*273–236 Reign of the emperor Ashoka in India. His capital is Pataliputra. **221–206** Qin Shi Huang Di expands the Chinese Empire and builds the Great Wall. **206** The Han dynasty succeeds the Qin.	*c.*400 Decline of Olmec civilization; destruction of their ceremonial centre at La Venta.
146 Carthage destroyed by the Romans. **30** Death of Cleopatra; Egypt becomes a province of the Roman Empire.	**185** Fall of Mauryan Empire in India. *c.*100 The Silk Road opens between China and the western world.	*c.*200 First settlement at Teotihuacán in Mexico. Hopewell Indian culture emerges in North America.

AD

Africa	Asia	The Americas
*c.*70 Christianity reaches Alexandria. **1st–2nd centuries** Alexandria becomes a major centre of international trade.	*c.*80 Hippalus, a Greek navigator, opens a direct sea route to India.	*c.*100 Beginning of the Basket Maker culture in the south-west canyons of North America. Large settlement at Cuicuilco in Valley of Mexico destroyed by an earthquake; Teotihuacán develops in its place. Accession of Yax Ehb' Xook, founder of Tikal's ruling dynasty.
*c.*250 Beginning of the decline of Meroë and its surrounding kingdom in Nubia.	**220** Han dynasty overthrown; Chinese unity breaks down.	*c.*250 Elaborate burials at Moche town of Sipán. **292** Date of oldest inscription at Mayan city of Tikal.
320–55 Reign of Ezana, who founds empire of Axum and destroys Meroë. Ezana adopts Christianity as official religion in Ethiopia.	**308–18** The Huns invade northern China, breaking up the Chinese Empire. **320** Beginning of Gupta Empire in India. *c.*335 Buddhism becomes the official religion of China.	**300–500** Two great Andean civilizations flourish in Peru: the Mochicas and the Nazcas. Teotihuacán grows into one of the largest cities in the world. **378** Tikal falls under control of Teotihuacán lord Siyak K'ak.
429 North Africa invaded and settled by Germanic tribe, the Vandals.	**5th century** Gupta dynasty first attacked by the Huns; within a century, Huns overthrow the dynasty. Asuka becomes capital of unified Japan.	*c.*400 End of Hopewell Indian culture. *c.*450 Tiwanaku civilization of Bolivia builds its own empire.
527 Alliance between Justinian and the kingdom of Axum against the Persians.	**581** Wendi, founder of the Sui dynasty, restores China's unity; new capital constructed at Chang'an.	**562** Defeat of Tikal by Mayan city of Caracol.
642 Arabs conquer Egypt.	**618** Tang dynasty succeeds in China; Chang'an is its capital.	*c.*600 Fall of Teotihuacán. **682–734** Reign of Hasaw Chan K'awil, Tikal's greatest king.
*c.*730 Arabs expand along the east coast of Africa.	**710** Nara becomes home of Japanese court. *c.*760–80 Construction of Borobudur – a huge Buddhist monument, 31m (100ft) high – in Java.	*c.*700 Pueblo Indian culture emerges from Anasazi Basket Maker culture in south-west North America.
*c.*800 Emergence of kingdom of Ghana; growth of trading towns in West Africa.	**800–50** Reign of Jayavarman II, founder of the Angkor dynasty in Kampuchea.	*c.*850 First large buildings appear at Chanchan. Foundation of Pueblo Bonito in New Mexico. **End of 9th century** Decline of Mayan civilization.
10th century The Fatimid rulers of Tunisia extend their empire to all parts of North Africa.	**904** Chang'an demolished and Chinese capital moves to Luoyang. **918** Foundation of kingdom of Korea.	**987** Traditional date of Toltec arrival in Chichen Itza.
11th century First stone structures built at Zimbabwe in south-east Africa. **1076** Capital of Ghana taken by Muslim Almovarid tribe.	**1044** Beginning of reign of Anawrahta, who builds the first monuments at Pagan in Burma. **1084–1112** Building at Pagan reaches a peak under Kyanzittha.	**11th century** Toltec Empire dominates highland Mexico; hybrid Toltec-Maya civilization emerges in Yucatán.
12th century The Yorubas found their first states in Nigeria. Beginning of the period of prosperity throughout the Ife kingdom.	**1113–50** Reign of Suryavarman II, builder of the temple complex Angkor Wat. **1177** Angkor sacked by the Chams of Annam; recovers and flourishes under Jayavarman VII.	*c.*1150 Cliff settlements built at Mesa Verde, North America. Peak of the Pueblo Bonito culture. *c.*1175 Collapse of Toltec Empire.
Around 1200 Kingdom of Mali becoming dominant state in West Africa. **Around 1250** Emergence of kingdom of Benin.	**1272** Kublai Khan conquers Song China. **1287** Pagan destroyed by the Mongols.	*c.*1200 Inca settlement established at Cuzco. **After 1200** Aztecs migrate towards Valley of Mexico after collapse of Toltec civilization.
14th century Ife kingdom at its height. **1340** Foundation of Songhay Empire in west Africa.	**1357** Siamese pillage Angkor.	*c.*1300 Pueblo Bonito abandoned. *c.*1325 Aztecs found Tenochtitlán on the site of present-day Mexico City.
1415 Ceuta in north Africa taken by the Portuguese: beginning of Portuguese exploration of mainland Africa. Prince Henry the Navigator encourages Portugal's seaward expansion. **1442** Beginning of the profitable native slave trade by Europeans.	**1460** Angkor finally destroyed by the Siamese.	**1438–71** Reign of Pachacuti Inca Yupanqui, founder of the Inca Empire. *c.*1450 Chimú kingdom of Peru at its peak. *c.*1490 Chimú kingdom becomes a province of the Inca Empire. **1492** Columbus reaches America.
16th century Final days of the Ife kingdom in southern Nigeria.	**1514** First Portuguese arrive in China. **1526–30** Babur conquers northern India; the Great Mughal Empire dominates India until the 18th century.	**1519–21** Aztec Empire destroyed by Cortés. **1532** Taking advantage of a civil war among the Incas, Francisco Pizarro puts the Inca Atahuallpa to death.

Discovering the past

Searching for sites

Many archaeological sites are visible as ruins – others are lost, submerged beneath the surface of the landscape. Sophisticated techniques are now used to pinpoint buried remains and identify areas likely to yield hidden treasures.

A bird's eye view

Sites long since invisible from the ground often become obvious when photographed from the air. Aerial photography reveals ridges and hollows, subtle variations in the colour or texture of soil, and differences in vegetation – particularly in cereal crops – which may mark the outlines of buried buildings, ditches, fields, and canals. Scientists use radar and satellite photography to locate sites in difficult terrain such as the rain forests of Central America, where Maya canals and raised field systems have recently been revealed.

EYES IN THE OCEAN   Modern submersibles allow marine reconnaissance at great depths. The thick walls of their spherical chambers resist crushing water pressure.

FLYING HIGH   Seen from the air, enigmatic lines etched into the arid plain near Nazca in Peru between 200 BC and AD 600 create huge geometric patterns, spirals, and pictures of birds and animals. The hummingbird is 50m (165ft) long.

Prospecting with electricity, magnetism, and sound

If archaeologists suspect that remains lie hidden beneath land or sea, they can pinpoint them using devices that measure the changes in electro-magnetic effects. On land, changes in the soil's resistance to the flow of electricity can be measured by passing a current through electrodes placed in the ground. The intensity of the current varies according to the resistance of the material through which the current flows. Since stone offers more resistance than soil, high resistance may indicate the presence of walls. Another device – a magnetometer – measures distortions in the magnetic field, which varies clearly where an object made of materials such as iron or burnt clay is buried. Sonar devices are also widely used, particularly in underwater reconnaissance. The sonar uses transmitted and returned acoustic waves to locate archaeological sites such as shipwrecks through murky waters and thick sediments impervious to other detection devices.

Probes and periscopes

In 1955 an Italian engineer, Carlo Lerici, devised a periscope that was to revolutionize Etruscan archaeology. Little was known about the Etruscans, who dominated central Italy between the 8th and 5th centuries BC. Although their artefacts

were usually buried with them in thousands of tombs, most had been looted and were empty – something usually discovered only after a tomb had been identified and opened.

Lerici's periscope could find out whether a burial chamber was worth excavating. Once a tomb had been identified, scientists drilled a small hole into it, lowered the periscope, and studied the interior before excavation – even taking photographs of it. By the mid-1970s, scientists had used the probe to examine some 7,000 tombs, while opening only 600.

Probes are now widely used – for example, in locating and examining hundreds of pits in the burial complex that also includes the terracotta warriors at Mount Li in China, and to reveal a wooden boat buried in a trench beside the Great Pyramid at Giza in Egypt.

Traces of the past

One method of research requires no special equipment other than a sharp eye and archaeological expertise. Occasionally, construction workers in the ancient world used stones from older, dilapidated structures when building new ones. Such stones are likely to be out of style with the rest of the new building, and suggest the existence nearby of ruined structures which may be buried.

Anomalies in the present-day layout of buildings or field boundaries are sometimes evidence of earlier buildings and settlements. These are created where builders have avoided earlier structures that have since disappeared. Documents such as parish registers and old maps may also provide clues about these features.

FIRM SUPPORT   The Inca wall beneath a church in Cuzco has survived earthquakes which have caused the church to be rebuilt.

Dating with accuracy

Since the middle of the 20th century, scientists have been able to establish the dates of archaeological discoveries with increasing accuracy. Methods range from investigating atomic particles to consulting the growth rings of the bristlecone pine.

ANCIENT ICEMAN The radiocarbon investigation of the frozen Alpine body nicknamed Ötzi, his tools, and grass stuffed into his shoes dated him to 3300 BC.

FINDING THE FAKES Thermoluminescence is used to distinguish fake Tang pottery – a popular target for forgery – from genuine pieces, such as the elegant lady found at Chang'an.

Radioactive remains

Carbon 14 is a radioactive isotope of carbon that occurs naturally and is absorbed by all living things. When a living thing dies (and stops absorbing carbon 14), the carbon 14 decays at a known rate – halving every 5,730 years (accurate to 30 years either way). By measuring the proportion of carbon 14 in organic remains such as bone or wood with a Geiger counter or a more modern tool – an accelerator mass spectrometer – a date of death can be calculated. The spectrometer's accuracy diminishes with the age of the object, but it can date remains up to 50,000 years old.

Secrets in the trees

Trees preserve a yearly record of seasonal changes in their annual growth rings. The thickness of the rings varies according to the effects of rainfall, sunlight, and temperature. Trees growing in a single area record the same conditions. By overlapping the rings of trees of different ages – even if the trees are dead, as in wooden beams from buildings – climatic calendars can be created. These allow wooden artefacts and ancient building timber to be dated accurately.

Dendrochronology was pioneered in the south-western USA. Climatic calendars created from the bristlecone pine of the American west have been dramatically successful. These pines live for up to 3,000 years, and with them scientists have built a record stretching back almost 8,000 years. Dendrochronology has been used to double-check carbon dating. Its climatic records highlight fluctuations in atmospheric carbon 14, and provide data to correct inaccurate radiocarbon dates.

Unleashing ancient energy

Ancient clay objects can be dated by measuring an effect known as thermoluminescence. After a clay pot is fired, crystals within its structure develop impurities through the process of ionization, in which electrons are stripped from the atoms of the minerals within the clay. These free electrons remain locked inside the crystals.

In thermoluminescence-dating the pot is once again subjected to fierce heat – effectively a second firing – until the trapped electrons emit photons, particles of light, which can be counted. Their number gives an idea of the age of the object – the older the pot, the more free electrons it contains. The technique also works on burnt flint.

A technique known as electron-spin resonance dating, which works on the same principle, is now being applied to other materials such as bones and tooth enamel, and has been used to date a number of early hominid teeth back to 250,000 years ago. Optical luminescence dating, another related technique, measures exposure to sunlight, and is used to date ancient sedimentary deposits containing archaeological remains.

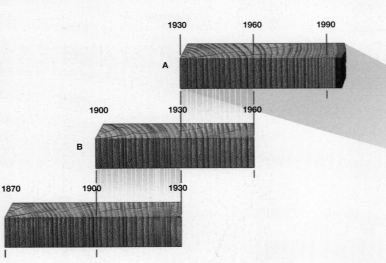

A YEARLY RECORD Rings in trees and wooden beams are correlated to build up a detailed climatic calendar. A section of wood from a living tree (A) matches the later part in a section from a dead tree or wooden beam (B). This beam is overlapped with an older beam (C). Sections from ever older trees or beams are added to build up a long-term record of rings.

Digging up the past

Sites are recorded in three dimensions as successive cultures leave evidence in uneven but distinct layers, often cut through vertically by features such as walls or ditches. An analysis of the layers reveals the history of the site through the ages.

Sifting through the strata

The remains of older cultures generally lie beneath those of more recent peoples. By studying the strata of successive cultures, archaeologists determine their sequence. These strata are of irregular thickness and extent, depending on what they represent – such as accumulations of domestic rubbish, the rubble from demolished buildings, man-made floors and roads, or soil resulting from natural erosion. The layers are usually dated by the age of the material contained within them.

Vertical features – upright structures such as walls, as well as pits and holes – will cut across the horizontal deposits into layers above and below. Such features will belong to the same era as deposits in the layer relating to them such as one containing the base of a wall or the top of a pit.

An excavation in progress

To reveal buried objects, workers first remove the topsoil, which is set aside and usually replaced when the excavation is complete. Next, archaeologists set up a grid of markers and string to record the positions of everything they find. The layers of the site are then carefully removed, in order. Often only a sample portion of an extensive layer is dug, while smaller features, such as hearths, are cut in half or excavated in their entirety. Fragile objects such as bones and jewellery are easily damaged – uncovering them requires infinite patience, and the use of precision tools such as dental picks and small brushes. Tiny shells, seeds, and other items too small to spot with the naked eye are recovered using wet sieving combined with

LAYERS OF HISTORY A 'section' records the different layers of a mound at Harappa in northern India, excavated in the 1940s. Harappa was a city of the Indus Valley civilization, which flourished in the 3rd millennium BC.

Surviving bricks from the wall of an Indus period house. The pit above was dug, probably between 500 BC and AD 500, to remove bricks for re-use.

A clay seal, known to come from the Indus period, was found here, helping archaeologists to date the deposit, or layer, to the 3rd millennium BC.

Pit created in modern times by the roots of a tree. Proof of its age was a coin found in the pit dating from AD 1910.

Deposit from the 'Historic' period, c.500 BC–AD 500. A coin found in this layer from the 2nd century AD helped to date it.

flotation techniques. Meticulous plans, drawings, and written notes record the location and context of each find before its removal – information that is vital to enable an accurate reconstruction of daily life on the site.

After the dig

Most of the material discovered on a site is sent to a laboratory for careful cleaning and treatment – allowing the investigation of tiny residues of food or other material left on the surface of tools and containers, which reveals what they were used for. Conservation is also undertaken to stabilize or restore decaying or broken objects. An army of specialists then sets to work analysing the finds – from pottery, metalwork, human bones, and animal remains to microfauna and plant remains – in order to extract every scrap of information that could shed light on life at the site, and its relationship to the local landscape and the wider world.

THE GENTLE TOUCH An archaeologist uses a hand-operated air pump (above) to blow sediment away from an Egyptian mummy discovered in the Bahariya Oasis.

FOR THE RECORD String marking out a grid (right) allows an accurate plan to be made of this burial site: an excavation in a cave near to the Pyramid of the Sun in Teotihuacán, Mexico.

Marine archaeology

When Jacques Cousteau and Émile Gagnan invented scuba gear in 1943, marine archaeology became a real possibility. The first to put it to use were a team under the American George Bass, who excavated a Bronze Age shipwreck off Cape Gelidonya in Turkey in 1960. Since then, many wrecks and other underwater sites across the world have yielded up their secrets.

Looking beneath the waves

Researchers investigating drowned settlements, submerged harbours, and shipwrecks use scuba gear in shallow waters and submersibles for deeper work. Remotely controlled submersibles can work in deep sea locations impenetrable by humans – they were used in the investigation of the *Titanic* and the recovery of material from the ship.

Underwater excavation often presents problems: poor visibility; currents disturbing sediments, equipment, and finds; and the physical limitations on the time investigators can spend under the water. As in land excavations, it is extremely important to record the position of finds. Measurements can be made from grids fixed to the seabed or suspended from a ship above, though these can be difficult to keep in position.

Making detailed plans of marine excavations is far easier today than in the past. Instead of hand-drawn plans, overlapping photographs are taken. These are used to create a mosaic which gives an accurate record of excavated structures or vessels. Video cameras, operated directly or from a remotely controlled submersible, can also be used to create a precise photographic record. The pictures can be manipulated by computers to produce not only plans, but three-dimensional reconstructions.

A new method of accurately recording the position of underwater sites uses GPS – the global positioning system. GPS receivers pick up signals transmitted by satellites in orbit around the Earth. The time lapse between the transmission and receipt of a signal is used to determine an exact position, regardless of bad weather and difficult conditions at sea.

MAKING PLANS   A diver measures the tagged remains of the Spanish galleon *San Diego* (top) off Fortune Island in the Philippines. The Dutch sank it in 1600 during a trade dispute.

RAISING TREASURE   A small chest containing blackened silver coins begins its journey to the surface in a crate attached to an inflated 'lift bag' at Silver Banks in the Atlantic Ocean.

Underwater excavations

The difficulties of recording underwater finds are often balanced by the ease of excavation. In land excavations, soil has to be laboriously dug or scraped away and then removed, but sediments in underwater sites can often be shifted simply by a gentle fanning of the excavator's hand. The underwater equivalent of the pick and spade is the suction dredger, a machine which sucks up the overburden of mud and sand through its manoeuvrable nozzle without clouding the surrounding water.

Small objects are placed in a bag or box and taken to the surface by divers. Larger objects are raised with the help of cables, flotation bags, and balloons. The timbers of wrecked ships are often badly decayed, but can be recorded in minute detail by using latex rubber to make moulds of the surviving fragments. Some well preserved wrecks have been raised to the surface in specially constructed cradles. Underwater sites often yield a wealth of organic remains, from massive timbers to tiny seeds, which will begin to decay when brought to the surface; the work needed to preserve them may involve expenses far greater than those of the excavation itself.

Çatal Hüyük

A sophisticated Stone Age settlement

A mysterious mound excavated in Turkey in the 1960s was to revolutionize archaeological thinking. For a large community had flourished on the ancient site 2000 years before the onset of civilization in Egypt and Mesopotamia.

In 1961 a team of British archaeologists led by James Mellaart travelled to the Konya plain in Anatolia, to a site about 320km (200 miles) south of the Turkish capital, Ankara. The purpose of the expedition was to excavate an artificial mound, known in Turkey as a *hüyük*, which rose beside the Çarsamba river more than 1,000m (3,281ft) above sea level.

As the digging proceeded, it became clear that this man-made hill – Çatal Hüyük – was the site of the largest, most important, and most fascinating Neolithic (Late Stone Age) settlement ever discovered in the Middle East. There were substantial dwelling-houses, cult-centres or shrines, and evidence of arts and crafts, and of extensive trade – mostly in local produce and artefacts, but also in more exotic articles.

Initially, radiocarbon dating placed the foundation of the settlement between 6250 and 5400 BC. But using a method called dendrochronology, counting rings in tree trunks to double-check radiocarbon dating, it became clear that it was established even earlier – between 7200 and 7100 BC.

A STONE AGE COMMUNITY

Çatal Hüyük consists, in fact, of two separate eastern and western mounds, divided by a branch of the River Çarsamba. Archaeologists have concentrated on the Neolithic eastern mound; the settlement shifted to the western mound in the succeeding Chalcolithic period. Only a small section of the 13ha (32 acre) eastern mound was excavated between 1961 and 1965, but since 1993 a large international team has expanded the investigations.

At the time of its discovery, Çatal Hüyük was unique. In recent years, similar contemporary sites have been discovered, including Umm Dabaghiyah in northern Iraq, Zagheh in northern Iran, Bouqras and Abu Hureyra in Syria, and Can Hasan, Suberde, and Erbaba in Turkey itself. But none of these settlements has shown quite the cultural and technical achievements of Çatal Hüyük – the site which gave archaeologists the first, tantalizing glimpse of an early farming settlement whose people cultivated cereals, crafted religious figurines, and traded with distant communities.

ANCIENT HUNTER The figure of a huntsman, dressed in a loincloth and leopard skin and carrying a bow, forms part of a great wall painting discovered in one of Çatal Hüyük's shrines, dating from about 5400 BC. The mural, painted in bold colours almost undimmed by the centuries, depicts a ceremonial hunt. Though settled in one place tending their crops, the people of Çatal Hüyük still lived a partly hunter-gatherer lifestyle.

Mellaart's excavations of the eastern mound uncovered one complete block of houses and shrines, part of another, similar block, and part of a third block which contained only houses. To the 1960s team, the shrines – rooms cluttered with relics such as bulls' horns and statuettes – seemed clearly distinguishable from the houses. But recent investigations have shown that most houses had domestic areas with hearths, beds, and storage bins in their southern section, and ritual features such as elaborate wall decoration in the northern section.

LIVING IN A MUD-BRICK MAZE

Each mud-brick house was surrounded by walls built directly up against its neighbouring buildings. It remained detached, though, and so could be demolished and rebuilt easily. Clusters of box-like, rectangular houses formed vast blocks, like cells in a honeycomb, interspersed with courtyards. A system of gutters moulded from plaster took the rainwater off the roof into the nearest courtyard and kept the house dry. There were no streets, so there were no front doors – houses were entered via the roof.

The reasons for using this method of building remain a puzzle. Evidence from other settlements in Iraq, Iran, Syria, and elsewhere in Turkey suggests that roof-entry may have been widespread in the Middle East in the 8th and 7th millennia BC. It may have been the best way to protect food and portable property from scavenging animals and light-fingered neighbours.

There are 14 known levels of building in Çatal Hüyük, spanning 800 years of cultural development, yet the basic design of the houses remains virtually unchanged throughout that period. Each house consisted of a main room, generally measuring about 6m (20ft) by 4m (13ft), with a storeroom along one side. On the roof was a small, ramshackle extra storey built of sticks and plaster which served as additional storage space and as a porch.

Wooden stairs or a ladder led from the roof to the kitchen area positioned at the southern end of the house. This consisted of a hearth or ovens and a fuel store. Cooking pots were kept in holes in the floor, and smoke

escaped through a hole in the roof. Some of the pots contained ancient 'pot-boilers' – stones heated in the fire then dropped into the pots to cook their contents.

Reed matting covered the centre of the floor. On two sides of the room, at the northern end, raised platforms covered with mats served as sofas and workbenches during the day and as beds at night. The discovery of traces of material suggests that felt was used to make bedding. The platforms had one further use – they also acted as family sepulchres.

The plaster surface of platforms was broken open to allow the burial of bones beneath them, 1.5m to 1.8m (5ft to 6ft) below the surface. The dead were buried with funerary gifts such as armlets, bracelets, copper beads, necklaces, obsidian mirrors, and weapons, as well as a wide variety of baskets and wooden vessels, which suggests a belief in life after death.

CITY ON THE PLAIN   Grass and weeds grow over the excavated ruins of Catal Hüyük. In the background spreads the Konya plain, once an area of swamps and forests, now the wheat bowl of Turkey.

Their bodies were laid to rest in a contracted position inside the platform, which was then plastered over again. More than half of the bodies found at Çatal Hüyük were of young children. Each platform seems to have been the burial place of a nuclear family. In several cases the latest burial was of a mature adult male whose interment was followed by the abandonment of the house, which probably then became an ancestral shrine.

THE DOMESTICATION OF THE HUNTER-GATHERER
The contents of each house were generally the same: the remains of food and matting; vessels made of pottery, wood, and occasionally stone; and beads, tools, and weapons made of obsidian – a glassy and extremely hard volcanic rock – or, more rarely, from flint.

The people of Çatal Hüyük kept domesticated dogs to guard their houses and, as one wall-painting shows, for sheep herding and for hunting. Human teeth from the site indicate that meat made up a large part of their diet; there is little evidence of the worn teeth that are prevalent among people who subsist mainly on cereals. The meat came from domestic stock and wild game. The number of bones found suggests

of oxen. Copper and lead also came from the Taurus Mountains. The obsidian used for implements such as arrowheads and knife-blades came from Cappadocia to the north-east. Sea-shells from the Mediterranean were also found at the site, along with Syrian flints, and a fragment of Syrian pottery.

The Çatal Hüyük craftsmen used many other materials not available in the local environment – they must have imported pigments such as red and yellow ochre; hard stone for toolmaking; limestone, shale, and aragonite; and minerals such as carnelian and blue and green apatite, which were fashioned into beads.

These finds are evidence of trade with faraway places. The discovery of Çatal Hüyük pottery in Cilicia, 160km (100 miles) to the south-east, suggests that the cultural influence of the settlement extended well beyond the Konya plain, perhaps even into the mountains surrounding it, across an area that may have been as large as $30,000km^2$ (11,580 sq miles).

HIGHWAY ON HIGH The roof levels in the honeycombed settlement of Çatal Hüyük were stepped to allow light and air into the closely packed houses. The inhabitants reached their homes by walking from roof to roof using steps and wooden ladders.

that mutton was their main protein, supplemented by other meats and fish. From wall-paintings as well as bones, it is clear that the Çatal Hüyük residents hunted wild goats, horses, and cattle, as well as wild boar and deer. Leopards, onagers (a species of wild ass), lions, gazelles, bears, and even wild cats were tracked down and killed for their skins.

Deposits of grain of different types suggest a fairly advanced system of cultivation and a variety of cereal foods. Grain was sometimes made into bread, but was more commonly served toasted, or in soup. The farmers also grew vegetables, and there is evidence that they processed oil from a type of mustard seed called shepherd's purse.

Foods eaten regularly included acorns, capers, crab apples, grapes, pistachios, and walnuts, gathered from swampy areas near the settlement and the forests on the edge of the Konya plain. Recent excavations have revealed that tubers were also an important element of their diet, including the marsh *Scirpus*, a bulrush that grew locally.

DIVERSE TRADE WITH DISTANT LANDS

Apart from food, the Konya plain had few natural resources beyond reeds and clay. Virtually everything else was imported. Timber – juniper, oak, and pine – was probably floated down the Çarsamba river from the Taurus Mountains about 80km (50 miles) to the south, then hauled to the settlement by teams

THE ROLE OF RITUAL IMAGERY

It seems likely that the stability of the community at Çatal Hüyük, and its links with other communities, owed much to a common religion. The shrines in the houses were elaborately decorated in three ways: with wall-paintings, plaster reliefs (frequently painted), and silhouettes etched into the plaster.

The wall-paintings range from simple red panels and geometric patterns to complex designs featuring symbolic figures and human hand shapes. Others depict vultures hovering over human corpses, a man defending himself from a vulture, a man

THE DAILY ROUND

Hundreds of everyday domestic objects were found in Çatal Hüyük's houses and tombs – homely items that give a vivid insight into the daily life of the settlement. The majority of the objects are carved out of wood or bone, or fashioned from clay. Particularly fascinating are several little bone spatulas, carved in the form of a fork, which the women used to apply make-up to their faces. Archaeologists also discovered wooden kitchenware in the form of large dishes with handles, plates, and bowls. Food was cooked in tall, double-handled clay pots which were either placed directly on the hearth or put into an oven to bake their contents.

SACRED ANIMAL Hunting probably had mythological significance in Çatal Hüyük. In a scene found in a shrine, tiny hunters with bows surround an enormous bull, 2m (6½ft) long.

carrying two human heads, a deer hunt, and an erupting volcano with a settlement in the foreground. Two of the shrines show bull-baiting and hunting dances.

The plaster reliefs explore a limited number of themes, which are frequently repeated. The most common figure is that of a goddess shown in the posture of childbirth, with her legs and arms lifted. Birth is a recurrent motif: there is a large female figure giving birth to a bull's head, and next to it is another female giving birth to a ram's head. In this second relief, three superimposed bulls' heads appear below the ram's head. Whether these represent previous births, or the 'heraldic' supporters of the goddess, is still not clear.

Bulls' heads appear in a great many of the buildings. In some cases their horns are real; in others they are moulded out of clay and plaster. The bull almost certainly represents the male element which, in the reliefs, is never portrayed in human form. The female element is represented in various forms apart from the figure of the goddess. Some figures are pregnant; others are slim and elegant. One particularly skilful image represents a woman whose arms and legs fit into sockets, like a child's doll. Many of the figures have no faces, suggesting that masks or headdresses may have been hung on pegs above the heads.

The third form of decoration, the silhouette style, depicts bulls, deer heads with antlers in profile, wild boars, and cows. Bulls' heads also appear with offerings laid beneath them, ranging from precious objects and weapons to cuts of meat and, in one case, a human head in a basket.

An exact interpretation of this religious imagery is impossible. In general terms it seems to celebrate the cycle of birth and death, a theme maintained in

GODDESS ENTHRONED A mother goddess gives birth to a human child, supported by wild animals. This clay figurine 12cm (4½ in) high, made between 5400 and 5200 BC, was found inside a grain-bin in a shrine.

ritual objects found at the site. Small statuettes – most less than 20cm (8in) tall and made of stone, though some are of baked clay – depict gods and demigods. They were found in the shrines, placed in groups, obviously to suggest some kind of connection between each set of figures. Several statuettes represent a bearded man, probably a god of hunting, sitting astride crudely carved animals. But the most remarkable sculpture is of the female deity seated on an animal throne, giving birth to a human child.

The richness of the ritual imagery at Çatal Hüyük hints at a high level of religious consciousness. Its nameless deities are the prototypes of later Anatolian gods and goddesses associated with birds, leopards, bulls, and deer.

MAKING A MARK ON HISTORY

So where did Çatal Hüyük's original settlers come from? On the south coast of Anatolia, traces have been found of the late Palaeolithic (Early Stone Age) culture that preceded the civilization of Çatal Hüyük.

In the caves of Kara'In, Öküzlü'In, and the rock shelter of Beldibi, there are wall-paintings and engravings of bulls, deer, ibex, and small human figures which may be the precursors of the art at Çatal Hüyük. It is possible that the first builders of Çatal Hüyük abandoned these caves and journeyed up to the plateau to found a new settlement.

The region continued to prosper for several thousand years. During the Early Bronze Age, there was a great increase in the number of settlements established in the Konya plain.

By 3000 BC, cities began to emerge, but by then the descendants of the Çatal Hüyük people had moved on to other sites. Strangely, shortly before 2000 BC, the region was virtually abandoned. A tiny trace of the Çatal Hüyük culture does, however, survive to this day.

The simple geometric patterns painted on the walls of the Çatal Hüyük houses – layers of red panels, with the imprints of human hands – can be seen in six modern villages near Çatal Hüyük: a creative idea which, astonishingly, has survived for 9,000 years.

The spread of agriculture

From about 9000 BC, the hunter-gatherers of the Middle East domesticated wild animals and cultivated grain. Around this time, agricultural activity began to evolve independently in places as far afield as China, Mexico, Peru, and northern Africa.

The expansion of farming

The earliest permanent settlements followed seasonal routines of sowing, tilling, and harvesting, and by 5000 BC irrigation systems were reducing their dependency on rainfall for watering crops. Intensive farming began with the arrival of the plough in about 4500 BC, and with the use of animals for pulling vehicles and carrying heavy burdens during the following centuries. The stability and wealth engendered by this Neolithic revolution led to the growth of urban civilization. The map and its colour key (below) show the dates at which agriculture first appeared across the world.

KEY TO DATES:

Before 8000 BC

Before 6000 BC

Before 3000 BC

Before 1500 BC

BEFORE 500 BC:

Hunters and gatherers

Uninhabited

Eastern North America
Squash

Central America
Animals:
Muscovy duck
Turkey
Crops:
Avocado
Cacao
Cotton
Lima bean
Maize
Pumpkin
Runner bean
Squash
Tobacco
Tomato

West Africa
Animals:
Guinea fowl
Crops:
Groundnut
Millet
Oil palm
Okra
Watermelon
Yam

Lowlands of South America
Chilli
Common bean
Manioc
Peanut
Pineapple
Yam

Andes
Animals:
Alpaca
Guinea pig
Llama
Crops:
Cocoa
Common bean
Cotton
Guava
Potato
Quinoa
Squash
Sweet potato

FRUITS OF THE EARTH
By 1500 BC, maize had become the staple crop of Central America. It was still a staple food 3,000 years later – a 16th-century drawing shows Aztec farmers harvesting their crops.

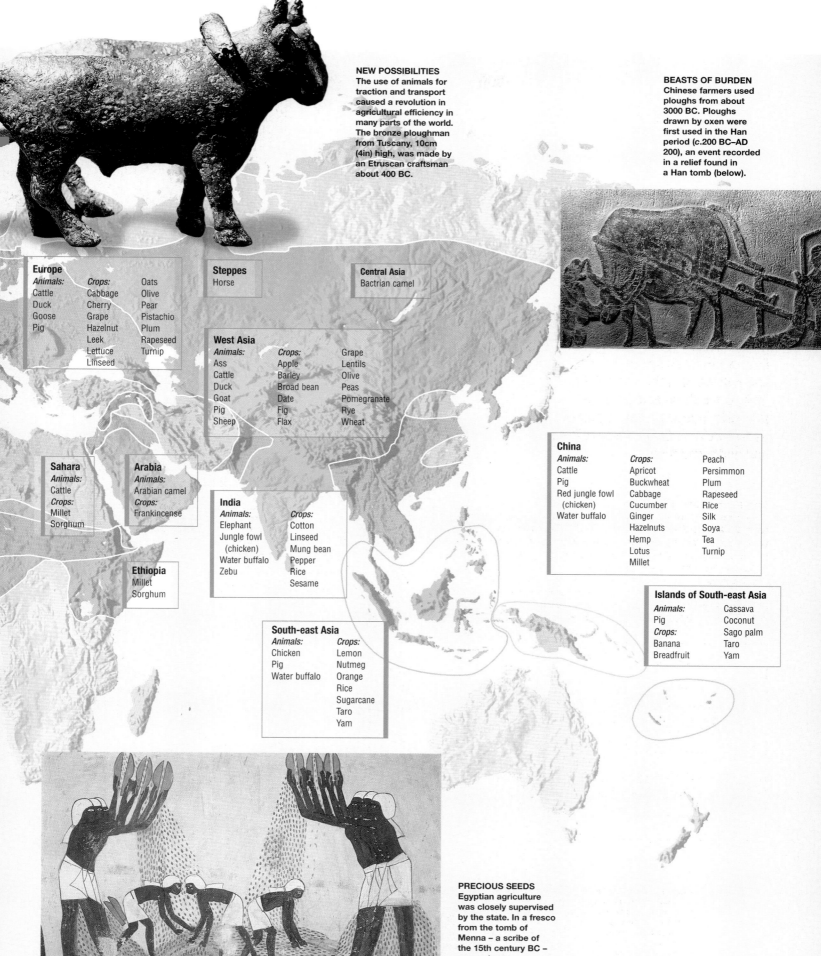

NEW POSSIBILITIES
The use of animals for traction and transport caused a revolution in agricultural efficiency in many parts of the world. The bronze ploughman from Tuscany, 10cm (4in) high, was made by an Etruscan craftsman about 400 BC.

BEASTS OF BURDEN
Chinese farmers used ploughs from about 3000 BC. Ploughs drawn by oxen were first used in the Han period (c.200 BC–AD 200), an event recorded in a relief found in a Han tomb (below).

Europe
Animals:
Cattle
Duck
Goose
Pig

Crops:
Cabbage
Cherry
Grape
Hazelnut
Leek
Lettuce
Linseed
Oats
Olive
Pear
Pistachio
Plum
Rapeseed
Turnip

Steppes
Horse

Central Asia
Bactrian camel

West Asia
Animals:
Ass
Cattle
Duck
Goat
Pig
Sheep

Crops:
Apple
Barley
Broad bean
Date
Fig
Flax
Grape
Lentils
Olive
Peas
Pomegranate
Rye
Wheat

Sahara
Animals:
Cattle
Crops:
Millet
Sorghum

Arabia
Animals:
Arabian camel
Crops:
Frankincense

India
Animals:
Elephant
Jungle fowl (chicken)
Water buffalo
Zebu

Crops:
Cotton
Linseed
Mung bean
Pepper
Rice
Sesame

Ethiopia
Millet
Sorghum

China
Animals:
Cattle
Pig
Red jungle fowl (chicken)
Water buffalo

Crops:
Apricot
Buckwheat
Cabbage
Cucumber
Ginger
Hazelnuts
Hemp
Lotus
Millet
Peach
Persimmon
Plum
Rapeseed
Rice
Silk
Soya
Tea
Turnip

South-east Asia
Animals:
Chicken
Pig
Water buffalo

Crops:
Lemon
Nutmeg
Orange
Rice
Sugarcane
Taro
Yam

Islands of South-east Asia
Animals:
Pig
Crops:
Banana
Breadfruit
Cassava
Coconut
Sago palm
Taro
Yam

PRECIOUS SEEDS
Egyptian agriculture was closely supervised by the state. In a fresco from the tomb of Menna – a scribe of the 15th century BC – peasants are winnowing the grain.

Susa

Home of the Elamites

Between the lowlands of Mesopotamia and the high plateau of Persia, the city of Susa emerged as a cultural crossroads. Here, the skills of those living on the plains merged with the vigour of the mountain people to produce a brilliant new civilization.

THE ANCIENT GREEKS KNEW SUSA as a royal city of the Persian Empire. Before them, the writers of the Old Testament referred to it as the capital of a land called Elam. But Susa's origins date back farther still – back to the shadows of prehistory, to an age before literate civilization began.

Today, Susa consists of a number of great earthen mounds situated in the plain of Khuzestan in south-west Iran. Each mound is composed of layer upon layer of mud-brick ruins. Mud-brick is a fragile material, and early archaeological investigations lacked the techniques needed to identify it. In 1897, a French geologist, Jacques de Morgan, embarked on an ambitious programme of excavation, seeking the origins of Elamite civilization. Valuable finds were made, but tonnes of the precious layers of earth and rubble were simply carted away and disposed of. What remains today does not give a full picture of the city of Susa, but a series of fascinating glimpses of its gradual evolution.

CRADLE OF CIVILIZATION

Susa lies on a lowland plain watered by rivers flowing from the Iranian plateau. Although it is in Iran, it is geographically part of Mesopotamia – the broad and fertile valley formed by the Tigris and Euphrates rivers. In these rich, alluvial lowlands, the rise of urban civilization began in the 6th millennium BC, when the inhabitants began to control river floods with irrigation schemes. Agricultural yields increased dramatically, and new wealth allowed specialist crafts such as pottery to flourish. Trade expanded, and great works of construction began; the building of temples signals the beginnings of organized religion. More than 5,000 years ago, the people of Mesopotamia invented writing, and went on to establish the first recorded kingdoms and empires.

By 4000 BC, a major urban revolution was in progress and the foundation of Susa dates back to this time. The city was to become the gateway to the Iranian plateau, a hub of trade routes linking the plains and mountains, for a period of several thousand years.

THE UNFINISHED TEMPLE
The kings of Susa undertook numerous building campaigns during its thousands of years as an Elamite settlement. The greatest Elamite king, Untash Napirisha, commissioned these mud-brick steps as part of a temple complex, the ziggurat, south-east of the city at Chogha Zanbil. The new complex was not a permanent success – after the king's death, further construction was abandoned.

KEEPING THE ACCOUNTS IN SUSA

Between 7000 and 6000 BC, farmers trading in the Middle East began to represent their goods with small, symbolic pieces of clay. The system was really no different from counting with pebbles. But in about 3500 BC, the plains of Mesopotamia and Susiana (the area extending to the east of Susa) saw a great advance. Here, a thriving trade in agricultural products made the development of a proper form of accountancy essential.

In order to represent large numbers of goods, an appropriate number of tokens was enclosed within a hollow clay ball. The ball was then authenticated by rolling a stone cylinder seal over its surface, in much the same way as later European letter writers authenticated their messages by stamping a signet ring into wax. A new development soon followed.

People began to indicate the number of tokens inside each ball by making marks or dents on the ball, or by listing the numbers separately on a clay tablet.

At this stage, the nature of the merchandise was not specified – whether it was a herd of cattle or items of furniture. But as symbols for these evolved, in the form of more elaborate tokens and then picture signs, a written language began to emerge.

A LIST OF GOODS The early Elamites developed their own script. It remains undeciphered, but this tablet of around 2900 BC is thought to be an inventory, with pits representing numbers.

COUNTING SHEEP The merchants of Mesopotamia used hollow clay spheres containing tokens to record quantities of commodities such as sheep or grain.

of Sumerian civilization in Mesopotamia, where a booming economy began to inspire new forms of art. It was a prelude to more significant developments.

In about 3400 BC, an age of monumental building began at the Sumerian city of Uruk, on the banks of the Euphrates south-west of Susa. Local artists of the time often depicted a priest-king figure, obviously the head of a centralized administration. Even more revolutionary, clay tablets bearing a form of written language had appeared. Symbols were used to list possessions or record business deals and land sales.

Susa felt the influence of Sumer, and developed in parallel. The city and its surrounding areas created a separate written language, also recorded on clay tablets. Similarly, a king-like figure begins to appear among relics of Susa from this period. The figure is depicted on engraved cylindrical seals which were used as stamps of ownership, much like signet rings, in both Susa and Mesopotamia. Despite this suggestion of a monarchy, the economy does not appear to have been centralized. Private merchants and traders probably controlled most of the wealth.

Susa's trading community began to take to the roads, setting up distant merchant colonies; there is evidence that merchants from Susa even reached Egypt. But once again, an era of history ended for reasons that have not been identified. In about 3000 BC Susa and its colonies were abandoned.

For 300 years after its foundation, Susa developed as the centre of a prosperous agricultural region. Funeral items from this early period, excavated from a vast cemetery containing more than 2,000 graves, include copper axes, suggesting an important traffic in the metal. The plain itself had no copper; it must have been brought from the Iranian plateau. The graves also suggest a tradition of fine pottery. The villages surrounding Susa produced elegantly simple pots painted with stylized birds and animals.

During this period, the inhabitants of the city built an enormous brick terrace, 80m (262ft) square, perhaps designed to carry a great temple. The sheer size of the work implies a strong economy capable of diverting a large workforce from food production to construction. It also suggests the existence of a powerful central authority, though no evidence of a king or ruling hierarchy exists from this time. Stone seals of ownership have been found, so riches are likely to have accumulated in a few private hands. Slim clues like these suggest some kind of civic democracy, but tantalizingly, the evidence stops there. At an unidentified date, the terrace was destroyed.

The next stage in Susa's evolution began in about 3700 BC, when its distinctive local pottery was replaced by plain, mass-produced ware which was flooding the Middle East at that time. This sudden new influence can be attributed to the meteoric rise

of Susa from this period. The figure is depicted on engraved cylindrical seals which were used as stamps of ownership, much like signet rings, in both Susa and Mesopotamia. Despite this suggestion of a monarchy, the economy does not appear to have been centralized. Private merchants and traders probably controlled most of the wealth.

Susa's trading community began to take to the roads, setting up distant merchant colonies; there is evidence that merchants from Susa even reached Egypt. But once again, an era of history ended for reasons that have not been identified. In about 3000 BC Susa and its colonies were abandoned.

A MEETING OF CULTURES

The abandonment is thought to have been brief. Excavations indicate that the city was soon reoccupied, and began a long period influenced at first by the hardy, inventive peoples of the Iranian plateau, then by the sophisticated Mesopotamians. Out of this fertile mixture of cultures, the civilization known to the Old Testament authors as Elam eventually emerged.

Initially, the newly occupied city looked to the upland peoples of the plateau, establishing commercial and diplomatic links with the peoples of the Fars region on the southern heights of present-day Iran. Among its new trading partners was a flourishing kingdom centred on the neighbouring town of

MAN OF CLAY Terracotta figurines were common in Susa. Some may have been toys, others perhaps votive offerings or images of gods. Men were usually bearded, like this figure of the late 2nd millennium BC.

Anshan. Examples of early Elamite writing have been discovered at both Susa and Anshan – distinctive and lively representations of animals impressed on soft clay. The culture of the civilization which produced them, known as Proto-Elamite, survived for some 200 years, until a new Mesopotamian upsurge caused Susa to renew its links with the cities to the west.

Susa was drawn even more closely into the Mesopotamian fold in about 2300 BC, when the mighty Sargon of Akkad, a warrior king from the north-west, overran the valley of the Tigris and Euphrates and united its kingdoms into a single realm. As a result, the local spoken language was replaced by the Semitic language of the Akkadians.

THE BEGINNINGS OF A NEW KINGDOM

Though politically and culturally part of Mesopotamia, Susa maintained its established trading links. It remained the gateway to the Fars plateau, hub of the well-trodden routes along which merchants carried precious stones and metals from the hills to the plain.

These routes were reaching ever deeper into Asia, and craftsmen on the Iranian plateau began to produce chlorite and later alabaster wares which were exported over vast distances. The most characteristic items were glazed seals made of steatite (soapstone) with cut-out patterns featuring a cross, an eagle, or a mythological figure. The seals reached Susa along the westerly routes; they have also been found in the steppes of southern Russia, and even as far east as the fringes of China.

Persia's prosperity was strongly felt by the people of Susa. After their long subjection to Mesopotamia, political and cultural links with the Fars region were restored when the Elamites brought about the downfall of Mesopotamia's ruling dynasty of Ur in 2004 BC. Susa and Anshan were reunited under one monarch, Kindattu – and the Elamite dynasty began. In about 1950 BC, the ruler's title of 'King of Susa and Anshan' was dropped in favour of 'Grand Regent'. The heir to the throne at that time was not the king's son, but his younger brother – the son was the second in line. This sensible arrangement gave the son time to mature, and the in-fighting so often connected in royal houses with the accession of a young heir was thus avoided.

Under the new dynasty, a suburb grew up on the northern outskirts of Susa which has been carefully explored by archaeologists. Houses were grouped in blocks, separated by well-defined streets. Each house had a fireplace, used for cooking and for heating in winter. Most of the houses were fitted with latrines with a drainage course to carry away waste water, and many of the inhabitants enjoyed the luxury of a bathroom with a terracotta bath.

One house contained its own private chapel – a tiny sanctuary housing a huge altar, elaborately decorated with reliefs. Tombs were dug underneath the houses, and fitted out with funeral furniture.

LIVING A NOBLE LIFE

The home comforts in the suburb of Susa all speak of modest prosperity, but it seems that the area was gradually adopted by a wealthier aristocracy. Funerary vaults replaced the simple tombs, and imposing buildings began to appear. In the 18th century BC, one of the suburb's housing blocks was transformed into the residence of a high official known as Temti-wartash.

Temti-wartash's house was a palace. After passing through three vestibules, visitors entered a lavishly tiled courtyard. A palatial doorway led to a reception room with an arched roof supported by four rectangular columns, and the rest of the building was laid out around secondary courtyards.

The records of the master of the house have been found. They mention the royal grants awarded to him, name his farm workers, and list the huge quantities of grain needed to sow his fields. They also reveal his extensive business interests, listing creditors in distant towns. He even had a debtor as far away as Liyan (present-day Bushehr) on the Persian Gulf.

Later, other dignitaries set up residence in the quarter, notably Rabibi, a royal chamberlain. His house, fitted out like Temti-wartash's, offers a delightful insight into daily life. There were classrooms where children learned the difficult cuneiform script of the period. Their exercises involved copying words, written by the teacher, onto large clay tablets, stored in holes in the ground to keep them cool and malleable.

THE ZIGGURAT OF CHOGHA ZANBIL

The ruined but majestic complex at Chogha Zanbil, built by Untash Napirisha, king of Susa, during the 13th century BC contains the remains of a huge temple dedicated to two gods: Inshushinak of Susa and Napirisha of Anshan. The union of the deities – one of the lowland plain, the other of the high plateau – reflected the twin influences at the heart of Elamite civilization.

The temple was built in two phases, almost as if its royal patron changed his mind after the first phase was complete. Workers began by constructing a huge courtyard, 100m (328ft) square, paved with unbaked brick. In the walls around it, vaulted chambers enclosed two sanctuaries and storage rooms for grain, jars, and building materials. Each of the walls had a central door.

After a time, the king decided to transform the building into a towering ziggurat – the tapering, terraced temple characteristic of all Mesopotamian civilizations. The brick-paved central courtyard was ripped up and the debris used to fill the vaulted rooms in its walls. Only one of the two sanctuaries was

preserved. The original construction became the first floor of the new ziggurat. Three more storeys were built up within the courtyard, each constructed of unbaked mud-bricks, with a casing of hard, baked brick, and a final outer layer of crushed baked brick.

The facade glittered with glazed blue and green terracotta. An internal staircase lead to a temple on the top floor, some 44m (144ft) up, decorated with glass and ivory mosaics. Piles of bricks at the site indicate that further building was intended when, in 640 BC, the Assyrian king Assurbanipal attacked the complex, precipitating its fall into ruins.

SANCTUARY ON THE PLAINS
The crumbling remains of the ziggurat include the two lowest storeys and the base of the third storey. They inspired the modern name for Al-Untash-Napirisha: Chogha Zanbil, or Basket Mound. Originally, the temple tower was more than 50m (164ft) high.

THE CONSTRUCTION The first building (1) with its central courtyard was constructed inside a walled enclosure. The courtyard was then filled in, and the three extra storeys (2, 3, 4) added. These consisted of concentric walls of brick, each resting on the ground rather than on the floor below it. A temple (5) topped the whole edifice.

Family vaults beneath the aristocratic houses have yielded numerous funerary items. To preserve the identity of the dead, portraits modelled from clay were painted and placed beside the corpse's head. They obviously seek to capture the likeness of the subject – unusual in the Middle East at a time when portraits usually conformed to conventional stereotypes. The most remarkable of them shows a man with a square-cut, fringed Elamite hairstyle. His doleful expression evokes the rough and ready peasant stock of a people living close to the mountains.

Women are shown smiling faintly, and wearing their hair plaited in a diadem. Small terracotta figures of naked women, probably from the same period, were excavated from the streets. They were broken when found. Pregnant women probably wore them as a charm, throwing them away once they had delivered their child. Couples intertwined in their beds and mothers suckling babies were also represented – imagery designed to encourage bigger families and, indirectly, a larger city.

LINKING THE TRADITIONS

Susa and Anshan gradually drifted apart, but in the 13th century BC the new Anzanite dynasty restored the union. Its princes declared 'expansionist' aims.

For hundreds of years, only the Semitic Akkadian script had been used at Susa. But the new kings had their inscriptions drawn up in the language of Anshan, as well as in Akkadian. It was a clear statement of pride in the traditions of the plateau.

Little is known about the greatest king of the line, Untash-Napirisha (*c.*1275–1240 BC), except for his great building programme. He also embellished Susa with masterpieces of metalwork. The most important surviving relic is a life-sized headless statue of his queen, Napirasu. Even without its head, this cast bronze figure weighs 1,750kg (almost 2 tons) – the largest metal statue ever found in the Middle East. But an even more impressive memorial to his reign is the temple and palace complex which he built for himself about 30km (18½ miles) south-east of Susa. This testament to his majesty was called Al-Untash-Napirisha, now known as Chogha Zanbil, which lies on the edge of a plateau dominating the river Ab-e Dez.

The approach to the complex was by river, then through the royal gate which also served as a law court (the custom in the Middle East). Within the first enclosure, a number of palaces were built for the use of the royal family. Below one palace were the tombs in which the king and his family would be buried. Banquets were held at each funeral, and the bodies cremated. Not far from this funeral palace was a temple dedicated to Nusku, the Mesopotamian god of light and fire. The high altar

IN THE NAME OF A GOD   Inscribed bricks in the ziggurat proclaim its dedication to Inshushinak, who was believed to ascend from his temple to the heavens each night.

TOYS FOR ETERNITY

The kings of Elam respected their queens and loved their children. As a final token of their tender feelings, they would leave favourite toys in the tombs of royal children, such as those beside the temple of Inshushinak at Susa. This lion and mother hedgehog, carved between about 1500 and 1000 BC, were made of limestone, with bases of bitumen – a tarry rock abundant in the region. The hedgehog was accompanied by two babies originally, but only the notches for their feet remain. Terracotta dolls' heads with clown-like faces were also favourites; some had holes in the neck so that cloth bodies could be sewn onto them. These objects belonged to royal families, but they give an idea of the toys that all children must have played with in Susa more than 1,000 years before the birth of Christ.

of the temple was exposed to the sky – it was possibly a cremation site, and certainly a centre of fire worship. Inside the walls of the first enclosure, a second enclosure housed the temples of various Elamite gods, and within, a third enclosure housed the major temples, including the sanctuary of the great gods Inshushinak, patron of Susa, and Napirisha, patron of the Anshan uplands.

The goddess wives of the two major deities also had temples dedicated to them. They were fully recognized alongside the gods, a tradition mirrored in the mortal world – Elamite women occupied powerful positions in both government and religion.

THE HUNT FOR TROPHIES

Not long after the construction of Al-Untash-Napirisha, the Elamite kingdom passed through a brief period of crisis. Then, in the 12th century BC, a new dynasty cast its eyes on distant horizons to restore the realm's prestige.

To the west, the Babylonian dynasty of the Kassites had been ruling for almost 500 years. The new Elamite king, Shutruk Nahhunte, overthrew the dynasty and captured an immense haul of booty. He returned to Susa with statues, monuments, and a host of other trophies.

This lust for treasure resulted in an invaluable service to posterity. Among the loot was a polished basalt stele, or engraved stone, from the Temple of Shamash at Sippar, north-west of Susa. The stele bears the fullest surviving text of the famous *Code of Hammurabi*, the most complete collection of laws to survive from ancient Mesopotamia. Hammurabi is shown standing in homage before the seated Shamash, the Babylonian Sun god. Nearly 300 laws – dealing with crime, trade, wages, marriage, and a host of other matters – are inscribed in vertical columns below the figures.

The new dynasty abandoned Al-Untash-Napirisha and set up a number of the captured monuments in Susa itself, where new temples were built in a distinctive style. The outer walls were made of glazed and moulded bricks, which depicted royal couples and the guardian spirits of the buildings. Only fragments of the bricks have been found, but a curious bronze model showing a religious ceremony has survived intact. It depicts two figures taking part in a ritual, and an inscription reveals that it illustrates the ceremony of the Rising Sun – Sit Shamshi.

The ritual takes place between two temples, probably those of Inshushinak and his wife at Susa. Offerings have been placed around the larger of the temples, beside some raised stones. Trees nearby indicate the existence of a sacred grove.

The piece suggests yet more unexpected affinities, in this case with the Semitic peoples of the Biblical lands far to the north-west: Syria, Lebanon, and Palestine. Though the temples are Elamite in style, the simple raised stones recall those worshipped as idols by the Canaanites. The wooded grove was revered by the Semites, who held all green trees sacred, and a miniature vase in the sculpture is similar to an item found in the Temple of Solomon in Jerusalem.

RELICS OF THE DEAD

Underground tombs beside the temple of the god Inshushinak in Susa contain the cremated remains of the royal dead. Partially burnt furniture has been found in these vaults, but the remains of precious gold and silver leaf bear witness to their original splendour. Statuettes of precious metal have also been discovered. Toys and games similar to modern solitaire had been buried there, too.

Ancient relics from earlier eras have also been preserved: stamp seals and cylinder seals, which were already more than 2,000 years old; and exotic axe heads. These relics, imported from eastern Persia, seem to have been placed in the tombs to

VOTIVE FIGURE Statuettes in precious metal found at Susa depict worshippers bearing offerings. This gold figure carries a kid. It is one of a pair; the other is crafted in silver.

SUN WORSHIPPERS A naked priest pours water onto the outstretched hands of another figure in the Rite of the Rising Sun. The Elamite king Shilhak-Inshushinak commissioned this bronze model in about 1150 BC.

civilization was doomed. At the end of the 8th century BC, an ambitious king of Susa called Shutur Nahhunte revived some of the splendour of the metropolis, and for a few decades its citizens enjoyed an uneasy peace through alliances first with Assyria, then with Persia. But it was not to last. In 646 BC, the Elamite capital was devastated once more, this time by the merciless ruler of Assyria, Assurbanipal (669–627 BC). Susa was looted, its royal tombs desecrated, and the images of its gods and kings were taken away.

But Susa refused to die. The Persians rebuilt the city in the 6th century BC, and it became the administrative capital of their empire. Later, in 331 BC, it fell to Alexander the Great. It continued its role as a trade centre until gradual decline set in during the late Middle Ages, reducing it into a cluster of deserted hillocks overlooking the barren plain of Khuzestan. But in one way the site preserved its history across thousands of years – it has retained its ancient name, in the form of Shush, from the time of the first written records until today.

reinforce the monarchy's claim to descent from the woman known as the Gracious Mother, the wife of the first Elamite king, Kindattu, who had reunited Anshan and Susa at the beginning of the second millennium BC. Safe in the vault, they survived the holocaust to come.

A LAND OF ASHES AND DUST

At the end of the 12th century BC the Babylonians recovered their supremacy and inflicted a crushing defeat on the Elamites. The ancient civilization crumbled as its enemies set it alight. The scale of the fire is almost unimaginable: a thick layer of ash covers the whole of the site of Susa – a terrible reminder of the size of the conflagration which ended Elam's most glorious period. Darkness fell over the conquered lands for some 400 years, and Elam never fully recovered. During those years, dramatic changes were to transform the Middle East completely.

In about 1000 BC, the plateau was engulfed by a wave of Aryan peoples from the Caucasus, from whom Iran derives its name. The Aryans founded the first Persian kingdom at Anshan. Meanwhile, a new power was rising in Mesopotamia – the empire of the Assyrians. Caught between these two power blocs, Elam's fallen

HIDING IN A SWAMP The Elamites were frequently at war with their Mesopotamian neighbours. In this relief from Nineveh, Elamites defeated by the Assyrian king Assurbanipal attempt to escape their foes while bodies of the slain float downstream.

Saqqara

Life in the Old Kingdom

Royal pyramids and noble tombs lie side by side in this vast and ancient cemetery along the banks of the River Nile. The Egyptians' preoccupation with death has enabled us to discover the richness of their daily life through the relics they left behind.

THE ANCIENT EGYPTIANS LUSTED AFTER IMMORTALITY – the mystery of death lay at the very heart of their culture. No other civilization has been quite so obsessed with the afterlife, or devoted quite so much energy to preparing for eternity. Egyptian corpses were mummified and their tombs generously furnished with the trappings of day-to-day living to create an 'eternal home'. Labourers and peasants found their eternal homes in holes in the sand, but pharaohs and high officials were buried in a huge cemetery, or necropolis, stretching up the west bank of the River Nile near Memphis, capital of Egypt's Old Kingdom of the 3rd millennium BC. The best known sites of the necropolis, or city of the dead, are the pyramids built for the pharaohs through the massed efforts of the populace as gigantic, impregnable tombs.

A TIMELESS LAND

The Old Kingdom spanned 500 years, from about 2700 to 2200 BC, and four royal dynasties, the 3rd to the 6th – the key period in the rise of Egyptian civilization. The necropolis was symbolically placed between the life-giving river and the wastelands of the dry Western Desert, spanning two zones of existence. The basic landscape of the Nile valley has hardly changed since then.

Many of the pyramids, like those at Giza, still tower above the landscape. Others are now small mounds of ruins. All are empty, pillaged by treasure-seekers. If they were all that remained, little would be known of the everyday life of the time, for hardly any documents survive. But the central plateau of Saqqara to the south of Giza, the area most dense in remains, has yielded a rich haul of clues.

Many of the tombs at Saqqara are more modest than the mighty tombs of the pharaohs. They are the resting places of princes and high officials, and are known as *mastabas* – an Arabic word meaning bench, which these box-like structures resemble. From the outside they look like a solid mass of stone, but underground the magnificent chambers are decorated with richly detailed bas-reliefs telling of daily life in the Old Kingdom.

CALM CONCENTRATION By the time of the Old Kingdom, the Egyptians had developed a complex system of hieroglyphics, a knowledge of which was shared among the elite – royalty, priests, and scribes. The number of statues of scribes, either reading or poised ready to write, displays their importance in the rise of Egyptian civilization. This figure, 51cm (20in) high, dates back to the 5th dynasty (c.2544–2407 BC).

The notables buried in the mastabas were all landowners, and the bas-reliefs vividly summarize the activities on their estates. Almost everything which brought wealth to their lands was recorded: agriculture, stock-raising, hunting, fishing, arts, and crafts. In these carvings, time stands still.

In one typical example, the lord sits at a table piled high with food and drink. His family is grouped around him. Musicians, squatting on their heels, play harps. A group of ladies clap hands to accompany the dancers. Farther on in the sequence, the master stands to receive queues of servants bringing crops, and game hunted for him in the desert. Farther still, the master is carried out on a sedan chair to inspect his lands. Peasants toil in the fields. A herdsman helps a cow to give birth while a butcher slaughters a bullock for tomorrow's great feast.

Ancient Egypt comes vividly to life in these works of art. Yet, strangely, one important image central to the whole civilization is rarely represented – the River Nile. Egypt's development cannot be fully understood without looking at the river's large and constant influence.

THE SWELLING OF THE WATERS

In prehistoric times the Nile was broader and its course much more irregular than today. North-east Africa was a swamp, and the vast expanse of marshland was inhabited by nomadic tribes who lived by hunting, fishing, and gathering wild cereals, berries, and tubers. But climate changes gradually turned the swamp into

When the flood peaked in September, the valley became a vast lake. Living space was reduced to exposed mounds of land, and boats were the only form of transport.

desert, and its inhabitants congregated in the river valley and learned to harness the forces of the river to give life to their crops.

At the time of the Old Kingdom, the Nile cut its way through the desert wastes in a long fertile strip. Every year, the valley's inhabitants watched the river flood their lands. Its waters gathered silt on the plateau of Ethiopia during the rainy season, and a few months later, towards the end of June, would inundate Egypt. When the flood peaked in September, the valley became a vast lake. Living space was reduced to exposed mounds of land, and boats were the only form of transport. Later, as the waters ebbed, they left a deposit of fertile silt over the valley.

FEEDING THE LAND

The flood was vital to survival in this desert land, but the Egyptians awaited it with great anxiety. If the waters came too lightly, some areas would not be irrigated. If they were too heavy, dykes would be breached and homes destroyed.

An entire industry developed around the cyclical event. Dykes were set up around threatened buildings, and when the waters receded, repairs were needed. A network of canals stored and distributed the flood waters to best advantage. The task of controlling the flood waters was immense, and a complex administration was required to deal with it. Upper and Lower Egypt were unified in a single kingdom in about 3100 BC, and from then on the country developed a planned economy.

From about 2700 BC, when the Old Kingdom was established, the state recorded the peak level of each flood so that the government could predict the size of the harvest and levy taxes accordingly. If it was a good year, reserves of grain would be put aside to provide for bad years. But if a series of bad years followed each other, disaster loomed.

THE BOAT BUILDER A relief in the tomb of a nobleman called Ty at Saqqara shows a carpenter sawing a trunk into planks to make a boat. The pole is set into the ground and bound in place to prevent it from slipping.

All resources, and the revenues they generated, were controlled by the state. The official administrators included an army of scribes who harnessed and supervised the labouring masses. Food subsidies were given in return for labour. The mastabas at Saqqara show that the scribes supervised every aspect of work in the fields: from the transport of grain and the storing of the harvest to the return of cattle to their stables and the noting down of all stock movements. When harvest-time arrived, the scribes would assess the likely size of the harvest. In ancient Egypt, agriculture was closely linked with religious faith. In Memphis, during the festival of Sokaris, a god of the

THE BIRD-CATCHERS Birds were caught using nets or throwing sticks. A scene from a vizier's tomb shows birds having their wings broken, before being caged and carried away to be fattened for the table.

dead and the underworld, the inhabitants enacted a symbolic mime representing the threshing of grain, and drove a herd of cattle around the city.

Wheat and barley, major crops in ancient Egypt, were used to make bread and beer, The phrase 'bread and beer' is engraved in all the mastabas in hieroglyphs, as if these three words represented the sum of all nourishment.

The cultivation of flax was also a major occupation. Flax was used to weave linen for clothing, for the dead as well as the living.

IN SEARCH OF PREY

In the age of the pyramids, the desert on either side of the Egyptian heartland was inhabited by wild animals. The Nile itself teemed with fish, and was a stopping-off point for countless flocks of migrating birds. Hunting and fishing were activities of great importance.

The master would go into the desert to hunt, accompanied by servants. Under the Old Kingdom, the prey was hunted down with dogs, or using a lasso. Greyhounds were the swiftest hunting dogs, unleashed upon gazelles, oryx, deer, and hares. Those killed by the pack were brought back to the lord's

kitchens. Others were captured alive and fattened in the farms before being eaten, or were interbred with animals already in stock to improve the breed.

Some kinds of hunt became a leisure activity reserved for the upper classes. But they may have had more than purely recreational value – stick-throwing hunts, harpoon-fishing, and hippopotamus hunts seem to have been imbued with magical significance. For centuries the Egyptians had fought nature to make the land habitable, and wild animals symbolized the forces of destruction. In massacring his prey, the master was attacking the visible forms of chaos – powers which threatened the land.

The mastaba in Saqqara of a nobleman, Ty, contains vivid hunting scenes. Ty is shown descending into the marshes of the delta with his hunting party. Mounted on a barge, he enters a vast jungle of papyrus. The swampland creatures around him seem oblivious of the human presence. A crocodile lurks in the shallows. Small birds are perched in nests set high in the clusters of papyrus. Under the water, fish glide about peacefully.

Ty is hunting two hippopotamuses, but he doesn't intend to risk his own life in this dangerous enterprise. Standing on his papyrus barge with a long stick in his hand, he watches his servants acting for him from another boat. One man at the rear guides the barge with a pole. Three others, completely naked, attack one of the hippos. First they throw a volley of harpoons. Then the shafts of the harpoons are withdrawn; only the sharp tips remain embedded in the creature's hide, each tip attached to a hunter by a length of cord. New spear-tips are fixed on and the beast is attacked again. One of the hunters now gathers the

CITY FOR THE DEAD Djoser's step pyramid was the centrepiece of a complex of buildings, designed to be lived in by the beings of the spirit world. It covered 15ha (37 acres) and was surrounded by a limestone wall.

cords in his left hand and grips them firmly. The hippo thrashes and tries to escape, but it is held fast. With his right hand, the hunter throws a last harpoon for the death blow.

TENDING THE CATTLE

Hunters often captured wild animals such as antelope, gazelle, and oryx with the intention of domesticating them, just as oxen, sheep, and asses had been domesticated at a much earlier stage. Many of their experiments were unsuccessful.

Asses were handled roughly – as roughly as labourers were treated by their foremen. In contrast, the Egyptians lavished immense love and care on their cattle. Oxen were objects of particular attention. They were carefully selected and copiously fed, sometimes fattened by hand with balls of bread dough.

Herdsmen seem to have been very low on the social scale. They are often represented naked in the bas-reliefs, with unshaven faces and a look of destitution. Their lives were ruled by the flood cycle. After the great waters had retreated, the herds of cattle, sheep, and goats were moved into the humid prairies. Then, during the hot season they were driven to the marshland fringes of the Nile Delta. Here, the herdsmen lived for long months alone with their grazing animals, killing fish or birds for food, which they roasted over a fire. At the end of the

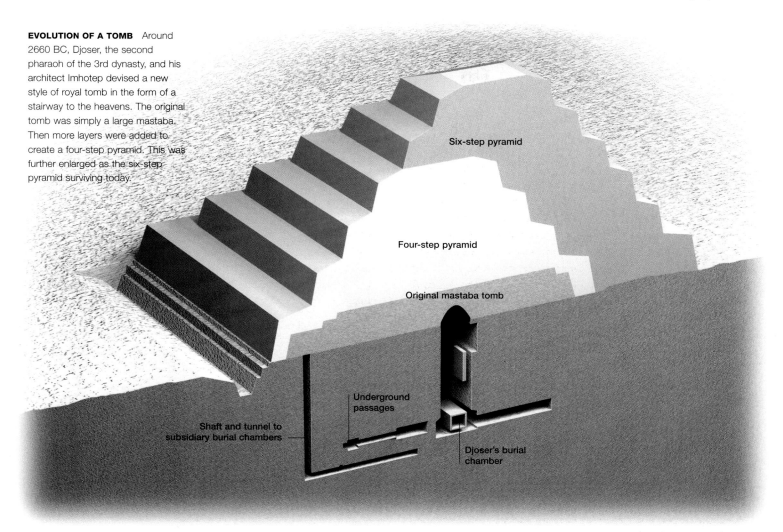

EVOLUTION OF A TOMB Around 2660 BC, Djoser, the second pharaoh of the 3rd dynasty, and his architect Imhotep devised a new style of royal tomb in the form of a stairway to the heavens. The original tomb was simply a large mastaba. Then more layers were added to create a four-step pyramid. This was further enlarged as the six-step pyramid surviving today.

Six-step pyramid

Four-step pyramid

Original mastaba tomb

Underground passages

Shaft and tunnel to subsidiary burial chambers

Djoser's burial chamber

season, the long journey south crossed canals and tributaries of the Nile – a common motif on the bas-reliefs of Saqqara. The herd swam across deep water, their great horned heads poking above the water. Their herdsmen crossed on barges made of papyrus, or forded shallow streams on stepping-stones.

On their return, the meat of the fattened bullocks was highly prized, and reserved for the upper classes. The flesh could not be preserved in the hot climate, and had to be cooked soon after slaughter. For this reason meat was often eaten at festivals, when many guests would arrive at a master's house and dispose of a whole carcass at one sitting.

RELICS OF THE ANCIENTS

Very little now remains of the towns of the Old Kingdom – nothing of Memphis, the capital, nor of Heliopolis, the 'city of the sun' which lay farther north towards the Nile Delta. The houses and even the royal palaces of these settlements were built of perishable materials: unbaked brick – silt mixed with straw and left to dry in the sun – and wood.

In contrast, Egypt's sacred architecture was built to last. Fine limestone was quarried at Tura near Saqqara and used to sculpt the pyramids. Granite was brought from Aswan and fashioned into columns and architraves. The transport routes for these

CITY OF THE DEAD Djoser's pyramid lay at the centre of a number of ritual structures, including this colonnade. The entire complex was the largest along the 6km (3¾ mile) length of the necropolis at Saqqara.

Carpenters and goldsmiths fashioned funerary furniture and jewellery. Weavers created decorative cloth. But death and religion were not the only inspirations. Objects found in the tombs reveal much about their work for the living.

There are some splendid examples in the 4,500-year-old tomb of Hetepheres, mother of Cheops, or Khufu – the pharaoh for whom Giza's Great Pyramid was built. The tomb lies near the Great Pyramid. It contains chairs with legs tapering to sculpted lions' paws and a box shaped like a grasshopper. Papyrus stems with spreading leaves support an armchair, and form the handle of a mirror.

The bas-reliefs in the Saqqara mastabas show craftsmen at work: carpenters, cabinet-makers, sculptors, goldsmiths, and potters. All contributed to the splendour of the master. Humble

materials lay along the valley of the Nile. The massive slabs of stone were carried by boat during the flood season, then heaved to the sites on huge wooden sledges pulled with ropes.

The architectural feats of the Egyptians were remarkable considering their sparse scientific knowledge; their mathematical system was limited, and though they mapped the stars, they made little progress in predicting their movements. Commitment and effort must have played a large part in the building works.

A LEAGUE OF ARTISANS

A huge number of craftsmen took part in constructing the necropolis. Architects, mathematicians, and astronomers designed the tombs. Sculptors carved statues and bas-reliefs.

HIPPOPOTAMUS HUNTING On the walls of the nobleman Mereruka's tomb, men with poles propel a boat through a thicket of papyrus plants teeming with water birds and game.

labourers are depicted too: in their
homes, praying in their temples,
or mourning the death of a relative.
Almost every visible aspect of daily life
is recorded on these stones.

Here and there in the reliefs,
hieroglyphic inscriptions represent
labourers chatting to one another.
'Leave this barley, it is husked,' says a
woman winnower in the mastaba of Ty,
and her companion replies: 'I do as you
say.' In the same mastaba, a tradesman
selling walking sticks proudly addresses
a customer, drawing a cane from its
sheath: 'Here is a very fine cane, my
friend! A measure of wheat for it!'
'I do like its knob,' the customer replies,
coming closer.

TIME FOR WORK AND PLAY

The reliefs give the impression that the
Egyptians of the Old Kingdom were constantly
at work. This can hardly have been the case.
Religious festivals must have lightened the
burden from time to time, despite their
demands on resources.

In the tomb of a 6th dynasty nobleman called
Mereruka, some rather dwarfish goldsmiths can
be seen adding the final touches to a necklace
which is almost bigger than themselves. 'It's
beautiful, my friend,' says one, admiring their
handiwork. Another, however, is nagging a
companion: 'Hurry up, finish it.' Such informal
asides hardly suggest a society brooding with
oppression. They evoke, on the whole, a nation
going about its business in good cheer, if mindful
of the scribes and overseers.

Mereruka's mastaba also contains scenes of adolescents at
play. Naked young men are shown performing acrobatics: a boy
balances on all fours on the outstretched arms of his companion.
Two teams of boys are having a tug-of-war, and a game similar
to leapfrog is also being played. Another scene shows young
men playing at soldiers: a boy with his arms tied behind his
back is being marched along by his companions; later in the
sequence the unfortunate prisoner has fallen to the ground and
is being vigorously kicked.

A particularly striking vignette in Mereruka's tomb
depicts a group of four maidens forming a kind of
human merry-go-round: two stand in the
middle, back to back, whirling their
companions around them.

A DIVINE ADMINISTRATION

For all the lightheartedness of its youth,
Egypt under the Old Kingdom was
unquestionably a powerful, ordered, and
conservative society. It imitated the
order of the gods, and the pharaoh, son
of the Sun, was divine in his own right.
He had been sent to preserve the stability
of society and to maintain justice in the
face of the forces of chaos. These forces –
symbolized by the daily victory of night over
day and the eternal bleakness of the desert –
were ever-present, always threatening.

To achieve order, the pharaoh oversaw a
remarkably advanced administration. The high
officials, often princes of the royal family,
controlled the country's ministers. Below these
aristocrats, the craftsmen and lower clergy
formed a tiny middle class. As for the peasants,
the lives of the poorest labourers were tightly
controlled. Captives of war provided an
additional labour force.

In principle, the king owned the whole
country. In fact, he often parcelled out his lands
as a reward to one or another of his relatives. As
a result, the royal domain gradually contracted
at the expense of great private estates. Each had
its own peasants, craftsmen, and herds, and
formed a small, self-contained community within
the larger community of Egypt. The estates began
to develop their own administrations, and their
growing independence was to bring the eventual
downfall of the Old Kingdom.

From prince to peasant, all Egyptians were
obsessed by death. They believed that a person
was made up of several different elements. Death
dispersed the elements, and reassembling them was
vital to survival into the afterlife. The body was one
element, and had to be efficiently preserved; the ka,
or spirit, was another. Everyone was born with a ka, which
stood beside them throughout their mortal existence. After
death, preparations had to be made so that it did not leave
them; the expression 'to go to one's ka' meant to die.

The Egyptians believed that the dead survived in their tombs,
or eternal homes. Obviously, the more beautiful a tomb was,
the more splendid the occupant's afterlife would be. Food and
drink had to be taken to the tomb, because the dead inhabitant

FROZEN IN TIME The largest mastabas had chapels, decorated like grand apartments. In Mereruka's tomb, an effigy of the dead nobleman stands above an altar, confidently facing the world of the living.

buried in pit-graves, their bodies unpreserved. But for the ambitious there was a chance of something better. The king often offered a fine sarcophagus as a reward for a lifetime of royal service. Within the stone coffin, the body would be preserved by mummification, a practice with origins dating back to the dawn of Egyptian history.

Even at the beginning of the Old Kingdom, it was known that a corpse's innards decomposed first, so the lungs, liver, and intestines were extracted from the body before embalming. The corpse was then coated with a preservative soda called natron, which dried out the tissues. Finally, the body was bound with bandages and placed in the sarcophagus.

By the end of the Old Kingdom, advances had been made in embalming techniques. Bodies were filled with linen and resin, and the outer bandages soaked in resin so that the deceased's features could be shaped and painted. Later techniques became even more elaborate. The brain was removed as well as the abdominal organs. Silty substances were injected between skin and tissue so that the shrunken flesh could be fattened out and moulded to make the corpse look more lifelike. Wigs were added, and artificial eyes inserted into the skull.

The rites performed at embalming and funeral ceremonies included the 'Opening of the Mouth', during which priests were said to re-endow a mummified corpse with the use of its senses.

Inside the tomb, a casket of cosmetics was sometimes placed next to the mummy, so that the ka could look its best in the afterlife. When the last accessories had been brought to the vault – fine furniture, jewellery, and crockery, to make the tomb into an eternal home – the entrance was sealed up.

– or rather his ka – needed nourishment, just like the living. If the corpse was neglected and allowed to decay, a second death would take place. This would be final, or would mean endless wandering in obscure realms – an atrocious fate in the eyes of the superstitious Egyptians.

Various explanations surrounded the concept of the afterlife. According to one tradition, the dead became stars in the sky. Another told of a mysterious kingdom of the deceased near the western horizon, where the sun went down. This is why the tombs were built on the west bank of the Nile.

PRESERVED FOR THE AFTERLIFE

Each king had a palace built below his pyramidal tomb on the outskirts of Memphis. A temple was built against the east-facing wall of the pyramid. Here, specially assigned priests would celebrate the cult of the dead monarch, living on the produce allocated to them by him. The mastabas were more modest than the royal tombs, but still only the privileged could afford them. The poor of ancient Egypt were mainly

From then until eternity, offerings had to be brought regularly to the tomb. In the minds of the Egyptians, this service was almost as vital as the preservation of the body. In order to guarantee that it was performed, the owner of the mastaba would make contracts with the priests before he died. In exchange for the revenue from a few fields, the priests would carry out regular sacrifices in the tomb's chapel, and deliver food and drink through 'false doors' – the means by which the dead communicated with the living.

LOOKING AFTER THE ANCESTORS

Each generation thus had to guarantee the funeral cult of all preceding generations, and the survival of the dead depended on the goodwill of the living. The Egyptians knew that their descendants might forget their obligations, so they took further precautions which hinged on the mysterious power of images.

An image was considered, in some magical way, to be the equivalent of reality. The ceremony of the 'Opening of the Mouth' could, they believed, bring a statue magically alive as easily as it could restore the senses to a mummy. So a statue was often placed in the serdab, a chamber in the mastaba behind the chapel where rites were performed. The ka of the dead person could come into the statue and partake of the offerings.

PRECIOUS METAL Gold was less valuable than silver in Egypt – it was easier to obtain. Workshops employed dwarves, believed to have special skills in making gold collars, as shown in this 6th-dynasty funerary item.

LEISURE IN THE OLD KINGDOM

From the bas-reliefs at Saqqara, it is known that the Egyptians relished games of skill and chance. Nobles enjoyed the occasional hunt for wild animals, or relaxed with the dancers and musicians of their harem. Boys of noble birth practised wrestling, perhaps as much a form of military training as a recreation, and also played games such as leapfrog. The Egyptians liked parlour games too, of which *senet* and *mehen* were the most highly regarded.

Senet was played by two people, using pawns on a board with 30 squares, as in the New Kingdom painting (below) in which a lion and an antelope pit their wits against one another. The players' aim was to win their rightful place in the afterlife. Mehen, or 'The Serpent', dates back to prehistoric times. It was played on a round table representing a serpent coiled around itself: the body was divided into segments, with the head in the centre. Players used small balls and pawns shaped like recumbent lions, and the serpent would try to 'catch' the pawns, or lions. The game had a symbolic significance probably derived from Egyptian methods of lion-hunting. These hunts involved digging a trap, in which the corpse of a servant was used as bait.

The Egyptians also believed that bas-reliefs and hieroglyphic inscriptions could be brought to life. So the image of the dead man was engraved on a stone slab or stele in the chapel. He was shown at a table piled with food and drink. If the priests neglected their duties, the scenes engraved on the walls could provide for his needs. Peasants sowing and reaping, servants making bread, and women weaving linen could all provide food and clothing, if the priests didn't keep their promises. Through the magic of images, the dead could also gain access to the things that they enjoyed during their mortal life.

THE PROMISE OF PARADISE

These beliefs changed gradually over the centuries and, in time, the cult of the god Osiris triumphed. The new deity was a benevolent god who was assassinated and brought back to life, promising resurrection to all in his paradise rather than a precarious existence in a magical tomb. But whatever visions of immortality were dreamed up by the priests, the Egyptians still insisted on one thing. Everything they held dear in life would go with them into eternity.

Mari

The lost city of Mesopotamia

When a large, headless statue was unearthed in Syria early in the 20th century, it turned out to be the first of a startling series of archaeological discoveries. A palace and temples followed – and soon an entire city was brought to light.

TELL HARIRI LIES ON THE WEST BANK of the river Euphrates in Syria, 12km (7½ miles) from the border with Iraq. In the early 20th century, the ruins at the site were considered to be of little interest – there were scores of similar sites, or tells, throughout the lands of the Middle East. But in the 1930s, while Syria was a French mandate, a Bedouin foraging among the ruins for a suitable gravestone discovered a headless statue. The statue bore an inscription in cuneiform – ancient, wedge-shaped writing. Casual digging at the site was hurriedly stopped by the local authorities, and the French archaeologist André Parrot was sent to explore the tell.

Parrot unearthed a large number of alabaster statues of the period known as Early Dynastic III, most of them inscribed with the Semitic names of kings, viziers, and priests. One, bearing a dedication to the goddess Ishtar, was inscribed with the name of the king of Mari – a find that unlocked the secrets of the site. Tell Hariri stood on the ruins of the lost city of Mari.

A MYSTERY IS SOLVED

The name of Mari had already cropped up in the records of the great Mesopotamian civilization of Sumer, discovered by earlier archaeologists. Sumer was centred on the delta of the Tigris and Euphrates rivers, where great cities such as Uruk, Nippur, Eridu, and Ur flourished some 3,000 years before the birth of Christ. Its people invented writing, and in early texts now known as the king-list, they named Mari as one of the dozen or so city-states struggling for supremacy between about 3000 and 2300 BC. But Tell Hariri was a long way from the known centres of Sumerian civilization – and its discovery revolutionized thinking about ancient Mesopotamia. Clearly its culture had been shared by other peoples living much farther up the Euphrates than had been imagined.

While working on the site in 1934, Parrot was visited by Henri Frankfort, a Dutch archaeologist then exploring Tell Asmar and Khafajeh, some 400km (250 miles) to the east. His findings were strikingly similar to Parrot's, suggesting that a single civilization spanned the entire breadth of Mesopotamia.

TOUCHED BY SUMER The figure of a steward called Ebih-II, clad in his goatskin skirt, is one of the most life-like in ancient art. Inscriptions on this and other statues unearthed at Mari were written in a Semitic language but used Sumerian cuneiform script. The city lay miles from the accepted centre of Sumerian civilization, but it was clearly in touch with Sumerian culture, and could offer its people trade links to Syria in the north-west.

DIVINE FLIGHT This lapis lazuli pendant, delivered by an envoy from Ur, is in the shape of the Anzu bird, associated with a hurricane god, Ningirsu. The bird's wings were said to beat rain from dark clouds, and thunder roared from its lion's head.

Parrot went on to reveal the true grandeur of ancient Mari. He discovered two royal palaces, one of which dated back to 2500 BC – the time of the Early Dynastic Period – and a haul of inscribed tablets, which helped to build up a vivid picture of the city's history.

A COMMERCIAL HEARTLAND

Mari's importance stemmed from its key position on the trade route linking Mesopotamia with Syria to the north-west. The Sumerian settlements of the delta were rich in agricultural produce, but they needed crucial raw materials from Syria to sustain their city culture. Sumer exported corn, leather, and wool in exchange for scarce building materials such as stone and timber. Silver and lead were brought down from the Syrian hills to supply Sumerian metalworkers. Copper came from as far away as the Taurus Mountains in Asia Minor, and from Magan (the Oman coast) in the Persian Gulf.

As trade expanded, military and diplomatic missions were sent to Mari to maintain links with its supply lines. During excavations of the Early Dynastic palace, André Parrot discovered a cache of objects, including several cylindrical seals, presented to the local ruler by Mesannepadda, king of the Sumerian city of Ur. The evidence indicated that an important diplomatic mission was sent to Mari in around 2500 BC. Mesannepadda's envoy was a scribe. With him, the king sent a message of friendship to Mari's ruler, an offer of alliance, and rich gifts, including a magnificent blue Anzu bird pendant of lapis lazuli imported from beyond the Iranian plateau and inscribed with the royal sender's name.

The journey was not difficult, for Ur at that time dominated many of the other Sumerian cities and nobody would have obstructed the caravan's progress. As it made its way up the valley of the Euphrates, the envoy would have noticed linguistic changes. But understanding the Semitic tongue was not a problem to a Sumerian scholar: Bedouin herdsmen often drove their cattle up and down the valley, and mixed freely with the city-dwellers in the south. Their language was understood in Ur.

In the dry uplands of the Euphrates, Mari loomed like an oasis, irrigated by networks of canals leading off the great river. A dyke protected the city from flooding, and ramparts of unbaked brick fortified its walls. The envoy was greeted at the gates by a royal official and conducted to the newly erected palace.

In the great visitors' courtyard, the envoy awaited an audience. At the appointed time, a group of dignitaries arrived – scribes, army officers, and relatives of the king – followed by the king himself. The king's costume was no different from that of his entourage, consisting mainly of goatskin from waist to ankle, but he was distinguished by the arrangement of his long hair, plaited in a diadem round his head with a double bun above the nape of the neck.

RICHNESS AND ROYALTY

After a short reception ceremony, the envoy followed the king through several halls to a courtyard with a decorated altar and walls inset with rectangular columns. From the courtyard two doors opened into a long chamber, the sanctuary, at the back of which was another room containing the sepulchre of the dynasty's ancestor. Above his tomb was an altar where the reigning king officiated as high priest and god.

On the walls, mosaics illustrated New Year festivals in which the king stood in for his god and the queen played the god's consort, acting out a divine marriage ceremony. If their union proved fruitful, it portended a fertile year. The mosaic figures were carved from mother-of-pearl imported from the Persian Gulf, and were mounted in bitumen on wooden panels. The content of the mosaics would have been familiar to the envoy – New Year's rites were similar to those practised at Ur – but the artistry would have seemed unusually refined.

The purpose of Mesannepadda's diplomatic mission was to tighten the bonds between Ur and Mari. Clouds were gathering to the west where the king of Ebla (present-day Tell Mardikh) posed a serious threat. This fearsome monarch had made vassals of his neighbours, and had conquered many more distant areas.

ROYAL ENTERTAINER A statue that once included a lyre, from the shrine of Ninni-Zaza, depicts one of the king's favourite musicians, Ur-Nanshe. His feminine features suggest that he may have been a eunuch.

The king of Mari was clearly anxious to show the importance he attached to the visit of the Sumerian envoy. Offerings from his own treasury had been prepared for burial beneath the new palace's foundations: copper, gold, and silver bracelets, silver pendants, and a series of cylinder seals from the city's workshops. There were also two statuettes of goddesses sent by a king of Syria, one of ivory, the other silver. Both were naked – shocking to a Sumerian. To this hoard of treasures were added the cylinder seals and pendant of lapis lazuli from Ur. All were placed in a large jug which was buried beneath the courtyard. The act symbolized, for the benefit of the gods, the splendour of the king of Mari, and the scope of his international relations.

THE COMFORT OF THE FAMILIAR

Over the centuries, Mari underwent developments like any other city. But even in 2400 BC, a century after the visit of Mesannepadda's envoy, a Sumerian traveller would have found much to remind him of home.

Mari's narrow, carefully laid-out streets resembled those of Ur. Near the palace stood the temple of Ninni-Zaza, a goddess also known at Ur. Through the temple's entrance hall was something rather less familiar to a Sumerian: a tapering stone set in the middle of the temple courtyard. In Mari, the gods not only took human shape – their presence also dwelt in stone. This belief, shared by Mari's western neighbours, was alien to the Sumerians. The stone would be regularly anointed with oil, and offerings of sacred cakes would be placed nearby.

Two doors led from the courtyard into the shrine of Ninni-Zaza, a long, rectangular chamber which was lit with oil lamps. At the end stood a wooden statue of the goddess

THE PALACE OF ZIMRI-LIM

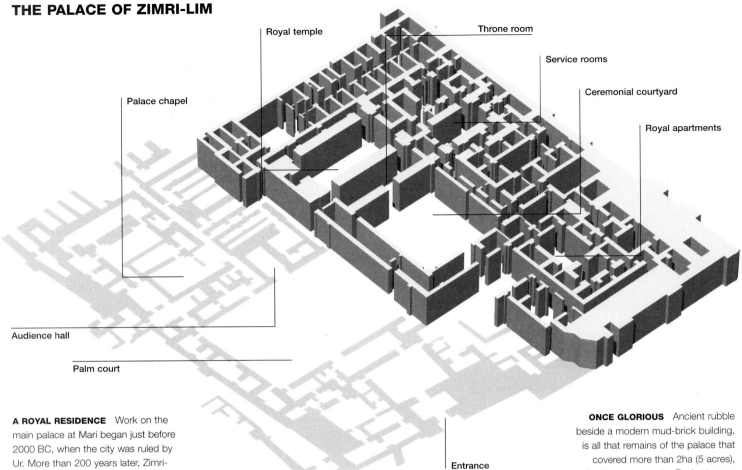

Royal temple

Throne room

Service rooms

Ceremonial courtyard

Palace chapel

Royal apartments

Audience hall

Palm court

A ROYAL RESIDENCE Work on the main palace at Mari began just before 2000 BC, when the city was ruled by Ur. More than 200 years later, Zimri-Lim completed it. In this diagram, part of the palace is shown reconstructed.

Entrance

ONCE GLORIOUS Ancient rubble beside a modern mud-brick building, is all that remains of the palace that covered more than 2ha (5 acres), looking out over the Euphrates, on which Mari depended for irrigation.

wearing a horned tiara. Below it, vases sunk into the floor received water poured by the priests. Offerings of food were placed on a nearby table.

On a brick bench facing the entrance stood a host of statuettes carved from white alabaster or limestone. They depicted the notables of Mari, in postures of reverence and prayer. One bore the inscription Iku-Shamagan, 'King of Mari'. Others represented Salim, the 'King's Eldest Brother', Mashigirru, the 'Country's Grandee', and lastly the 'Royal Cup-bearer', 'Steward of the King's Household', and 'Great Scribe' (the prime minister, Ipumsar). The inscriptions were in a Semitic language, but the script was Sumerian and easy enough to decipher since the symbols represented concepts as much as sounds.

Religion at Mari differed in some important ways from that practised at Ur. Images on cylinder seals found at the site depict the Sun god, patron deity of Mari, at the prow of a serpent-shaped vessel, brandishing a leafy branch. The god is sailing the celestial ocean which was believed to span the world and feed the Earth's rivers. He reigned the Universe as the master of all life, in particular of plants. In this capacity he was also the patron of ploughmen, and a plough was

depicted at his side. Ur's patron deity, the moon god Nanna, was represented in a more down-to-earth fashion. Nanna was the highest in a hierarchy of gods: each deity had a particular sphere of influence and wielded his or her power through spirits who fulfilled specific roles.

But for all the power of the gods, and the alliance with Ur, Mari was soon to fall. Sometime between 2350 and 2300 BC, the city was destroyed. Historians are unsure of the invader: perhaps the ruler of neighbouring Ebla, or perhaps the mighty Sargon of Akkad who, from his capital near Babylon, conquered lands between the Persian Gulf and the Mediterranean to establish the first Mesopotamian empire. When Mari became part of this empire, the rebuilding of the ruins began. But Sargon's supremacy crumbled within a century, and was eventually replaced by a Sumerian empire based at Ur. Mari's rulers were vassals to Ur from about 2111 to 2003 BC.

This period was marked by deep disturbances. Nomadic peoples from the Syrian desert and beyond were gradually moving into Mesopotamia. They became established at Mari, and one of their princes marched from the city on Ur, joining forces with the Elamites of the Iranian plateau to the east to destroy the

> *Nanna was the highest in a hierarchy of gods: each deity had a particular sphere of influence and wielded his or her power through spirits who fulfilled specific roles.*

last Sumerian dynasty. Ur's glory was at an end. But the new rulers, the Amorites, adopted the civilization of the conquered peoples and restored the kingdom. At the end of the 19th century BC, the Amorite Yagit-Lim founded a dynasty at Mari. Trade flourished, and the city's workshops thronged with craftsmen. Mari became famous for its metalwork, producing everything from fish-hooks to ploughshares.

But the city did not stand alone as a major power. During the rule of Yagit-Lim's son, Yahdun-Lim, the Assyrian king Shamshi-Adad controlled the middle valley of the Tigris from his base at Ashur. Shamshi-Adad looked jealously at the stretch of the Euphrates controlled by Mari, and had Yahdun-Lim assassinated, placing his own son, Yasmah-Addu, on the throne. But the Assyrian prince was weak, and when his father died, Mari was seized by a usurper, Ishar-Lim. The legitimate heir took his opportunity, and returned from his refuge at Aleppo to drive out the usurper. The name of the rightful king was Zimri-Lim.

INSIDE THE ROYAL CHAMBERS

The palace taken over and extended by Zimri-Lim (c.1780–1759 BC) became the administrative heart of the kingdom. According to its contemporaries, it was one of the wonders of the world. For the archaeologists, it was a major find. The fortress-like building had a single entrance flanked by towers. A series of quadrangles beyond the entrance led to a large courtyard shaded by palm trees.

This 'palm court', as scholars call it, was the site of Mari's old administrative centre. From it, a sacred way led to the palace chapel – a shrine built over the ruins of the old palace's sanctuary. An audience hall opened onto the courtyard. The walls of the courtyard were covered with paintings dating from before Zimri-Lim's time. They depicted Mari's king making a libation to the Moon god.

To the west of the palm court, Yahdun-Lim and Zimri-Lim added private apartments for the royal family. The queen's chamber had two terracotta baths positioned beside a hearth, which was used to heat water. Near to the state rooms, apartments reserved for distinguished visitors contained bathrooms with latrines and well-equipped kitchens.

The building's plumbing arrangements were remarkable. The bathrooms had coatings of bitumen on the floors and lower walls to protect against damp. Brick gutters were set into the paving, and clay pipes lined with bitumen were sunk 9m (30ft) into the ground. While excavating the palace, André Parrot discovered how efficient the drainage system was. When a sudden cloudburst soaked the site, creating a chaos of mud and water in the pits and trenches, the waters subsided in minutes, carried away by the 4,000-year-old plumbing system.

The royal apartments were connected to the domestic wing and service rooms, and to a ceremonial courtyard about 29m (95ft) long and 26m (85ft) wide. An enormous door led from the courtyard to the throne room, which opened onto a vast royal temple. The throne stood on a dais at the back of the temple, facing a gallery. This was the inner sanctum of the dynastic cult, where royal statues of Mari's ancestral kings stood on plinths.

An interesting feature of the palace is the apparent absence of windows. Daylight probably entered through broad doorways opening onto the courtyards, or through circular skylights.

LETTERS FROM THE PAST

The construction details of the palace, including decrees for the building of canals, dams, and embankments, were recorded by the tireless scribes of Mari, and archived in rooms adjoining the ceremonial courtyard. More than 20,000 tablets have been found, providing a mass of information on court life and royal administration.

Some of the most human touches are found in the letters of wives writing to their lords who were away on military campaigns. They give family news and express affection and respect. This, for example, is from a queen identified as Shibtu: 'May my lord beat his enemies and may my master then return to Mari safe and sound with joy in his heart.'

INSIDE THE ROYAL KITCHEN

The royal archives deal with daily life. Many letters concern the provision of food, which was prepared and cooked in impressive kitchens beside the steward's offices. Some of the documents read like pages from a caterer's notebook: '70 measures of wholemeal bread; 17 measures of leavened bread; 3 measures of semolina; 2 measures of gruel, 2 measures of beans. Total: 94 measures . . . for the king's meal.' Other documents refer to wine imported from Syria: 'Tell this to my lord: thus speaks Kibri-Dagan, your servant. I have been ordered by my lord to take jars of wine for Atamrum in ships of the people of Emar. Assisted by Atamrum's cup-bearer, I had several jars of wine brought up to the quay; 90 jars of wine were selected. The rest were sent back. I therefore arranged to load these 90 jars of wine for shipment.'

FINE CUISINE Several hundred decorative moulds including the cake mould (right) were found near the palace kitchens, along with ice-storage facilities.

Affairs of state were also recorded, such as imports and exports, and the details of censuses taken to assist taxation and military conscription. Although the census was accompanied by an issue of free beer and bread, the tribes of nomads within the city's frontiers showed a marked reluctance to be counted.

From the mass of tablets, the kings of Mari emerge as responsible and respected administrators. Inscriptions record many appeals for mediation in disputes, and countless gifts from loyal subjects. Public order seems to have been firmly maintained. One tablet records that a child's mutilated body had been found outside Mari: a full inquest was promised.

From these documents, it becomes clear that the main concern of the kings of Mari were the raids of nomads from the Syrian desert: the savage Suteans, most fearsome of all; the Yaminites (or

Benjaminites), who were herdsmen like the patriarchs of the Bible; and the Haneans, who were eventually assimilated and provided excellent soldiers.

Yet it was not the unruly nomads who brought about Mari's downfall. In Babylon to the south, a new star was rising. King Hammurabi had become master of lower Mesopotamia. Much of what is known of his reign comes from Mari's archives.

A FINAL GESTURE

Hammurabi and Zimri-Lim were at first close allies, controlling between them the entire length of the Euphrates. But once Hammurabi had conquered central and southern Mesopotamia, he began to look north, towards the valuable trade routes leading from Mari to the Mediterranean. The Babylonian monarch suddenly turned on his ally. In 1759 BC, he defeated Zimri-Lim in battle and reduced him to vassalage.

Zimri-Lim was spared at first. Perhaps to reinforce his waning authority, he ordered a large mural to be painted on an outer wall of the ceremonial courtyard, near the door to his throne room. On the upper section, the king, draped in an elaborately fringed costume, is honoured by Ishtar, goddess of war. The mural was framed by tall panels with stylized trees, birds, and mythical animals.

The painting was the most richly ornamented of any found in the palace, but the gesture was in vain. Two years later, Hammurabi marched on Mari, captured it and destroyed it by fire. Although the site was settled by Assyrians in the first millennium BC, its significance had been eradicated – the ancient city was never to rise again to its former glories.

SOLEMN RITUAL A wall painting from the main palace at Mari shows a procession of figures leading a bull to sacrifice. The figure on the right is the king, probably Yasmah-Addu, shown much larger to reflect his importance.

Harappa

Advanced planning on a vast scale

More than 4,000 years ago, a merchant people built great cities of brick at Harappa and elsewhere in a valley of what is now Pakistan. They developed a written language that remains an enigma, and left an indelible mark on Indian culture.

IN 1856 TWO BRITISH ENGINEERS, the brothers John and Robert Brunton, were contracted to build a railway link between Lahore and Multan in what is now Pakistan. They were immediately faced with a problem. The alluvial soil of the Indus Valley through which the proposed railway was to run was a rich landscape for cultivating crops, but almost completely lacking in stone to act as ballast for the railway tracks. The Bruntons solved this problem in a way that must have impressed their employers, but which created an archaeological disaster. Near the village of Harappa in the north, they had discovered huge deposits of ancient, baked mud-bricks. These would make perfect ballast for their building project, the Bruntons decided, and they laid 160km (100 miles) of track on the ancient bricks.

After the brothers' plunder, Britain's then director-general of archaeology in India, Sir Alexander Cunningham, carried out a small excavation at Harappa. He concluded that little was left, but he did publish details of an inscribed seal found earlier at the site which bore a picture of a bull and six strange symbols. More than half a century elapsed before this enigmatic clue to India's early history was pursued.

REWORKING THE ANCIENT MAP

In 1921, under a newly appointed director-general, Sir John Marshall, detailed excavations began at Harappa. Marshall's team uncovered the scant remains of a large city – a find that turned out to be the first of a series of epoch-making discoveries proving the existence of a hitherto unknown culture, the Indus Valley civilization, which flourished more than 2,000 years before the birth of Christ.

A year later, excavations began on a second city near the railway at Mohenjo-Daro, the 'Hill of the Dead', 640km (400 miles) to the south. The discoveries here shed light on the mysteries of Harappa. Further investigations uncovered the remains of smaller settlements over a vast area, from present-day Karachi to the mouth of the Narmada river, and eastwards almost as far as modern Delhi.

BEJEWELLED SPLENDOUR
Mother goddess figurines wearing elaborate headdresses and jewellery were common in Indus cities such as Harappa. The terracotta statuettes were probably votive offerings made for ritual uses, and followed a religious tradition established by earlier settlers, who occupied the Indus region for centuries before the great urban centres emerged.

The earliest settlers in the Indus Valley arrived in the 4th millennium BC. Between 2700 and 2600 BC, uniformly planned towns and cities emerged and the entire Indus region became culturally unified. The massive city walls of Harappa were constructed during this time of transformation. Since the discovery of Harappa and Mohenjo-Daro, other ancient Indus cities have been found, such as Dholavira in Gujarat and Ganweriwala in Cholistan, giving archaeologists further insight into the urban lifestyle of the Indus civilization.

THE RISE OF THE RIVER VALLEY CITADELS

Harappa's most prominent feature was its citadel, built on an artificial hill to the west. Its outline remains, enclosing an area of about 396m by 198m (1,300ft by 650ft). Indus citadels contained ritual structures and public buildings, but no palaces. The Mohenjo-Daro citadel housed a structure now known as the 'Great Bath' – a rectangular pool 12m (39ft) long, 7m (30ft)

MASTER PLANNING The kiln-fired bricks of Harappa were laid out on a grid plan on the left bank of the Ravi river, now a dry riverbed. Since 1986, an American team has been carrying out comprehensive excavations.

wide, and 2.4m (almost 8ft) deep which may have hosted immersion ceremonies – an intriguing precedent for the bathing rituals of later Hinduism.

At the foot of the citadel in Harappa were workshops and brick-paved floors, some of which may have been used for husking grain. North of these is a structure once identified as a granary, now thought to have been a large public building. Mohenjo-Daro contains a similar building. In the small Indus town of Lothal, near the western coast in Gujarat, the citadel held a large warehouse containing clay seals which bore the imprint of the cloth packaging to which they had been fastened.

Spacious residential quarters stretched out beneath the Harappan citadel. Recent surveys have revealed the staggering size of the Indus cities, much of which lay hidden beneath deep layers of alluvium: Harappa covers more than 150ha (370 acres); Mohenjo-Daro sprawls across 250ha (618 acres).

South of the citadel at Harappa lay the cemetery. The graves of the Indus Valley people were built on the same generous scale as their cities. The average size was 3.3m by 1.2m (almost 11ft by 4ft), though some were as large as 4.5m by 3m (almost 15ft by 10ft). Recent work at Harappa has revealed new information about burial practices. The dead lay on their backs or sides, their heads towards the north, and were sometimes wrapped in a textile shroud. Objects buried with the bodies included copper rings, stone and shell necklaces, and mirrors of polished copper. Pots were the main offering, usually filled with food and drink; frequently, they were placed in the grave first and covered with soil, and the coffin was placed on top of them.

LAID OUT TO A PLAN

The most astonishing aspect of all Indus cities was their advanced system of town planning. Within the thick outer walls – probably a defence against flooding – large blocks of houses were separated by a grid of broad roads. Houses were terraced; they varied in size, but were all designed around an inner courtyard, usually with a staircase leading to an upper floor. Much of the daily life of the citizens took place in the courtyard, as it does in Indian homes today.

The people were fastidious about personal hygiene. The houses contained bathrooms, and often brick lavatories, which were connected to a system of drains which followed the routes of the streets, punctuated by manholes, gutters, and wells. The houses contain slight traces of elaborate woodwork, and the plastered walls and floors may have been painted or covered

with mats and hangings. Finds of jewellery, vivacious figurines, and lively painted pottery show that the Indus people did not lack artistic imagination or colour in their daily lives. But there seems to have been little room for more permanent secular or even religious art, only sparse evidence of which has survived.

Apart from a few elaborate sculptures, no large statues have been discovered in the region – only a vast quantity of clay figurines. Some figurines represent naked, bearded men, but most of them are well-rounded female forms, full-breasted and wide-hipped – probably images of the great mother goddess who was worshipped in various guises throughout the Middle East at the time. Their bodies are adorned with heavy necklaces and fantastic bulging headgear in which lamps could sometimes be mounted. Other figurines include a large number of toys such as ox-drawn carts. Some of these models may have been intended as religious offerings rather than as mere playthings.

BOUNTIFUL WATERS

The climate in Harappa was probably as hot and dry then as it is today, and the crops – with the exception of rice and millet, which were not cultivated until around 2000 BC – were the same: wheat, barley, peas, sesame (from which oil was extracted), and cotton. In the 3rd millennium BC, the bounty of the Indus was matched or exceeded by another river system running parallel to it to the south – the 'lost Saraswati', which

survives today only in the form of minor rivers such as the Hakra. The area watered by this mighty river was probably the breadbasket of the civilization.

The Indus people certainly ate fish from the rivers and hunted big game – wild ox, elephant, tiger, and rhinoceros – which was more plentiful then than now. Some farmers kept chickens, cattle, buffalo, sheep, and goats; others specialized in herding animals, driving them between seasonal pastures.

THE SOCIAL HIERARCHY

Nothing is known for certain about the social system of Harappa and the other Indus cities. A class of priestly rulers probably governed the communities. Peasant farmers, fishermen, and nomadic pastoralists were the backbone of society. Artisans such as carpenters, metalworkers, potters and workers of gemstones would have occupied the next level up in the social order. Craftsmen shaped tools from stone, copper, or bronze – iron was unknown; bowls and jars were created mainly from clay or wood. Other crafts, notably spinning and weaving, would have been practised in every household.

Rich merchants may have comprised an elite class above the artisans, trading with the other cities of the Indus Valley and, according to ancient texts from Mesopotamia, with places as far away as Sumer in modern Iraq. Indus merchants established trading communities in Sumerian towns, and Indus ivory, gold, carnelian, and agate beads, timber, and other goods had an important place in the Sumerians' import business; in return they

> *The prosperity of the Indus merchants was based not on military superiority – all the evidence shows that they were peaceful people – but on intellectual sophistication.*

may have exported fine textiles, perfumed oils, and other perishables of which no trace survives.

The Indus people also traded with neighbouring hunter-gatherers and the fishing communities of Gujarat and the Aravalli hills, south of the river valleys – regions that supplied ivory, carnelian, agate, copper, tin, and many other raw materials. Goods were carried between settlements in ox carts with solid wheels; for longer journeys, the merchants used pack animals or river craft resembling today's Indus houseboats.

The towns of the Iranian plateau to the west and Turkmenia to the north-west had long been trading partners of the Indus people and their ancestors. This trade took a new turn when the Indus authorities established an outpost at Shortugai, far to the north, to control the supply of lapis lazuli – the most valued commodity in West Asia, which at that time came only from Badakshan in Turkmenia (in present-day Afghanistan).

WRITING ON SEALS

The prosperity of the Indus merchants was based not on military superiority – all the evidence shows that they were peaceful people – but on intellectual sophistication. The cities

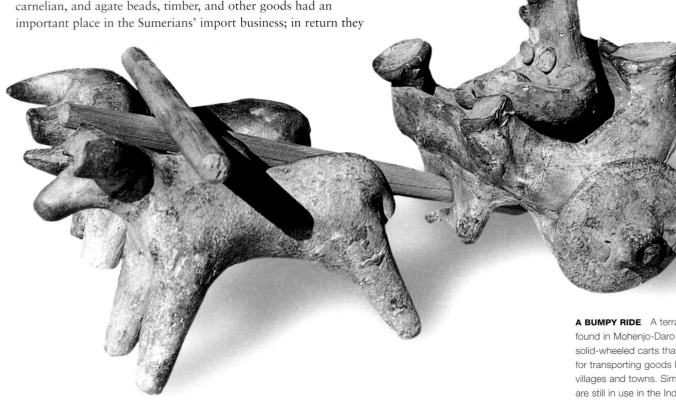

A BUMPY RIDE A terracotta model found in Mohenjo-Daro shows the solid-wheeled carts that were used for transporting goods between villages and towns. Similar vehicles are still in use in the Indus region.

UNSOLVED MYSTERY Merchandise seals used by the Indus people usually bear between four and ten symbols – insufficient evidence from which to decode them. The animal on the seal is a rhinoceros.

mythological creature have been found. Some seals show a grotesque animal with a man's head, a bull's horns, an elephant's trunk, a ram's forequarters, and a tiger's hindlegs.

One bizarre image has fascinated archaeologists: a man seated in a yogic position, wearing horned headgear. He has been identified as a prototype of the Hindu god Shiva, a deity known as the Destroyer but also as a lord of fertility. The goddesses that feature on some seals closely resemble the forms taken by Shiva's consort – variously known as Kali, Parvati, or Durga.

The Indus cities also used standardized weights and measures. The basic unit of weight was equivalent to just under 14g ($^1/_2$oz); linear measurements were based on a 'cubit' of about 53cm (21in), from the length of a man's forearm. Archaeologists found a bronze ruler at Harappa marked with cubits.

used a written language, for example. Excavators have discovered numerous square seals, mainly of soapstone, engraved with animals and other symbols. The seals were used as signatures, stamped onto bales of merchandise to identify the owners or issuing authority. Most scholars believe that the symbols derive from an early Dravidian language, from the same family as Tamil and other languages of southern India.

The keenly observed animals pictured on the seals offer the most impressive surviving examples of the Indus people's artistic skills. The most common motif is a one-horned antelope. It is shown in profile and could represent a two-horned creature with one horn hidden. More probably, it represented a unicorn – terracotta figures of this

ASHES TO ASHES A cemetery at Harappa reflected the changes taking place as the Indus civilization declined in the 2nd millennium BC. The dead were now often cremated: this dish was used to cover a funerary urn.

A FRACTURED POPULATION

By 1600 BC the great cities of the Indus Valley had been abandoned. Quite why the people left is uncertain. Perhaps repeated flooding or shifts in the riverbeds destroyed the harvests and wrecked the once buoyant economy. The gradual drying up of the great Saraswati river caused a serious decline in agricultural productivity. There is also evidence of malaria and probably cholera, which must have taken their toll. The arts of city life, such as writing, disappeared. Although some regions continued to prosper, notably Gujarat in the south-west, many areas saw a decline in their population.

Eventually, Indo-Europeans from central Asia invaded the valley and settled among the existing population. Many farmers and pastoralists moved into adjacent regions in the south and east, and, slowly, sand and silt buried the ruins of the cities. But the Indus culture did not die.

Although the Indo-Aryan languages of the new settlers from the west eventually prevailed, the indigenous Dravidian languages had a strong influence on their vocabulary, grammar, and pronunciation. The Hindu religion that crystallized in the 1st millennium BC combined elements introduced by the Indo-Aryans with the earlier beliefs of the inhabitants of Indus Valley settlements such as Harappa. Today, many features of modern Indian life have their roots in the Indus civilization – the first great flowering of culture in the subcontinent.

The first towns

The advent of agriculture led to dependable food supplies and the first permanent settlements. In the 3rd millennium BC, communities set aside areas for administration, craftwork, and worship, and the city took shape. The map below shows some of the most important early settlements.

KEY TO MAP: DATES OF FOUNDATION

- Before 3000 BC
- 3000–1000 BC
- 1000–1 BC
- AD 1–1000
- AD 1000 to present

Cliff Palace: canyon town of Mesa Verde

Long before the Spanish conquistadores arrived, some Latin American communities were living in urban settlements known as pueblos. Cliff Palace at Mesa Verde in Colorado is among the most remarkable, sheltered by a vast natural cavity in a cliff. The settlement – a complex of dwellings stacked together on a succession of terraces – flourished between AD 1150 and 1300. Scattered among the houses were several kivas – circular buildings used for worship.

L'Anse aux Meadows: the first European home in America

L'Anse aux Meadows, Newfoundland, is proof that the Vikings arrived in America. The farmstead consisted of three houses made of turf laid over a framework of local driftwood, each containing several rooms and a central stone hearth. The site also included cooking pits, five outbuildings used as worksheds, and a smithy where local bog-iron was worked into tools. The insubstantial houses and small quantity of domestic debris suggest that the settlement, founded about AD 1000, was only occupied for a short period.

VIKING HOMESTEAD The houses of L'Anse aux Meadows have now been reconstructed.

Skara Brae: a Stone Age cooperative

Skara Brae in the islands of Orkney off Scotland was a tight-knit village. Paved alleyways ran between its dry stone huts, each of which had a single room with a central hearth and stone furniture. Contemporary communities in the Mediterranean were building more substantial settlements, such as the village of Los Millares in Spain and the Greek town of Lerna.

Skara Brae 3rd millennium BC

L'Anse aux Meadows 11th century AD

Skara Brae ground plan

Cliff Palace 12th century AD

Teotihuacán 1st millennium BC

CANYON FORT The 217 rooms and 23 kivas of Cliff Palace were built in an almost inaccessible location to guard against intruders.

Teotihuacán: metropolis of the sun

Teotihuacán in the Valley of Mexico was founded in the late 1st millennium BC. Its site was a cave from which the sun, moon, and first humans were believed to have emerged when the world began. The city was one of the largest in the world with some 200,000 inhabitants at its peak in the 6th century AD. A wide avenue flanked by pyramids and temples formed its ceremonial centre. The surrounding city covered more than 20km² (7.7sq miles), and was divided into complexes housing different social groups, such as craftsmen. On the outskirts dwelt the peasant farmers who cultivated the rich valley soil.

TIME CAPSULE Skara Brae has now been excavated. Originally the whole structure, including the alleyways, was roofed over.

A CEREMONIAL PATH The Avenue of the Dead in Teotihuacán leads from the Pyramid of the Moon (far left) past temples, palaces, and the vast Pyramid of the Sun to the Great Compound and the Temple of Quetzalcoatl in the ceremonial heart of the ancient city.

Dura Europos: a Greek city on the banks of the Euphrates

Not every culture developed urban civilization by its own devices. The cities founded by Alexander the Great and his successors in areas such as Ai Khanoum in Afghanistan introduced the Greek way of life to new regions. Dura Europos on the Euphrates in Syria, founded about 300 BC, is an example of a 'planted' Hellenistic town. Its grid-plan streets centred on an *agora*, or Greek marketplace. It became a caravan city under the Parthians from 100 BC. When the Romans took over in AD 165, they converted many of the houses into barracks and added Roman structures such as a bath-house.

GRID-PLAN CITY Dura Europos was founded by one of the generals in the service of Alexander the Great – Seleucus I Nicator. By the 2nd century AD, its boundaries enclosed 180ha (445 acres) of rectangular city blocks.

Nippur: the religious heart of Mesopotamia

A cuneiform tablet dating back to the 13th century BC provides the world's earliest-known city map (right). From it, archaeologists have been able to identify parts of the great Sumerian metropolis of Nippur, founded in about 5000 BC. On the left are the waters of the Euphrates. Inside a double line of ramparts is the Kirishauru, a garden which adjoined an enclosure. A canal ran through the city centre, and to the right of this was the E-kur, a shrine dedicated to Enlil, patron god of Nippur and head of the Sumerian pantheon. This association gave the city supreme religious status throughout Mesopotamia.

Dura Europus
3rd Century BC

Jericho
9th millennium BC

Nippur
5th millennium BC

Mohenjo-Daro
3rd millennium BC

Mohenjo-Daro: city of the Indus

Mohenjo-Daro in southern Pakistan dates from before 2600 BC, and was one of the earliest settlements to be laid out according to the principles of town planning. A grid of wide streets was intersected at right-angles by narrower lanes. Houses were spacious; they had their own wells and many home comforts, including bathrooms. The facades overlooking the streets had no windows, and the only access to the houses was through the narrow alleys. The city also had a mains-drainage system.

Mohenjo-Daro ground plan

Jericho: Jordan Valley town

A spring attracted some of the world's earliest farmers to settle at Jericho about 9000 BC. They built circular houses of mud brick (the earliest structures known in this building material), and by 8500 BC Jericho may have housed as many as 1,500 people. A massive stone wall surrounded the settlement – a unique feature at the time of its construction, which was intended to provide a defence against invaders, animals, or floods, or as a sign of prestige. Apart from occasional periods of abandonment, the site would remain a major settlement for a further 8,000 years.

LOOKOUT POST The ruins of a stone tower 10m (33ft) wide houses a stairway which once led to the top of Jericho's wall.

RITUAL BATH The citadel mound in Mohenjo-Daro contains the Great Bath, a pool sealed with bitumen, once used for ceremonies which are now a mystery.

Ur

A city known to Abraham

For thousands of years a sandy hump brooded over the desert of lower Mesopotamia, covering the silent remains of a thriving urban community. It is the site of ancient Ur, a city whose discovery cast light on a forgotten chapter of history.

'AND THEY SET OUT FROM UR OF THE CHALDEES . . .' declares the Book of Genesis, describing how the family of Abraham left their native city for Canaan. The episode is of great significance in Biblical studies, for it was after leaving his place of birth that Abraham made his covenant with God, and from his seed – numberless as the stars – sprang the children of Israel.

In the mid-19th century, scholars discovered that some scriptural passages had their origins in real people, places, and events. Exciting finds at Nineveh and Khorsabad in northern Mesopotamia had cast dramatic light on Assyrian kings named in the Old Testament. In this period of awakening interest, an English diplomat, J.E. Taylor, set out in 1854 to explore a site in southern Mesopotamia known to the locals as Tell al-Muqayyar: an ancient mound of mud-brick ramps and terraces. But archaeology was then in its infancy, and sites were studied more for their relics than for the information they could reveal. Taylor's main hope was to find artefacts to display in a museum.

UNCOVERING A LEGENDARY CITY

After preliminary excavations at the bottom of the mound, Taylor ordered his workmen to the summit. The team found only clay cylinders with cuneiform (wedge-shaped) inscriptions, which were sent to London for examination. When the site was abandoned by the archaeologists, local Bedouins scavenged the mound for bricks, and its contours dissolved into dust and rubble. The depredations continued until the First World War, when a British officer, Major R. Campbell Thompson, once an assistant in the British Museum, tried to restore some of the damage. His enthusiasm had repercussions. The clay cylinders found by Taylor were for the first time given serious attention. Once deciphered, they disclosed that the mound was the site of a tower erected in the 3rd millennium BC by a Mesopotamian king, Ur-Nammu. The name of Ur was well known from the Bible. If the king ruled Ur, this desecrated site had to be the city of Abraham.

FUNERARY FINERY A goat reaching for the succulent leaves of a shrub – fashioned from gold, lapis lazuli, silver, and mother-of-pearl – is the work of goldsmiths of the Early Dynastic period at Ur (2600–2100 BC), who produced objects of exquisite artistry unmatched by craftsmen of later periods. It stands about 50cm (19½in) high and was discovered in the royal cemetery.

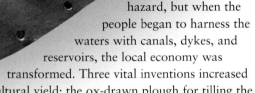

GILDED SPLENDOUR A helmet belonging to a prince was unearthed from the royal cemetery at Ur. It was hammered from a single sheet of gold alloy around 2500 BC. A padded lining was attached to the helmet by laces threaded through the holes.

In 1923, an Anglo-American expedition headed by Sir Leonard Woolley revealed the full grandeur of Ur. The team uncovered temples, storehouses, workshops, spacious residential buildings, and countless articles of everyday life. But the most dramatic discoveries were made in a royal cemetery dating back nearly 3,000 years before Christ. Here, a series of vaults contained a wealth of treasures which ranked for splendour with those of Tutankhamun, discovered in Egypt a year earlier. Yet these were older, dating from some 1,000 years before the Egyptian pharaoh came to the throne.

AN EMERGING CIVILIZATION

Excavations in Mesopotamia were building up a picture of an astonishingly advanced people. The culture which flourished on the lower Euphrates is known as the civilization of Sumer, and marked a turning point in the history of mankind. The key to Sumer's emergence from the shadows of prehistory was the soil – the primary source of the area's wealth. The long rivers Tigris and Euphrates ran together for some 160km (100 miles) from their respective mouths, depositing rich alluvial silt along the lower reaches on the inland plain. Irregular flooding was a hazard, but when the people began to harness the waters with canals, dykes, and reservoirs, the local economy was transformed. Three vital inventions increased the area's agricultural yield: the ox-drawn plough for tilling the fields, the wheeled wagon for transporting goods, and the milking of animals to provide a sustainable supply of protein.

These developments liberated some of the population from toil in the fields. Settlements grew into towns, where specialist skills such as pottery, weaving, and metalwork began to flourish. It is possible that the metalworkers of Ur first developed the lost-wax process. This method of creating moulds is thought to have been invented in the 4th millenium BC. An object would be modelled in wax in fine detail, then placed inside an earthen mould and covered with plaster or clay. The clay was then fired, and molten wax flowed out through holes, leaving a finely detailed hollow mould into which molten metal could be poured.

Sumer had no rocks or forests, so its merchants had to trade the produce of its fields and the creations of its artisans for stone, timber, and metal ores. Commerce created its own needs: writing became a essential skill, and a system of arithmetic had to be devised.

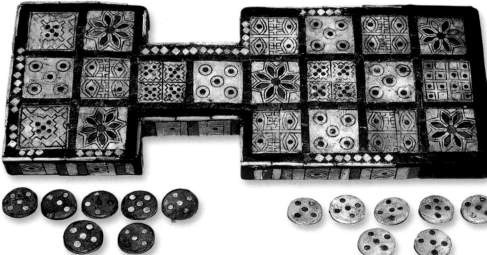

CRAFTED FOR PLEASURE Wooden gaming boards inlaid with shell, bone, red paste, and lapis lazuli were found in the graves at Ur. The game, for two players, had 14 counters and may have been similar to ludo.

From about 3000 BC onwards, a cluster of city-states grew up in Sumer: Ur, Uruk, Eridu, Lagash, and Nippur among them. Farther upriver, other trading partners, such as Mari, shared many of their achievements. These cities had become true urban communities ruled by centralized administrations, with temples, palaces, and specific quarters allocated to groups of craftsmen.

Because of its position on the Euphrates, Ur must have been an important warehousing centre. At that time, too, the city was probably on the sea-coast at the head of the Persian Gulf – sediments carried down by the Tigris and Euphrates have since then pushed the coastline farther south. By the early centuries of the 3rd millennium BC the city had become prosperous.

In 1927, Woolley's team excavated the royal cemetery to the south-west of the city. They found 2,000 graves dating from between 2600 and 2100 BC, within what is known as the Early Dynastic period. The tombs were densely packed – often one on top of another. Many had been plundered by grave-robbers, but from the few that had survived intact, the excavators reaped a golden harvest of fine artefacts.

ROYAL RICHES AND SACRIFICE

Many of the tombs contained rich grave offerings, and 16 pit graves with funerary chambers of stone or brick yielded startling contents. The tomb of Queen Puabi, who lived around 2500 BC, contained a wooden chariot decorated with mosaics of coloured stone and white shell. Nine fantastic headdresses were found, shaped from lapis lazuli and carnelian and hung with gold beaten flat in the shape of beech and willow leaves.

The glister of gold was everywhere. Even a bundle of spears bore heads tipped with the precious

MUSIC OF THE AFTERLIFE The tomb of Queen Puabi at Ur contained an elaborate harp. A reconstruction (right) shows its rich ornamentation – it sported a bull's head of pure gold, with piercing eyes of lapis lazuli.

metal. All of the artefacts were of the most exquisite quality. With these riches came evidence of macabre burial rites. The royalty of the Early Dynastic period seem to have been interred with their entire households. The golden spears were in the hands of skeletal soldiers, and the fantastic headdresses framed the skulls of sacrificed women. From the tombs, Woolley reconstructed the grim majesty of the ceremonial burials.

With a handful of attendants, each royal body had been laid to rest at the bottom of a long, sloping shaft. The chamber was then sealed up, and a doomed procession of courtiers, soldiers, servants, and musicians followed down the shaft. In their gorgeous apparel they were, in Woolley's haunting words, 'part of the tomb furniture'. Each figure bore a cup containing a lethal potion, which they drank as they prepared themselves for eternity. The musicians played on to the end before taking the poison, then the grave was filled in. Fires were lit above ground and a funeral banquet held.

The 16 royal tombs all contained evidence of mass sacrifice. In some cases as many as 80 people were interred with their sovereign.

IMAGES OF WAR AND PEACE

The largest grave of all was found almost empty, its contents plundered with the exception of one unique relic – a magnificent mosaic made of shell and lapis lazuli on a wooden box 45cm (17½in) long.

The box became known as the Royal Standard of Ur. It is made up of two long rectangular panels with two triangular end-pieces. The two rectangular panels illustrate war and peace; the end-pieces display mythological images. The peace scenes show a royal feast with servants in attendance, and the war scenes depict images of battle, with chariots and light and heavy infantry engaging a naked enemy. The soldiers wear copper helmets and long, hooded cloaks. Their weapons are axes and short spears. These were Ur's shock troops, men who marched right up the Euphrates in the 3rd millennium BC, perhaps as far as the Mediterranean coast. They were needed for the defence of the homeland, too, for even in the Early Dynastic period, nomadic invaders threatened the Sumerian frontiers.

CONQUEST BY FORCE

For centuries Sumer had been infiltrated by Semitic tribes from the Syrian and Arabian deserts. They had founded their own cities in the heart of Mesopotamia, and traded with those under Sumerian control. The peoples of Mesopotamia formed a fairly homogeneous culture, but had never been a unified nation. Sovereignty among the cities was exercised by whoever happened to be strongest at the time.

But in about 2334 BC, everything changed. A Semitic king, Sargon of Akkad, overthrew the ruler of Uruk (then the leading city), and from his capital near Babylon, went on to conquer Mesopotamia. The realm founded by Sargon lasted less than 150 years, but shortly after it fell, Ur became the leader of the

Ships from Ur traded along the Arabian coast, sailing through the Strait of Hormuz, around Iran, and into the Indus Valley. Wealth poured into Ur-Nammu's city.

Mesopotamian community. Under its Third Dynasty of rulers (2113–2004 BC), the city reached the pinnacle of its glory as an imperial capital of Sumer. This outstanding period in Ur's history was inaugurated by the reign of Ur-Nammu (2113–2095 BC), who built on Sargon's realm to carve out an empire of his own.

Trade extended Sumer's influence still farther. Ships from Ur traded along the Arabian coast, sailing through the Strait of Hormuz, around Iran, and into the Indus Valley. Wealth poured into Ur-Nammu's city. Wood, precious stones, and silver flowed down the Euphrates from Lebanon and the Amanus mountains (Nur Daglari) in Hatay province of modern Turkey. From Arabia came gold and incense, and a great trading depot grew up on Dilmun, the island of Bahrain in the Persian Gulf. Tin and lapis lazuli reached Ur from Iran and the Caucasus. Copper arrived from Oman, a place known to the Sumerians as Magan. From Meluhha, the Indus region, came timber, and beads of agate, carnelian, and ivory.

THE VICTORY FEAST The Royal Standard of Ur records a peacetime banquet. On the top panel, the king sits on a throne faced by his officers. The figures all wear simple sheepskin skirts. Below, servants bring food and tributes from the royal domain.

A FIGHTING FORCE On the war panel of the Royal Standard (below), infantry soldiers are accompanied by solid-wheeled Sumerian chariots, drawn by onagers (wild asses). At the top centre, the king receives prisoners.

A CITY ON A GRAND SCALE

Merchants arriving at Ur would first have passed through the immense mud-brick ramparts erected by Ur-Nammu to protect his capital. They completely encircled the city, 'like a yellow mountain', in the king's own words.

The capital was also almost entirely surrounded by water. A man-made canal, acting as a moat, extended the natural course of the Euphrates which washed the western walls. Two harbours lay to the north and west of the city, with bustling docks, warehouses, and quays.

Ur-Nammu was a builder of astonishing energy. Monuments dedicated by him during his reign have been found throughout the city, which covered an oval area of some 60ha (148 acres), and housed an estimated population of 24,000 people.

Towering above all other buildings in the city was a great staged pyramid dedicated to the Moon god, Nanna, patron deity of the settlement. The pyramid was a ziggurat, the characteristic staged tower of Mesopotamian civilization – a raised sanctuary, protected against floods. Despite the erosions of time, it remains the best preserved ziggurat in all of Mesopotamia.

The three levels of the monumental structure were joined by a harmonious geometry of stairways and facings. At the top stood a temple dedicated to Nanna. There was a large courtyard around the bottom of the tower, and a smaller one to the north-west. Both were surrounded by shrines for cult worship. The temples had inner courtyards where animals were sacrificed, and cooking areas. The sacred enclosure included workshops, and storehouses for tribute to the Moon god: grain, oil, wool, fruit, and cattle. There was also a royal palace used by the king on ceremonial occasions. Just outside the enclosure was another royal cemetery. But the tombs had been extensively plundered,

TOWERING TEMPLE The imposing remains of the great zigurrat of Ur, repaired and restored, loom large in the desert. Built around 2100 BC, the building was originally 17m (56ft) high.

and held no treasures comparable to those of the earlier graves. The streets running through Ur were narrow, some constructed in straight lines, but most simply meandering between small blocks of houses. Sumerian texts describe broad avenues and large public gardens, but the remains of these larger spaces have not been located by archaeologists.

THE DAILY LIFE OF RICH AND POOR

The homes of the poorer inhabitants were modest, each arranged around a courtyard. The houses of the wealthy may have had an upper storey, with rooms opening onto an internal raised gallery made of wood. The richest families possessed whole suites of rooms, with bedrooms, living rooms, kitchens, washrooms, servants' quarters, and often a private chapel.

Furniture was scanty. The most common items were high stools, sometimes collapsible, or high-backed chairs. Low tables were also used. Household goods such as pots and plates were stored in chests. Floors were generally paved with unbaked bricks or mud plaster and covered with reed mats or hides.

Documentary material found engraved on clay tablets provides a vivid picture of domestic life at Ur. The father enjoyed a privileged position in the family, according to a complex system of legal codes drawn up by Ur-Nammu and his successors. If a husband wanted to separate from his wife, he only had to pay a fixed sum in silver. But if a wife wanted a divorce, 'she must be thrown into the river'. If a married woman took a lover, she was put to death; but a husband could take concubines and philander to his heart's content.

The children of the poor toiled beside their parents in field or workshop from an early age, unless their father had invoked his right to sell them as slaves. School, called the 'house of writing tablets', was open only to the children of the rich. Gaining an education involved learning the 600-odd signs of the Sumerian cuneiform script, and was a long and costly process. Every day, each child would study a tablet which the master had written out the day before, and attempt to copy it. The texts included epic tales, legends, hymns, and sayings, as well as simple groups of words such as the names of animals, vegetables, and minerals, and of countries and towns. Teachers also instructed pupils in grammar and mathematics. At the lunch-time meal, a 'holder of the whip' ensured strict discipline. One Sumerian schoolboy has left a rather miserable account of a day at school. On his arrival, he was whipped for gazing

around in the street; then for being 'improperly dressed'. During the course of the day he received four more beatings: for talking in class, for standing up, for walking outside the gate, and for producing bad work. From this austere discipline emerged a class of scribes on whom the entire Sumerian religious and administrative system was based.

Writing was a cherished and exclusive skill, which must have seemed magical to the mass of the people. Writing tablets give the names of 500 scribes and their origins, adding up to a

THE ZIGGURAT OF UR
The Tower of Babel would have looked something like this, for the ziggurat at Babylon was a scaled-up replica of the one at Ur. It has been suggested that terraces were hung with plants. The ziggurat rested on a base measuring 60m by 45m (197ft by 147ft). Spacious stairways led from ground level to the three upper floors and to the temple of the moon god, Nanna, at the top. Bitumen was used as cement for the outer shell of baked bricks. The mud-brick core was reinforced with wooden beams and reed matting, used for ties. The god was believed to alight in the upper temple and descend the stairs to a larger temple which stood nearby. The ziggurat thus provided the link between heaven and earth.

roll-call of privilege. The list includes the sons of civic officials, ambassadors, governors, temple officials, priests, scribes, archivists, accountants, tax collectors, officers, ships' captains, foremen, and stewards. Only one woman is mentioned in the entire list. Perhaps she was educated at home, for schooling seems to have been a male prerogative.

FITTING INTO THE SOCIAL HIERARCHY

The scribes formed the apex of the administrative hierarchy in Ur, headed by the sovereign himself. Promotion within the administration depended perhaps as much on political muscle and royal favour as on ability. Nonetheless, there seems to have been considerable social mobility. The humble role of

courier, carrying messages or escorting convoys between capital and provinces, launched many an ambitious scribe on a career of glory. A certain Ir-Nanna, for example, began as a courier, came to head the whole courier service, and later also acquired the post of an *ensi* (governor) of six towns, and a *shagin* (prefect) of the eastern provinces.

The wealth of Ur came partly from the tributes it received from subject towns and from the estates owned by king and priesthood. But the city also profited from industry. Wool was mass-processed in workshops by female spinners using fleeces and goats' hair. Linen was also woven, though it was reserved for use by priests. A group of male artisans formed a class of their own, the *eren*.

THE BASKET-BEARER During the Third Dynasty, copper pegs were used to anchor public buildings and temples symbolically to the ground. The upper part of the peg depicted the building's founding monarch – this peg represents Ur-Nammu.

A craft was generally passed on from father to son, and residential quarters were allocated to specific trades, such as carpentry or engraving. Guilds of goldsmiths and other metalworkers were closely supervised by state foremen. Generally free men, they worked not for themselves but for the state, which supplied them with raw materials and took charge of the finished goods. Finished artefacts were handed over to the workshop manager, who issued a receipt. A chief controller examined the item to make sure that none of the original ore had been sold off for private gain, then countersigned the receipt. Goldsmiths, like other workers, were paid in measures of barley.

THE RIGHTS OF SLAVES

At the bottom of society were the slaves – prisoners of war, bankrupted free men, or people who had been sold off by their parents, usually to pay debts. The slaves' lot was not totally abject: they had the right to set up in business, to own property, and to buy their freedom. They could also marry free citizens, and their children would be born in liberty.

In Third Dynasty Ur, the state owned much of the land, as well as all of the industry. Most Sumerians were not city dwellers but field workers who farmed the alluvial plain. Much of the work revolved around maintaining the irrigation system: clearing channels, repairing dykes, and operating sluice-gates in times of drought. Fields were ploughed with wooden ploughshares fitted with funnels through which the seed was sown. This apparatus was the first known seed drill, which was a testament to the Sumerians' extraordinary inventiveness – no comparable device was used in Western Europe until the Englishman, Jethro Tull, reinvented the seed drill in the 18th century AD.

A whole mythology of germination, death, and rebirth accompanied this seasonal toil. Ceremonies were held in honour of Dumuzi, the god of vegetation, whose autumn death and descent into the underworld was celebrated by a procession of female mourners, who grieved his passing to the sound of a flute. Other festivities marked Dumuzi's resurrection, when he grew once again amid the new crop of wheat.

Separate from the cornfields, were the gardens and orchards, which produced cucumbers, gourds, lentils, melons, onions, and pomegranates destined for the markets and the palace and temple warehouses. Beyond the fertile valleys, sheep and goats grazed in the pastureland that spread along the desert margin. The coarse grasses were not suitable for feeding cattle, so they were fattened on stocks of barley brought from the plain. Official caravans passing through these upland regions to gather tithes went with escorts of soldiers armed with lance and dagger. The routes were well-worn, but raiding tribes from the desert were always a menace.

In about 2000 BC, the Amorites from the west and the Elamites from the foothills of Iran to the east descended on the capital in a cloud of destruction. Sir Leonard Woolley's team unearthed the evidence: temples had been sacked, monuments had been smashed, and buildings had been razed to the ground. Yet Ur not only survived but continued to flourish, although on a reduced scale, into the time of Abraham, who is thought to have been alive in about 1500 BC.

THE BIBLICAL CONNECTION

Could this great city really have been the home of Abraham, a Semite always thought of as a tent-dwelling nomad? If Abraham's family lived in Ur, they can only have done so temporarily – by 1500 BC the city was an age-old metropolis, and its citizens had been living the urban life for more than two thousand years.

It is likely that the tribe of Abraham was one among many who drove their flocks from the wastes of Arabia into the fertile plain. They must often have passed through the swarming, urban communities that sprawled before them. Coming from the calm silence of the desert, they would have experienced an acute culture shock as they gazed on the city's grand palaces, temples, and busy workshops. And Sumerian legend left its mark on the tribe in one immensely significant respect: in the

RICH ADORNMENTS Heavy jewellery of beaten gold, lapis lazuli, and other precious stones were among the extravagant array of ornaments that graced the ladies buried in the royal tombs of the Early Dynastic period.

Bible story of the great flood. The Sumerians' royal chronicles allude to a colossal rising of the waters which once engulfed their land. The flood legend is also at the heart of the Epic of Gilgamesh, a favourite myth of their civilization. Gilgamesh – half-god, half-man – was said to have been king of the powerful city-state of Uruk.

Part of the epic relates how the gods decided to wipe out mankind in a deluge. Only one faithful believer, a certain Utnapishtim, was to be spared from the catastrophe. He built an ark and loaded it with the 'seed of all living things'. The storm raged for six days and nights, and on the seventh, it subsided. 'All mankind had turned to clay,' and the ark lay stranded on a mountain top. Three birds were then sent out in succession, just as in the Bible, to look for dry land.

EVIDENCE OF THE FLOOD?

When exploring Ur, Woolley came upon something which seemed to tie the flood to a specific time and location. Digging below the royal cemetery he discovered a clear layer of silt 3m (10ft) thick interrupting the continuous evidence of prehistoric human habitation. Broken vessels dating back to about 4000 BC were discovered above and below the silt, but not within it. The clean clay was a flood deposit: the sign of a massive inundation which partially buried the original settlement.

Was this evidence of the flood described in the scriptures, a huge deluge that had engulfed the entire valley of the Tigris and Euphrates? Initially, Woolley thought it might be. Today, scholars are more cautious. The inundation was not as extensive as Woolley first believed. Other major floods had occurred at

The clean clay was a flood deposit; the sign of a massive inundation which partially buried the original settlement . . . Was this evidence of the flood described in the scriptures . . . ?

various times in Sumerian history. And since flood myths are found all round the world, it is even conceivable that all date back through tribal memory to the melting of the waters at the end of the Ice Age in around 8300 BC. Cultures as distant as Aztec Mexico and Hindu India speak of a great purification of the earth by water. Whatever the truth, it is clear that the Sumerian myth caught the imagination of the Semitic tribe of Abraham, and helped to shape the form which the Biblical version was to take.

THE SHINING CITY FADES

Much of modern civilization can be traced back to the inventive Sumerians: the wheel, the plough, patterns of city life and social organization – even the art of writing itself. It seems incredible today that this vibrant culture could ever have been forgotten. Yet such was its fate.

During the course of the 1st millennium BC the centre of civilization in the Middle East shifted from Mesopotamia to the Iranian plateau, where a Persian dynasty with alien gods was building a mighty empire. The ancient cities of Sumer declined. Various rulers of Ur tried to restore the city to some of its former glory – notably Nabonidus, a 6th-century Babylonian king who rebuilt parts of the great ziggurat. But Ur was slowly dying and, in about 316 BC, an unexpected event dealt a fatal blow to the great city. The Euphrates, whose waters had so long nourished the prosperity of Ur, changed its course. It started to run some 14km (8½ miles) east of the city. Ur was starved of its shipping trade. The canals which had once watered the fields were dry, and the city was stranded like a beached leviathan on a flat desert waste.

The remaining inhabitants abandoned the site. Wind and sandstorms did the rest, eroding walls and monuments and heaping up accumulations of dust, until all that remained was a series of gentle hillocks overlooked by a hump-backed monument – a hump which the Bedouins called Tell al-Muqayyar – the Mound of Pitch.

Knossos

Luxury in the land of the Minotaur

Bathed in shimmering Aegean light, Knossos saw the first flowering of civilization in Europe. Its myriad courts echoed to laughter. Then silence fell – a silence so absolute that for centuries ancient Crete was thought of only as a myth.

FEW CIVILIZATIONS HAVE BEEN SO COMPLETELY LOST as that of Minoan Crete. Even the ancient Greeks knew this astonishing culture only as a timeless folk memory – the source of myths and legends. It had been, according to Homer, 'a rich and lovely island, set in the wine-dark sea, densely peopled and boasting 90 cities'. The most famous of the Greek legends describe how the island was ruled by an awesome king, Minos (hence the term 'Minoan'). The king, it was said, possessed a bull-monster called the Minotaur, which dwelt in the heart of a vast maze known as the labyrinth. A young Athenian called Theseus slew the monster in its lair, finding his way in and out of the maze by following a thread given to him by the king's daughter, Ariadne.

Until the late 19th century AD, the Crete of King Minos was assumed to be nothing but a myth. But in 1899, an English archaeologist, Sir Arthur Evans, purchased the land on which the ancient Cretan town of Knossos stood and began excavations. Within a year, he had uncovered the ruins of a huge palace.

A COURTLY COMMUNITY

Evans's work was to continue for more than 40 years, until his death. What he brought to light was more than a lost settlement – it was an entire civilization whose existence had not even been suspected.

Its people had lived a life of unimagined luxury in graceful surroundings. The palace at Knossos was a dazzling feat of construction built on several levels, with walls covered in exquisite paintings. Frescoes and figurines restored by Evans vividly evoke the life of the palace: the chatter of its courtly ladies; the splendour of its half-naked princes; the agility of its acrobats; and the euphoria of its ritual dancing.

The people of Minoan Crete were the first civilization to arise in Europe, predating the emergence of classical Greek culture by more than a thousand years. The sophistication of their palaces indicated a community which had learned to take advantage of Crete's key position in the midst of Mediterranean commerce.

RITUAL PROCESSION
Frescoes represent the pinnacle of Minoan art. A procession of men holding vessels decorates one wall of the palace in Knossos. The short wrapped skirt was standard attire for Minoan men – women wore long, flounced skirts and tight bodices. The archaeologist Sir Arthur Evans painstakingly restored many frescoes at Knossos, but has been criticized for going beyond what could be accurately reconstructed.

Today, the landscape of Crete is dominated by a beautiful, desolate skyline of bare hills and mountains. But in prehistoric times the ranges were thickly forested, and the woodlands abounded with deer, hares, and rabbits.

It seems that the island was first settled by a Stone Age farming people who arrived in about 7000–6000 BC. Tracts of land were sown with cereal crops, and pigs, sheep, cattle, and goats were raised. The settlers probably supplemented their diet with game hunted in the forests, and mackerel, tuna, and mullet from the coastal waters. Carpentry, pottery, spinning, and weaving developed, and village communities began to emerge. The villagers settled in rectangular houses in which several small rooms were arranged around one large room.

A RECIPE FOR CHANGE

By 3000 BC, changes were in the air. In Anatolia, communities of metalworkers had already become well established, and the influence of these settlements extended to the offshore islands. Crete was easy to reach through a series of island hops via Rhodes, Kárpathos, and Kásos without ever losing sight of land, and contact with the Anatolian communities brought new ideas, and possibly new people.

As metalworking became widespread, profound changes took place in Cretan society. Craftsmen began to specialize, working with particular metals or precious stones. A huge variety of metal tools and building equipment emerged. The people began cultivating vines and olives, and breeding sheep for wool. Wheeled vehicles drawn by animals were introduced, and circular, vaulted tombs began to appear. The Bronze Age had arrived, and with it came population expansion and new patterns of social organization.

The period from 3000 to 2000 BC was one of consolidation in Egypt and the Middle East, when priest-king figures were emerging at the heads of centralized governments. The urban communities of Mesopotamia were developing extensive trade links with their neighbouring peoples, and, in Egypt, the Old Kingdom was established and the first great pyramids were built. Crete felt the effects, and with its sea-girt frontiers was in a good position to profit from the stable and flourishing civilizations surrounding it.

Links with Anatolia were consolidated, and new links were established with Egypt, and with Ugarit and Byblos on the eastern seaboard of the Mediterranean. Along this part of the coast, new commercial centres began handling goods from Egypt and Mesopotamia. In Crete itself, the building of roads, bridges and aqueducts all speak of increasing social cohesion. Wheeled carts became increasingly prevalent, and Cretan merchants took to the sea in masted sailing vessels.

From about 2000 BC, several urban centres with imposing palaces developed on the island at Phaestos, Mallia, Zakro, and Knossos. Knossos, founded on the ruins of the Stone Age settlement, soon emerged as the dominant court, and its kings exercised sovereignty over the other rulers. The kings of Knossos bore the title of Minos – probably an official term rather than the name of an individual monarch.

The earliest palaces showed the influence of the civilizations with which Crete was in contact: Egypt, Syria, Anatolia, and Mesopotamia. But they bore signs of originality, too. At Knossos, a complex of chambers, porticoes, and corridors sprawled out from a central court. Distinctive features included sunken bathrooms, light wells, balconies, and terraced and porticoed gardens.

> *As metalworking became widespread, profound changes took place in Cretan society . . . The Bronze Age had arrived, and with it came . . . new patterns of social organization.*

Around 1700 BC, a sudden and terrible earthquake almost destroyed this first flowering of Minoan civilization. But the disaster did not halt Crete's growth. On top of the rubble, the survivors laid out new plans. Collecting up the scattered building materials, they erected a new, even more luxurious palace on exactly the same site – and from the ashes of a near-catastrophe, the great age of Minoan Crete arose.

THE NEW HEART OF KNOSSOS

The new palace at Knossos is the one to which Sir Arthur Evans devoted most of his labours, and the one you can visit today. It is, by any standards, a stupendous achievement: an urban complex rather than a single building. Like other great palaces of the period it was not only a royal residence, but a manufacturing centre, a storage depot, the heart of religious life, and the administrative hub of the kingdom.

The double-headed axe, a symbol of the dynasty of Minos, appears throughout the palace. The Greek word for the symbol is *labyros*, from which the term labyrinth derives. The palace itself resembled a labyrinth, with its maze-like conglomeration

A LIFE OF LUXURY The palace at Knossos sprawled across more than 2ha (5 acres) of ground. The buildings were grouped around a central courtyard measuring 60m by 30m (197ft by 98½ft). The view (above) shows part of the west wing, whose colonnaded facade faced onto the central courtyard. The colonnades were designed to keep the palace well ventilated and comfortable in the hot, dry Cretan climate.

MODERN DECOR Figure-of-eight shields, characteristic of the Aegean, decorate the walls of the upper hall in the palace's royal apartments. Evans sometimes used modern materials to reconstruct the ancient palace: the columns shown here are made of reinforced concrete.

identifying it as an early form of Greek – the script used by the Mycenaeans, the inhabitants of the Greek mainland. It was developed from Linear A, and provides many clues to the spelling of words in Linear A. But the words of Linear A make up a language unrelated to any that are now known, and it remains a mystery.

The inscriptions shed little light on the Minoans. Almost everything that is known about their civilization has been deduced from the wordless evidence of archaeology. Much of their written information was probably kept on parchment, which must have perished. The finding of inscribed tablets in private houses as well as palaces reflects the existence of a substantial literate bureaucracy, but the lack of other written records suggests that most of the population was illiterate.

THE HEIGHTS OF ECSTASY

Excavations have revealed that Knossos was a centre of cult worship. Yet temple buildings do not dominate the palace as in the Middle East, and there is no obsession with death – none of the preoccupation with evil spirits so common in Egypt and Mesopotamia. What emerges instead is a picture of a culture

> *The Minoans had a taste for spectacle . . . During torchlit nocturnal festivals, women performed sacred, ecstatic dances to enter into contact with the deity.*

founded on a love of life and the celebration of music. The Minoans had a taste for spectacle, and musicians, poets, female dancers, acrobats, and jugglers, all lived at the palace. A paved floor, surrounded by tiers of seats, served as a theatre for some displays; others were performed in a great central court.

During torchlit nocturnal festivals, women performed sacred, ecstatic dances to enter into contact with the deity. A clay goddess from Gazi, near Knossos, is shown wearing poppies in her crown – it has been suggested that the Minoans may have used opium to enhance states of religious trance. Homer evokes the mesmerizing quality of the dances held at Knossos as he describes a scene depicted on the shield of Achilles: 'Now they ran ever so lightly with cunning feet, as when a potter sits gripping his wheel with his hands and tries to see how it spins. Now again they ran in lines opposite each other. A big crowd stood around enjoying the passionate dance; and two acrobats spun around in their midst, setting the rhythm of the performance.'

The Greek myths describe a dancing floor built at Knossos for Ariadne, daughter of the Minos. A complex ritual dance performed on the floor mirrored the labyrinthine construction of the palace itself. The dancing floor may have been patterned to guide the steps of the performers.

Another spectacle with obvious ritual overtones centred around the island's extraordinary bull games – a long tradition which dated back to at least the 2nd millennium BC, and is represented at Knossos in many reliefs, figurines, frescoes, and

RITUAL SPECTACLE A fresco of *c*.1500 BC in the east wing of the palace at Knossos shows an acrobat somersaulting over a bull. In Minoan art, men were represented with dark skin and women with fair skin.

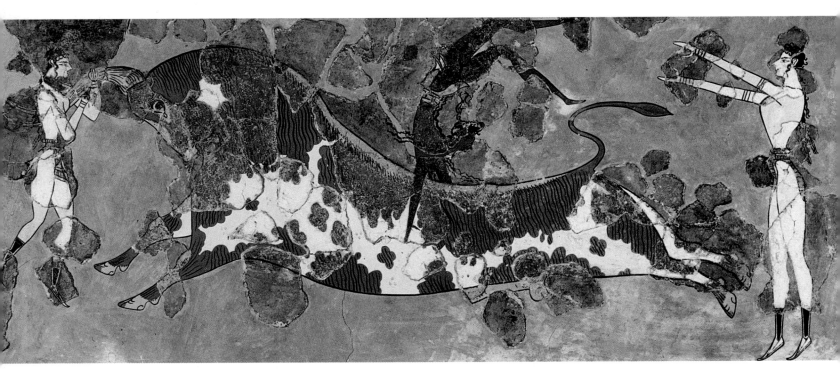

FLEETS OF THE MINOS

The rulers of Knossos became masters of the sea. Their fishermen had been plying the coastal waters in canoes since Stone Age times. From about 2000 BC onwards, methods of maritime navigation were developed, and international trading began on a large scale. The first sizeable sailing vessels appeared in the Mediterranean.

Minoan ships are clearly depicted on many seal engravings. They had both oars and sails. The hull was crescent-shaped, with a high prow and stern, rather like the Egyptian and Phoenician vessels of the period. A deck was often erected between the sides. The ships sat high in the water so that they could be hauled up onto beaches without too much difficulty. The square or rectangular sail was set up on a central mast. Rigging included stays to support the mast, a pole to support the sail, and halyards to raise or lower the sail. Two steering oars kept the vessel on course.

This type of cargo vessel rarely measured more than 12m (39ft) long, though a few exceptionally long vessels existed, with teams of oarsmen numbering up to 30 men.

With elegant little craft like these, the kings of Knossos dominated maritime traffic on the Aegean and the whole of the eastern Mediterranean. It is a testament to the sturdiness of their design that very similar vessels were being sailed around the Aegean islands until the Second World War.

ALL AT SEA A fresco from the island of Thera shows a fleet of crescent-shaped Greek ships sailing between towns. The towns' inhabitants have turned out to watch the spectacle.

SACRED DANCE The mother goddess descends towards the priestesses who are summoning her in a shimmering ecstatic dance depicted on a gold ring found in a royal tomb at Knossos.

seal engravings. The games were probably staged in a wooden arena to the east of the palace, and both men and women took part. It was the most highly rated Minoan spectacle, and involved many incredible acrobatic feats. One act involved running towards a bull head-on, grasping its horns, performing a handspring over its head and landing on its back, then quickly jumping down into the arms of a waiting attendant. Modern toreadors have doubted whether the feat is possible – yet the evidence is there at Knossos, along with pictures of other forms of bull-leaping. Bull-leaping had a big following – it is often shown with crowds of spectators, watching with bated breath.

THE GODDESS AND THE MINOTAUR

The significance of the bull games may have been rooted in religious beliefs. How the games evolved can only be guessed – it is possible that they derived from the dangers attending the capture of wild bulls, and went on to develop ceremonial overtones. The bull was a symbol of male potency, and is a recurring motif in Minoan art, depicted on vases, frescoes, and buildings – symbolic bulls' horns are a feature of Minoan architecture. Religious ritual connected with the bull took the form of the worship of a young male god – a practice that began to emerge during the Minoan period.

The main religion of Crete revolved around a mother goddess, worshipped in effigy at shrines and rock shelters from the earliest times. She is often represented with symbols of living things, such as snakes, birds, or flowers. In the early period, before 1700 BC, worship took place in sanctuaries high up on mountain peaks.

Offerings were made in the form of clay models which reflected the concerns of the worshippers. The models frequently depicted parts of the human body or domestic animals; some were related to fertility. Larger offerings may have taken the form of a sacrificial bull – perhaps slaughtered using a double-headed axe, the symbol of Minos which so often appears in the palace at Knossos.

The relationship between the mother goddess and the bull is a subject of great controversy. According to the Greek myths, the Minotaur was a hybrid monster – a man with a bull's head.

MISTRESS OF THE BEASTS
The mother goddess is often shown with living symbols such as snakes and cats. This statuette from the main chapel at Knossos may represent the goddess or a priestess.

The beast was said to be the fruit of the Cretan queen Pasiphae's lust for a bull, and its origins may lie in a Minoan cult involving a sacred marriage between the mother goddess and the bull. In ritual, the king may have worn a bull mask.

The bull may also have been seen as the divine origin of earthquakes, whose ominous subterranean rumblings were calmed by the mother goddess. The initial tremors of the violent earthquakes which destroyed the early palaces of Crete in about 1700 BC seem to have inspired a unique rite. At the shrine of Anemosphilia, on the lower slopes of Mount Juktas near Knossos, a young man was bound and sacrificed, his blood flowing out as an offering to propitiate the angry gods. But the sacrifice was in vain: before the rite could be completed, tremors of even greater violence destroyed both the shrine and the officiating priest and priestess.

PASTIMES OF THE RICH AND POOR
Besides the sacred dances and acrobatic bull-leaping, the Minoans' love of games included activities such as boxing and wrestling. A large conical vessel known as the Boxer Vase has been discovered at the palace at Ayia Triadha, near Phaestos. The vase shows pugilists wearing short cloth skirts and necklaces, equipped with helmets and knuckledusters.

The wealthy could enjoy playing games on chequerboards inlaid with gold and crystal. A magnificent specimen framed with ivory and measuring about 1m by 50cm (just over 3ft by 1½ ft), was found by Evans at Knossos. The board bears an elaborate design of circular plaques and rectangular bars, and may have been mounted on wood to form the lid of a box which held the pieces.

Such exquisite leisure items obviously belonged only to the nobility; the poorer people of the island may have played much humbler variations of these games. A simple knucklebone dice marked from 1 to 14 has been found in the harbour area of Knossos, with two sets of gaming pieces.

The poorer people spent most of their time working the land, maintaining a rhythm with the seasons. Harsh winters followed the baking hot summers. There were vines to be tended, and fields to be tilled and sown. Even the most arduous toil seems to have been carried out in good spirit. One vase shows a rollicking harvest homecoming. The men bear sickles over their shoulders and are apparently led by a priest. One man is going in the wrong direction – perhaps he is drunk, or just causing pure mischief.

Peace, comfort, and a relaxed exuberance permeated the fabric of society. The seas protected the frontiers of the island, and none of the palaces was fortified. There must have been some fighting – in some Minoan tombs, narrow rapier-like swords have been found, nearly 1m (about 3ft) long. The pommels are heavy, to counterbalance the length of the blade, and some are fashioned from stone, ivory, or gold-plated wood. In the later Minoan period, these long, thrusting weapons gave way to shorter, broader swords.

Helmets were usually conical and sometimes plumed. Large shields – made of bull's hide stretched over a wooden framework – seem to have been the traditional means of defence in battle. An armoury building in Knossos yielded a large number of metal arrowheads and tablets bearing symbols of chariots. It is not known whether skirmishes were fought chiefly with outsiders or within Crete itself.

CRAFT AND COMMERCE
Minoan artistry was of the most refined quality, expressing a love of nature and movement. Motifs with martial themes are rare – it seems clear that the Minoans took little pride in mere feats of arms. One example, on a vase, depicts two soldiers presenting arms. A few soldiers with typical Minoan equipment are also shown in one of the frescoes on the island of Thera in the Cyclades, which may have been under Minoan domination.

No large statues have been found in Crete; its artists excelled at exquisite miniatures. Animals, birds, flowers, and marine life were depicted with intense vitality, particularly on the fine

Minoan pottery which was much in demand on the Greek mainland and in Anatolia, the Levant, and Egypt. The most remarkable items found on the island are in carved ivory, faience, gold, and bronze.

Gold was finely worked for jewellery, and silver was used to craft luxury vessels. Stone carvers used local materials such as marble, soapstone, alabaster, and limestone, and more exotic imported stones, such as obsidian.

Crete owed its wealth to the maritime trade generated by its position at the hub of Mediterranean seagoing commerce. The Egyptians, the principal power in the region for much of the 2nd millennium BC, employed the Minoans as middlemen to transport goods and materials.

The coastline to the north of Knossos harboured many fishing villages, and Amnisos, the teeming international harbour, stretched out along the foot of the cliffs. The royal fleet was anchored there, and the road between the palace and the port was constantly busy with merchants and freight.

A multitude of nationalities would have thronged the quays: islanders from the Cyclades standing alongside traders from Byblos and Ugarit. Dockers unloaded cargoes from mainland Greece, and from Asia, Africa, and the Middle East. On the quayside ready for embarkation were cereals, cattle, oil, wine, pottery, and textiles. At the height of the Minoan period, Cretan ships journeyed to every part of the eastern Mediterranean, distributing their island produce.

THE FALL FROM GLORY

Archaeology has revealed few clues to the downfall of Minoan civilization. It is known that during the 15th century BC, a rich warrior culture emerged in Greece. From Mycenae on the mainland, bronze-clad raiders began to invade the undefended coasts of the island.

The Mycenaeans may have come in the wake of another calamity – in about 1450 BC, fire ripped through the island's settlements, and all of its major

TRAILING TENTACLES Minoan potters produced their best work between c.1500 BC and c.1450 BC. Dark-on-light designs and marine motifs predominated – a style shown on this storage jar from Knossos.

palaces were abandoned, with the exception of Knossos. The original cause of this devastation is unknown, but a sizeable earthquake and volcanic eruption are both possibilities. The Mycenaeans took over and rebuilt the palace at Knossos. A cross-cultural civilization emerged, in which native Minoan traditions were mixed with those of Mycenae. The old ways lingered on in Crete for over 300 years, but the island was now a territory of the Mycenaean realm.

The decline became irreversible. Thucydides, a Greek historian of the 5th century BC, thought that the civilization of Crete was finally extinguished by an invasion of a Greek people known as the Dorians, who overran the entire Mycenaean world. But modern historians believe that the Mycenaean civilization crumbled from within. Whatever the background, it is clear that in around 1100 BC the maritime trading links with Egypt and the Middle East were abandoned, commerce slumped, and the once flourishing society was reduced to subsistence farming.

All that survived from Crete's taste of glory were folk memories – legends passed from generation to generation. They remained embedded in the culture of the Greek people, finding expression in myth and religion.

The name of Minos survived, but it was remembered in two distinct ways. On the one hand, the Minos was the scourge of Athens – the possessor of a terrifying beast, the Minotaur. On the other, he was remembered as a king of great wisdom, so renowned for this quality that he was called upon to act as a judge in Hades. The confusion of these contrasting images suggests that two kings from different periods may have been remembered as a single monarch.

In the 5th century BC, Greek historians trying to trace the origins of their people took an interest in this legendary figure. For example, Thucydides, in the first book of his *History*, wrote: 'Among the characters known from folklore, Minos is the first to have owned a fleet and dominated the greater part of . . . the Greek Sea'. But little beyond this vague memory survived: all the reality had been lost – the magnificent palaces, the busy merchant fleets, the ritual dances, and the spectacular bull games. All evidence of Minoan existence remained buried beneath the earth of Crete – the small Aegean island which saw the first great flowering of European civilization.

Mycenae

The melting pot of ancient Greece

In 1876 a German archaeologist excavating a rocky hilltop in the Peloponnese uncovered treasures which proved that the Mycenaeans were much more than a mythical people invented by the poet Homer. They were, in fact, the first Greeks.

FOR MORE THAN 3,000 YEARS, THE GODS AND HEROES of ancient Greece have held the world in thrall: the kingly Zeus, toying with human destinies and striking down his enemies with thunderbolts; the brave Achilles, vulnerable to wounds only in his heel; the wanderer Odysseus, a hero with courage and cunning. Homer's world of honour, vengeance, incest, adulteries, and human sacrifice has achieved immortality.

But how much is imagination, and how much is a poetical recounting of history? It is now thought that many of Homer's heroes may have been based on real people – heroes from the Bronze Age civilization of Mycenae. The Greek Bronze Age, today known as the Helladic period, lasted from about 3000 BC to about 1050 BC, and is divided into three eras. The Late Helladic period, or Mycenaean Age, which began in about 1600 BC was its final flowering, the culmination of centuries of growth, fostered by contact with other Bronze Age civilizations such as those of Crete and Egypt.

OF MYTHS AND MORTALS

According to the ancient Greek myths, Mycenae was founded in the mists of time by the hero Perseus who asked a trio of one-eyed giants called the Cyclopes to build the city's fortified walls. Later rulers of Mycenae were mortals, but their names are no less steeped in myth.

The most famous, the warrior king Agamemnon, controlled much of southern Greece. Legends tell how Paris, prince of Troy, abducted Helen, the wife of Agamemnon's brother, Menelaus, and took her back across the sea to his home city. His actions began a spiral of violence that was to end in tragedy. To recover Helen, and to avenge the wrong done to Menelaus, the Greeks mustered a powerful army and laid siege to Troy. Agamemnon, as ruler of the leading Greek city of the day, commanded the troops. After a ten-year siege Troy was captured when the Greeks withdrew leaving a colossal wooden horse containing a secret band of warriors at the city gates.

ROYAL MEMORIAL The graves of the elite of Mycenaean society, which yielded rich treasures when excavated, were important to the city's inhabitants. The circle of tombs from the 15th and 16th centuries BC was included within newly extended city walls during the 13th century BC. The stone slabs lining the circle were also erected at the later date.

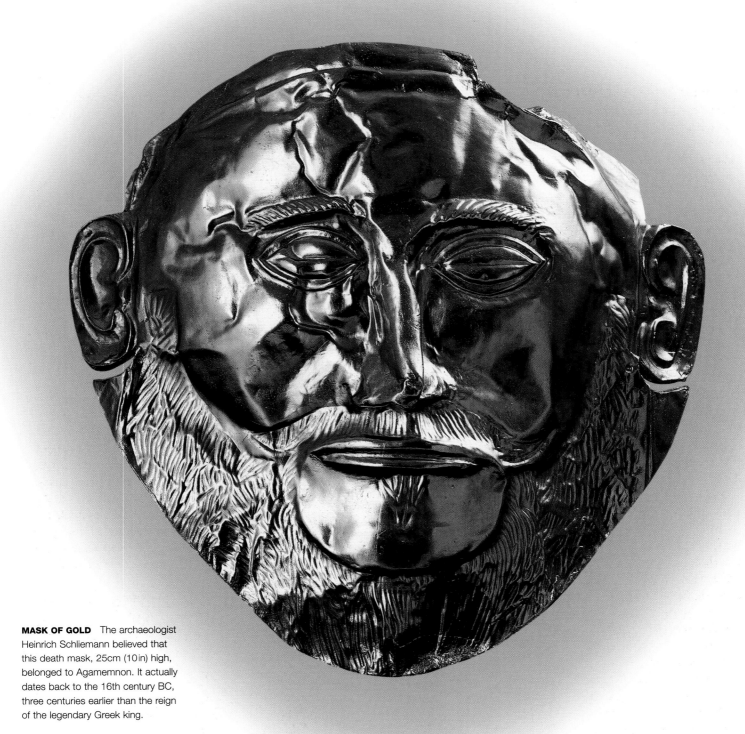

MASK OF GOLD The archaeologist Heinrich Schliemann believed that this death mask, 25cm (10in) high, belonged to Agamemnon. It actually dates back to the 16th century BC, three centuries earlier than the reign of the legendary Greek king.

Intrigued, the Trojans rolled the horse into Troy and when night fell the Greek warriors in its belly crept out and opened the gates to their awaiting army who sacked the city. Now that the wrong done to Menelaus had been avenged, the Greek leaders – Odysseus, Achilles, and Agamemnon – returned home as heroes. But all was not well in Mycenae. During his ten-year absence, Agamemnon's wife, Clytemnestra, had taken a lover called Aegisthus, and together they plotted to seize the throne. They welcomed their returning king, but in his hour of triumph, murdered him – the first step in a saga of bloody revenge.

These deeds were more than just stories to the Greeks. To play-going Athenians of the 5th century BC, they were part of a creed of established beliefs, embroidered and embellished to illustrate the fickleness of human fortunes and the controlling hand of the gods. But little thought was spared for Mycenae itself, by then a small town of no great importance.

In 480 BC, men from Mycenae fought with the Spartans at the great battle of Thermopylae in an attempt to resist the Persian king Xerxes' invasion of Greece. A year later, more Mycenaean troops helped to defeat the Persians at the battle of Plataea. But in 468 BC, when Mycenae refused to accept the leadership of the powerful neighbouring city of Argos, the town was sacked without warning.

For the next few centuries, the city which had coloured legends and played a central role in the formation of Greece was consigned to obscurity.

INSPIRED BY AN ANCIENT POET

When the Greek traveller Pausanias visited Mycenae in the 2nd century AD, the city walls and major tombs were tourist attractions. The site then fell into oblivion for 1,700 years. It was not until 1876 that the work of Heinrich Schliemann brought Mycenae to the world's attention.

As a boy, Schliemann had been inspired by Homer's epic poems, and he nursed a passionate desire to prove that the poet's account of the siege of Troy was more than just a figment of the imagination. It must have seemed a daunting task for a grocer's messenger boy. But Schliemann grew into a determined man. First, he taught himself Ancient Greek so that he could read the works of Homer in the original. Then he amassed a fortune as a merchant banker which enabled him to retire in his early forties.

His first ambition was to find the remains of Troy. He believed that the ancient city was sited on Hissarlik, a mound 50m (164ft) high opposite the Gallipoli peninsula, and in 1871 he set about excavating its northern face. After two years of digging through nine layers of remains, a dazzling prize spread before him: a hoard of 8,700 objects made of pure gold – cups, vases, bracelets, and a glorious diadem of 16,000 pieces of gold which hung from brow to shoulders. Schliemann believed that the treasure belonged to Helen of Troy. In fact, the diadem dated back more than 1,000 years before Helen was born. The excavated mound did contain the remains of Troy – but Schliemann had dug straight through its mud-brick ruins.

Next, Schliemann moved on to Mycenae, hoping to locate the grave of Agamemnon. According to the writings of Pausanias, the legendary king had been buried within the city walls. In 1876 Schliemann explored the area south of the monumental entrance gate – the Lion Gate – with spectacular results. He discovered five graves containing gilded vessels, jewellery, and golden death masks of astounding quality.

Mycenae, which Homer had described as a city 'rich in gold', had indeed lived up to the archaeologist's expectations. Schliemann was convinced that the tombs belonged to Agamemnon and his contemporaries. The graves have since been dated

THE LION GATE The lions carved above the main entrance to Mycenae in the 13th century BC symbolized the power of the rulers of Mycenae. Through it, visitors entered the western end of the citadel.

back to centuries earlier than the period in which the story of Agamemnon seems to fit, but there was no doubt that they lay in the city once ruled by the legendary king.

FRESH INSIGHTS INTO THE PAST

Schliemann's investigations lent substance to the myths surrounding early Greece, and opened up new horizons which are still the subject of intense research. At sites such as the Acropolis in Athens, the palace at Pylos, and the tombs of Dendra, 11km (7 miles) south-east of Mycenae, other clues about this previously unknown society have since been unearthed. Today, much more is known not only about Mycenae, but also about the role it played in Bronze Age Greek civilization.

The Homeric epics which caught Schliemann's imagination, the *Iliad* and the *Odyssey*, now exist in written form, but probably originated from oral poems composed and recited by travelling minstrels. The ancient Greeks did not know who Homer was, nor when he lived. References within the poems to various scenes, a statue and a shield known to date from the 8th century BC led historians to decide that the *Iliad* and the *Odyssey*, in their present form, cannot date from much before that time. But a number of references date back much further. Objects such as helmets made from boars' tusks, large shields, and an ornamental cup, refer to legends of the Mycenaean Age.

Even more surprising is the catalogue of ships in Book Two of the *Iliad*. This lists the Greek forces which set out to capture Troy. The picture it provides of the balance of power in Greece at the time differs from what is known about the political situation in the 8th century BC, but corresponds closely to the Greece of about 1200 BC, at the end of the Bronze Age.

The poems have preserved the glorious reputation of the Mycenaean Age from its heyday between the 15th and 12th centuries BC into the classical Greece of the 8th century BC and beyond. Clues from them have now been linked with archaeological evidence to build a more detailed impression of the Mycenaeans.

A ROYAL RECEPTION

Mycenae was well placed as the chief stronghold of Bronze Age Greece. From its rocky eminence, Agamemnon's citadel commanded views of the surrounding countryside. The palace and the houses of the nobles were safely guarded behind stone walls. Some of the scenes in Homer's *Odyssey* capture the flavour of Mycenaean palace life. The story of a visit by Telemachus, the son of Odysseus, to King Nestor of Pylos, echoes the archaeological discoveries at Mycenaean palaces.

Telemachus travels to Pylos to find out when his father is likely to return from the Trojan war. Nestor tells him of the fate of some of the kings who returned home to Greece from Troy – and, in particular, of the bloody end met by Agamemnon

> *The sight of Menelaus's palace amazes the young Telemachus. The building gleams with a collection of stupendous treasures in amber, copper, gold, ivory, and silver.*

at the hands of his wife and her lover. Telemachus prepares to sleep on board his ship during his stay, but is firmly told that it must not be said that Nestor was unable to offer the hospitality and comfort proper for a visitor.

A bed is found for Telemachus in the porch, while Nestor and his queen retire to their own room at the back of the building. The next day, a heifer with its horns covered in gold leaf is sacrificed to the goddess Athena, and Telemachus is given a ceremonial bath by one of Nestor's daughters.

The archaeological records of Mycenaean palaces confirm that an inner room was set aside for the use of the king and queen. Guests slept in one of the outer courts or porches. In one of the graves at Mycenae, a cup has been found in the form of a black bull's head with beautifully gilded horns. It fits Homer's description of the sacrificed heifer. Finally, in Nestor's palace at Pylos, a bathtub has been excavated which may have been the one in which Telemachus bathed.

Telemachus also travels to the court of Menelaus in Sparta, where he is treated to a similar round of hospitality. The sight of Menelaus's palace amazes the young Telemachus. The building gleams with a collection of stupendous treasures in amber, copper, gold, ivory, and silver. When Telemachus leaves, he is presented with a large mixing bowl of solid silver with a rim of gold, which was originally a gift to Menelaus from the king of Sidon. Such generosity explains the rich hoards of gold and silver treasures found in Mycenaean palaces.

A NEW POWER REVEALS ITS STRENGTH

Homer's account of courtly society is often corroborated by archaeological research, so historians can rely on it to piece together a vivid picture of life in ancient Mycenae. It was a society which set great store by the veneration of royalty, the appeasement of the gods, and the arts of war. So who were the Mycenaeans? And what exactly did they leave behind?

Since the Early Helladic period (3000–2000 BC), the inhabitants of Greece had been using handmade pottery, some of it glazed or patterned, and had been proficient at fashioning bronze, gold, and silver. The ships depicted on their pottery illustrate their involvement in trade. Their main commercial contacts were Crete and the Cycladic islands. In the Middle Helladic period (2000–1600 BC), overseas trade became less important. Settlements became poorer, perhaps as a result of

GREEK FORTRESS The citadel of Mycenae stands on a spur between two ravines. Its main features can still be distinguished: the Lion Gate (1), Grave Circle A (2), the houses of the aristocracy (3), and the royal palace (4).

THE IMPORTANCE OF ARMS AND ARMOUR

In the *Iliad* and *Odyssey*, Homer accurately described the weapons of the Mycenaeans – a fact which surprised archaeologists when they unearthed impressive amounts of arms during excavations at Mycenaean sites. The importance of warfare to the Greeks is confirmed by Linear B tablets, among which inventories of weapons are common. The number of different words used to describe these weapons is a sign of their significance in Mycenaean society.

Offensive weapons included bows and arrows, slings, spears, javelins, swords, rapiers, dirks, and daggers. Defensive armour included leather helmets decorated with wild boars' tusks, linen breastplates reinforced with small metal plates, cheek plates, arm

guards, knee and shinplates, and shields. Most of the arms and armour were crafted in bronze; more elaborate pieces were used for show rather than combat.

The Greeks used chariots as a mobile fighting platform for elite warriors. Ordinary footsoldiers may also have been carried into battle on chariots. Dismounting to fight alongside their chariots, they would have been responsible for protecting them and fighting the occupants of disabled enemy vehicles.

EXQUISITE WEAPONRY
Leopards in gold and silver leaf prowl the blade of a bronze dagger with a gold handle, from the 15th century BC.

society becoming less centralized. Houses were generally simple in design, and there are few obviously important buildings. One of the features of this period is a style of plain grey pottery known as Minyan ware.

Then came the blossoming of the Mycenaean Age (or Late Helladic period) from 1600–1050 BC. Why there was such a sudden explosion of power and wealth on the mainland of Greece is not really known. Some scholars have suggested that a new people may have arrived in Greece at the time, and that it was their culture which grew into the Mycenaean civilization. But the Mycenaeans themselves were neither a new nor a foreign element in Bronze Age Greece – their ancestors had been established on the mainland since 1900 BC.

What changed was that from about 1500 BC, the people of mainland Greece, led by Mycenae, began to assert their authority over the peoples of the Mediterranean – until then, a world dominated by the Cretans, the Egyptians, and the Hittites. It seems that the emergence in Mycenae of a line of powerful warrior kings made this possible. They commanded craftsmen of the highest order and increased their influence by widening their trading contacts with other Mediterranean peoples.

During the course of the following century, the positions of Mycenae and Crete were slowly reversed. Art and artefacts from this period show increasing contact between the growing Mycenaean power and the fading glories of Crete.

THE MYCENAEAN TAKEOVER

In about 1450 BC, the palaces of Crete were destroyed by a catastrophic fire. Archaeology is unable to reveal the original cause of the destruction, but it is likely to have been some kind of natural disaster such as an earthquake or volcanic eruption.

By the time the Cretan sites had recovered from the blow, they were occupied by the Mycenaeans. Clay tablets of this date found on the island are written in Mycenaean rather than Cretan script. The takeover of Crete's palaces gave Mycenaean civilization an extra impetus. Contacts between the two cultures

had already been established through trade and diplomacy, and had resulted in a fusion of artistic styles in metalwork and pottery. After the takeover of Crete, Mycenaean establishments modelled on Cretan palaces flourished. Control of Crete taught the Mycenaeans how to run royal households, and how to create the written records which were essential to efficient organization. For the next 200 years the Mycenaeans were a major force in the Mediterranean, with trading contacts as far afield as Italy, Egypt, the Near East, and Northern Europe.

CHAMBERS OF EXOTIC RICHES

Archaeology provides the most accurate account of Mycenae's development. Two circles of graves discovered by Schliemann are the earliest visible features. Circle A, which is inside the city walls, contains graves formed by vertical shafts cut into the rock, marked by upright stones bearing carved decoration.

The six graves found so far date from between 1600 BC and 1450 BC. Three graves sunk during the second half of the 16th century BC yielded the richest treasures – gold and silver vessels – including the bull's head cup, and a cup shaped like a stag used for making offerings to the gods; personal ornaments; jewellery; and exotic imported objects, such as ostrich eggs set in gold mounts. Among the most remarkable finds were gold face masks for the dead.

As well as this ostentatious display of wealth, there were also more practical objects, including bronze armour and bronze and pottery vessels. Fragments of helmets fashioned from boars' tusks have been discovered, along with swords and daggers. The bronze blades of many of these are inlaid with a strip of darker material decorated with scenes picked out in gold or silver.

The 24 graves in Circle B, left outside the 13th-century BC walls, date from the 17th and 16th centuries BC. Many of them consist of shafts cut into the rock which were roofed over after receiving the bodies. Inside, excavators found weapons, pottery, and bronze vessels, which may have contained a last ritual meal for the departed.

Few of the grave goods from Circle B can rival the wealth and splendour of those from Circle A, but some fine gold and silver ornaments have been found. One particularly interesting find – probably an import from Crete or Egypt – was a rock-crystal bowl carved in the shape of a duck, with its tail forming the spout and its head elegantly turned back to form the handle.

In the 15th century BC, the shaft graves in the two circles fell into disuse. From then on, major burials of commoners in Mycenae took place in chamber tombs. The dead were normally buried in family vaults cut into the rock of a hillside, with an entrance passage leading to it. Royal families had a far more elaborate form of tomb known as the *tholos*, or beehive tomb. The full development of this type of tomb can be seen in the so-called Treasuries of Atreus and Clytemnestra, constructed in the 13th century BC. Their entrance passages were cut into the hillside, and led into a tall, circular chamber. Blocks of stone lined the passages, and the tomb chambers were roofed with a corbelled stone vault.

THE PALACE AND ITS PANTHEON

The hilltop of Mycenae bears little trace of permanent settlement before the 14th or 13th century BC, although abundant finds of pottery show that it was occupied earlier. The grandest building on the site, at the top of the rocky hill, is the palace, the building of which may have begun in about 1400 BC.

The most important of the palace's rooms is the *megaron* – a large, colonnaded hall. Visitors approached the megaron by means of a staircase, of which one flight is well preserved. This led to a forecourt, which opened onto a courtyard, passed a room where guests were housed, and finally reached the porch of the megaron. The megaron itself consisted of an inner and an outer room; it had a circular hearth in the middle and a roof supported by columns. There is evidence that most of these rooms were highly decorated, but little of the original plasterwork and frescoes survives.

Several other houses have been found south of the palace, within the walled citadel. These probably once belonged to

GOLDEN GOAT Mycenaean art was influenced by Minoan craftsmen who worked on the mainland. Minoan jewellery often featured dangling roundels, a feature of this pendant found at a Mycenaean site.

influential nobles, relatives of the ruling dynasty, important court officials, or wealthy merchants. Most of them are known by modern names, after the objects found inside them. The Granary, for example, is so called because barley and wheat were found in storage jars in its basement. The House of the Warrior Vase is named after a striking pottery vase discovered in its rooms, which depicts troops marching out to battle.

A series of rooms near these houses are thought to have been used for cult worship. In one room archaeologists unearthed an altar used for animal sacrifice. Other chambers contained human idols and coiled snakes made of terracotta. These clues suggest that this was the centre of an underworld cult. Other rooms appear to have been used by cults of war and fertility. Some of Mycenae's most impressive frescoes have come from this area of the city. These include the portrait of a richly dressed lady with long black hair – perhaps a priestess – bedecked with jewels.

The shrines at Mycenae illustrate how the ancient cults were the forerunners of classical Greek religion. Clay tablets from Knossos reveal that in about 1400 BC, after the Mycenaean takeover of Crete, some of the classical Greek gods were already being worshipped. These included Poseidon, the god of the sea; Zeus, the king of the gods; Athena, the goddess of wisdom; and Paian (later known as Apollo), the god of light, healing, music, and poetry.

Tablets found at Pylos record an equally illustrious pantheon, including Hermes, the messenger of the gods, and Artemis, the goddess of hunting, as well as Zeus and his consort, Hera. A recently discovered archive of tablets in the palace at Thebes refers to the worship of Maka, probably the mother goddess associated with cults of snakes, bulls, and other animals. At other sites, the goddess is referred to as Potnia (The Lady) – a figure identified with the goddess of agriculture, Demeter, and her daughter Persephone – two aspects of the same deity.

MOTHERLY LOVE Ivory figures found in a Mycenaean shrine wear the bare-breasted garments of Minoan Crete. The figures may represent early versions of the goddess Demeter and her daughter, Persephone.

The terracotta figures of gods and goddesses found in the shrines often had horrific faces, and their heads were uplifted in prayer or supplication. Pottery snakes with reared heads have also been found, which may have been used as a form of protection against evil.

A LEGACY OF ART

One of the richest sources of information about the inhabitants of Mycenae lies in the city's legacy of artefacts, many of which were found in the craftsmen's workshops in the eastern wing of the palace. The city's potters were particularly skilled, although they owed something of the calibre of their work to the quality of the light red or yellow clay that they used, which gave their pots a distinctive sheen. To begin with, they imitated Cretan forms, sometimes embellishing them with original features. Eventually, they began to develop their own distinctive style, characterized by a highly polished cream or buff surface with painted decoration.

Mycenaean pottery came in several basic shapes, such as the *kylix*, or goblet, the *krater*, or large mixing bowl, and jars with a handle and a narrow neck. One of their specialities was the *rhyton*, a funnel-shaped vessel used for pouring libations to the gods. At first, decoration consisted mainly of geometric designs. Later Mycenaean potters created more abstract motifs and stylized pictures of natural subjects.

Pottery was used to transport oil made from Mycenaean olives. Perfumed oils scented with aromatic substances such as terebinth resin from the Levant were exported in small, elegant vases which became valuable in their own right. The people of Italy, with whom the Mycenaeans traded, made their own imitations of these vessels.

Mycenaean metalworkers worked in bronze made of copper from Cyprus and Sardinia and tin from the Near East. One of the most remarkable finds has been a full set of bronze armour from a tomb at Dendra. It consists of several pieces which were originally stitched together: shoulder pieces, a breastplate, and plates to protect the abdomen. The suit also included a boar's tusk helmet with bronze cheek pieces and a pair of bronze greaves – plates to protect the knees and shins.

The work of the jewellers of the Mycenaean world was more delicate. Their favourite material was ivory, from which they fashioned small decorative plaques for furniture and wooden boxes. The most exquisite pieces are small sculptures fixed to furniture as ornaments or used as religious statues. These include a carving of a helmeted warrior, and a statue of two richly bejewelled women found in the cult centre at Mycenae. The women probably represent the dual aspects of the mother goddess, or Potnia. They are sitting down, and a child, possibly a demigod, is climbing onto the knee of one of the women.

DECIPHERING A BRONZE AGE CODE

The discovery of painted symbols on some early pottery vases suggested that the Mycenaeans had a knowledge of writing. But it was not until the discovery of inscribed clay tablets that archaeologists realized that the Late Bronze Age world was highly literate. Several thousand engraved tablets have been found at Mycenaean sites across Greece and Crete – though few have been found in Mycenae itself. The oblong tablets, which are about 7.5cm (3in) long, were made from soft clay and engraved with a wooden stylus. The engraved clay was left in the sun to dry. Where tablets have survived, it is because they were accidentally burned at a later date, as at Pylos and Knossos – this firing made them even harder.

Research has shown that two distinct scripts existed in the Late Bronze Age. One of these was confined to Crete and is now known as Linear A. So far, Linear A has not been deciphered. Until recently it was thought that many of its symbols were taken over and used by the Mycenaeans to create their own script, now known as Linear B, in around 1450 BC. But a Linear B inscription from the 17th century BC found at Olympia in 1994 has led scholars to reconsider Linear B's ancestry.

Linear B is composed of 87 different symbols, each of which represents a spoken syllable rather than a single letter. The type of information recorded on the tablets shows that they were used to keep an account of the day-to-day business carried out at the sites where they were found.

TRADE SECRETS FROM A SHIPWRECK

The Mycenaeans were active participants in a trade network linking Egypt, the Levant, and Anatolia with the Aegean. Their ships, often crewed by Mycenaeans or Canaanites, travelled a circular route around the eastern Mediterranean, carrying local produce from each region to customers elsewhere. Copper came from Cyprus, for instance. Glass, aromatics, timber, and Syrian ivory came from the Levant, and Egypt supplied ostrich eggshells and goldwork.

A remarkable demonstration of this trade came with the discovery in 1982 of a ship that had gone down at Kas (Uluburun) off the coast of Anatolia in around 1350 BC. It carried ingots of tin and blue glass, ivory tusks, and 100 amphorae of the valuable aromatic resin, terebinth. The ship probably started out from a Canaanite port, and called at Ugarit and then Cyprus, where it had been loaded up with its major cargo – 200 copper 'ox-hide' ingots. Other goods on board included Mycenaean pottery and swords, and a tiny gold scarab from Egypt bearing the name of Akhenaten's queen, Nefertiti.

PRECIOUS CARGO The copper ingots found on the wreck were shaped like cured ox hides.

It was a British architect, Michael Ventris, who deciphered Linear B. First, he identified several recurring groups of symbols. These, he suggested, were place-names – an assumption that was to prove reasonably accurate. Ventris theorized that the language represented by the symbols was related to Ancient Greek. In 1952, during the course of the excavations at Pylos, archaeologists unearthed a tablet that was to be decisive. The tablet, an inventory, consisted of pictures illustrating tripods, or three-legged vessels, and vases with different numbers of handles. Each picture was accompanied by the Linear B word for the object. The word for a tripod was *ti-ri-po* – a syllabic version of the Greek word *tripos*. The vases, too, were accompanied by words which translated into Greek as 'four-eared', 'three-eared', and 'no-eared'; descriptions which corresponded exactly with the different vase symbols.

The tablet supported the theory that Linear B was a form of early Greek. The discovery radically altered established ideas about Greek prehistory. Historians now knew that a recognizable form of Greek was spoken about 1,000 years before the familiar alphabet of the language emerged in the 8th century BC.

THE DIVISION OF THE CLASSES

The discoveries at Mycenae and other major sites such as Pylos, Tiryns, Thebes, and Dendra have yielded a rich store of information about Mycenaean society. At the top of the social scale, after the king, came the courtiers. Tablets found at Pylos refer to the king or *wanax*, to a man called a *lawagetas* (a sort of grand vizier) who perhaps led the warriors, and to several other

officials – *telestai, damos, hequetai,* and *guasileus*. Although the rank and function of these officials are not known, rough translations of their names give an idea of their role. The *telestai* were possibly tax officials. *Hequetai* were 'followers' or 'companions'. *Damos* may have been landholders. The *guasileus* was the leader of a small group – often of craftsmen – or of a small outlying district. The corresponding word in classical Greek, *basileus*, means 'king' – a sign that the significance of the role may have been misinterpreted after the chaos that accompanied the downfall of Mycenaean civilization.

The officials probably lived in the houses built below the palace at Mycenae. Their tasks included keeping detailed accounts of tax collections, and inventories of the palace's contents and stores. Information was recorded on clay tablets: a census records the number of children in Mycenae; the number of pigs delivered to the palace; the weight of bronze allotted to metalworkers for making 500,000 arrowheads; the food rations doled out to the servants of the royal bathroom; the number of chariot wheels stored in the palace armoury; and the amount of oil, wheat, honey, wine, cheese, and meat required for offerings to the gods.

Clay tablets were an unwieldy way of storing information – they were little more than tallies, and were probably kept for about a year. Permanent records may have been kept on papyrus sheets or parchment, which have since perished.

The skill of writing was not widespread in Mycenae. It was a tool of administration rather than a token of education or civilization. The ability to write was a specific talent cultivated by the scribes in the civil service. Such men were craftsmen, as specialized in their own fields as potters or metalworkers. Along with the traders and merchants, they earned more than the rest of the common people. As a result, a middle class may have begun to emerge in Mycenaean society – although its political power was held in check by the controls exercised on behalf of the king.

The middle classes clearly aspired to slightly grander houses than those lived in by the common people. Perhaps the largest of these private dwellings are to be found below the palace at Mycenae. The House of the Oil Merchant, for example, had 12 rooms on the ground floor. Here, archaeologists discovered a consignment of jars of oil, ready for despatch, which had never been sent. Other houses nearby, decorated with fresco-adorned walls, contained Linear B tablets and the remains of finely carved ivory ornaments. Evidence of upper storeys showed that they had, at one time, been substantial dwellings. At the bottom of the class system were slaves. A number of slaves lived inside the palace – the majority of these were most probably war captives, taken during Mycenaean raids on the lands of the eastern Aegean. The slaves performed general domestic chores around the palace, or wove textiles.

The majority of the population were peasants living outside the city in the countryside. Here, herdsmen looked after sheep, pigs, goats, cattle, or horses; farmers ploughed the arable land to provide cereal crops and pulses, and grew olives, vines, and figs. They lived in simple one-roomed houses made of unfired brick. Originally, most of the countryside surrounding Mycenae was common land. But the king gradually appropriated more and more land as he granted sections of it to his senior officials in exchange for their loyal services. The result was the emergence of a property-owning class.

Like most ancient societies, Mycenae owed its prosperity to agriculture. Crafts and commercial activities sprang up as a result, making possible a culture of increasing complexity. Crete had a great influence over Mycenaean culture – for several generations before the Mycenaeans finally took over the island, almost every pursuit was influenced by techniques and ideas which filtered to the mainland from the Cretan civilization.

INTO THE DARK AGES

Archaeologists have shown that in the 13th century BC, the fortifications surrounding many Mycenaean sites were strengthened, and that some time after 1250 BC a number of the sites were damaged by fire. Mycenae itself was dealt a series of savage blows from which it would never fully recover.

One explanation for the destruction of the Mycenaean world comes from later Greek historians. Thucydides (*c*.460–*c*.400 BC) describes an invasion of the Peloponnese by Dorian people from the north. A massive wall built across the Isthmus of Corinth around 1200 BC may have been a last attempt to keep these invaders

A HIDDEN LANGUAGE The Linear B tablet, the first to be publicized by Sir Arthur Evans, has pictograms, such as the sign for a wheel, to reinforce other information, given in syllables and occasional numerals.

out. Certainly, 300 years later, when Greece emerged from its Dark Ages, the Dorians had become well established in the Peloponnese. But archaeologists have found little evidence for such a dramatic invasion. A more convincing explanation is that Mycenae's downfall was caused from within – brought about by the chaos of internal strife and rebellion.

It is possible to look for historical clues in the epic stories of the *Iliad*. Could the story of the Greek assault on Troy be an allegory illustrating the Mycenaeans' fear in the face of a powerful rival, whom they attempted to eliminate by concerted action? And do the stories of the problems faced by the Greek heroes on their return suggest that this external pressure aggravated internal strife and rivalry?

ENEMIES FROM ACROSS THE SEA

The excavations at Troy show traces of destruction that could well have been caused by enemy action in about 1250 BC. This evidence supports the theory that the 50 years following the Mycenaean success at Troy were difficult ones at home. The Mycenaeans' troubles may have been exacerbated by one other factor. There are a number of references in Egyptian records from about 1200 BC to the Sea Peoples – bands of raiders who were repulsed in Egypt, but who could have been responsible for at least part of the unease in the Mycenaean world in the late 13th century BC. This explanation for the decline of Mycenae is supported by a series of tablets from Pylos which record information about stationing troops along the coastline to guard against raids.

When the Mycenaean civilization finally died, the Greek world went into hibernation. When it awoke three centuries later, it scaled new heights of artistic and political achievement founded on memories of the Mycenaean Age, from the Greek language to the pantheon of Greek gods. Last but not least of these survivals – the Homerian epics – kept the names of Agamemnon and Mycenae alive beyond the emergence of classical Greece to this day.

Ugarit

At the crossroads of the ancient world

More than 1,300 years before the birth of Christ, a nation of merchants and craftsmen became the rich middlemen of the Middle East. Their need to break down the barriers of language led them to invent the world's first alphabet.

TOWARDS THE END OF THE 1920S, a peasant was tilling his field near the harbour of Minet el-Beida on the northern coast of Syria, when his ploughshare suddenly jarred. Squatting down to investigate, he found several flat stones that had been partially turned over, revealing a dark vault under the earth filled with wonderfully painted vases. He could not have guessed the significance of his find. This colourful windfall was to lead to the discovery of a little-known city and unlock the secrets of the alphabet – the basis of modern written language.

An expert at the Louvre in Paris identified the jars as fine pottery imported from Mycenaean Greece some time before 1000 BC – a sign of trade which excited great curiosity. In 1929 Claude Schaeffer, one of France's leading archaeologists, took an expedition to Minet el-Beida to explore the Syrian coastal area further.

A DISPLACED PEOPLE

Until Schaeffer's investigations, knowledge about the earliest peoples of Syria, Lebanon, and Israel had been scant. The only information came from Biblical texts, which referred to them as the Canaanites, and from the accounts of the Greeks and Romans, who knew them as Phoenicians. The two sources did not match. The Canaanites occupied much of Palestine – the Promised Land which the Israelites entered under Joshua. But the Phoenicians were a seafaring people, inhabiting a narrower coastal region. The discrepancy reflects important changes that took place in the Middle East towards the end of the 2nd millennium BC.

Joshua is thought to have led the Israelites into Canaan in the 13th century BC at a time when others were also arriving in the country, including traders from Mycenae. Around 1200 BC, a group of Sea Peoples from the Aegean and Mediterranean known as the Philistines occupied Canaan's southern plain, and about 200 years later, the nomadic Aramaeans took over the lands in the north. The Canaanites were slowly squeezed out of much of their territory, and the culture they had created disappeared – until the discoveries by Schaeffer in 1929.

THE FIRST ALPHABET To be successful, Canaanite merchants had to deal in all the languages of the ancient Near East, which used five different scripts. By using symbols to represent consonants instead of syllables, they could record multilingual transactions. This tablet bears the seal of Mursil II, a king of the Hittites, Ugarit's overlords from the 14th to the 12th centuries BC.

The Aramaeans pushed the Canaanites back to the coastal fringes of present-day Lebanon, an area rich in timber and with fine harbours, known to the Greeks as Phoenicia. The displaced people developed their maritime skills, and established an empire in the western Mediterranean with colonies in Cyprus, North Africa, Malta, Sicily, and Spain.

When Schaeffer's expedition began, Phoenicia was already a subject of scholarly research. During excavations at Byblos (modern Jubayl) in Lebanon just after the First World War, archaeologists had discovered an unusual 13th-century BC inscription on a royal sarcophagus. Previously discovered ancient writing used signs representing whole syllables and ideograms – symbols based on pictorial representations. But in this Phoenician script, the symbols represented single sounds. What had inspired the Phoenicians to refine hundreds of symbols into an alphabet?

Schaeffer hoped to find an answer. Near Minet el-Beida, he found more underground vaults, rich in treasures, proving that a complex civilization had flourished there during the 2nd millennium BC. Something else became clear: Minet el-Beida had been no more than a port for a much more important place – a great city buried under the rubble at nearby Ras Shamra. Schaeffer moved to Ras Shamra and began excavating. One of his first finds was a collection of clay tablets, known as the

> *Something else became clear: Minet el-Beida had been no more than a port for a much more important place – a great city buried under the rubble at nearby Ras Shamra.*

Library of the High Priest, inscribed with a previously unknown type of cuneiform (wedge-shaped) writing. The script was made up of a small number of symbols representing 30 basic sounds: an alphabet. When the language was identified as Semitic (belonging to the same family as modern Hebrew and Arabic), it became apparent that this was not the form of Phoenician known to the ancient Greeks, but an older Canaanite dialect.

THE FIRST GLIMPSE OF A LEGENDARY CITY

Scholars pieced together the history of the site. They identified it as an ancient city known as Ugarit, the existence of which had been suggested in the archives of two Egyptian pharaohs, Amenhotep III and Akhenaten, from about 1400 BC. Schaeffer found five levels of occupation, dating from 6500 to 1200 BC.

In 1948, the archaeologists discovered a great palace with another hoard of tablets, both literary and administrative. Royal seals impressed on the tablets identified one of the city's early

PALACE RUINS Ancient stones are all that survive of the palace at Ugarit. The main entrance, on the right, led into a courtyard giving access to the throne room and royal apartments.

HIDDEN SECRETS A fortified wall surrounds the entire city. The palace complex is visible to the left. To the right, trenches revealing parts of residential areas indicate how much of Ugarit remains unexplored.

rulers, King Yaqaru. This confirmed that it was once the capital of a kingdom dating back to the early 2nd millennium BC. Very little is known about this remote period. Yaqaru was probably the leader of a tribe of Amorites, nomadic people of Semitic origin who seized Ugarit because of its position as a trading post with Crete.

The king may have visited the city of Mari on the Euphrates, the palace of whose ruler, Zimri-Lim, was considered a wonder of the world at the time. Although Yaqaru's palace has not been found, a later palace discovered at Ugarit reflects a similar plan.

In the 14th and 13th centuries BC, successive kings added new wings to the later palace, which eventually covered more than 1ha (2½ acres). A grand entrance with wooden pillars led to a paved courtyard which served the royal quarters. Next door were the royal burial chambers, with a wing built over them; beyond, two large suites of rooms housed the treasury and the palace archives. A chancellery, and furnaces used for firing clay tablets, were added later.

East of the palace lay the royal craftsmen's workshops where ivory carvings were found – perhaps made as gifts for foreign kings. These included the carved head of a young prince or warrior god, encrusted with bronze and gold. The minister for trade lived in a house nearby. Beyond that were stables, more than 29m (95ft) long, and a riding school and coach-house.

THE GODS OF CANAAN

Ugarit's two high temples, dedicated to Hadad, the god of thunder (later called Baal) and Dagon, the god of agriculture and fertility, originally date from Yaqaru's reign. Both were rebuilt in the 14th century BC, at a time when the Egyptians controlled Palestine and were maintaining a naval base and garrison at Ugarit. The temples were positioned along a north-south axis to conform to the religious tradition of the Middle East – the temple of Solomon at Jerusalem followed the same plan. A square antechamber opened into the main shrine from which a staircase led up to the treasury. Most of the sacred rituals were performed in an open courtyard to the south.

The Old Testament patriarchs considered Canaanite fertility ceremonies an absolute abomination, the seductions of which tested the Israelites' faith through the centuries. The documents found at Ugarit gave flesh and form to these Canaanite deities for the first time. El was the father, the 'creator of all creatures', a merciful, wise god. By his wife, the goddess Athirat – known

SKILLED CRAFTSMEN AND TRADERS

The Phoenicians, like their ancestors the Canaanites of Ugarit, occupied a crossroads in the ancient world and were skilled middlemen in commercial activities. But they were craftsmen as well as traders. Many of the luxury goods they exported to Mesopotamia were made in their own workshops. In exchange they imported raw materials and products unobtainable at home. The centre of the Phoenicians' commercial activities was the great city of Tyre on the coast of Lebanon.

The Bible provides a graphic description of Phoenician trade. Chapter 27 of the Book of Ezekiel describes how merchants went to Tarshish (possibly Tartessus in Spain) and returned to the markets of Tyre 'with silver, iron, tin, and lead'. Edom (which bordered ancient Israel in the south) was a source of 'purple garments, brocade and fine linen, black coral and red jasper'. The Israelites 'traded . . . wheat . . . and honey, and oil, and balm'.

OCEAN TREASURE Glass ingots, 12.5cm (5in) across and dyed with cobalt (left) and copper (right), were recovered from a 14th-century BC shipwreck off the Anatolian coast. Glass was exported to Egypt for vase and bead manufacture.

in the Bible as Asherah – he fathered the lesser gods, principally Baal and the goddess Anat, who was Baal's wife as well as his sister. Baal, the god of thunder and rain, was also known as the son of the fertility god Dagon.

Baal and Anat waged war against Mot ('death'), the god of drought. Mot defeated Baal, who descended into the land of the dead. Anat pleaded for Baal's life. When Mot refused her, she killed him: 'With the blade did she cleave him, with the basket she winnowed him, in the fire did she burn him, with the millstone she ground him . . . ,' and El restored Baal to life. Anat's treatment of Mot, reaping, winnowing, and grinding, re-enacts the harvesting process and the turning of grain into flour – a familiar process in Canaan. Canaanite mythology followed the cycles of the seasons – its people were farmers, to whom the difference between drought and rain was the difference between life and death.

THE GREAT GODDESS An ivory box lid from the 13th century BC, found at Minet el-Beida, depicts a vibrant mother goddess. The carving is Mycenaean in style, and may have been made by immigrant craftsmen.

Baal is singled out for attack by the Hebrew prophets. As the Canaanites' most revered deity, the rain god was a special threat. The Israelites had begun to farm the land, like the Canaanites, instead of tending flocks – and no doubt prayed earnestly for rain in the dry seasons. But the patriarch's imprecations were more than just propaganda. They reflect a moral struggle to sustain Israel's identity in an alien culture. Baal's incestuous relationship with Anat must have seemed outrageous to the Israelites' moral sensibilities, and Anat herself was a figure of barbaric violence. One Canaanite text describes how 'she waded up to the knees, up to the neck in blood ... she tied the heads of her victims as ornaments upon her back, their hands she tied upon her belt.'

A LUST FOR INDEPENDENCE

During its heyday the Ugarit kingdom was surrounded by powerful neighbours, and its kings had to exercise their skills of diplomacy to ensure its survival. In the south, the Egyptians had established a vast empire which included much of Syria. It was not possible for them to administer their outlying territories directly, so they were content to allow vassal

DIVINE ICON In the artisans' district in the south of Ugarit, precious stones, gold and silver ingots, and gold-plated statuettes of the gods were discovered, including this figure which may depict Baal, the god of thunder.

kingdoms such as Ugarit a certain degree of independence. But during the reign of the pharaoh Akhenaten, whose stubborn preoccupation with religious reform created chaos in Egypt, a new menace arose: the Hittites.

The Hittites were settled in Hattusas, in what is now central Turkey, and their king decided to take advantage of the situation in Egypt to annex Syria. The kings of Ugarit skilfully negotiated to retain a measure of independence, while becoming vassals of the enlarged Hittite state. Throughout the 14th and 13th centuries BC they paid tribute to the Hittite monarchs; in return, the Hittites gave them protection. The people of Ugarit were thus able to concentrate on trade.

THE FRUITS OF COMMERCE
The city grew rich. The houses of the princes and noblemen, east of the palace, were luxuriously equipped, with bathrooms and lavatories fitted with waste-pipes. One of the king's advisers, Rapanu, lived in a house with 34 rooms on the ground floor alone.

The eastern part of the city was devoted to business. Here, Schaeffer discovered the warehouse of an olive oil dealer, which contained hundreds of oil jars labelled in cuneiform script. The dealer's prosperity was obvious from the treasure found in the graves of his children: toys and jewels, and an Egyptian statuette of a African dwarf holding a vase.

By far the most striking aspect of Ugarit was its profusion of libraries. After Schaeffer's discovery of the great Library of the High Priest, archaeologists discovered more and more tablets, revealing a collection of religious literature that preceded the texts

of the Old Testament. One library in the central square of the artisans' quarters was a school for scribes, containing literary and astrological classics, and a fascinating collection of maxims and sayings in the form of a dialogue between a father and his son. The library in Rapanu's house possessed a comprehensive selection of dictionaries of various cuneiform languages – including Akkadian, the language used in commerce throughout the ancient world – as well as private correspondence and state papers.

AN ALPHABET OF EXPEDIENCY
In Ugarit, intellectual and commercial activity were inextricably linked. The people of Ugarit were essentially middlemen – their city was a trade centre from which the luxuries of Crete and Cyprus were distributed throughout the East. Its merchants had to be able to trade in many different languages, from Sumerian and Akkadian to Hurrian, Hittite, Egyptian, and Minoan, as well as in their own Ugaritic tongue.

The only answer to this linguistic problem was simplification. Canaanite scribes devised a simple method of writing down the languages of their trading partners. Taking their inspiration from the Akkadian cuneiform script in common use, they created 30 symbols to represent single consonants instead of syllables. From the necessities of commerce, the invention which forms the basis of modern writing emerged.

Ugarit was destroyed by the invading Sea Peoples at the beginning of the 12th century BC. The Canaanites who settled on the coast of Lebanon became known as the Phoenicians, and carried their alphabet with them across the Mediterranean. They abandoned clay tablets and began writing on papyrus in a new alphabetic system called Proto-Sinaic, invented around the 17th century BC using Egyptian hieroglyphs as the basis for 22 alphabetic symbols.

Fragments of Phoenician papyrus survived through the centuries to tantalize modern scholars about the origins of the alphabet, but not until the discovery of Ugarit was the truth revealed: that the Phoenicians' Canaanite ancestors had developed the alphabet through centuries of patient experiment; and that the purpose of all that toil in the libraries of Ugarit had been to make life easier in the counting-houses.

The written word

Since the dawn of human existence, our earliest ancestors used visual signs, from cave paintings to symbols etched on the landscape, to convey information. The first pictorial writing system was developed around 3300 BC. It marked an evolutionary milestone allowing knowledge to be shared and recorded for future generations.

KEEPING THE ACCOUNTS These tokens and the clay token container were used by traders at Susa in south-west Iran in about 2900 BC.

Concrete records

From about 8000 BC, Near Eastern communities used clay tokens in trading transactions. Geometric shapes represented commodities such as measures of grain and individual animals. When towns emerged in the 4th millennium BC, tokens were shaped to resemble the commodities they represented. Tokens for a single transaction were kept together in a clay envelope marked to indicate its contents. Gradually, traders realised that the marks alone recorded all the necessary information.

DAILY ALLOWANCES A tablet from Jemdet Nasr, Iraq, written around 2900 BC, lists items issued as rations on individual days across five columns. The symbol at the bottom of each column means day. The series of horizontal lines each represent a number.

Writing in pictures

Around 3300 BC, the first writing appeared in Sumer. Pictorial signs were pressed into flat clay tablets. Many different signs were invented to depict a large range of commodities and to express new meanings, such as the verb 'to eat' – made by combining a person's head and a bowl. Several transactions were recorded on a single tablet, in separate boxes or columns.

Sumerian writing became very versatile. Pictograms were used not only for objects but for related words – extra lines or marks were added to extend meaning. Pictures began to represent sound rather than meaning. This allowed the scribes to string syllables together to create new words.

The invention of cuneiform

Sumerian writing was executed with a wedge-shaped reed on a clay tablet, so curved shapes were difficult. By 3000 BC, signs were being modified into a series of straight lines – cuneiform (wedge-shaped) writing. The signs quickly assumed conventional forms bearing little

---

FROM THE SCRIBES OF EGYPT

The Egyptians were beginning to develop writing by 3000 BC, perhaps inspired by Sumer. The signs of Egyptian hieroglyphic script were beautifully pictorial and, unlike Sumerian script, remained so over the millennia. By 500 BC, several thousand symbols existed. Knowledge of the script was restricted to the elite – royalty, priests, and scribes.

Like the symbols used in Sumer, hieroglyphs came to represent sounds as well as words. Only the consonants were written: the reader mentally supplied the vowels. When the script reached maturity, it was mainly composed of signs which represented one consonant or sequences of two or three consonants.

Hieroglyphics were used throughout Egyptian history for important records, such as royal inscriptions carved on public monuments and biographies painted or engraved on the walls of tombs. For writing with pen and ink on papyrus, a simplified, cursive (joined together) version developed, known as hieratic script.

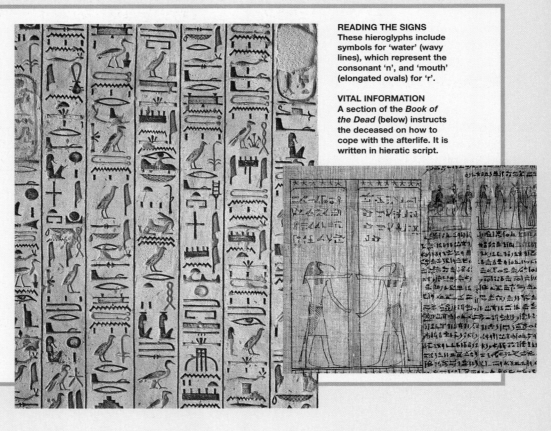

READING THE SIGNS These hieroglyphs include symbols for 'water' (wavy lines), which represent the consonant 'n', and 'mouth' (elongated ovals) for 'r'.

VITAL INFORMATION A section of the *Book of the Dead* (below) instructs the deceased on how to cope with the afterlife. It is written in hieratic script.

HEAVEN'S MYSTERY
This 7th century BC inscribed tablet was found at Nineveh in Mesopotamia. It bears an astronomical text written in cuneiform.

resemblance to the original pictograms. By 2600 BC, Sumerian script could be used to write any word in the Sumerian language. Writing was used for many purposes – economic transactions, royal inscriptions, labels, seals, and literature. The script was modified to write another language spoken by the ancient Mesopotamians – Akkadian. Other Near Eastern communities adopted cuneiform as they began to write.

A giant step for mankind

Around 1700 BC, the Canaanites of the Levant took a revolutionary step. A number of single-consonant Egyptian hieroglyphs were assigned the sound of the beginning of a Canaanite word – for example, the hieroglyph for 'house', *betu* in Canaanite, gave the sound 'b'. These signs formed the first alphabet, from which many other writing systems developed, including Hebrew, Aramaic, and Brahmi. The ancient Greeks introduced symbols for vowels, creating the basis of most later European scripts.

The language of divination

Chinese script was invented by the Shang dynasty in about 1700 BC. By 1200 BC, it was being used to inscribe bones for divination. Its pictographic signs, which signify whole words and syllables, were not developed into an alphabet. As a result, modern Chinese script, still based around the same system, uses thousands of characters.

ALPHABET STONE By about 1400 BC, the city of Ugarit in the Levant had devised its own alphabetical script, applying the notion of single-sound letters to cuneiform shapes rather than Egyptian hieroglyphs. This inscription shows the Ugaritic cuneiform alphabet in 'abc' order.

CALENDARS AND KINGS

Around 500 BC, Central American cultures began using signs to record dates. Later civilizations such as the Aztecs developed scripts that could record information such as names, but only the Maya developed a script that fully recorded spoken language. Maya script is still being deciphered, in the process revealing the history of kings and cities. The script uses devices such as puns, but is largely syllabic, formed by highly ornate glyphs and pictograms.

WORK OF ART Part of a Maya inscription from Palenque, dated AD 644, shows two symbols from a repertoire of more than 800, based on animals, people, and objects.

THE INDUS SCRIPT

The people of the Indus civilization invented a script which has not been deciphered – partly because it died out when the civilization declined, and partly because the inscriptions, mostly on seals, are very short. Many symbols probably represent names or official titles. Patient detective work and computer analysis have revealed the direction of writing (right to left), the probable type of script (combining syllables and words, rather than alphabetic), and the fact that it probably belonged to the Dravidian language family still spoken in parts of India. It may prove impossible to go much further in cracking the Indus code.

UNBROKEN CODE The typically short inscription on this seal found in Mohenjo-Daro shows just four of about 350 symbols used by the Indus civilizations.

Amarna

Capital of a heretic pharaoh

It was a dazzling moment in Egypt's history when Akhenaten ordered the worship of a single deity – the Aten, or Disc of the Sun. But the old gods took revenge through his successors, who buried the heart of his city beneath a sea of cement.

THE RELIGION OF ANCIENT EGYPT embraced a pageant of human and half-human deities, from Isis, the horned goddess, and Osiris, lord of the dead, to hawk-faced Horus, and Thoth, god of intelligence, depicted with the beak of an ibis. Scores of lesser divinities were also worshipped – snake-gods, cat-gods, jackal-gods – in a long tradition derived from ancient cults. Their worship bonded Egyptian society for thousands of years.

During the reign of Amenhotep IV (1379–1362 BC), the pantheon was swept aside. The pharaoh ordered that only one god was to be worshipped: the Sun, or more properly, the Aten ('Disc of the Sun'). The new monotheistic religion was revolutionary, exalting universal harmony, the beauty of nature, and love among all mankind – and represented nothing less than a cultural revolution.

THE POWER OF AMUN

When the renegade pharaoh mounted the throne, Egypt was at the height of its power. Since the founding of the 18th dynasty in 1570 BC – the beginning of the era known as the New Kingdom – Egyptian wealth and might had grown immeasurably. The nation ruled the largest empire the world had yet seen, encompassing Upper and Lower Egypt and the greater part of Nubia, beyond the fourth cataract of the Nile to the south.

The empire received tributes from subject kingdoms, and Thebes, the capital, became a city of fabulous riches. Much of the wealth reached the priests of the capital's main deity, Amun – 'The Hidden One'. The figure of Amun encompassed many divinities, most notably Ra (the Sun), and the gods of war and conquest. His cult was Egypt's official religion, and his Temple of Karnak at Thebes became one of the biggest religious complexes ever built. The priests of Amun wielded immense power – enough to threaten the throne.

By the time of Amenhotep III, decadence was beginning to taint Egyptian society. The empire's frontiers seemed secure, and warlike skills were neglected. Art had become more mannered, and the religious monopoly of Amun was breaking down. Amid the wealth and splendour of the civilization, a feeling of disquiet pervaded.

THE LIGHT OF LIFE In a stone relief found in the grand palace of Amarna, Akhenaten, his queen, Nefertiti, and one of their daughters present lotus flowers to the solar disc or Aten. The cult of the Aten came to Egypt at a time when accepted religious practices were fracturing. New cults were beginning to emerge, and older traditions were revived, allowing scope for a new approach to faith and ritual.

HAND IN HAND Akhenaten wanted his artists to move away from stylized art towards realism. This limestone statue displays all his imperfections – sunken chest, pot belly, and almost feminine hips. It gives no hint of the beauty of Queen Nefertiti.

The name of Aten, Disc of the Sun, first appeared on some monuments as another title for the Sun god, Ra. The cult may have been given royal sponsorship in an attempt to break the powerful grip of the established priesthood on Egypt's political life. It was in this setting that the drama of Akhenaten unfolded – a drama which was to shake Egyptian society to its roots.

THE COMING OF A NEW GOD

Amenhotep IV came to the throne in 1379 BC surrounded by all the usual pomp and ceremony of the established cult of Amun – even the name Amenhotep means 'Amun is content'. But the new pharaoh had a particular zeal for Sun worship.

Amenhotep began installing monuments dedicated to Aten in the Temple of Amun at Karnak. This must have stirred a whirlwind of fury among the established priesthood. As the pharaoh's religious ardour increased, he began closing the temples of Amun and persecuting the priests. The name of the god was obliterated from monuments throughout the country, and Amenhotep decided to take a new name, Akhenaten, 'He who is pleasing to Aten'.

It was not only the cult of Amun which was disbanded; those of the other ancient deities – Isis and Osiris, Horus and Thoth – were swept away, too. At the expense of a company of gods who had coexisted since the dawn of Egyptian civilization, Akhenaten imposed monotheism: the belief in a single, universal deity. He dismantled an entire universe, leaving the vulnerable Egyptians protected only by the blank gaze of a celestial disc.

The strength of the pharaoh's religious beliefs suggests some kind of personal revelation. A great hymn surviving from the period, which may have been composed by Akhenaten, reveals a fresh and sparkling vision of the world. It is a paean to the supreme life force, the Sun, and names Akhenaten as the son of the solar divinity – the sole intermediary between mankind and the divine:

'You arise in beauty in the horizon of the sky, oh living Aten, creator of life … Earth lights up when you appear on the horizon, Aten who shines throughout the day.

'You chase the darkness and bless us with your rays. The two countries [Upper and Lower Egypt] rejoice. The people awaken, they stand upright.

'It is you who have caused them to rise … trees and plants grow green. The birds fly from their nests, praising your spirit with their wings. All creatures leap in frolic …

'No one knows you but your son Neferkheperure Waenre [another name for Akhenaten]. You have informed him of your ways and of your power.'

AMARNA TAKES SHAPE

It was obvious that Thebes was still too devoted to the ancient gods to allow the new Sun cult to flourish. A new capital was needed, untainted by the worship of other gods, and a place known today as Tell el-Amarna was selected.

It was named Akhetaten – 'the Horizon of the Disc'. The site lay on the east bank of the Nile, at a point where the river's fierce waters had once gouged out a huge natural amphitheatre – a desert space some 12km (7½ miles) long and 5km (3 miles) wide, bordered by a wall of cliffs to the east.

The northern and southern extremities of the site were marked with inscriptions on stone slabs known as frontier *stelae*. The engravings are surmounted by images showing the king and his queen, Nefertiti (meaning 'the beautiful one has come'), making an offering to Aten. The stones declared the boundaries of the area dedicated to the celestial father. More inscriptions were placed in the cliffs to the east, and on the west bank of the Nile. The cliffs were patrolled, and all newcomers were checked.

erected with sun-dried mud brick. In the heart of Amarna, the official quarter was constructed, comprising the royal palace, the Temple of Aten, and administrative buildings. The house of the vizier, head of the administration, was about 1.5km (1 mile) from the palace, and could be reached quickly by chariot.

The palace overlooked the Nile on one side, and on the other it faced the Royal Highway – a broad avenue running through the middle of the city. The ruins of the palace extend for more than 400m (1,312ft), a labyrinthine sprawl of courts and chambers from which archaeologists have identified the principal areas. A large central courtyard contained colossal statues of the pharaoh and his queen, and led to a harem and an immense throne room containing more than 500 pillars.

The king did not live in the palace – it was reserved for official functions. His personal residence, a more modest villa with gardens and outbuildings, lay on the opposite side of the Royal Highway. The two complexes, official and private, were connected by a covered bridge across the avenue, and this structure played a vital role in the life of the city. From a balcony in the middle of the bridge, the pharaoh would toss shimmering hoards of gold to his most favoured subjects.

A PHARAOH UNMASKED The long face, thick lips, and other unflattering features of Akhenaten (above) have led scholars to suggest that he may have suffered from a glandular or metabolic disorder. A bust from Amarna shows Queen Nefertiti's contrasting beauty (right).

The soil of Amarna was somewhat above the flood level of the Nile, and therefore infertile. In order to maintain a supply of agricultural produce, an expanse of arable land on the left bank was colonized. Amarna was founded not just as a royal capital, but also as a self-sufficient community.

Some of those who accompanied the pharaoh must have been true believers, motivated by faith in his vision. Others must have clung silently to their ancient beliefs. Whatever the background of its people, the original community of Amarna was large enough to form the nucleus of a metropolis which expanded over the years that followed.

Surrounded by cliffs and water, the site was hard to reach. Transporting large stone slabs for temple-building proved difficult, so to speed things up, only stones of modest size were used, and then only to face the walls. Houses were hurriedly

THE GOLD OF RECOMPENSE

It had long been the custom of the pharaohs to reward loyal subjects with gifts. Under the Old Kingdom, the royal bounty often took the form of a stone coffin or a funerary adornment for a tomb. Under the New Kingdom, gifts of gold became more usual – the precious metal satisfied the material cravings of a more commercially minded age. Gold could be used in trade, but it also had religious associations – it was an incorruptible solar substance symbolizing immortality.

An award of the 'gold of recompense' was considered the highest honour in Amarna, and the scene is often depicted in the city's tomb paintings. The honoured subject is generally shown standing on the Royal Highway at the foot of the palace bridge. The royal family appear above him, and articles of gold are tossed down: cups, bracelets, and heavy necklaces which servants fasten around the neck of the receiver. Ecstatic crowds witness

FEASTING FOR ETERNITY
The pleasures of life in the New Kingdom are recorded in the tomb paintings of the time, which typically depict events in the lives of those buried there. In this scene, discovered in the tomb of an 18th-dynasty official at Thebes, a banquet is in full swing, complete with musicians and dancing girls.

the subject's day of glory: colleagues, friends, and servants – all of whom bow down before their ruler. After the ceremony comes dancing and celebration, and the gifts are taken back to the home of the favoured one. Akhenaten certainly knew how to nurture the faith of his followers.

RITUAL IN A SUN-DRENCHED TEMPLE

The great Temple of Aten was situated slightly to the north of the private palace, in a vast sacred enclosure measuring 800m (2,625ft) by almost 300m (984ft). Like other Egyptian temples, the sanctuary consisted of a series of courtyards radiating from a single axis, and the entrance to the complex was framed by two pylons – huge, tapering stone masses. But the likeness to traditional temples ended here, because the Temple of Aten had been conceived in a revolutionary way.

In traditional temples, such as those at Karnak and Luxor, a courtyard led into a succession of increasingly dark and small rooms, with lowered ceilings and raised floors, culminating in the sanctuary itself, away from the crowds and from daylight. But the temple at Amarna had no roof – the walls acted merely as partitions between chambers open to the sky. Akhenaten was anxious that nothing should block the Sun's holy rays.

Reliefs from Amarna evoke the grandeur of the ceremonies held inside the Sun-drenched sanctuary. Events are presented frame by frame, with an almost cinematic effect. The king drove his own chariot to the temple. Nefertiti drove a second chariot. Behind came the princesses and ladies of the court, and soldiers carrying standards ran beside the procession. At the temple,

servants led the horses and their chariots away, and priests greeted the royal couple with a bow. Women beat tambourines, and subjects raised their arms in homage.

Luxury verging on decadence is apparent everywhere. The women wore diaphanous pleated dresses. The king and queen were similarly attired in fine fabrics revealing the contours of their limbs. Feathers decked the horns of the sacrificial oxen, whose bodies were so fattened that they could barely move.

Within the temple enclosure, the king approached the main gate. The little princesses trooped in after their parents. The children were naked and their heads were shaved, except for a single lock of hair, as was the practice for Egyptian children. Each of them carried a *sistrum*, a musical instrument used in Egyptian religious ceremony. It consisted of a metal ring fastened to a handle. Rods loosely attached to the ring tinkled when the instrument was shaken. The sound was associated with love and joy, and was credited with warding off evil spirits.

HONOURING THE ATEN

The music of the sistrum provided a familiar background to the ceremonies, but the rites of Aten were startlingly new. Egyptian gods were traditionally worshipped in effigy: a statue would be washed, dressed, and perfumed exactly like a living being, and presented with offerings of food. No such idolatries attended the new religion. The Aten had no statue; it was never represented in human or animal form. Offerings were piled on a great altar – gifts of bread, poultry, beef, and garlands of flowers – and the Disc of the Sun witnessed the rites as the pharaoh consecrated gifts, burned incense, and poured water, with the queen officiating at his side.

The temple site contains an astonishing number of lesser altars – some 2,000 in all – which may have been used by Amarna's citizens. The possibility that the king and his subjects worshipped the Aten in the same sacred space indicates another revolutionary departure from the conventions of earlier Egyptian rites.

... the Disc of the Sun witnessed the rites as the pharaoh consecrated gifts, burned incense, and poured water, with the queen officiating at his side.

HOMES TO A UNIFORM DESIGN

Residential areas grew haphazardly to the north and south of the city's official buildings. The homes of the wealthier citizens were spaced out along the streets at irregular intervals, and humbler citizens occupied the areas in between, different classes living side by side.

Whatever their size, whether humble dwellings or princely palaces, houses in Amarna were laid out according to the same basic plan. All were divided into three parts: an antechamber, a living room, and a private area with bedrooms. The antechamber was a long and often beautiful room, its ceiling supported by wooden columns, and it was sometimes surrounded by a suite of smaller rooms.

COMMUNITY CRAFTS Craftsmen shape *djed* pillars, symbols of Osiris, in the top centre of an 18th-dynasty tomb painting. In Amarna, groups of people practising the same craft settled together in neighbourhoods in the northern part of the city.

The square living room was the centre of the house. The walls were not open to the sun, so the room temperature was cool and comfortable. They led up to a ceiling higher than that of the rest of the house, supported by wooden columns. Daylight entered through small windows set high in the walls.

The private apartments consisted of the master's chamber and rooms reserved for family and guests. There were no true bathrooms – a simple chamber provided a space where servants would shower family members with water from a jar. A small adjacent room provided somewhere to relax, and a staircase led to the terrace roof where the family might sleep if the summer heat made the house unbearable.

The wealthier houses at Amarna were like miniature estates. They included gardens and many outbuildings, all enclosed by a rectangular wall, and were largely self-sufficient. The kitchens were always situated in the outbuildings, as were the cattle-sheds, stables, kennels, a well, and the servants' quarters. Grain brought from the west bank of the river was stored in a large courtyard equipped with grain lofts.

Soil had to be brought in from outside the city to enrich the gardens, which were tended with exceptional care. Trees planted in rows according to species were often arranged around a large, rectangular pond. Most gardens contained a chapel, with an engraved stone showing the royal family making an offering to the Aten. Images of the Disc and of Akhenaten, his prophet, were everywhere in the city. In the desert space outside the city, the pharaoh built a number of royal palaces where he and his family could retreat for relaxation.

FAMILY LIFE Akhenaten liked to have himself depicted in intimate scenes of domesticity. A relief from an Amarna villa shows the royal couple playing with their daughters under the life-giving rays of the Aten.

couple heartily enjoy a meal. Akhenaten holds a chop, Nefertiti a piece of chicken; they are eating with gusto. Another relief shows the royal couple side by side on a chariot, Akhenaten holding the reins and Nefertiti embracing him. Such displays of intimacy must have outraged traditionalists.

Charmingly casual though the scene often was, the royal couple were always represented with the Disc of the Sun blazing overhead. The rays of the heavenly body were drawn as long lines terminating in a hand which held a looped cross – an *ankh* – the hieroglyph symbolizing life.

Even in death, the image of the pharaoh and Aten accompanied the citizens of Amarna. Tombs were built in the wall of cliffs along the eastern frontier of the city. Like other Egyptian burials, they were decorated with scenes from the dead person's earthly existence. But at Amarna, Akhenaten himself, crowned by the rays of the Sun, always dominates the pictures.

All the mythology of the Egyptian underworld was swept away by Akhenaten's reforms. The occupants of the tombs faced the unknown under the protection of the pharaoh alone. It was he who illuminated his subjects' burial places, and he acted as their exclusive guardian against the terrors of the afterlife.

An entire village for the tomb workers was built near the cliffs, laid out according to a careful plan. Five streets ran between its terraced houses linking some 70 dwellings, all more or less identical except for the foreman's larger house. The village limits were marked by a mud-brick wall.

THE FACE OF THE NEW KINGDOM

Death masks and casts have been excavated from the villa of a sculptor named Thutmose. The modelling room and studio contained chisels and drills, and models of heads fashioned out of gypsum plaster. Such likenesses were the sculptor's stock-in-trade, from which portraits would later be carved in stone.

At Maru-Aten, to the south of the town, he constructed several artificial lakes, the largest of which might have been used for water sports. In the middle of another lake, on an island, were three pavilions – an oasis of calm which may have served as the pharaoh's summer palace.

Another royal residence to the north of the town seems to have included a zoological garden. Frescoes here and elsewhere in the city bear tribute to Akhenaten's delight in nature, depicting an exotic world of flowers, birds, and water plants.

QUESTIONS OF LIFE AND DEATH

The Egyptians had always lived close to nature, and the animal kingdom featured prominently in their art. The Amarna period brought greater spontaneity – a more vibrant sense of life, independent of its mythological associations. The rigid lines of conventional art melted into more fluid forms. Representations of the human figure, for instance, began to show how people really looked, rather than following an established stereotype. Musculature was examined, the casual gesture revealed.

These new developments are most evident in the countless representations of the pharaoh and his family. Many carvings show scenes from their private life. On one relief, the royal

Many customers were private individuals, from fairly low-born citizens who had profited by Akhenaten's favour to the highest in the land. The head of Nefertiti found at Amarna is the work of Thutmose. The piece combines the formal simplicity of traditional Egyptian art with the naturalism encouraged by Akhenaten. It has none of the distortions which mar some of Amarna's stone reliefs.

While Thutmose was clearly one of the foremost artists of his day, he was not the sculptor-in-chief. That high title belonged to a certain Bak, whose father had been head sculptor under Amenhotep III. Whether Bak resented Akhenaten's personal influence on the arts is not known. Like everyone else at Amarna, he paid at least token homage to the pharaoh's new vision of the world, styling himself as chief sculptor, 'whom his majesty himself taught'.

Other excavations at Amarna have revealed little new information about the ordinary routines of daily life. Most of the workers were involved in farming the land; irrigating the fertile banks of the Nile according to age-old traditions. But frescoes and figurines from the period do reflect important changes in high society since the days of the Old Kingdom.

STYLISH CUT This head of a young woman, made of blue glass, dates from the Amarna age. Her hair is cut short and rounded, falling in a style that was fashionable among the high-born ladies of Amarna.

These are nowhere more evident than in the styling of clothes.

Under the Old Kingdom, the Egyptians had always dressed simply. Men wore nothing more than a loincloth, long or short, sometimes pleated, sometimes starched. Women wore long, tight-fitting dresses fastened at the shoulder with straps. The material in both cases was plain white linen. The difference between the clothing of the rich and the poor lay principally in the fineness of the fabric.

FOLLOWING THE FASHION

Fashion, in the modern sense of fluctuating styles of dress, evolved side by side with the wealth and taste for luxury which arose under the New Kingdom. Chic Egyptians began to wear fuller and more complex garments. Short-sleeved blouses became popular, and the traditional loincloth was covered with a large piece of transparent drapery. In Amarna, the front of

A NEW REALISM Akhenaten's artists strove to break with the rigidity of tradition. A painting of two of the six royal princesses shows the faces in profile, as usual, but the bodies are depicted with a more realistic fluidity.

AN EGYPTIAN HOME A villa discovered in Amarna was surrounded by a wall 70m (230ft) long and 60m (197ft) wide. Two entrances led in from the street, one through the garden, one straight into the main house, for the use of servants. The house is constructed of sun-dried mud-brick, with stone doorsteps and lintels. The walls are pebble-dashed in white, and decorated with friezes of plant life.

1 Main entrance	9 Stables
2 Porter's lodge	10 Servants' quarters
3 Chapel	11 Storage room
4 Central hall	12 Kitchen
5 Harem	13 Cattle sheds
6 Master's bedroom	14 Garden with pond
7 Dressing room	15 Grain silos
8 Workshops	16 Servants' entrance

this piece of fine linen was folded upwards to form a long pleated pocket. New, discreetly voluptuous forms began to replace the austere lines of traditional wear. Women's dresses, full length and flared, were knotted under the breasts, sometimes leaving them bare.

Whether male or female, all high-born Egyptians lavished great care on their complexions. Men shaved regularly with bronze or copper razors: a high-ranking Egyptian never wore facial hair, a custom that distinguished him sharply from his Asiatic neighbours. On bas-reliefs, Syrians are immediately recognisable by their beards.

Men's hair was cut short, and a curly wig worn on top. Women wore heavier artificial hairdos, especially for banquets, when the wig was plaited and fell to the shoulders in a mass of ribbons and flowers, often crowned with a jewelled diadem.

The jewellery of the New Kingdom was magnificent. Women's necks were adorned with beaded necklaces, their wrists with arrays of bracelets.

SUN WORSHIP Akhenaten's great Temple of Aten never had a roof – it was designed to be open to the Sun-god's rays. The foundations have now been uncovered, and one of the great pillars of the temple has been reconstructed.

Materials varied according to the wearer's station: from pottery or glass paste to gold, silver, ivory, and precious stones such as lapis lazuli, turquoise, or malachite.

This iridescent splendour reflected more than wealth or high rank. Decorative amulets of magical significance were shaped in the forms of hieroglyphs meaning 'Life', 'Health', or 'Longevity'.

SOFT LIVING – THE FATAL FLAW

Even before the Amarna period, the distinction between men's and women's clothing was becoming blurred. In Akhenaten's time, this tendency reached its high point. It is clear from portraits that the king had a strangely feminine appearance, and under his rule characteristics traditionally associated with women were exalted: love, tenderness, affection for nature, and domesticity. At the same time, conventionally masculine skills of warfare and statecraft were being abandoned – a move that was to have catastrophic consequences for the empire.

The reign of Akhenaten lasted 17 years. During that time, Egypt's hard-won dominion over Palestine and Syria disintegrated. A cache of state archives, written on clay tablets, was discovered at Amarna in 1887. Many of the tablets are letters from the rulers of contemporary states such as Mitanni, discussing diplomatic gifts. Others present a vivid picture of an empire in decline. They include letters written by vassals of Egypt in the Middle Eastern territories, begging for help against rival states, or complaining about Egypt's failure to send troops.

In fairness to Akhenaten, the process of decay must have set in before he came to the throne. Many of the letters are addressed to his father, Amenhotep III. Some scholars have suggested that it was official policy to keep the eastern states quarrelling among themselves, on the time-honoured principle of 'divide and rule'. If so, the policy backfired. A people now known by their Biblical name of the Hittites were emerging as a major power in the Middle East. They profited from Egypt's neglect by seizing Syria.

No evidence survives to suggest that the loss worried Akhenaten in his secluded world on the banks of the Nile. While night stole across the imperial domain, Amarna bathed in the rays of a setting sun. The last years of the pharaoh's reign are shadowy. Queen Nefertiti disappears – she may have died or fallen from favour, or she may have moved to Thebes as the pharaoh's representative. Her place at Akhenaten's side was taken by her eldest daughter, the princess Meretaten.

BANISHING A HERESY

In 1362 BC Akhenaten died, and was succeeded by his son-in-law, Smenkhkare, husband of Meretaten. Smenkhkare reigned for a mere two years, and was succeeded by another son-in-law of Akhenaten, Tutankhaten. Already Egypt was turning away from the god which had failed to keep the empire intact. The new sovereign changed his name to Tutankhamun, reflecting a reversion to the ancient dynastic deity previously worshipped in Thebes.

The name of Tutankhamun became famous after the discovery, in 1922, of his tomb in the Valley of the Kings. His reign was short, but significant for the restoration of the traditional gods. Deserted shrines were rebuilt in splendour, and their priesthoods returned. But the taint of heresy lingered about the royal house. The efforts of Tutankhamun and his successors to appease the angry heavens did not go far enough. Around the end of the 14th century BC, one of Tutankhamun's chief advisers, a general called Horemheb, came to the throne, and set about annihilating Akhenaten's memory.

THE PRIESTS' REVENGE

Amarna, already partially deserted, was obliterated. Statues of Akhenaten were smashed, monuments razed to the ground. Particular vengeance was reserved for the great temple; the walls were demolished, and thousands of stone slabs ferried along the Nile for re-use in temples dedicated to the ancient gods, as though to atone for the outrage committed against them. In a final gesture, a layer of cement was poured over the foundations of Amarna's temples.

Under the new dynasty of pharaohs, Egypt's old imperial ambitions were revived, and the Amarna episode was committed to oblivion. Yet, in a curious paradox, it is the only major Egyptian city of which a fairly clear picture survives.

Urban centres in the populated regions have all disappeared under successive layers of habitation, but the remote site of Amarna was never re-occupied. In addition, the cement which Horemheb poured over the foundations of the temple protected them from erosion, and the layout of the town survives exactly as it was in the age of Akhenaten – a blueprint of Egyptian town planning preserved.

An extraordinary mystery surrounds the fate of Akhenaten himself. The pharaoh had prepared a family tomb to the east of the city, and this has been excavated. One of the royal princesses, who had died young, was buried there, but no other members of the household reached their appointed resting place. Four granite coffins have been unearthed at the site – they had been shattered. Somehow, the Egyptians denied the dead pharaoh his intended burial, perhaps wishing to forget the son of the Aten and his divine, faceless father.

Hattusas

Heart of the Hittite Empire

Near an isolated village in Turkey stand the ruins of a once-bustling capital, the hub of an ancient superpower. Hattusas was the capital city of the Hittites, masters of warfare who shook the might of ancient Egypt.

ACCORDING TO THE BOOK OF GENESIS, the Hittites were one of the warlike tribes living in Palestine when the Jewish people returned from slavery in Egypt to the Promised Land. They are often mentioned later in the Old Testament – for example, the great Jewish kings, David and Solomon, both took Hittite wives. It is clear that by about 1400 BC the Hittites were considered as formidable a military power as the Egyptians, and their sphere of influence was spreading across Syria and Palestine.

Until the early 20th century, the Hittites could only be glimpsed indirectly, through the eyes of other cultures who had come into contact with them. The few rock carvings and inscriptions attributed to them had proved difficult to interpret. Then, in 1906, a dramatic archaeological discovery rescued the lost civilization from oblivion.

In that year, German archaeologists were working through the remains of a fortified city on the heights overlooking the remote Turkish village of Bogazköy (present-day Bogazkale) in central Anatolia. They unearthed some 2,500 inscribed tablets – part of the state archives of a forgotten people. In the decades that followed, further excavations led to the recovery of a total of some 10,000 tablets. Deciphering the inscriptions on the tablets revealed that the fortified city was Hattusas, ancient capital of the Hittites.

SETTLERS FROM THE STEPPES

The Hittites were originally nomadic Indo-European herdsmen and warriors. They descended on the Middle East from the steppes of southern Russia during the third millennium BC, and settled in Anatolia in about 2300 BC. Their domain was not built on lightning conquest – initially, they seem to have integrated peacefully with the local people. But by 1700 BC, they had united several scattered kingdoms into what was to become a large and powerful empire. By 1350 BC, under Suppiluliumas I, they became a major Middle Eastern power, contesting supremacy with both the Egyptians and the Mitanni of northern Syria and Iraq.

SUSTAINING A GROWING CITY
The Hittites first occupied the site of Hattusas in the 17th century BC. Between the 15th and the 13th centuries BC, the city doubled in size. Inside its massive defensive walls lay five sanctuaries, each of which had storage facilities for grain, oil, and wine. The ruins of the main temple complex, dedicated to the Hittite weather god, include a series of huge storage jars, taller than a man, half sunk into the ground.

SPINNING A YARN A royal lady spins wool while a child looks on, holding a writing tablet and stylus (above). This 8th century bas-relief from Marash is evidence that the culture discovered among the ruins of Hattusas (below) survived the fracturing of its empire in the 13th century BC.

The essential instrument of Hittite might was the horse-drawn chariot – a two-wheeled vehicle manned by a driver, a fighter armed with a bow and a lance, and a defender with a shield. The war chariot was not an innovation; the Egyptians used a similar, though lighter, vehicle with a crew of two men. But Hittite chariots were technically superior – they were swift and easy to manoeuvre – and enabled their makers to maintain control over Syria, despite the opposition of ancient Egypt.

Egyptian records describe an epic encounter with Hittite war chariots which occurred some time in the early 13th century BC. The Hittite king Muwatallis II engaged Pharaoh Rameses II in the first battle of massed chariots in recorded history. The sides met at Kadesh on the River Orontes in Syria. The Hittites and their Syrian allies lined up some 2,500 vehicles. Rushing forward with a thunderous roar, they overturned the light Egyptian chariots and routed their infantry in a cloud of dust.

The personal intervention of Rameses at the head of his forces saved the Egyptians from disaster. His records claim the battle as a victory for Egypt, but the tablets found at Hattusas, and the fact that the Egyptians subsequently abandoned the north of Syria to the Hittites, clearly indicate the real victors.

INSIDE THE CITY WALLS

The Hittite capital reflected the warrior traditions of its people. The site – a large arena of hills enclosing an undulating area dominated by a citadel – was protected by 6km (3¾ miles) of fortifications. The walls were made of huge stones erected in double ranks, with rubble packed in between. They were punctuated by square towers and gateways flanked by carved lions or gods. A lower wall was erected 6m (20ft) in front of

FIERCE DEFENDERS The fortified walls of Hattusas included two gates with sculptural decorations: the Lion Gate (above), set in the south-west, and the King's Gate, inscribed with a warrior god, in the south-east.

the main wall. A tunnel beneath it allowed Hittite troops to emerge suddenly and surprise the enemy. The city itself was spaciously laid out. Houses were detached, separated by gardens. Many were built of mud, then whitewashed or roughcast.

These materials were fragile and needed constant maintenance, but they were easy to rebuild following damage by war or earthquake. Stone was used only in the lower structure of religious and administrative buildings. Five sanctuaries have been located in the city, all conforming to the same basic plan. Storerooms surround a rectangular courtyard, with a shrine at one end. The most important temple in Hattusas was sacred to Tarhun, the great weather god. His consort was Arinnitti, the Sun goddess of Arinna and the patron deity of the king and his empire. Arinna is the name of a pre-Hittite town in Anatolia, suggesting that the conquerors had adopted the beliefs of an existing cult.

THE ARCHIVES OF AN EMPIRE

The inscribed tablets were discovered in the administrative buildings and palaces of Hattusas. Codes of law, treaties, and royal correspondence are recorded in cuneiform script, alongside religious and educational texts and literary works. The tablets touch not only on affairs of state, but also give an impression of everyday life in the thriving Hittite capital.

THE ART OF METALWORK

When the Hittites conquered Anatolia, they inherited an already thriving metalworking culture which may have been one of the earliest in the world. The first metal used for utensils was copper. Bronze, an alloy of copper and tin, was produced in the third millennium BC.

Copper ore was roasted in furnaces, melted down in crucibles, and heated again. Furnaces were fanned with bellows made from animal skins. To make bronze, the molten copper was mixed with tin and cast in blocks or ingots which were distributed to metalworkers. After further founding, the metal was cast into sandstone moulds.

The Iron Age began in Anatolia and the Near East towards the end of the second millennium BC. Iron ore came from the Taurus Mountains and Armenia. The Hittites learned ironworking – Egyptian records mention royal gifts of iron objects sent by Hittite rulers.

Ironworking required more elaborate techniques than those used to shape copper or bronze. Ancient wood or charcoal furnaces could not reach high enough temperatures to melt the metal – they were capable only of softening it. Softened iron had to be pounded on an anvil with a heavy hammer to remove impurities and produce the required form.

RITUAL OBJECT A bronze standard from a royal burial near Hattusas.

The empire was ruled by a king who governed with the help of the *pankus*, a council of elders and notables. This body had legal powers, and could even censor the king's orders. The queen also took an active part in government.

The royal subjects were divided into two classes: free men and slaves. Free men were arranged in a hierarchy headed by priests and nobility. The slave class were bonded to the land, living like serfs in feudal Europe rather than in total bondage. When land was sold, the slaves working it became the property of the new owner. But slaves were allowed to own land in their own right. Married slaves could not be separated from their families, nor could their belongings be seized for any reason.

EVERYDAY LIFE IN A HITTITE CITY

Whether free or enslaved, every Hittite had a home. Houses were one or two storeys high with a number of windowed rooms, and were topped by a flat terraced roof reached by a wooden ladder. People slept on mats on the roofs on hot summer nights.

Furniture varied according to a person's means. The poor would own little more than a mat to sit and sleep on. They would use a terracotta brazier fuelled by charcoal for cooking and heating. Clothes might be kept in a wooden chest. Wealthier people possessed a range of items, from gate-legged tables and raised beds to high-backed, carved wooden seats.

Grain, oil, and other foodstuffs were kept in large jars in storerooms. Some storerooms contained ovens and equipment for grinding grain, used to make bread and beer. Only the rich could afford the luxury of wine.

The streets were particularly lively near the city gates where the markets were held. Among the crowds were stocky Anatolians dressed in short tunics or wide cloaks and long, pointed leather shoes. Hittite women swept by in long gowns, their heads covered with a fringed scarf.

There were visitors from far afield: Syrians with pointed beards dressed in embroidered garments, and Achaean Greeks from Cyprus or the shores of the Aegean, recognisable by their sleeved tunics. Assyrian merchants in heavy cloaks, their beards carefully groomed, mingled with the crowds, taking a particular interest in local supplies of lead, copper, iron, and silver.

The price of almost all goods was fixed by law on the basis of a specific standard, the silver shekel, though dealing was usually carried out by barter. A garment worth 20 shekels might, for example, be exchanged for a carthorse of the same value. A set measure of grain was worth one-third of a shekel; a cheese was worth a little more – half a shekel.

Citizens brought their garden produce to market: apples, pears, pomegranates, figs, onions, leeks, lentils, peas, or olives. Artisans offered manufactured goods such as footwear, elegantly shaped pottery, mirrors, bronze objects, and gold and silver jewellery. From the fields outside the city, peasants brought grain, oil, mules, cattle, and sheep. Mules were in demand in this mountainous country, and were expensive at 60 shekels – four times as much as a horse and 60 times as much as a sheep.

Land sales are also likely to have been carried out in the markets. One hectare (2.5 acres) of irrigated land was worth three shekels. If planted with vines, its value rose to 120 shekels – clear evidence of the scarcity of wine in the region.

ENTERTAINMENT FOR THE MASSES

The colour and bustle of Hittite street life were not confined to the markets. The military went by in chariot processions, and great caravans of muleteers carried the tributes of the Syrian princes to the palace. Open-air displays were performed by acrobats, sword-swallowers, and lute-players.

Religious ceremonies also played their part in the life of the people. The Hittites' most imposing sacred monument was the great sanctuary known as Yazilikaya ('Inscribed Rock'), built at the mouth of two natural rock galleries, about 1.5km (just under a mile) from Hattusas. Its function remains a subject for speculation, though it was possibly the site of an annual festival.

The Hittites also loved physical exercise. Chariot-racing and hunting were favourite activities. Armed with bows and spears, young men would seek hares, stags, and wild boars on the high plateaus of Anatolia. Mounted on chariots, javelin in hand, they hunted antelopes and lions on the plains.

TIME TO MOVE ON

For all the city's vigour and prosperity, the days of Hattusas were numbered. Its fortifications were extended in the 13th century BC to enclose the plateau of Büyükkaya to the east – an area only recently investigated by archaeologists – but as the century drew to a close, the empire began to disintegrate. The principal enemies were the Sea Peoples. This assortment of marauders emerged from the Mediterranean islands and from Anatolia; they were peoples of

SACRED MONUMENT The Yazilikaya sanctuary (below) is built on the sides of two natural gorges (1, 2 in the plan, right), on which images of gods and royal personages were carved. A monumental gate (3) gave access to a temple (4) built by Hattusil III.

A REFLECTION OF NATURE Hittite pottery, made of ochre or red clay, often featured stylized shapes inspired by the natural world, such as this jug of *c.*1700 BC with a spout shaped like the head of a bird of prey.

the Mycenaean world, which was itself collapsing. They forced the Hittites from their homeland, and many travelled south to form neo-Hittite city states in northern Syria, in places such as Malatya, Karatepe, and Carchemish. These states flourished for almost 400 years, until their annexation by Assyria in the 8th century BC. Bas-reliefs discovered at these sites are reminders of the time when Hattusas stood proud on its rocky heights. These relics, together with the written records of Egypt, the only kingdom to resist the onslaught of the Sea Peoples, show that the nomadic spirit of the Hittites helped their culture to survive.

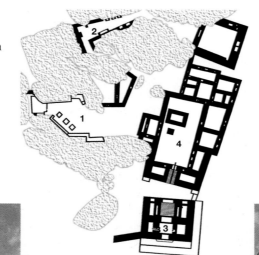

Anyang

A Chinese capital in the Bronze Age

Masterpieces of sculptured bronze attest to the brilliant civilization of the Shang dynasty. Another Shang legacy – a collection of bones etched with questions for the ancestral gods – reveals clues to the birth of the Chinese language.

TOWARDS THE END OF THE 19TH CENTURY, Chinese peasants tilling their fields near Anyang, in the northern province of Henan, unearthed hundreds of ancient bones inscribed with strange writing. They sold their discoveries to apothecary shops, believing that they were dragons' bones charged with magical healing powers. Scholars soon realized that the bones were of great historical interest, but serious excavations in the area did not begin until 1928.

Under the direction of Dr Li Ji of the Academia Sinica (a Chinese research institute, now based in Taipei), archaeologists unearthed thousands more of the inscribed bones, which had been carefully stored in chronological order. The inscriptions were questions for the ancestors of the mighty Shang kings, who ruled from 1750 to 1027 BC. They were the only written records of a vanished civilization.

In the 14th century BC, the warrior-king Pan Geng had initiated a new era in the Shang dynasty when he moved his capital north from Yan – a place not yet identified – to the site of Anyang. He called his new city Yin, and historians refer to this second Shang era, which lasted until 1027 BC, as Yin, and to its rulers as Shangyin. Little was known about the period until the excavations at Anyang. By 1937, more than 100,000 objects had been unearthed, and the inscribed 'bones' – including ox shoulder-blades and the lower shells of turtles – were recognized as tools of divination.

ROYAL RITES AND RICHES

Yin spread across several sites near present-day Anyang. At the nearby village of Xiaotun, the foundations of 53 large buildings were excavated, including those of a single-storey royal palace built on several large terraces. The buildings had evidently been part of an important ceremonial complex – following an earlier tradition, hundreds of human sacrifices had been placed beneath them. The victims may have been prisoners, captured in the wars waged against neighbouring communities by Shang kings such as the great Wuding of the 13th century BC. The palace itself was the heart of Yin, the last capital of the Shang dynasty.

CAST FOR A RITUAL Hundreds of bronze vessels dating from between the 15th and 12th centuries BC were found in the tombs at Anyang. This vessel, 35cm (14in) high, takes the form of a tiger protecting a man. It is a *you* – used for pouring libations of millet wine. The vessels were made in ceramic moulds of several pieces which were assembled for casting.

WATCHFUL FACES Animals were sacrificed in a ritual bronze vessel known as *ding*, or *fangding* if rectangular. More than 30 such vessels still exist, dating from the 14th to the 11th centuries BC.

The 20 buildings which made up the palace had been built along both sides of a central street. The larger buildings were about 40m (131ft) long and 10m (33ft) wide, and – on the evidence of the marble sculptures, woodcarvings, and bronzes discovered in the royal tombs – richly decorated.

Space, light, and luxury were the exclusive privileges of the royal family and the court. The ordinary people of Yin lived in holes in the ground, in pits and dugouts of many shapes and sizes. The pits, which were probably roofed with thatch, were between 3m and 4m (10ft and 13ft) deep. Steps led down to a rammed earth floor, in which smaller pits were dug for storage purposes.

BONES AND BURIALS TELL THEIR STORY

The inscriptions on the bones found at the site offer the most important evidence about life under the Shang dynasty. These inscriptions preserve the earliest known Chinese writing and confirm the historical basis of some legends; they also record everyday life in Yin. Many inscriptions seek predictions for the day's hunting. This pastime seems to have been a royal sport – to provide animals for sacrifice rather than for food.

The Shangyin were essentially farmers. Questions inscribed on the bones reveal their staple crops:

'Is this a year to grow rice?'
'Is this a year to grow millet?'

Back came the answers inscribed by diviners:

'This year is a good year for sorghum.'
'Go out and harvest the wheat.'

Some inscriptions show that the Shangyin knew how to breed silkworms and make silk fabrics. Traces of silk wrappings have been found in one of the Yin tombs, around a bronze vessel.

Of the hundreds of bronze vessels discovered in the tombs, more than half were used for wine. Alcohol played an important role in the social life of the city, and in its religious rituals. Wine made of fermented cereals was used in sacrificial rites, and libations were poured onto the ground after burials.

The royal burial chambers lay at Xibeigang, north of Yin. Each tomb contains several bodies, and is surrounded by subsidiary tombs.

On the death of a Shang king, his intimate followers and servants were buried with him – as many as 500 people were sacrificed at each royal death. In most of the tombs, the skeletons of dogs were found next to the royal sarcophagus, guarding their master against the evils of the spirit world. In one area, an entire company of soldiers and four charioteers with horses and vehicles had been buried.

Twelve Shang kings ruled between the founding of Yin and the end of the dynasty, but it is known that only 11 of them were buried at Xibeigang. The last Shang ruler, Di Xin, was killed in about 1027 BC by Wu Wang, who became the first ruler of the Zhou dynasty, and the defeated king was not allowed to rest with his ancestors. But there are 13 great tombs at Xibeigang; if 11 contain the Shangyin kings, the other two may be the tombs of important queens.

Although the tombs had all been plundered, their surviving contents are among the most treasured relics of ancient Chinese culture. Perhaps the most spectacular was a bronze vessel known as Si Mu Wu Fangding, from the dedication inscribed on it; this indicated that it had belonged to a deceased queen mother. The vessel is more than 1.2m (4ft) high and weighs more than 180kg (397lb). It was once used to sacrifice animals – a whole sheep or pig could be boiled inside it.

Vehicles found at Anyang show that the Shangyin used the wheel – for chariots, for making pottery, and for agricultural work. Chariots were probably the principal means of transport for the nobles. Other treasures from the tombs offer glimpses of another aspect of life in the Shang capital – fashion. One statuette shows a Shangyin man wearing a short jacket and a short, belted skirt. His shoes have long, pointed tips which curl up at the ends. An engraving on jade shows a Shangyin lady in a tall hat – the women adorned their hats with turquoise ornaments, and wore ivory combs and pins in their hair.

On their foreheads they wore a carved jade disc with a hole in the centre; other small jade carvings hung from their belts, depicting everything from human faces to animals such as bats, tigers, pigeons, frogs, and cicadas.

THE WARRIOR QUEEN

Many of these ornaments were among the spectacular grave goods in the only royal tomb that has been discovered intact; it was found in 1976 south-east of the palace at Xiaotun. Inscribed bronze vessels identify it as the burial of Fu Hao, a consort of king Wuding. Oracle bones and later historical records show her to have been a formidable character, who not only bore children to the king but also led his armies in campaigns against neighbouring tribes and states. Many of the articles in her grave were probably war booty.

A mere 16 people had been sacrificed to accompany Fu Hao to the grave. This relatively modest retinue suggests that the grave goods in her tomb may also have been modest in number. Even so, there were more than 1,600 different objects. The treasure included 440 bronze vessels, nearly 600 pieces of precious jade, a large collection of weapons and tools, and a rare ivory container inlaid with turquoise.

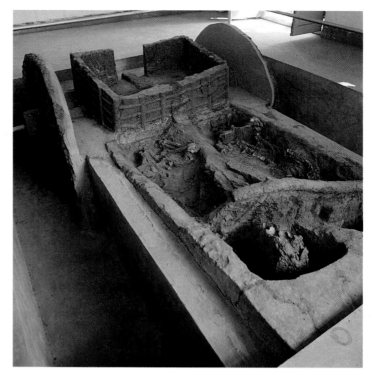

GHOSTLY CHARIOT The wood of chariots buried in the royal tombs disintegrated many centuries ago, but soil casts have survived.

THE SECRET OF THE ORACLE BONES

The inscribed bones unearthed in Anyang were found in storage pits. The bones were used to divine the future by inscribing a question to the ancestral gods of the kings. The diviner would then heat the bone, either on red-hot stones or with a burning stick, until a crack appeared. The diviner interpreted the crack and incised the answer of the gods onto the bone and, next to it, the date and the name of the king.

Apart from providing priceless information about the life and customs of the Shangyin – such as the facts that they used a lunar calendar, and that they practised the art of astronomy – the bones are a clue to the origins of the Chinese language.

The written characters are mainly pictorial. The word for music, for example, is composed of two root-words for silk and wood, indicating that the musical instruments of the Shang had wooden frames and strings made of silk.

LOOKING FOR ANSWERS Inscriptions to the gods covered every subject from military campaigns to domestic concerns such as agriculture and childbirth.

Many of the artefacts and materials found in Fu Hao's tomb and elsewhere in Anyang were obviously not made locally. Where, for example, did Shang bronze come from? Copper was abundant in northern China at that time, but tin – the other constituent of bronze – was not, and must have been imported.

Cowrie shells must also have been brought in from southern China. Many were found in Fu Hao's grave. The evidence of the oracle bones suggests that cowries were the currency of the Shangyin and that they were hung, in groups of five, on strings – shells found at the site were pierced with holes.

These objects may have come to Yin as tribute from subject kingdoms beyond the borders of China. Alternatively, the Shang may have been involved in far-reaching trade; extensive trade networks, particularly to obtain jade, had already been in operation over much of China for hundreds of years.

THE BEGINNING OF A NEW ERA

For two centuries the royal capital of Yin flourished, but about 1027 BC, the rulers of the western principality of Zhou in the valley of the river Wei rose up against Di Xin because – according to one account – the Shang king had allowed himself to be dominated by an unscrupulous concubine called Da Ji.

The new dynasty established by the princes of Zhou was to last for almost a millennium; a period that saw the flowering of Confucian philosophy – the study of the meaning of life and the right way to live. But in that time a city died. The magnificent Shang capital of Yin fell into ruins, and was abandoned and forgotten until the ancient oracles of Anyang brought the past back to life.

Nineveh

A symbol of Assyrian power

Sculptured reliefs found amid the rubble of a ruined city tell the story of a royal capital – home of the leader of a race of fearsome warriors, whose reputation for savagery has been immortalised by the writers of the Old Testament.

NOT A TEAR WAS SHED BY ASSYRIA'S SUBJECT PEOPLES when, in 612 BC, the Medes from north-west Persia sacked the Assyrian capital Nineveh and brought their subjection to an end. 'Woe to the bloody city. It is all full of lies and robbery,' thundered the Old Testament prophet Nahum. 'Nineveh is laid waste; who will bemoan her?'

According to the Bible, the history of the Assyrian Empire is a sickening catalogue of sackings, enslavement, and torture. But it was not until the 19th century AD that archaeological discoveries corroborated the bitter Biblical tirades about the mighty race that once ruled all the lands of the Middle East.

THE CITY ON THE FERTILE PLAIN

The Assyrian plain enjoys a cooler climate than Babylonia, its southern neighbour. Through the ages its fertile pastures have been watered by two tributaries of the River Tigris, the Great and Little Zab. This region was part of a great arc of land in the Middle East where, 11,000 years ago, people began producing their own food – a way of life that gradually supplanted the nomadic existence of the hunter-gatherer. It was here, around 4,000 years ago, that the Assyrians turned from a peaceful agricultural life to a career of brutal conquest.

The Assyrians' landlocked location forced them to fight wars in order to keep their trade routes open. For a time their expansion was blocked by the Hittites to the north. But when the Hittite Empire collapsed in the 13th century BC, there was no major power to stand in Assyria's way.

In the 9th century BC, after a period of revolt and disarray, the Assyrians set about establishing an empire. Their army was a formidable fighting machine, hardened by many years of rigorous campaigning and organized into corps of swift-moving chariots, cavalry, bowmen, and lancers. Their iron-headed battering rams could breach seemingly impregnable walls. And their soldiers were sustained by a fierce religious fervour, illustrated in their art by the figure of the god Assur hovering over them as they go into battle.

WARRIOR KINGS From the 9th to the 7th centuries BC, Assyria expanded under the leadership of a series of great rulers. This relief from Nineveh shows the last great Assyrian king, Assurbanipal, out hunting, poised to shoot his prey. Assyrian kings enjoyed hunting almost as much as war – it provided an opportunity to display their heroism, and good training for battle.

In the words of Byron's poem, *Destruction of Sennacherib*, the Assyrian army came down on their helpless foes 'like the wolf on the fold'. For nearly 300 years, great rulers such as Assurnasirpal II (883–859 BC), Shalmaneser III (858–824 BC), Tiglath-Pileser III (744–727 BC), Sargon II (721–705 BC), Sennacherib (704–681 BC), Esarhaddon (680–669 BC), and Assurbanipal (669–627 BC) led their armies on almost yearly raids to secure trade routes and frontiers, and to obtain booty – all for the greater glory of their national gods.

Babylonia, Syria, Israel, Egypt, and Elam fell under Assyrian domination. Rebels were flayed, buried, or burned alive, impaled on stakes, blinded, or mutilated in some other way, while whole nations were deported and resettled.

Mass deportations were a powerful instrument of Assyrian tyranny. The Old Testament describes how the Jewish population of Samaria was deported from Israel, and their homeland resettled with outsiders: 'And the king of Assyria brought men from Babylon, and from Cuthah, and from Ava, and from Hamath, and from Sepharvaim, and placed them in the cities of Samaria, instead of the children of Israel.'

The dismemberment of communities was intended to break down their sense of national identity and, with it, the will to resist. The new inhabitants of Samaria were a hybrid people with alien gods. They were shunned by the Jews, as the New Testament parable of the Good Samaritan recalls.

TRACES OF AN ANCIENT POWER

The Assyrians campaigned throughout the Middle East. By the time of Assurbanipal, their empire stretched for more than 1,600km (995 miles), from the Valley of the Nile in Egypt almost as far as the Caucasus mountains in Armenia, and from the Phoenician cities of the Mediterranean to the Persian Gulf. As they carved out an empire for themselves, the Assyrians operated from a succession of capitals. In the Old Testament

AERIAL VIEW Assurnasirpal II built a huge city at Kalhu (present-day Nimrud), covering a 360ha (890 acre) site. In the south-west corner of the city he built a palace, the remains of which have been excavated (left).

The city walls can be seen running north (1) and east (2) of the palace complex. In the foreground of the aerial photo are palaces built by later kings. In the Temple of Nabu (3), and the Governor's Palace (4), Assyrian archives have been discovered.

In the northern portion of the palace, a courtyard (no longer visible) once opened onto a throne room, flanked by public rooms within the white-roofed building (5). To the south of these were the royal apartments (6) where, between 1988 and 1990, the tombs of three royal ladies were discovered – possibly the wives of some of the Assyrian kings, from Assurnasirpal II to Sargon II. The tombs were lavishly furnished with gold jewellery, including some extraordinarily fine filigree work.

THE ASSYRIAN WAR MACHINE

The function of the Assyrian monarchy was essentially religious, for the kings were the gods' deputies on Earth. The army was the instrument of the gods, and only went to war at their behest – after consultation with soothsayers who would accompany the soldiers into battle.

According to Assurnasirpal II, the Assyrian army was 50,000 strong, although a vast arsenal built at Nimrud by Shalmaneser III was capable of equipping twice that number. For a long time recruitment was feudal, each great family undertaking to send along a batch of slaves. The poorer sectors of society, or *hupshi*, were forced to perform military service. They made up the light infantry and the vanguard responsible for breaching the walls of enemy cities. Mercenaries and contingents from Assyria's allies swelled the ranks and, as a result, Assyrians were outnumbered – though they held the monopoly on the officers' ranks.

During the heyday of Assyrian military strength, the army was almost permanent. In addition to the troops of Assyria's allies – which during Sargon's reign in the 8th century BC comprised 150 chariots, 1,500 cavalry, 20,000 archers, and 1,000 lancers – there were also the crack Assyrian troops. The troops were divided into squads of ten, then into sections of 50 men under the command of a captain, then into armies under a general who was at the same time a provincial governor. The king was always the commander-in-chief.

In the 9th century BC, the Assyrian army's light infantry wore a short tunic and carried a cone-shaped helmet and a round shield for protection. The heavy infantry wore a long robe covered with small iron plates – a very early form of armour which dated back to the middle of the second millennium BC. The armour was so clumsy, however, that it was later abandoned in favour of a short, well-fitting leather breastplate which did not hamper movement. The infantry's weapons included the pike, the sling, and a simple form of longbow which was less effective than the double-curved bow of the Persians, who served as auxiliaries. The two-horse chariot was used extensively in battle, but it was so heavy that it was gradually replaced by horsemen equipped in the same way as the foot soldiers.

The most sophisticated machine of Assyrian warfare was the mobile assault tower. These terrifying wheeled, wooden constructions, with battering rams at the base and archers on the top, were used to breach city walls.

SLINGS AND ARROWS The tactics of the Assyrian infantry made them well-nigh invincible. Spearmen with pikes (left) presented a barrier on which horses impaled themselves; from the rear, bowmen and slingers (above) delivered a rain of missiles.

Book of Jonah, one of these capitals, Nineveh, is referred to as a gigantic city which took three days to cross on foot. Historians found it impossible to make such details tally with the vague information provided by the Greek geographers, who hardly knew on which bank of the Tigris the city was sited. Then, in the middle of the 19th century, remains of the city were discovered at the village of Nabi Yunus, on the eastern bank of the Tigris opposite the town of Mosul.

The find came after a British archaeologist, Sir Austen Henry Layard, unearthed stone bas-reliefs at Nimrud, south of Mosul. From Nimrud, he moved on to excavate a man-made mound, or tell, called Kuyunjik, near the village of Nabi Yunus. And there, just south-east of the tell, he came upon the palace of Sargon's son, Sennacherib – concrete evidence that the tell did indeed mark the site of Nineveh.

BUILDING A NEW CAPITAL

Sennacherib founded a capital at Nineveh in about 700 BC to replace Sargon's capital at Khorsabad, to the north-east. Massive ramparts 11km (7 miles) long surrounded the city. Each of the 15 gates which studded the walls was probably guarded by fearsome statues of winged bulls with human heads – protective genies to Assyrian eyes, designed to strike terror into the hearts of their enemies.

A small stream flowed through Nineveh, but this was hardly enough to serve the city and irrigate the surrounding countryside. So Sennacherib ordered water to be drawn from springs in the hills near Bavian, 50km (31 miles) away. This proved to be a colossal task, and involved the building of a huge aqueduct supported by five stone arches, 22m (72ft) wide and 9m (29½ft) high, crossing a ravine almost 300m (984ft) across.

The sophisticated construction methods that made this feat possible were recorded in bas-reliefs decorating the walls of the new palace.

THE PLANNING OF A PALACE

One of the best ways to understand how an Assyrian king lived is to look at the palace built by Assurnasirpal II at Kalhu (present-day Nimrud). Kalhu was the centre and symbol of Assyrian imperialist policies in the 9th century BC.

Exploration of the site, begun by Layard in the 19th century, resumed in 1949 in the hands of the British archaeologist Sir Max Mallowan and his wife, the novelist Agatha Christie. Just as readers would unravel the threads in one of her mysteries, Agatha Christie and her husband solved the puzzle of how an Assyrian palace was run. Their answers threw light on the discoveries at Nineveh.

The palace unearthed at Nimrud was divided into two parts, the *babanu* and the *bitanu*, each of which contained a courtyard. The *babanu*, near the main entrance, played host to unimportant visitors, along with government departments such as the treasury and chancellery. At the end of the courtyard, monumental doors flanked by winged bulls with human heads opened onto the

> *... Sennacherib ordered his artists to depict his victorious campaigns against the kingdom of Judah. The carved wall reliefs ... are a vivid record of events from Assyria's history.*

throne room at the heart of the palace. The walls of the throne room were covered with brightly painted bas-reliefs which depicted the king's noble deeds as a skilled huntsman and warrior. A relief near the throne showed him worshipping a tree symbolizing the fertility of Assyria.

The throne room led onto the king's apartments, or *bitanu*. These consisted of several small private chambers and two long rooms running side by side, decorated with bas-reliefs depicting scenes of a royal banquet. The rooms opened onto an inner courtyard from which further apartments could be reached.

On the site of the outbuildings archaeologists have unearthed magnificent ivories once used as ornamentation for the royal furniture. Some had been captured as booty during campaigns in Syria and Phoenicia. Others were probably made locally by Phoenician artists who mixed Egyptian motifs with local themes.

SURROUNDED BY SCENES OF WAR

The layout of the Nimrud palace was reproduced on a much larger scale by Sargon II for his palace at Khorsabad, but Sennacherib made several alterations to the basic plan for his residence at Nineveh to create what he called the 'Palace Without a Rival'. Next to his throne room, he installed a lavishly decorated bathroom. He also modified the king's living quarters. Two identical suites of rooms flanked the courtyard, and the state rooms were arranged at one end. The new layout was used as a model for later palaces at Babylon and Susa.

In these apartments, Sennacherib ordered his artists to depict his victorious campaigns against the kingdom of Judah. The carved wall reliefs, now in the British Museum in London, are a vivid record of events from Assyria's history.

A ROYAL CAMPAIGN The king – either Sennacherib or Assurnasirpal II in this relief – took an active part in military campaigns, and inspected the spoils of battle from a chariot drawn by richly caparisoned horses.

FIT FOR A KING A painting by the British archaeologist A.H. Layard shows Assurnasirpal II's throne room at Nimrud. The overall impression is probably close to the room's original richly coloured appearance.

For Sennacherib, the climax of the campaign was the siege and capture of the city of Lachish. The reliefs show Assyrian troops charging triumphantly down hillsides covered with olive groves. Archers and armoured siege engines draw up around the walls of the heavily fortified city. Civilians flee in terror, Jews with wild and woolly hair are driven into slavery and exile, and defeated commanders are flayed alive. The king watched the rout from a safe distance. The inscription on the relief boasts: 'Sennacherib, king of the world, king of Assyria, sat upon an ivory throne and passed in review the booty from Lachish.'

THE GREAT LIBRARY OF ASSURBANIPAL

During the excavations at Nineveh, archaeologists discovered more than 25,000 clay tablets covered in cuneiform script which once belonged to Sennacherib's grandson, Assurbanipal. Assurbanipal was brought up in the palace, and recorded his love for it in writing – revealing a sentimental streak that is surprising in a conqueror. Although, like most Assyrian rulers, Assurbanipal was a man of action, he was happiest in his library, surrounded by his clay 'books'.

The task of deciphering the tablets fell to a brilliant young Assyriologist, George Smith. In 1872, one of Smith's discoveries fired the imagination of Victorian England: among the archives, he found a version of the Biblical story of the great flood.

The tale of the flood told in the tablets forms part of the Sumerian Epic of Gilgamesh. Though written long before the Bible, its parallels with the Old Testament story are startling. The gods prepare to destroy mankind in a mighty deluge, but decide to spare the hero of the tale. He tears down his house and builds a boat, into which he brings his family, his craftsmen, and a host of animals, both wild and domesticated. When the terrible storm is over, his boat is left grounded on a mountain top, and he sends first a dove, then a swallow, then finally a raven to see if the waters have abated.

When Assurbanipal's library was unearthed, it was by far the largest collection of ancient inscribed tablets that had been discovered in the Middle East. As well as painting a vivid picture of Assyria's violent history, the tablets reveal much about its culture and society. The Assyrian king with his square-cut,

Assurbanipal, in particular,
succeeded in marrying the
two most ancient traditions of
Mesopotamia – war and
words. His library forms the
basis of the modern
knowledge of Mesopotamian
science and literature. His
scribes copied the work of
Babylonian scholars to make
huge compilations of omens,
rituals, incantations, points of
law, and grammar – as well as
recording the heroic deeds of
their king.

THE JEALOUS BROTHER
When Assurbanipal took the
throne in 669 BC, just as his
grandfather commissioned
reliefs of the siege of Lachish,
he had a number of rooms in
the palace redecorated to
depict his victories. The
pictures record a family
drama – his accession had
not gone smoothly.

In 729 BC the Assyrians
under Assurbanipal's father,
Esarhaddon, had seized the
city of Babylon, but had
found it difficult to control.
For this reason, Esarhaddon
divided the empire between
his two sons. To his elder son,

curling beard and cruel lips was more than a mere warrior. He
was also the chief priest and central figure in the cult of Assur,
the most important of all Assyria's gods. It was only at Assur's
command that the country went to war.

TURNING OVER A NEW LEAF
Assyria's genius was concentrated on advancing military
technology, imposing ruthless discipline, and on finding the
best uses for naked terror. But the tablets also disclose a less
brutal side. Contact with Babylon, which they seized in the
8th century BC, inspired the Assyrians to educate themselves.

Shamash-shum-ukin, he gave Babylon, and to Assurbanipal he
left the rest. Shamash-shum-ukin resented the fact that his
younger brother had the lion's share. By devious plotting, he
embroiled his neighbours from the country of Elam in a war
with Assurbanipal, without taking any part in it himself.

This was the campaign, fought in 653 BC, which a group of
artists recorded in the palace at Nineveh for Assurbanipal.
Inscriptions explaining the course of the action were added to
the pictures, like the speech bubbles in a comic strip. One of
the reliefs proudly records the execution of Teumman, king of
Elam, and his son Tamaritu: the royal headgear has been dashed

SYMBOL OF MAJESTY ˙ Assurbanipal spears his prey – lion hunting was the duty of the king. Mesopotamian lions were smaller than African lions, and sometimes the king is shown gripping a standing lion by the throat.

to the ground beside the banks of the river which marked the border of Elam. Gently, the flowing waters carry away the carnage of a defeated army. 'Teumman, the king of Elam was wounded in a ferocious battle,' reads Assurbanipal's brutally simple inscription. 'Tamaritu, his eldest son, took him by the hand and, together, they fled for their lives, hiding in a thicket. With the aid of the god Assur and the goddess Ishtar, I killed them and cut off their heads.'

Assurbanipal now faced a coalition comprising his brother, king Teumman's vengeful nephews, and a league of desert Arabs, Syrians, and Egyptians. It was an uncomfortable alliance, and Assurbanipal soon took advantage of this. First he stormed Babylon, where his brother was burned to death in the blazing palace. Then, in a single campaign, he subdued the Syrians and the Arabs. Only the Elamites were left.

A SHORT-LIVED VICTORY

In 646 BC the Assyrians destroyed and pillaged Susa, the capital of Elam. Inscriptions describing the victory are filled with delight: 'According to the word of the gods Assur and Ishtar, I conquered Susa, great and holy city, seat of the Elamites' mysteries. I entered its palace; I lived there and rejoiced . . . I destroyed the ziggurat . . . Thirty-two royal statues cast in gold, silver, and copper, and carved in alabaster did I take to the land of Assyria. My soldiers entered their sacred groves

ARTISTIC LICENCE A vast quantity of carved ivories were discovered at Nimrud. This plaque is Syrian in style: the figure shows Egyptian influence in the headdress and lotus, but is dressed like an Assyrian.

which had never before been approached by a stranger. They saw their secrets and destroyed them by fire. I devastated the tombs of their kings and took away as booty to the land of Assur the daughters and wives of the kings, the inhabitants male and female, and the livestock large and small.'

When Assurbanipal had this story recorded in his palace at Nineveh, he could hardly have imagined that his own cities would suffer a similar fate just 30 years later. When he died in 627 BC, war broke out between his two sons. At last Assyria's enemies, who had been biding their time like vultures, perched on the borders of the empire, had an opportunity to swoop.

In 614 BC the Medes from northern Persia joined forces with the Chaldaeans from southern Persia, who had taken power in Babylon. Together they seized Ashur (present-day Qal'at Sharqat), the religious capital of the Assyrians, south of Nineveh. Two years later, Nineveh itself was besieged. Its inhabitants, entrenched behind the massive ramparts, managed to hold out for three months. But eventually the city was captured and destroyed, and its inhabitants massacred or deported.

The mighty Assyrian Empire was consigned to the rubbish tip of history. All that remains of their once-proud capital are the sculpted figures in the bas-reliefs, the writings in Assurbanipal's great library, and the city's ruined walls.

Early warfare

In the Stone Age, wars were little more than ritual skirmishes fought to resolve tribal grievances. But the development of agriculture brought larger conflicts. As people settled, territorial rivalries grew, and communities coveted the possessions of their neighbours. Warfare found new objectives – the plundering of goods and the re-drawing of frontiers.

TOOLS OF COMBAT
Sumerian troops carry spears on Ur's Royal Standard of 2600 BC (above). The Sumerians also used bows and arrows, first adapted as weapons during the Stone Age, as shown in a Spanish cave painting of 6000 BC (far left).

The first armies

As city-states such as Ur in Sumer developed centralized government, their rulers organized disciplined armies to defend their interests and extend their territories. Success depended on combined muscle-power. Soldiers fought in close ranks, wearing uniform helmets and protected by formations of shields. They carried metal-tipped arrows and spears, and copper-headed axes.

Technology and tactics

The growth of urban civilization brought new dimensions to warfare. Penetrating the defences of a large city required huge, disciplined armies, and technological innovations had to be quickly adapted to support a new style of fighting. In the 3rd millennium BC, metal tools led to metal weapons, and the first organized armies emerged. As armour became heavier and stronger, infantry formation and battle tactics became more sophisticated. Gradually, the limitations of human strength were overcome, as cavalry, chariots, siege engines, and battleships became part of the military arsenal.

HEAD PROTECTION
In the 8th century BC, armoured Greek footsoldiers known as hoplites fought in massed groups. This bronze hoplite helmet was found in Thessaloniki.

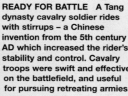

READY FOR BATTLE A Tang dynasty cavalry soldier rides with stirrups – a Chinese invention from the 5th century AD which increased the rider's stability and control. Cavalry troops were swift and effective on the battlefield, and useful for pursuing retreating armies.

Arms and armour

The equipment used by early soldiers reflected their status. Officers usually wore bronze breastplates or iron mail; infantry wore armour made of leather or padded cotton with, at best, a metal helmet. Most men carried spears, although Roman armies equipped all their troops with swords – usually seen as a prestige weapon. Bows and slings were used for long-distance attacks – a practice perfected by Chinese, Roman, and Carthaginian units.

Cavalry and beasts of burden

By the 9th century BC, the well-organized Assyrian army included cavalry units. By 500 BC, the Chinese state of Jin had developed cavalry forces to counter threats by the horsemen of the northern steppes, and the idea caught on among the other Chinese states. Horses were not the only military animal – Arab forces of the 1st millennium BC had camels as mounts, and in India, China, and South-east Asia, elephants were used to transport generals, charge the enemy, and frighten enemy horses. The generals of Alexander the Great introduced military elephants to the West.

RITUAL HUMILIATION
In South America war captives were often stripped naked: this wooden figure depicts is a captive of the Moche, who dominated northern Peru from the 1st to the 8th centuries AD.

Phalanx against legion

The phalanx – a block of heavily armed infantry standing shoulder to shoulder – was perfected by Philip II of Macedonia in the 4th century BC. The Macedonian version comprised 16 massed ranks of troops armed with lances more than twice their height. This tight formation seemed invincible until Roman legions defeated it at Pydna in 168 BC by splitting its ranks as shown here.

BATTLE TACTICS The phalanx developed gaps as it crossed rough terrain, allowing small groups of opposing troops to split it up. The enemy front line then charged its broken ranks.

Roman legions

Macedonian phalanx

Sacrificial prisoners

Among many of the cultures of Central and South America, battles were fought specifically to take prisoners for torture and sacrifice during religious ceremonies. This practice reached its peak in the 'Flowery Wars' – a term used by the Aztecs to describe such campaigns. In the 15th and 16th centuries AD, Aztec ceremonies required a regular supply of hundreds of sacrificial victims.

SUPERIOR STRENGTH Pharaoh Tutankhamun (reigned 1361–52 BC) conquers a mob of Syrians in one of his tomb paintings (below).

Cities under siege

Many of the world's earliest cities were walled for defence, and the siege of such fortifications was a major enterprise. The Assyrians were the first masters of siege warfare, using siege engines to batter enemy walls and ladders to scale them, as well as mining underneath them. By the middle of the 3rd century BC, the Greeks had developed powerful wooden catapults which threw spears 700m (nearly 2,300ft) over fortifications, but it was the Romans who perfected siege technology. Their devices included the ballista (a giant crossbow) and a siege tower which cast a drawbridge across the top of the enemy's walls, allowing Roman troops instant access to the city.

ENGINE OF WAR The armies of the Assyrian king Sennacherib (reigned 704–681 BC) used siege engines with battering rams to destroy city walls.

Chariots of war

War chariots were used in Mesopotamia during the 3rd millennium BC, drawn by donkeys or asses, and later by horses, which were domesticated on the eastern fringes of Europe about 4000 BC. Initially, chariots were used to carry elite warriors to the battlefield, but by the 16th century BC the Egyptians were using them as a shock weapon. The first great chariot battle in history was fought between Egyptians and Hittites at Kadesh in Syria in the early 13th century BC.

The might of the navy

The development of warships lagged behind other military technology. To wage war at sea, vessels had to be large enough to contain a significant fighting force, yet still be swift and manoeuvrable. The Greek trireme, with three tiers of oarsmen, was an important advance in ocean warfare. The great bronze buffer at the prow could be used as a ram, or could smash the enemy's oars when two ships came alongside one another.

Babylon

The city of Nebuchadnezzar

An immense mud-brick stump in present-day Iraq is all that is left of Babylon's most infamous building, the Tower of Babel. But the tower was once a wonder of the ancient world, in a great city that surpassed in splendour all others of its time.

THE GREEKS DESCRIBED BABYLON'S 'HANGING GARDENS' as one of the Seven Wonders of the World. The Book of Genesis referred to its tower, which soared more than 90m (295ft) above the surrounding countryside, as the Tower of Babel. For the Old Testament writers this attempt to reach heaven represented the ultimate in human vanity.

But there was once good reason for this vanity: the city of Babylon was the pounding heart of an empire which stretched all the way from Egypt in the

west to the old kingdom of Elam (south-west Iran) in the east. All that remains today of what was once the largest city in the world is a dun-coloured field of dried mud ruins. And, until the 20th century, all that was known about Babylon came from the writings of the Greek historian Herodotus (*c*.484–425 BC) and from Biblical denunciations. 'Babylon the Great', thunders a New Testament writer, 'the mother of harlots and abominations of the earth.'

GREEK IMPRESSIONS

Herodotus's view differed. Around 450 BC the much-travelled historian made the journey from Greece across the mountains and deserts of Syria and down the river Euphrates. What he saw impressed him. He described a vast capital straddling the Euphrates protected by a gigantic rampart so wide that there was enough space for a four-horse chariot to turn. He told of walls more than 86km (53 miles) round, and studded with 100 bronze gateways.

Babylon, he wrote, 'surpasses in splendour any city of the known world'. He also recounted some of the customs of the city's inhabitants: how, for example, every woman was obliged, once in her life, 'to reside in the sanctuary of Aphrodite and unite with a stranger'; how auctions of women were held every year, when the most beautiful were acquired by the rich, and the plainer-looking fell to the lot of the poor.

ISHTAR GATE Babylon's main gate, reconstructed in Berlin's Pergamon Museum, was dedicated to the goddess of love and war, Ishtar. Wild bulls and horned dragons adorn the blue enamel glaze of the gate's brickwork. The Babylonians were famous for the use of glazed bricks to decorate their buildings.

PROCESSIONAL WAY Beyond the magnificent Ishtar Gate lay the Sacred Way. The religious processions passing along it were a spectacular sight – especially at the New Year festival.

1792 to 1750 BC was undoubtedly glorious. One by one he crushed all his enemies, most of whom were Amorites like himself, until he had set up an empire which embraced all of southern Mesopotamia – north into Assyria, westward towards the Mediterranean and southwards to the Persian Gulf. His genius for unification was reflected in his legal code, a concisely written body of common law.

But he knew little about the history of Babylon and had not even heard the name of Nebuchadnezzar II, its emperor from 605 to 562 BC. It was not until the start of the 20th century that historians could begin to disentangle fact from fantasy.

In 1899, German archaeologists under the architect Robert Koldewey undertook the first intensive exploration of Babylon. Their excavations continued until 1917. It was delicate work, for the temples, palaces and houses in Mesopotamia – the fertile valley bounded by the rivers Tigris and Euphrates – were built of sun-dried brick, extremely crumbly and difficult to distinguish from the surrounding soil.

UNEARTHING A LEGEND

Nonetheless, Babylon's high walls, some of them coated with glazed bricks, were finally unearthed. The ghost of a ruined city rose from the dead, and a picture of its history gradually took shape before the archaeologists' eyes.

As the excavation work continued, students of Assyrian history deciphered the thousands of texts that were uncovered. From these they learnt that Babylon was a relatively young city – at least measured against the history of Mesopotamia. The Sumerian cities of Ur, Uruk and Nippur, for example, had been founded hundreds of years earlier.

In about 2000 BC the Amorites, a nomadic people from the Syrian desert, overran much of Mesopotamia and founded a series of kingdoms in Ashur and Mari and, farther south, gained control of the old Sumerian cities, including Babylon. Here, at the start of the 19th century BC, they founded their first royal dynasty. Hammurabi was this first Babylonian dynasty's fifth king, and his reign from

AFTER ORDER, CHAOS

No treasures from Hammurabi's time remain in Babylon itself, partly because its valuables were scattered during the maelstrom that followed. For 1,000 years after Babylon's founding, the warring peoples who populate the pages of the Old Testament disputed Mesopotamia. The Kassites – from the Zagros mountains in western Iran – took and held Babylon for four and a half centuries. After that, invading Elamites carried off many of the city's riches to their own capital, Susa. These included the stele that shows Hammurabi receiving the contents of his laws from Shamash, god of justice.

In the 13th century BC Babylonia fell victim, for the first time, to the Assyrians, and from the 9th century onwards it was a vassal state of Assyria. Babylon found its subjugation intolerable. There were several revolutions, and during the course of the 7th century BC the Assyrians destroyed the city twice.

Then, in 625 BC, its governor, Nabopolassar, proclaimed Babylon independent and himself king. By making an alliance with the

LAW GIVER The god Shamash delivers a code of laws to Hammurabi, Babylon's fifth king. Details of the sophisticated code, loosely based on Sumerian tradition, also appear on this basalt stele, which was discovered at Susa in 1901.

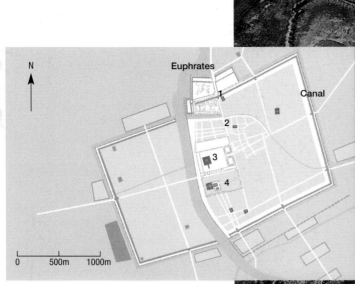

BABYLON FROM THE AIR   A vast field of ruins (right) is all that remains of Nebuchadnezzar's magnificent city. At the centre, the huge square foundation of the Tower of Babel is still visible. Above: The plan shows the Sacred Way (2) leading from the Ishtar Gate (1) to the Ziggurat (3) and Temple of Marduk (4).

Medes (from Iran) Nabopolassar defeated Assyria in 612 BC and destroyed its capital, Nineveh.

When Nabopolassar's son Nebuchadnezzar mounted the throne in 605 BC, the entire area known as the Fertile Crescent – from Jerusalem to the Persian Gulf – was his. All he had to do was to eradicate the last pockets of Assyrian resistance and to restore Babylon as a capital worthy of his ambitions.

Under Nebuchadnezzar, the city re-emerged as the queen of the civilized world, built along both banks of the Euphrates, with the main buildings on the east bank. A double exterior wall, 18km (11 miles) long, enclosed an area that was barely inhabited and may have served as a refuge for villagers and their herds in time of war. This outer line of defence was reinforced to the north by the fortress of Babil, which still stands 22m (72ft) high; it once contained the summer palace of the king. An inner wall, the shape of a quadrangle and surrounded by a canal, protected the main part of the town. This brick rampart consisted of a front wall 6.5m (21ft) wide, and a second wall more than 3m (10ft) wide, between which was built a third wall. Each of the city's eight gateways was under the protection of a different god.

The main palace and the main gate – dedicated to Ishtar, the goddess of love and battle – were also protected by a fortress. A sacred processional way skirted the fortress and passed through the Ishtar Gate before entering the city. Here, it ran alongside a double wall which defended the royal palace, making it an impregnable citadel right in the heart of Babylon.

HOME FOR AN EMPEROR

The construction of the palace was begun by Nabopolassar, Nebuchadnezzar's father. His living quarters consisted of two large halls and three private rooms, opening onto a courtyard. Nebuchadnezzar kept the palace but enlarged it. To do this he merely added to it four identical 'palace units'. These complexes stood side by side and were connected by passages. In one of the units the place of the living quarters was taken up by an enormous hall: the throne room.

Outside the palace, the processional way continued as far as the Temple of Marduk, patron god of Babylon. The temple was a square fortress with a central courtyard. In line with its

BRONZE DRAGON'S HEAD
Called *mushhushshu*, the dragon was a composite creature with horns and a viper's head. It symbolized Marduk, Babylon's patron god, who was worshipped in the great temple of Esagila.

fertility rites. He reported that there was a bed and gold table on the top storey of the tower, but no statue of a god. 'Only a woman chosen by the god would spend the night alone there,' he wrote, adding that 'sometimes the god came into the temple and slept in the bed.'

The French archaeologist André Parrot linked the name of Babylon – literally 'gateway of the god' – with Jacob's vision in the Book of Genesis. As Jacob dreamed, he saw a ladder which reached from the earth up to heaven's gate. Parrot suggested that the Babylonians, too, saw the tower, with its monumental staircase, as a 'gateway of the heavens' and as a resting-place between the heavenly home of the god and his earthly residence in the temple.

BALANCING COSMIC FORCES

The Babylonians' religious beliefs were rooted in a tradition which dated back over 2,500 years to the origins of Sumerian civilization. Every Sumerian city was ruled by a monarch – the representative of his city's god who, surrounded by his court, was also master of a specific area of the world. The god assured the prosperity of the city by keeping in balance the cosmic forces upon which the fertility of the earth and its occupants depended. Quite how this balance was maintained in the Babylonian scheme of things is not known. But some scholars conclude that, in Babylonian belief, the god shared his power with a mother goddess whom he wed afresh each year.

It was at these ceremonies that the king and the high priestess acted out the role of the divine couple. The mythical son to whom they gave birth personified the new year's growth of crops. Months later, harvest time heralded the god's death.

entrance, a door opened into the sanctuary of Marduk. His golden statue was small and light enough to be carried during processions such as the one held at the new year. Another room in the temple was reserved for Marduk's throne; another housed the bed intended for the symbolic weddings of the gods; and some rooms were dedicated to lesser gods – for, like any earthly king, Marduk had his court.

A TOWER TO RIVAL HEAVEN

Alongside the temple, and isolated within a high wall, was an immense tower, or ziggurat. It had been built hundreds of years before the reign of Nebuchadnezzar, but had fallen into disrepair. The king ordered it to be rebuilt so that its top 'might rival heaven'.

Nebuchadnezzar's tower of sun-dried brick rested on a square base and rose like a pyramid some 90m (295ft) above the city. Its seven storeys were crowned with a temple. According to the historian Diodorus of Sicily, in the 1st century BC, the tower was an observatory for Chaldaean astrologers from southern Mesopotamia. Herodotus thought it was used for sacred

Although he was mourned, it was recognized that his death formed an essential part of the natural cycle.

The gods were organized into a pantheon, whose purpose was to maintain order throughout the world. Anu, god of the sky, Enlil, god of the wind and atmosphere, and Ea, god of the water, were the supreme gods. Then came Sin, the Moon; Shamash, the Sun; and Ishtar, the planet Venus. Marduk was one of the young warrior gods. When Babylon became the centre of the Middle Eastern world, Hammurabi

BABYLONIAN WORLD MAP With west at the top, this map marks Babylon in the upper rectangle. Assyria lies on the right and Susa at the bottom. Outside the encircling ocean are strange lands, which are described in the accompanying text.

declared that Marduk – as the city's patron – occupied too modest a position in the pantheon. To put this right, he proclaimed that the top three gods had made Marduk their leader.

His theologians were expected to justify the proclamation, so they set to work gathering together the oldest traditions about the creation of the world. A long poem was composed which recounted battles between the elemental beings – Tiamat, salt sea, and Apsu, fresh water – and the gods to whom they had given birth. Tiamat, they said, had created an army of monsters to kill the gods and to hurl the world back into primordial chaos. Terrified, the gods refused to give battle until the young Marduk stepped forward as their champion and agreed to defend them on one condition: that they grant him supreme power. After an heroic struggle, Marduk became first among the gods. The other gods survived, but as personifications of Marduk's many powers.

The Babylonians also concerned themselves with less spiritual aspects of the heavens. They mapped the stars, named and studied the movements of the planets, and tried to predict eclipses of the Sun and Moon. They were travellers and traders, buying produce from Arabia and India, Syria and Persia. They were exporters too – of wool and woven fabrics, and barley.

THE LEGENDARY 'HANGING GARDENS'

And they were gardeners. Although no contemporary Babylonian text describing the 'hanging gardens' exists, historians such as Diodorus of Sicily rated them one of the wonders of the world.

Elaborate gardens with artificial hills, for which water was brought in by aqueduct and raised using bronze Archimedes' Screw devices, were built by the Assyrian king Sennacherib at Nineveh. Some archaeologists believe that these 'Hanging Gardens' of Nineveh were mistakenly attributed to Babylon.

Others accept that Babylon also had magnificent gardens, but have not established their location. Traces of a garden have been attributed to a building behind the servants' quarters. Its rows of vaulted corridors could have once supported plant-filled terraces. But corridors such as these were commonly used in the East for storing barrel-shaped jars. The building more probably contained the palace storerooms. A corner bastion of the palace on the edge of the Euphrates may also have been a retaining wall for a garden.

Whatever their location, they were a credit to Nebuchadnezzar's brilliant reign. But the brightness of his capital was soon to dim. In 559 BC Nabonidus, the son of a priestess of Sin, mounted the throne as Nebuchadnezzar's successor. He very soon exasperated Marduk's clergy by giving preferential treatment to the temples of Sin

> 'Mene, mene, tekel, upharsin … Thou art weighed in the balances, and art found wanting. Thy kingdom is divided, and given to the Medes and the Persians.'

STAR-GAZING IN BABYLON

Astrology was just one of the many methods used in the East to establish omens, but towards the end of Babylon's history it became the favourite. The Babylonians believed that every event on Earth had a corresponding event in the heavens. Over the years records were kept of omens that were particularly likely to be repeated, so that it could be worked what celestial phenomena 'led to' which kinds of events. Most of the records deal with the Moon and Sun, the other planets, stars and constellations, and the weather, all of them the domains of different gods. The priests then sent their report to the king, with advice on how to avoid misfortune.

VENUS TABLET A tablet from the 7th century BC lists six years' observations of the planet Venus. The Babylonians had been recording this kind of information since the 17th century BC.

in Ur and in Harran, in northern Syria. And life under Belshazzar, last of his line, was no easier. He held in contempt the Jews whom Nebuchadnezzar had brought in captivity to Babylon after the sacking of Jerusalem in 587 BC.

There were many in Babylon who welcomed Cyrus, the king of the Medes and Persians, as a liberator. In 539 BC Cyrus and his army entered Babylon while Belshazzar was enjoying a great festival. The city was so vast that according to the fanciful account of Herodotus, the outskirts were captured without the people in the centre knowing anything about it. At the same time, according to the Jewish prophet Daniel, there 'came forth fingers of a man's hand … and wrote upon the plaster of the wall of the king's palace … and this is the writing that was written … *Mene, mene, tekel, upharsin* … Thou art weighed in the balances, and art found wanting. Thy kingdom is divided, and given to the Medes and the Persians.'

Cyrus declared himself a worshipper of the god Marduk; and one of his first acts was to free the captive Jews in the city. But while the Persians did not destroy Babylon, it had lost its independence for ever. Two centuries later, Alexander the Great established his empire throughout the Middle East, and planned to restore the city to its former brilliance. After his death, however, the idea was forgotten, and the inhabitants of Babylon soon abandoned their home to the plunder and neglect of the next 2,000 years.

Tarquinia

An Etruscan city-state

The torch of Etruscan civilization ignited quickly and burned with a pure, brilliant light for centuries, until it was extinguished by a brighter, fiercer flame: the rising sun of its neighbour, Rome.

FOR HUNDREDS OF YEARS, while Rome was in its infancy, a powerful and prosperous people influenced much of Italy and the western Mediterranean. The Etruscans, whose origins remain a mystery, developed a high level of civilization in a remarkably short space of time. During the first millennium BC, they not only established trading contacts with Greece and Carthage, they were also directly responsible for much of the cultural and architectural development of Rome. Etruscan kings of the Tarquin dynasty ruled in Rome during the 7th and 6th centuries BC, and from them the Romans acquired some of their most cherished skills and traditions. But as Rome grew and achieved dominion over the known world, it overwhelmed its illustrious forebear, and Etruria vanished from the map.

A RICH AND RADIANT LAND

Ancient Etruria, the land of the Etruscans, lay in the beautiful region of central Italy now known as Tuscany, stretching between the Appenines – backbone of the peninsula – and the Tyrrhenian Sea on the west coast. It is bounded in the north by the River Arno and in the south by the Tiber.

The loveliness of the landscape has been celebrated since ancient times. But it was the region's rich mineral resources, rather than its natural beauty, which made Etruria the cradle of civilization in Italy. The soil is exceptionally fertile, watered by many rivers and enriched by volcanic ash, but it also contains valuable reserves of metal ores – from iron, lead, and tin to copper and silver.

Bronze Age farmers and herdsmen founded settlements on Etruria's isolated hilltops during the 9th century BC. Mines were opened during the next century, a period which saw the expansion of the settlements and a dramatic upsurge in trading activity.

In the 8th century BC, Greek and Phoenician merchants from the east were engaged in a frantic search for new sources of metals. Their seafaring explorers established colonies and trading posts throughout the Mediterranean basin, and when they penetrated Italy, the natural wealth of Tuscany was exposed.

WANDERING MINSTREL Cultural enjoyments such as music were important to the Etruscans. Their favourite instruments were the lyre and the *aulos*, or double flute (right). Flautists accompanied such diverse activities as athletic contests, religious ceremonies, pastry-making, and hunting. The musician shown here provides an accompaniment for a banquet in the 5th century BC Tomb of the Leopards in Tarquinia.

The origins of the Etruscan people are not known. In the 5th century BC, the Greek historian Herodotus claimed that the country was first settled by emigrants from Lydia, a state in Asia Minor, led by a prince called Tyrrhenus. But writing in the 1st century BC, Dionysius of Halicarnassus insisted that Etruscan culture was not imported, and modern scholars favour his view. Although many outside influences can be traced in the Etruscans' swift rise, it seems likely that the bulk of the population was of local origin. They grew rich on international trade, and profited greatly from foreign interest in their mineral resources.

The Etruscan language sheds no light on the problem, but creates a mystery of its own. The people of Etruria began writing in the 7th century BC using an alphabet derived from the Greek. But their grammar and vocabulary are unlike any other known language of the ancient world. Etruscan is assumed to have been the last remnant of a form of speech extinct elsewhere, and has still been only partially translated. It bears no relation to the Latin tongue of the neighbouring Romans.

Thousands of Etruscan funeral inscriptions have survived, many of which are now understood. But the range of words in these dedications is limited. Day-to-day writing was probably done on perishable wax tablets or scrolls. These have not

> *The people of Etruria began writing in the 7th century BC . . . But their grammar and vocabulary are unlike any other known language of the ancient world.*

survived, and neither have the works of any native historians or scribes. A tiny handful of longer works still exist: a scroll used to wrap a later Egyptian mummy, two dedicatory gold plaques from the port of Pyrgi, and a bronze tablet from Cortona recording a land transaction.

To illuminate the history of this baffling people, experts have had to turn to the archaeology of Etruscan sites and the writings of their contemporaries: the Greeks, and later the Romans.

EXCITING FINDS AT THE 'CITY OF TARCHON'

By the 6th century BC, Etruria had reached its maturity as a federation of 12 independent city-states, each with several satellite towns and villages. The states had grown up in isolation from one another, and each had preserved its own distinctive traditions. One settlement in particular has left a rich heritage of archaeological evidence, and was often alluded to by Roman historians: the state of Tarquinia.

According to legend, the 12 cities of Etruria were founded by Tarchon, the son or brother of Tyrrhenus. Tarquinia, or 'city of Tarchon', must have occupied an important place among the 12 cities to have earned its grandiose title. The settlement seems to have emerged during the 9th century BC. Its strategic location, on a rocky spur of compacted volcanic ash overlooking the coastal plain of southern Etruria, brought great prosperity to its inhabitants. Its port, Gravisca, commanded all the maritime traffic passing the coast.

Exciting finds have been made in the region since the 18th century, and excavation is still going on. Tarquinia's city walls have been unearthed, and the base of a colossal temple called the Ara della Regina (Altar of the Queen) has been found. But the heart of the city is yet to be uncovered. Some parts are overlaid by later levels of Roman occupation, others have been razed by centuries of agriculture. In 1976, sophisticated scanning equipment produced a complete layout of Tarquinia's houses and streets, promising a wealth of enlightening material for future excavators.

The most fascinating aspect of the current excavations of Tarquinia is its cemetery, sited on the rocky ridge of Monterozzi to the south of the city. More than 10,000 people were buried here between the 9th and 2nd centuries BC in chambers carved out of the rock. A few of the burial chambers are decorated with magnificent frescoes revealing many details of Etruscan life. Protected in their subterranean vaults, the colours have hardly faded since they were painted.

In recent years, archaeologists have used photographic probes to explore new chambers. A tiny hole is dug to allow the insertion of a small flashlight camera into the tomb, then a complete photographic record is obtained before the contents are exposed to the light during excavations.

THE NECROPOLIS At Tarquinia, most were buried deep underground. This cemetery, known as Fondo Scataglini, is exceptional in that the tombs are laid out along a road, rather than being cut into the ridge.

The Tarquinian tomb paintings evoke a world of happiness
and festivity. The scenes show banquets, music, dancing, sports,
hunting, and fishing. In some cases the execution is of the
highest quality, in others it is rather clumsy, but all share an
exceptional sense of colour and movement.

VIVID SCENES IN THE BURIAL CHAMBERS

In the oldest tombs, only the fronts of the doors were
decorated. The images often represent lions and tigers. Vaults
are covered with geometrical designs, or plant motifs. Later
tombs are decorated in more riotous colours, and a Greek
influence becomes apparent.

Tarquinia's artists were obviously impressed by the works of
their sophisticated trading partners, but their frescoes are not
slavish imitations. The Greeks aimed for a harmonious ideal; in
Etruscan works, a more earthly realism always intruded. The
finest examples date from the second half of the 6th century BC,
by which time the local artists had developed a distinctive style.

Greek myths sometimes provided themes for tomb paintings.
A burial chamber of the mid-6th century BC known as the
Tomb of Bulls shows the hero Achilles lying in wait for Troilus,
the son of Priam. Troilus wears a strange helmet with a cockade
and Etruscan footgear. He is moving towards a tall fountain
behind which Achilles is hiding, armed with a Greek shield and
helmet, but clad in a short skirt in the Etruscan fashion.

Another chamber, the Tomb of Augurs, is covered almost
from floor to ceiling with frescoes. In one scene, two stocky
naked athletes can be seen wrestling. A referee raises his hand,
giving the signal for the fight to start. A spectator turns
impatiently to a servant bringing a folding chair; another
servant, squatting on the ground, is fast asleep.

Spirited scenes of dancing are common. One image, from the
Lionesses' Tomb, shows a naked man cavorting opposite a
woman in diaphanous robes. The figures are symmetrical and
stylized, but are imbued with a sense of vigour.

The natural world is always present, and the Hunting and
Fishing Tomb contains glorious seascapes. Birds of many colours
soar and glide in the sky, while dolphins plunge through the
waves. Fishermen cast their nets from a shallow boat; a hunter
shoots a catapult at the birds; and some distance away, a man
executes a perfect dive into the calm sea below.

Banqueting scenes, above all, evoke the Etruscans' love of
the good life, and their determination to enjoy their wealth. An
example from the Leopards' Tomb of the 5th century BC shows
three couples reclining on couches. Musicians are in attendance.
One man holds an egg, the symbol of continuity in life. Another
calls for more wine from a servant who seems happy to oblige.

REALISTIC EFFIGIES OF THE DEAD

The scenes in the burial chambers are the richest and most
original expressions of Tarquinian art, but they are not the
only examples of native craftsmanship. The tombs were
furnished with sculptures in stone, sandstone, and terracotta.
Like the paintings, the sculptures reflect the outside influences
brought to bear on an emerging civilization. Early tombs from
about 700 BC often contain sandstone slabs, sculpted in relief.
Their spiral edgings, worked with plant motifs, animal figures,

THE GOOD LIFE In the Tomb of the Leopards, Etruscan men and women recline to enjoy a banquet. Wealthy Etruscans ate their food from silver plates. Their diet consisted chiefly of poultry, venison, cakes, and fruit.

and occasionally human figures, were probably inspired by carpets from the Middle East. Later, as the impact of Greek art becomes more marked, the lids of stone sarcophagi are decorated with effigies of the deceased. Bas-reliefs inspired by mythology or the afterlife adorn the sides. Greek influence is evident, but the Etruscan effigies are truer to life than the idealized forms of Greek statuary.

The lively carvings and exuberant frescoes of the tombs do not, of course, reveal the whole story about Etruscan society. Little is known, for example, of the lives of the poor; still less of the vast class of slaves. Rich in detail as the frescoes are, they were created to serve a specific religious function: furnishing the burial chambers of the great with all the good things of life.

THE ARTS OF DIVINATION

Etruscan religion absorbed many foreign deities, especially those of the Greeks, but was characterized by a belief in predestination. The destiny of every Etruscan was believed to be ordained by the gods, and each person had to live out their allotted fate in accordance with divine will. Interpreting

portents was central to every aspect of life – a key figure in Etruscan mythology was a legendary boy seer called Tages, who was said to have brought the sacred arts of divination to the people when he sprung from a Tarquinian ploughman's furrow.

One divination technique involved making observations of lightning, and noting its point of origin and the direction in which it was travelling. Others involved studying the flight patterns of birds, or examining the entrails of sacrificed animals, particularly their livers – an art known as haruspicy. An inscribed bronze model of a sheep's liver has been found at Piacenza in northern Italy, and apparently served as a sacred manual of the art. The liver is divided into sections, each one allocated to a group of gods. The heavens were divided in similar fashion – it was believed that living things contained a model of the Universe in their entrails.

Texts on the sacred learning were collected in the *Etrusca Disciplina*, a book of ritual and divination known and respected by the Romans. The sacred heritage of the Etruscans played an important part in the Romans' own obsession with fate.

A common religion must have given the Etruscans a sense of national identity – something that their political systems could not provide. Etruria never became a unified nation. Its cities grew in isolation from one another, making war and peace independently with their neighbours or with each other.

State representatives would meet once a year at a festival held in the city of Volsinii (present-day Bolsena). The festival included games, probably in emulation of the Greek Olympics.

All the contests of the Olympics were known in Etruria: boxing, wrestling, races on foot and on horseback, javelin and discus throwing, and long jump. But the Etruscans are also credited with introducing a new and sinister spectacle – the gladiatorial contest, fought to the death.

LAYING SOLID FOUNDATIONS

The Etruscan genius for building left an enduring legacy. New towns were planned on a grid system, laid out with broad streets and careful provision for water supply and drainage. The later Roman masterpieces of plumbing and town planning had their origins in Etruria.

Like so many aspects of Etruscan life, the foundation of a town was governed by omens. Seers would select a favourable day for starting work, then a single ploughman would mark out the city walls, raising his plough from the furrow only when he reached the sites designated for the gates.

The foundations of buildings were constructed from stone; the dwellings themselves were made of perishable mud-brick and wood. Very little Etruscan architecture survives – only a few impressive gateways and bridges. In Tarquinia, a rare example of stonework completely unconnected with funeral rites has been found – a magnificent high relief of two majestic winged horses, dating back to about 400 BC, which once decorated the front façade of the city's huge temple, the Ara della Regina.

Inside the houses, the couch seems to have been the central piece of furniture in the Etruscan household, used both for sleeping and to recline on at mealtimes. Possessions were kept in trunks or baskets, or they were hung from hooks on the walls. An immense variety of pottery vessels was used in

LOCKED IN COMBAT Wrestlers form the handle on the lid of a 3rd-century bronze vessel, made by skilled Etruscan metalworkers. The theme was probably drawn from Greek mythology.

BRONZED WARRIOR Etruscan bronzes of human figures are often curiously elongated. This tall, slim 6th-century warrior from Castiglione Fiorentino, near Arezzo, is fairly close to normal proportions in comparison with many other examples.

everyday life, from tiny perfume phials to vast amphorae, in styles that were often influenced by Greek models.

But it was in metalworking that the Etruscans excelled. Their workshops developed a long tradition of excellence which made them famous throughout the ancient trading world. Care was lavished on the humblest of utensils. Metal rakes for the fire often ended in the shape of a human hand; ladles were shaped like an animal's head. The houses of the rich were lit by magnificent bronze candelabra.

Luxury articles for women included exquisite mirrors – discs of bronze polished to give a reflection. Some were held in hinged cases, others mounted on bone or ivory handles. The reverse sides were engraved, or worked in relief, with scenes from mythology or daily life.

Metalworkers also made everything from jewellery, cups, and vases to armour, harnessing, and even chariots. Their wares were exported throughout the known world, reaching deep into the heartlands of Europe, and were prized as much by barbaric Gaulish chieftains as by sophisticated townsmen.

THE POWER BEHIND THE CITY-STATES

In early times the Etruscan city-states were ruled by kings, but it seems that these were later replaced by assemblies of notables. The fasces, a bundle of rods with a protruding axe, was an Etruscan symbol of magisterial authority, later appropriated by the Romans and more recently by Mussolini's Fascists in 20th-century AD Italy.

The notables drew their members from the great families of the day, and clan pride ran deep in the aristocratic houses. Generations of family

ETRUSCAN FASHION

Until the 5th century BC, Etruscan dress had a certain originality, though it was influenced by styles from the Middle East. Thereafter, Greek fashions predominated. The paintings at Tarquinia give an idea of the diversity of colours and fabrics used.

Clothes were worn draped, and kept in place on the shoulders by clasps, *fibulae* (ornate safety pins), or by a type of button which made it possible to form sleeves. Men wore short cloaks or tunics, tight or loose, which barely covered their thighs. Arms were left bare. Fuller tunics might reach the knee, and leave one shoulder uncovered. Fishermen and other labourers might simply wear a loin cloth.

Women's tunics were sometimes of transparent material, reaching to the calves or ankles. Etruscan women wore few jewels, though cosmetics were often applied, judging from the number of make-up accessories found in the tombs. Low ankle boots with long pointed tips were a common form of footwear for both men and women.

members might be buried in a single tomb. An individual's funeral inscription often included the names of their father and mother as a sign of respect.

Women occupied an equal position to men in Etruscan society. Banqueting scenes show couples reclining on the same couch: a shocking public display in the eyes of the Greeks, who exalted manly virtues and excluded women from important social functions. These disapproving observers circulated malicious stories about the freedom and promiscuity of Etruscan women.

THE BEGINNINGS OF ROME

The Etruscans ruled about half of Italy at their height in the 6th century BC. Etruscan fleets defeated the Greeks and forged an alliance with Carthage. Their overland trade routes passed over the Alps into the forests of central Europe, while a powerful navy protected their merchants' interests in the western Mediterranean.

During these early years, Rome – founded in 753 BC – presented no real threat. The township of Rome was just 70km (43 miles) from Tarquinia, less still from the Etruscan cities of Veii (present-day Veio)

and Caere (Cerveteri), and it grew slowly in the shadow of the neighbouring civilization. To protect itself, Rome developed a system of government by elected monarchs. Strong kings were chosen to rule for life. Two of these monarchs were Tarquinians: Tarquinius Priscus (616–579 BC), and the last king of Rome, Tarquinius Superbus (534–510 BC).

The two Tarquins are credited by Roman historians with many innovations. Their achievements are sometimes confused, but between them they are said to have laid out the Circus Maximus, built the city's sewage system, and founded the Temple of Jupiter on the Capitol. Priscus, a great general, is said to have celebrated a triumph by being borne through the streets of Rome on a chariot, clothed in robes of purple and gold.

PRECIOUS ADORNMENTS Etruscan goldwork was of an exceptionally high standard. Techniques included granulation – the soldering of tiny gold balls onto the surface of objects such as the earring (left). Rings were often decorated with miniature figures or three-dimensional designs (above).

EQUAL PARTNERS The harmonious couple on a 6th-century sarcophagus from Cerveteri reflect the sexual equality of Etruria. Women, like the men, attended festivals and games and undertook business transactions.

But the citizens of Rome eventually came to resent their overlords. The resentment reached its peak, according to legend, when a son of Tarquinius Superbus raped Lucretia, a highborn Roman lady of beauty and virtue. Riots broke out. Superbus was expelled, the monarchy abolished, and a republic installed in its place. These events, occurring in 509 BC, had immense significance both for Rome and Etruria.

A SENSÈ OF FOREBODING

The Etruscans tried repeatedly to regain the government of the upstart republic; again and again they were repulsed. It is hard to see how Rome could have withstood the might of the Etruscans and gained the initiative over them, but over the next 200 years of tension and warfare, it did just that. Rome gained in confidence as the power of Etruria waned.

It has been suggested that the very roots of Etruria's success – its fertile soil and profitable trading links – contributed to its downfall by making its people lazy and complacent. Petty rivalries between its city-states had prevented the formation of a strong and united front against any external threat. And Etruria had more than just Rome to contend with – in 474 BC a Greek fleet from Syracuse inflicted a crushing naval defeat off Cumae, an ancient Greek colony 19km (12 miles) west of Naples. Meanwhile, Gaulish raiders were pressing down on the rich northern cities of the region.

In 396 BC after a 10-month siege, an Etruscan city, Veii, fell to the Romans. One after another, more Italian territories were annexed by the disciplined Roman war machine. In 309 BC, the last outposts of independent Etruria were swallowed up.

The Etruscans' fatalistic outlook became more abject in the face of these disasters. It was as if they surrendered all freedom of spirit to the will of a malevolent destiny. In Tarquinia, in the 4th century BC, the exuberance of the earlier tomb frescoes gave way to a sense of grim foreboding. Demons began to appear in banqueting scenes. The effigies of the dead reflect both sadness at leaving the earthly life, and a dread of the Beyond. This tendency is markedly obvious in the Tomb of Orcus, which is decorated with macabre figures of the underworld.

As time passed, the Latin tongue of the Roman masters replaced the Etruscan language, and Etruscan settlements were occupied and overlaid with new buildings. The ceremonies, skills, and superstitions of the Etruscans were assimilated by the Romans, along with their taste for all things Greek. But the distinctive culture that had once characterized the landscape of central Italy had been extinguished, and Etruria ceased to exist.

The Heuneburg

A mysterious Celtic fortress

Why, in the damp climate of central Europe, did Iron Age people build a massive wall using sun-dried bricks better suited to the Mediterranean? This exotic structure throws new light on the early contacts between two cultures.

ON A SPUR NEAR THE SOURCE OF THE DANUBE in southern Germany rises a plateau known as The Heuneburg. Today, it commands a fine view over woodlands and the peaceful river valley. In the Iron Age, more than 25 centuries ago, it was surrounded by mystery, untamed beauty, and danger. The Heuneburg lay in a forested wilderness stretching as far as distant mountains – the domain of bears, wild boar, and wolves. Within this wilderness, the clearings made by Celtic tribesmen were no more than tiny islands in the sea of forest.

Iron Age remains still abound in the forest: burial mounds, up to 13m (42½ ft) high in which Celtic warrior chieftains were interred. The biggest mound, the Hohmichele, was excavated in 1936. In the centre was a large wooden burial chamber, which had been pillaged. An adjoining chamber, still intact, contained the bodies of a man and a woman buried beneath a four-wheeled vehicle. The wagon had been interred complete with its rich harness, but without its horses.

The chamber also contained funerary objects, including silk textiles from China – a testament to the remarkable distance luxury goods could travel as a result of early trade links. The layout of the burial was characteristic of the Celts of the 6th century BC.

A MEETING OF CULTURES

The burial mounds provided rich finds for archaeologists, but The Heuneburg offers more – a direct glimpse into the Celtic world between 700 and 450 BC. Excavations began in 1950 and continued for 25 years.

The most startling discovery was the remains of a wall which once encircled the summit. Nothing like it had been seen before north of the Alps. It was flanked by bastions jutting out at right angles, a feature alien to Iron Age central Europe. The upper level had been constructed of unbaked bricks – an unlikely material for the damp climate. The structure had clearly been influenced by the advanced cultures of the Mediterranean. At the time, central Europe must have been – in modern terms – a developing country, envying and imitating the products of the civilizations to the south.

RIVER FORTRESS The Heuneburg plateau, in the centre, slopes down steeply to the Danube Valley with its surrounding marshes, lakes and wooded hills. The remains of a fortified wall which encircled its 2.8ha (7 acre) summit were first attributed to the Romans. But pottery found inside the bastions dated back to 600 BC – several hundreds of years before the rise of the Roman Empire.

Before about 800 BC, central Europe was inhabited by scattered communities of farmers and herdsmen led by warrior chieftains. Bronze tools and weapons were widespread, but iron implements were rare. The people buried the cremated remains of their chieftains in funeral urns grouped in flat cemeteries.

Over the next 200 years, vital developments occurred. The use of iron – harder and more easily available than bronze – spread through Europe. The influence of nomadic horsemen from the steppes of eastern Europe began to spread. Iron horse bits and iron-rimmed wagon wheels appeared. Burial customs also changed; chieftains were interred with funeral accessories in wooden chambers buried beneath mounds of earth.

South of the Alps, the Mediterranean was experiencing a cultural explosion. Greek city-states such as Athens, Thebes, and Sparta emerged, and began to flourish. Greek traders founded settlements on the coast at places such as Massilia (Marseille), and Emporion, in Spain, and Phoenician seafarers plied their wares along the shores. Meanwhile, in northern Italy, the first Etruscan towns were growing up around the rich mineral deposits of Tuscany.

Writing was unknown in central Europe at the time, but the Mediterranean cultures were literate. The sophisticated Greeks referred to the people living among and beyond the Alps as the 'Celts'. In about 500 BC, the Greek historian Hecataeus of Miletus mentioned that the city of Massilia had made contact with 'Celtica'. In the Iron Age, Greek and Etruscan trade routes began to reach up the valley of the Rhône and over passes in the Alps into the heart of central Europe. The Heuneburg is an example of the influence exercised by these Mediterranean cultures.

THE ARRIVAL OF SOUTHERN STYLE

The Celts must have been fascinated by the Mediterraneans. The first exotic foreign wares were probably acquired by the warrior chiefs: oil, wine, fine pottery, jewellery, and weapons. In exchange, they may have offered raw minerals, crops, perhaps even slaves. As trade expanded, goods from the south began to permeate the whole of Celtic society. Archaeological evidence confirms that, from about 550 BC, foreign products flooded central Europe, and southern styles and technology were adopted by local craftsmen.

LAID TO REST The tomb of a 6th-century chieftain was discovered at Hochdorf in Baden-Württemberg. Bronzework in the tomb included a couch, dishes piled in a cart, and a cauldron. The chieftain wore gilded slippers and golden jewellery.

Social and political upheaval accompanied these changes. Large hilltop fortresses were established, especially along the trade routes. The Heuneburg is one example; there are other, similar sites, including Mount Lassois on the Upper Seine in Burgundy. Yet mystery surrounds the origins of The Heuneburg. The style of building indicates much more than a passing acquaintance with Mediterranean building techniques. Did the local chieftain commission a southern architect to build his citadel? Did a native learn the necessary skills in a long apprenticeship among Greek or Etruscan craftsmen?

The warrior chief for whom it was built must have been a man of considerable power. The task was colossal. The construction work required hundreds, perhaps thousands of workers acting under strict supervision. Merely producing the food and supplies necessary for the workers must have been a gigantic operation in itself.

The wall's unbaked bricks rose nearly 4m (13ft) above a limestone footing. The footing itself was two-thirds buried in the ground, acting as a foundation, and also protecting the bricks from the dampness of the moist, central European soil.

A lime-based rendering had to be applied to both sides of the brickwork – it may have been painted on annually by The Heuneburg's inhabitants. Charred woodwork had fallen around the foot of the wall on both sides, indicating that it had once held a wooden parapet, and that it had, at some time, been destroyed by fire.

FIRE IN THE FORTRESS

Rival tribes repeatedly subjected the citadel to fire and siege during its lifespan, from 600 to 450 BC. Work on the walls was a continual process – they were rebuilt seven times.

In about 550 BC, the original superstructure of unbaked bricks was destroyed by a great fire. It was not rebuilt in its original form: new walls were erected on the ruins using a construction method more typical of Iron Age Europe.

BRONZE WARRIOR A fierce Celt stares at his enemy with glass paste eyes. This votive offering of the 1st century BC was buried in a sanctuary at Saint-Maur-en-Chausée in France.

Two faces of bonded stone were set up around a solid framework of wooden beams, and the gap between was filled in with rubble. This building technique was much admired by the Roman emperor Julius Caesar, who referred to it 500 years later as the *murus gallicus* (Gallic wall).

In about 450 BC, the Celtic fortress finally succumbed to a great fire. It is not known whether the fire began by accident or was started deliberately by attackers. But the archaeological evidence suggests that after this fierce blaze consumed the site, the citadel was abandoned forever.

INSIDE THE WALLS

About 40 per cent of The Heuneburg's interior has been excavated – enough to enable the archaeologists to reconstruct a fairly accurate idea of how people lived. Within the fortified walls, all available space was utilized. The population was densely packed. The residential quarter in the south-east corner of the citadel, near the gate leading to the Danube, included the workshops of Celtic craftsmen who fashioned items from bronze, gold, and coral, and created fine pottery. Many furnaces and hearths have been found in this area, along with fired clay smelting crucibles and foundry debris, such as slag and broken moulds.

The houses were made of wood. They were crowded together in narrow alleys – surely a contributing factor to the frequency of fires; the living quarters were razed and rebuilt about 18 times. Many houses were surrounded by ditches which channelled rainwater into a drain passing under the foundations of the citadel's outer wall.

An alley ran alongside the defences, giving the inhabitants rapid access to the wall, and the parapet walk could be quickly reached by wooden stairways or ramps. Clearly, the residents of The Heuneburg lived in constant fear of attack at the hands of hostile neighbours or marauding beasts.

The range of finds within the living areas is very limited – each time the fortress was taken it must have been pillaged from top to bottom. Pieces of rubbish and broken ceramics are by far the most common finds. Whole items are much rarer. Discoveries include

THE FORTRESS OF VIX
AND THE CELTIC PRINCESS

Mount Lassois is a limestone outcrop overlooking the Upper Seine in the Côte d'Or region of France. In 1947 comprehensive excavations began on the remains of an Iron Age site known as Vix perched on its summit; it was soon revealed as one of the leading Celtic trading centres of its time.

Vix was a fortress. Like The Heuneburg in Germany, it enjoyed remarkable prosperity at the end of the 6th century BC. Its location on a trade route connecting the Mediterranean and Celtic worlds allowed it to take control of the transportation of tin from Brittany to the Greek colony at Massilia, at the mouth of the Rhône. The Seine ceases to be navigable at Mount Lassois, so Vix became a key link in the busy trading network. The tin had to be unloaded there, then reloaded onto convoys heading south for the workshops of northern Italy and Greece. The Celtic dynasties of Mount Lassois would have grown immensely rich from this traffic.

· In 1953 the site yielded up one of the most spectacular discoveries ever made in French archaeology. A tumulus at the foot of the outcrop was excavated, revealing a lavish burial tomb. Among the rich furnishings were many items of Greek and Etruscan origin.

The most remarkable piece was the Vix *krater* – a wine-mixing vessel with a capacity of 1,100 litres (240 gallons). It was made from a single sheet of cold-hammered bronze. It is an extraordinary feat of metalwork, one of the most beautiful vases surviving from ancient Greece. The neck is adorned with a frieze showing Greek soldiers and chariots.

DIPLOMATIC GIFT The Vix *krater* (left) may have been designed to suit the Celts' warlike tastes. Its neck (above) depicts Greek figures armed for battle.

An exquisite statuette of a woman with a haunting smile decorates the lid. The vessel may have been given to the local chief by Greek merchants as a diplomatic gift.

The tomb housed the body of a woman. She was interred on a burial wagon draped with embroidered blue and vermilion cloth. A golden torque around her neck, her amber beads and necklace and bronze anklets and brooches all proclaim that she was a Celtic princess of great wealth and influence.

brooches, needles, and ornaments dropped in the rain-sodden ground, which lay undiscovered until excavated by archaeologists. Sewing needles scarcely differ from modern ones.

Animal bones found at the site suggest that cattle and pigs accounted for about four-fifths of the meat consumed. The rest was made up of sheep and goats, and a small amount of game. It seems that the people of The Heuneburg were mainly stock-breeders and farmers. Though the forests were thick with game, hunting may have been a privilege enjoyed by the lords. Food was served on coarse earthenware vessels. Earthenware cooking pots and enormous storage vessels have also been found. Sets of kitchen utensils were stacked in the bastions of the great wall.

Fine paste ceramics found at the site show the skill of the Celtic potters. Although almost always made without a wheel, they are of excellent quality. The vessels are thin-walled, their red and black polish still as bright as ever. Greek and Etruscan inspiration is common, but the influence of the pottery of Provence, in southern France, is also evident.

The fortress chiefs must have had extensive foreign contacts. Fragments of great amphorae – two-handled jars often used for transporting wine – have been found. At that time, wine was a

luxury which the Celts could not produce for themselves. Other discoveries include brooches with springs and catches like safety-pins, and hairpins, often encrusted with coral and amber. The Celts loved to adorn themselves – many fragments of earrings, torques (ornamental metal collars), and bracelets in bronze, lignite, or jet have also been found. Beads were valued; those found at The Heuneburg were locally produced, from horn, jet, amber, and green glass.

Great quantities of waste bronze sheet have been unearthed – clear evidence that the production of bronze was an important activity. During the Iron Age, it was still used to manufacture bowls, cauldrons, and other vessels. A great number of items found in the burial of a contemporary chieftain at Hochdorf in Baden-Württemberg were made of sheet bronze.

BEYOND THE CITADEL GATES

Initially, the settlement was not entirely enclosed within the citadel's fortified walls. Many people lived outside the gates – the surrounding area seems to have been densely populated. At the time when the unbaked brick walls were erected, the area west of the fortress was a town whose inhabitants may have been in the service of the fortress chiefs. Ceramics and foundry moulds found in the outer town suggest that potters and metalworkers had workshops there during the settlement's early years. But the town existed only for as long as the wall encircled the fortress – when the mudbrick defences were destroyed by the fire of 550 BC, this residential area was abandoned.

A FEARSOME RACE

Under Graeco-Etruscan influence, Celtic society crystallized, and a recognizable culture emerged. Mediterranean interest in central Europe waned from about 400 BC onwards, but the arts, social customs, and religious beliefs of the Celtic people began to spread, reaching as far west as Britain, and as far east as Asia Minor. The cause of this expansion is not known.

In about 390 BC, the Celts forced their way onto the stage of Classical history by streaming over the Alps and sacking Rome. From then on, the shadowy inhabitants of The Heuneburg and other, similar sites could no longer be ignored by Greek and Roman historians. The Roman author, Livy, vividly describes the Celtic attacks on Italian cities: 'Strange men in thousands were at the gates – men such as the townsfolk had never seen, outlandish warriors armed with strange weapons who were rumoured already to have scattered the Etruscan legions on both sides of the Po . . .'

Many writers dwell on the Celts' pride and belligerence. We also know what they looked like, from statues as well as literature. The men were tall, with fair or ruddy complexions. Their eyes were fierce, and their voices harsh. They wore moustaches, and their hair swept back from their brows in shaggy manes. Warriors wore torques around their necks as magical talismans, and sometimes went into battle naked, except for this single item. Their weapons were long, slashing swords. Their everyday clothing included trousers, tunics, and cloaks made of brightly coloured fabric.

> *Warriors wore torques around their necks as magical talismans, and sometimes went into battle naked, except for this single item. Their weapons were long, slashing swords.*

The Celtic women were also tall and warlike, stamped in an Amazonian mould. A wife was highly respected in Celtic society, and quick to defend her husband in a quarrel. The 4th-century Roman historian Ammianus Marcellinus described one such figure: 'Swelling her neck, gnashing her teeth, and brandishing her great pale arms, she begins to strike blows mingled with kicks, as if they were so many missiles hurled from a catapult.'

The characteristics of the big-boned, brawling Celts dwelt upon by Roman writers probably differed little from those of their ancestors, who lay buried beneath the earth in the misty forests surrounding The Heuneburg, and at many other Iron Age sites. The culture they had created was to survive for many centuries.

As the Celts developed their sophisticated metalworking techniques – working in gold and bronze as well as iron – their farming techniques improved, and later Celtic communities built on these strong foundations. Peasants and herdsmen, bound by loyalty to their lord, formed the basis of a barbarian world which was to survive the Roman Empire and endure, through centuries of turmoil, until the feudal age.

STATUS SYMBOL The skill of Celtic craftsmen is obvious from the variety of torques which still survive, from this German example in silver-plated iron to more elaborate creations in gold.

Persepolis

A royal capital of the Persian Empire

A forest of huge stone columns and terraces is all that remains of the splendour of Persepolis, the city founded by Darius, the King of Kings. In its time it was the ceremonial capital of the greatest empire the world had ever seen.

SINCE THE MIDDLE AGES, EUROPEAN TRAVELLERS HAVE MARVELLED at the ruins of the ancient Persian city of Persepolis (now Takht-e Jamshid), which lies at the foot of a rocky cliff in the southern plains of modern-day Iran. Major excavation to unearth the half-buried city began in 1930. Among the stonework, archaeologists uncovered graphic bas-reliefs which reveal much about the religious and social hierarchy of the city.

Persepolis was built by Persian kings during the 6th and 5th centuries BC, by a dynasty whose empire subjugated all the early civilizations of the Middle East. On the bas-reliefs, the peoples of 31 nations can be seen paying homage to the might of Persia. The roll call of the defeated is impressive, including the Egyptians, Libyans, Thracians, Cilicians, and the people of Cyprus. All had been overcome in a hurricane of conquest.

THE PERSIANS RISE UP

Iran (Land of the Aryans) lies at the crossroads of Europe, Asia, and Arabia. The landscape is one of plains, interspersed with deserts and mountains. In the centuries before 1000 BC, Aryan tribes from the Caucasus overran the region and created two separate kingdoms, the Medes settling in the north and the Persians in the south. The Medes were the first to show their strength, conquering their southern neighbours and, with the aid of the Babylonians, destroying the Assyrian Empire in 612 BC. Then, around the middle of the 6th century BC, came a dramatic Persian upsurge.

The founder of the Persian Empire, Cyrus the Great, who ruled from 559 to 530 BC, rebelled against his Medean master, seizing his kingdom and territories to the east as far as present-day Afghanistan. Cyrus then conquered the kingdom of Lydia, which held Greek settlements on the coast of Asia Minor. Babylon was next to fall; the onslaught seemed unstoppable. Cyrus's victories stemmed from the supremacy of his bowmen – the Persians excelled at archery. He avoided fighting at close quarters by overwhelming the enemy with a hail of arrows and harassing them with swarms of cavalry.

A SIGN OF STRENGTH
The heads of bulls decorate the towering pillars which once supported the *apadana*, a great audience chamber where the king received subjects and visitors. Surrounded on three sides by open colonnades, the *apadana* measured more than 60m (200ft) square.

UNITING THE EMPIRE

By 539 BC, Cyrus the Great had united his conquests in a single domain stretching from India in the east to the Mediterranean in the west. It is known as the Achaemenid Empire, after Achaemenes, an ancestor of Cyrus. From his capital at Pasargadae, the monarch set about ordering his realm. He was no mere warlord – he treated his subjects generously, allowing them to maintain their customs and religious institutions. In place of massacres and deportations Cyrus introduced tolerance and the rule of law.

When he died, his son Cambyses II (530–522 BC) continued to expand the empire, conquering Egypt. After Cambyses' death, for a brief period it seemed that the empire might fall apart. But then Darius I (522–486 BC), another Achaemenid, came to power and set about consolidating his ancestors' achievements.

Darius controlled what was virtually a world empire. Reflecting this grandeur, he took for himself the title of 'King of Kings', and administered his provinces through governors known as satraps. Each territory was required to pay tax in local produce, precious metal or, in the west, in gold coinage. The gold daric, a coin named after the king, became international currency throughout the western part of the empire.

Darius founded two new capitals to replace Pasargadae. One was at Susa, which became the administrative hub of the empire, close to the thriving urban centres of Mesopotamia. The other, known as Persepolis, was built on the remote plain of Marv Dasht in the Persian homeland. This city's role was primarily ceremonial – to reinforce the imperial majesty of the Achaemenid dynasty. Here, for example, the coronations of kings were to be held.

The two capitals were the twin hearts of the empire, with arteries reaching its farthest corners. The Persians constructed a royal road from Sardis near the Ionian coast all the way to Susa, a distance of more than 2,570km (1,600 miles). An eastern extension led to Persepolis. Mounted couriers operated a relay system along the highway, switching horses at 111 post stations, and covering the whole distance in as little as a week.

CEREMONIAL HEART OF THE EMPIRE

The building of the ceremonial capital was begun by Darius and continued after his death by his son, Xerxes (486–465 BC). A township surrounded the core of Persepolis – a great complex of halls and palaces built on a single, immense stone terrace, 450m (1,476ft) long and 300m (984ft) wide.

MAJESTIC ENTRANCE Columns 12m (40ft) high supported the huge Gateway of All Nations. Inside, three great doorways led into different parts of the king's even taller audience hall.

OFFERINGS FROM MANY NATIONS
The reliefs decorating the staircases leading up to the *apadana* may depict the city's New Year celebrations, when delegates from across the empire travelled to Persepolis bearing tributes.

To reach the terrace, Xerxes built a broad stairway in the north-west corner, leading up to a colossal gatehouse. This 'Gateway of All Nations' was guarded by huge statues: monstrous figures with the head of a man and the body of a winged bull. The gatehouse gave access to a gigantic audience hall, the *apadana*, supported by stone columns about 20m (65ft) high. Bas-reliefs surrounding the hall showed delegates from all the nations of the empire. Stone figures of officials were originally shown converging on Xerxes as he sat on his throne, encircled by his counsellors, with his eldest son standing at his side. After an abortive palace coup by some of these officials, their figures were replaced with carvings of guards to remind the people that the king alone was master.

Delegates came and went constantly on official business. The reliefs show the variety of racial types with their local offerings: humped bulls from Babylon, rams from Cilicia, fabrics from the Greek cities of Asia Minor, and elephant tusks from Ethiopia.

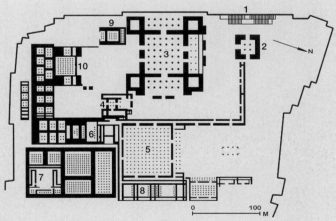

IN THE PRESENCE OF A KING
The raised palatial terrace dominated the town of Persepolis. Left: The columns of the audience chamber or *apadana*, where the king received foreign visitors, still stand, with the Marv Dasht plain stretching out behind. Above: Features of the terrace included the entrance stairway (1); Xerxes' Gateway of All Nations (2); the *apadana* (3); the Tripylon, where the king received Persian and Medean noblemen (4); the Hall of 100 Columns (5); the harem (6); the treasury (7); the royal stables (8); and the private palaces of Darius (9), and Xerxes (10).

HONOURING THE SUPREME GOD
Reliefs on the royal tombs at Naqsh-e Rostam show the universal deity, Ahura Mazda, spreading his wings over Darius the king, who raises his hand in a gesture of reverence.

Only the chief delegates could enter the great hall. They are shown mounting a flight of steps leading onto a huge verandah with corner towers. From the verandah, doors opened out onto a room of staggering proportions, the height of a modern seven-storey building. Thirty-six columns reached into the high roof, each topped by the stone figure of a bull. The great king would sit as shown on the bas-reliefs, enthroned on a low dais in the centre of the hall. His robes were rich, and the canopy above him was decorated with a winged disc, the emblem of the dynasty. Smoke rose from censers smouldering in front of the high-backed throne.

The buildings at Persepolis are laid out according to a single basic principle. The main feature is the square hall in the centre, with its roof supported by a forest of columns. In the *apadana*, the columns were of stone, but in less important buildings they were made of wood and mounted on fluted stone bases. The broad verandah running around the walls, with its doors leading into the hall, acted as a shady promenade. This characteristically Persian layout had already been established by the time Cyrus had built his capital in Pasargadae.

BEHIND THE SCENES

Behind the great audience hall was a smaller palace, the Tripylon, where Persian and Medean noblemen would be received. The king would enter, shaded by a parasol and accompanied by a servant. The throne was set up on a high platform, supported by statues of the subject peoples.

The Tripylon led into the rear of the citadel where the treasury and harem were housed. Darius, Xerxes, and their successors built private palaces here, and constructed smaller residential apartments nearby.

A third palatial complex was isolated behind a wall – the king's military headquarters, where he acted in his capacity as supreme head of the armed forces. The complex was larger than the *apadana* in area, but not as high. Its roof was supported by 100 columns, and its sculpted doors showed the king enthroned on a platform supported by Persian and Medean soldiers. The palace and its adjoining government offices opened onto a courtyard where the king could review detachments of his troops.

TESTIMONY TO FAITH

There is no temple at Persepolis. But that does not imply that the court had no religion. The best clues to the religious beliefs of the empire appear on the tombs of Darius and three of his successors. The burial chambers, carved out of a cliff face at Naqsh-e Rostam, about

FINAL RESTING PLACE Above the entrance to the tomb of Xerxes I at Naqsh-e Rostam is a carving of the king carried by his subjects.

13km (8 miles) north of Persepolis, are built to look like palaces. The sculpted façade of Darius's tomb has a flat floor on which the King of Kings is depicted, carried on an enormous platform by all the peoples of the earth. Darius stands with his bow resting on one foot, which is slightly ahead of the other. He is worshipping a sacred fire burning at an altar. Above, a soaring figure inside the winged disc symbol of the dynasty blesses the king: this figure is Ahura Mazda, the Wise Lord, personification of divine goodness. The religion of the Achaemenids revolved around this universal deity, believed to be visible in the light of the sun and the purifying effect of fire.

The worship of Mazda played a key role in the Achaemenids' notion of government. They were the supreme people, and Mazda was the supreme god, light of the world. They had achieved dominion through his will, and they were conscious of the responsibilities conferred by their power.

THE GREAT ADMINISTRATOR

When Darius came to the throne, he reorganized the government of the 312 subject nations into 20 provinces, or satrapies, dividing power between the local officials. Each satrap, or governor, was chosen from among the Persian and Medean nobility. The command of the local troops was in the hands of a separate general. A third dignitary was responsible for the tax collecting, and a 'secretary' supervised the general administration of the province through a staff of inspectors – 'the Eyes and Ears of the King'. A well-organized network of roads ensured the empire's economic and administrative cohesion, maintaining open lines of communication with the seat of central government in Susa, and allowing the king's inspectors to travel across the Persian territories and supervise local officials personally.

BEARING GIFTS The nations pay tribute – sculptures at Persepolis show two Lydians bearing vessels of gold and a Babylonian with a length of woollen cloth arriving to visit the royal court.

MURDER AND MAYHEM

Throughout the period of Achaemenid greatness, the emergence of the Greek city-states was a constant problem. In 490 BC, the Greek subjects of Persia had risen in revolt and Darius had led a punitive expedition against the mainland. But on the field of Marathon, at the gates of Athens, the unbeatable Persian archers had been vanquished.

Ten years later, Xerxes launched a campaign against Athens and Sparta. Again the Persians were defeated, on land at Plataea, near Mount Cithaeron in Greece, and on the sea off Salamis, an island in the Aegean. These military disasters exploded the ancient world's belief in Persian invincibility.

Decline set in. Greek historians record the assassination of Xerxes in 465 BC. It seems that as Xerxes grew older, the reins of power fell increasingly to his vizier, Artapan, and his eunuch chamberlain, the police chief Aspamites. One night Aspamites admitted Artapan into the royal apartments, where the vizier stabbed the king to death. The two accomplices then persuaded the young prince Artaxerxes that the crime was the work of his elder brother, Dariaios.

The ruse worked. Artaxerxes had the guiltless Dariaios executed, and assumed the throne. With an inexperienced young monarch as nominal ruler, the assassins were the effective masters of the empire for seven months. Not satisfied, they hatched a plot to eliminate their sovereign. But the plan failed. Most of the army stood by the king, and Artapan and Aspamites were put to death.

It was then that the relief of Xerxes surrounded by his counsellors was removed from the great audience hall. The treacherous officials were represented on the original carving: Artapan in Medean costume – short tunic, trousers, and high round cap – with Aspamites standing behind. Artaxerxes had the relief taken down and placed in a private part of the citadel.

The whole affair was followed by a plague of palace plots. Disorders broke out, too, among the tribesmen of the mountains and deserts, leading to insurrections in the empire's fringe territories. The empire, now ruled by Darius III, survived but the enemy was uniting. The Greek states, overcoming their internal feuds, had become capable of toppling Persia from its pedestal. The catastrophe came in 334 BC, when a young Macedonian general named Alexander led an invasion force from Greece across the Dardanelles. Forty thousand men crossed over into Persian territory, and in a series of spectacular victories Alexander took Asia Minor, then the Mediterranean coastlands.

The Persian army crumbled. Alexander thrust into Mesopotamia; Babylon fell and Susa was occupied. In 331 BC the Macedonian general arrived at Persepolis. Acting in revenge for the Persian burning of Greek temples, Alexander decided to put the city to the torch. Persepolis was not entirely destroyed, but it survived merely as an outpost of Alexander the Great's empire. Only the ruins of the citadel remained as an epitaph to the ancient ceremonial capital of the Persian kings.

Carthage

Gateway to rich Western trade

Ancient Carthage was once Rome's most dangerous rival, but the Phoenician city perished in a single orgy of destruction, leaving barely a trace of a powerful civilization that embraced both high culture and horrific ritual.

CARTHAGE STANDS BESIDE ATHENS AND ROME as one of the main centres of wealth and power in the ancient Mediterranean. In fact, it almost supplanted them both as the forerunner of all Western civilization. In 216 BC, the Carthaginian general Hannibal came within a shade of destroying Rome and changing the course of history. But it was Carthage's fate to be wiped off the face of the earth only 70 years later.

Today, little remains of the great city which once overlooked the Gulf of Tunis. It was so thoroughly obliterated by the Romans that only a shadowy idea of Carthaginian achievements survives, gleaned from the biased and incomplete writings of its Greek and Roman enemies – and from the patient work of archaeologists.

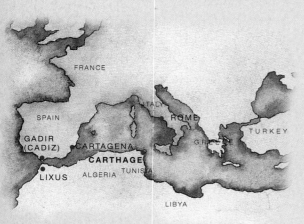

THE SEARCH FOR TREASURE

Carthage was founded by the Phoenicians, ancient inhabitants of the modern Syrian and Lebanese coasts in the eastern Mediterranean. The Phoenicians were related to the Jews of the Old Testament, sharing their Semitic languages and cultural heritage. The Bible refers to them as Canaanites or Tyrians, and the Hebrew patriarchs were scandalized by their idolatry.

The Bible also portrays them as businessmen and seafarers who voyaged to distant lands in search of valuable minerals. The Greeks knew the Phoenicians mainly as merchants, in particular through their exports of a highly-prized purple dye extracted from a shellfish native to the Lebanese coast.

The eastern cities of the Phoenicians enjoyed their heyday between the 12th and 8th centuries BC. The mineral riches of the West drew the Phoenicians like a magnet, and it is known that voyages to the western end of the Mediterranean were taking place as early as the 12th century BC. They set up new trading bases, and established regular communications with outposts as far away as the Atlantic coast, at Lixus in Morocco, and at Gadir (Cadiz) in Spain – an area especially valued for its precious ores. Carthage was founded on the route to these treasures.

RAZED AND REBORN
Strategically situated on the Tunisian coast, Carthage has been a prime location for settlement through the ages. The Carthaginian Empire vied for dominance with the rising Roman state, and a century after the Romans in turn razed the city, they refounded it as a colony. This Roman bathhouse was commissioned by Antonin in 142, then destroyed by the Vandals when they took the city in 439.

Some uncertainty surrounds the city's origins. The traditional date of its foundation – 814 BC, as recorded by the Greek historian Timaeus – was long considered an exaggeration. But recent discoveries of remains from the early 8th century BC give the date some credibility.

Carthage is said to have been founded by a group of exiles from Tyre (in present-day Lebanon), under the leadership of the king's sister, Elissa (or Dido, as the Roman poet Virgil calls her). The reality is probably that political rivalries forced a section of the Tyrian ruling class into exile with their followers, and that they eventually settled at a key point on the trade routes. Virgil's story makes Dido, founder of Carthage, a contemporary of the Trojan prince Aeneas, founder of Rome, and tells of their love but ends with Dido's suicide as Aeneas follows the instructions of the gods and sails away to Italy and his destiny.

The name Carthage derives from the Phoenician Qarthadasht, or New City. Occupying the seaward end of a peninsula jutting out from Tunisia's northern coast, it is not far

WATER IN THE DESERT The Romans, famed for their feats of engineering, built an aqueduct stretching 80km (50 miles) to bring water from a spring on the mountain of Zaghouan to Carthage.

from the point where the southern and western shores of the Mediterranean are closest. Carthage, then, had strategic importance, commanding the narrow passage between the Mediterranean's eastern and western seas.

THE CITY SPREADS ITS ROOTS

Nestling on its promontory, Carthage began to profit by an expansion of commerce in the Mediterranean. Meanwhile, in the east, Phoenicia's light was failing. Its small city-states of Tyre, Sidon, and Byblos (present-day Jubayl) were being eclipsed by the growing might of Assyria. After the Assyrian Empire collapsed at the end of the 7th century BC, Babylon and Persia successively cast long shadows over the Phoenician homeland.

Phoenician culture maintained its characteristics over the centuries (its bold seafarers are even credited with having sailed round Africa in about 600 BC), but it was left to Carthage to carry the torch as the centre of Phoenician civilization.

Carthage began to develop colonies of its own. By the 4th century BC, settlements with Phoenician-speaking inhabitants dotted the coast of North Africa. Parts of southern Spain, the whole of Sardinia and western Sicily were also settled.

Rivalries with Greece and Etruria (in northern Italy) led to warfare over trading frontiers such as Corsica and Sicily. Carthage suffered a dark period towards the end of the 4th century BC when Agathocles, ruler of Syracuse (the chief Greek

MAGICAL MASKS The Phoenician settlers made miniature faces out of glass paste measuring 4cm to 7cm (about 1½in to 2¾in) across. They were used in jewellery, perhaps as charms to ward off evil spirits.

power in Sicily), took an army to North Africa. After the wars, the Carthaginians relied less exclusively on commercial networks and more on territorial control as the basis of their power.

In Tunisia, they looked inland. Some of the most fertile land in North Africa was within reach of their city. By the time of Agathocles's invasion they were farming it, producing cereals, livestock, fruit, and vegetables. A Sicilian historian, Diodorus, gives a vivid impression of Agathocles's soldiers gazing open-mouthed in awe at the abundant orchards and rich country houses of Cape Bon, north-west of the city.

Meanwhile, Carthage extended control over the trading bases on the North African coast and the Mediterranean islands. Almost accidentally, an empire was born, and Carthage came to rival the most advanced cities of the Greek world. Its population was estimated by the geographer Strabo at 700,000. This seems excessive; Athens itself had no more than about 250,000 inhabitants. The figure may refer to Carthage and the territories it administered but a six-figure population is plausible for a city which, at its height, covered an area of 5km² (nearly 2sq miles), with a further 15 to 25km² (6 to 9½sq miles) of suburban villas.

KEY EVIDENCE OF A GROWING METROPOLIS

Archaeological evidence, once meagre, has grown rapidly since UNESCO launched a 'Save Carthage' campaign in 1972. It has emerged that Carthage was every bit as magnificent as the descriptions suggest. The heyday of the city is termed Late Punic, referring roughly to the years between 300 and 146 BC. (Punic is simply a term for Phoenicians of the west.)

The key period in the city's expansion corresponds with the era when the Carthaginians started farming and established themselves as an imperial power. But remains of an earlier, more modest Carthage have also been found – tombs, a sacrificial precinct, and the debris of a few buildings.

The position of these tombs provides fascinating evidence of the city's growth. Historians believe that, like the Greeks and Romans, the Carthaginians had religious taboos about burial within the city limits, and moved their burial places farther out as the settlement grew bigger. But early cemeteries lie beneath the later town. For example, 6th century BC burials lie under 3rd and 2nd century BC houses on the hill which dominates the city.

WHAT THE RUINS REVEAL

The hill is the Byrsa, or citadel, of Carthage – mentioned in ancient texts as the last bastion of the defenders under the final Roman onslaught. On its slopes, archaeologists have discovered one complete *insula* or block of buildings, with its surrounding streets, and parts of neighbouring *insulae* and streets. From this evidence the shadowy city begins to take form and substance.

The main buildings were grouped around a large market square, which served as a meeting place. On top of the Byrsa was the Temple of Eshmun, the Carthaginian god of healing. The other buildings on the Byrsa – shops and houses – date back to the city's later days. They seem to have been two storeys

high, built of sun-dried brick and stone. Their walls were faced with plaster, and their floors decorated with mosaic or coloured cements. The shops opened onto the street, and people gained access to the houses behind them through corridors leading to small courtyards.

Other houses, found by German archaeologists working down on the coast, reveal the same basic plan, but are larger, with colonnades surrounding the courtyards. These were the seaside homes of the wealthy – though the sea view must have been obstructed by the massive city wall in front of them.

The wall, according to an ancient text, was over 12m (39ft) high and 9m (29½ft) thick, with arsenals and even stabling for elephants set into its stones. This daunting fortification enclosed the whole of the city, including the harbours and some suburban areas, over a circuit of 32km (20 miles).

The harbours were among the most striking features of ancient Carthage. The two man-made basins, one for merchant shipping and one for military fleets, were connected by a channel of water. Covered dry docks could take in a fleet of 220 vessels. British excavations in the military basin revealed sheds for vessels measuring about 5m (16ft) across and 30m (98ft) in length.

The warships would have been shallow-bottomed oared galleys, which relied on speed for their effectiveness in battle. The harbours were only about 2m (6½ft) deep, but were extensive; the merchant basin covered some 6ha (15 acres) or more, and the military some 5ha (12 acres). Scooping them out was an impressive feat – it would have yielded some 191,150m³ (6.75 million cu ft) of soil. The work seems to have been carried out as late as the 3rd century BC.

LAYERS OF CITY UPON CITY

Ancient Carthage is still being excavated, but only glimpses of the city are likely to be revealed. Not only is the site overlaid by the remains of a later Roman city, but modern Carthage, a suburb of Tunis, lies on top. The only overall view of a Punic city clear of the debris of later habitation lay to the north-west, at the small town of Kerkouane on Cape Bon.

Little evidence of early Carthaginian produce has survived. Textiles were woven for the domestic market and for export, and recent excavations uncovered purple-dye works in a suburb of the city, and in Kerkouane. Salted fish and slaves were major exports as well as being in great demand in the city.

The eastern Phoenicians were renowned craftsmen in ivory and metals, and the Carthaginians maintained

SHIPS FOR BATTLE Most Carthaginian and Roman warships were quinqueremes with up to three banks of oars on each side. Some vessels, like this Roman flagship (above), had a single bank with five, or even six, men to each oar. In Carthage (right), some quays, on land that has now sunk beneath the sea, faced onto the Mediterranean. Behind them, the sheltered merchant harbour was the hub of commercial shipping, leading to the inner military harbour.

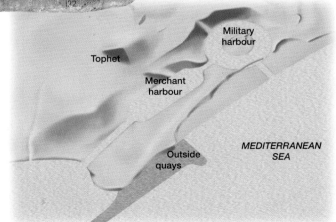

Tophet

Military harbour

Merchant harbour

Outside quays

MEDITERRANEAN SEA

INSIDE A CITADEL Plaster-lined cisterns for collecting rainwater nestled beneath the ground floor storage rooms of the buildings on the Byrsa hill. The occupants probably lived on the first floor.

these high standards. They took inspiration from the products of their neighbours and combined this with their own ideas to create distinctive Carthaginian pieces. Their workshops manufactured a wide variety of objects, from gaudy trinkets to exquisite jewellery and fine furniture.

Domestic crafts were probably overshadowed by the city's many imports, from Etruria, Egypt and Greece. Nearly all of the fine pottery found at Carthage is of Greek or Graeco-Italian origin. But Carthaginian workshops did produce small terracotta figurines and extraordinary terracotta images of grimacing faces, perhaps once hung in homes to protect against evil spirits.

And Carthage excelled at food production. After the 4th century BC, shipments of Carthaginian grain are recorded in Athens. In a famous incident in the Roman Senate, Cato the Elder brandished Carthaginian figs while expounding on the threat that the city posed to Rome.

IN THE SPIRIT OF EXPLORATION
The Carthaginians were valiant seamen. A tantalizing reference in a later Roman text credits one Himilco with a northward voyage of many months that may have reached Brittany and even Cornwall. The merchants of Carthage are known to have dealt in Cornish tin ore, but there is no evidence that the city's own ships made such a long and perilous voyage; Spanish or Gallic traders were probably the link with distant Britain.

One great Carthaginian sea voyage has been recorded. In the 5th century BC, a man named Hanno is said to have travelled down the west coast of Africa, reaching as far perhaps as the modern Ivory Coast. On his return, he recorded his journey on a bronze tablet at Carthage, and a version of the text survives in Latin. The account remains controversial. Only part of the narrative

Seeking gold, the Carthaginians would spread out their wares and signal to attract the natives. The natives would then present their offerings of the precious ore.

is straightforward reporting – for example, a section describing how the explorers took colonists to Lixus in Morocco. More intriguing passages describe pygmies, wild animals, a volcanic eruption, and various geographical features such as rivers and mountains. The order of the text is jumbled, and the full length of the journey is unclear; colourful inventions seem to have been mixed with factual statements.

In their more far-reaching ventures, Greek writers relate, the Carthaginians used a so-called 'silent barter' for trading with primitive tribes. Seeking gold, the Carthaginians would spread out their wares and signal to attract the natives. The natives would then present their offerings of the precious ore. If it was sufficient, the Carthaginians would take it, leaving their own goods in payment; if not, they would wait until more gold was brought. Both sides apparently respected the system.

IDOLATRY AND ANCIENT RITUAL
Like the Greeks and Romans, the Carthaginians believed in gods and goddesses with their own special roles. There were two main deities: Tanit, who was patron goddess of Carthage and an earth mother who also presided over the moon; and Baal, the sky god. Between them they represented the very basic powers of human and agricultural fertility – powers that a primitive society depended on for their survival.

The people also worshipped various lesser deities – gods who sometimes corresponded to minor deities venerated in Greek and Roman religion. Where the

Carthaginians differed most strikingly from their contemporaries was in the survival of primitive religious practices – in particular, the rite of human sacrifice.

This dark practice had been known in Bronze Age Greece and elsewhere, but it horrified the writers of classical times. The Carthage ritual is described in detail by Diodorus, the Sicilian Greek historian.

Sacrifices took place at night before a great bronze statue of the supreme god, Baal Hammon. The parents brought their sacrificial child to the site – an infant between two and three years old, sometimes older. The ceremony included loud music and a great deal of festivity (which would drown out the crying of the child), and at the appropriate moment the child was taken by a priest to have his or her throat slit in a secret ritual. The body was then placed on the statue's outstretched arms, from which it rolled off into the flames of a fire. During the crisis in the 4th century when Agathocles besieged Carthage, 200 children are said to have been sacrificed.

EXAMINING THE EVIDENCE

There is no question of the nightmarish ceremonies being merely an invention of enemy propaganda. At Carthage and other Punic sites, archaeologists have discovered sanctuaries with urns containing the ashes of infants. The sanctuaries, known by modern writers as tophets after a place of sacrifice in the Bible's *Book of the Prophet Jeremiah*, are walled enclosures, open to the sky. The urns were buried in pits, and a stone monument or stele about the size of a modern gravestone was erected nearby.

The Carthage tophet contains some of the earliest reliable evidence of Phoenician settlement in the West: fragments of pottery discovered at its lowest level date back to about 725 BC. From then until the city's fall, layer upon layer of urns containing the remains of thousands of sacrificed children were deposited, along with commemorative steles. The area of the Carthage tophet eventually stretched across some 2ha (5 acres).

Most children seem to have been sacrificed individually, and studies of teeth found among the charred bones confirm that most were two years old

A DIVINE SIGN A votive stele found in the Carthage tophet, where the ashes of children were buried, bears the symbol of the goddess Tanit, consort to Baal Hammon.

THE TRADING EMPIRE OF CARTHAGE

When Carthage replaced Tyre as the chief city of the Punic world, it inherited a powerful group of merchant enterprises. Carthage controlled its own market, buying in raw materials – mainly precious ores such as gold, silver, tin, and copper – and selling the products of its own industry: ceramics, textiles, arms and armour, small glassware, jewellery, trinkets, and furniture. And it acted as a middleman for goods produced and used by other peoples. Carthaginian shipping lanes extended throughout the western Mediterranean and into the Atlantic beyond. Besides colonies in North Africa, settlements and trading posts were set up along the southern coast of Spain and the Balearic Islands. Sardinia came within the Punic fold, as did western Sicily. And the smaller islands of Malta, Gozo, Lampedusa, and Pantelleria were used as staging posts by Carthaginian sailors.

or younger. Some were newborn. Occasionally, two children have been found in one urn, characteristically a newborn with a small child. Perhaps the parents promised to surrender a child in advance of its birth – if the child was stillborn, they would have to present their elder infant.

Why did this barbaric practice persist among such a sophisticated people living in one of the most advanced civilizations of the classical world?

During the last 200 years or so of Carthaginian civilization, the grave steles are often inscribed with a standard dedication: 'To the lady Tanit and her consort Baal Hammon, —, the son of the son of —, dedicates this in fulfilment of a vow.' The family's social status is frequently indicated – those sacrificed were always of the property-owning class.

Trying to understand why only the children of the rich were sacrificed, and why the brutal tradition survived for so long, American excavators speculated that the practice may have had a social purpose: the sacrifices may have been a convenient form of family planning, allowing the property-owning class to prevent their wealth being divided between too many heirs. Cynical as it sounds, there are parallels elsewhere. The Greeks, for example, used to expose unwanted children on hillsides.

POLITICS AND POWER

Carthage was unusual in the ancient world in having a constitution acknowledged by the Greeks. In the Greeks' opinion, the Carthaginians, like the Romans, did not entirely qualify for the label 'barbarians'. Although evidence of the city's constitution is sketchy, it is clear that

DARK SANCTUARY The urn in this Roman vault, built over the Carthage tophet, contains the remains of a sacrificed child. Archaeologists estimate that 500 children a year were sacrificed in the city's heyday.

by the 4th century BC, three elements of authority existed side by side: monarchy, oligarchy (rule by a small dominant faction), and democracy.

Before about 450 BC, something approaching kingly authority had been held by one family, the Magonids (among whom was Hanno the navigator). But later, the great merchant families and the landowners used their political muscle to guarantee a share in government. The kingly element survived in the role of two principal officers of state, known as the *suffetes*. They were similar to the Roman consuls: two were elected annually from among the most influential families.

Leading citizens were represented in a Council comparable to the Roman Senate. From the several hundred Council members, who held their positions for life, two powerful committees were chosen: one to carry out day-to-day policy, the other to administer justice and review the actions of the generals.

A citizen body represented the democratic element in the constitution. The body could vote on proposals put before it, and had the power to elect certain administrators. In practice, its influence was small throughout most of Carthage's history. When the *suffetes* and Council decided on a course of action, they rarely allowed the issue to go to a popular vote.

ON A COURSE TO DESTRUCTION

The closing chapters of the city's history began in the 3rd century BC, when Rome moved into the world of Mediterranean politics after taking control of the Greek cities in southern Italy. Almost by accident the Romans and Carthaginians – previously allies in wars against the Greeks – fell out over the control of Sicily. The disagreement was to spark the first of the three great Punic wars.

The first brought 23 years of intermittent fighting by land and sea (264–241 BC). It ended in victory for the Romans, and Sicily became their first overseas province. Following the loss of Sicily, and later of Corsica and Sardinia, the Carthaginian

general Hamilcar Barca launched a masterly campaign to seize the southern half of Spain. Here, Carthagena, 'the New Carthage', was founded in 221 BC. But the contest with Rome had not been resolved. Hannibal Barca, son of Hamilcar, now led the army. When a second Punic War broke out in 218 BC he crossed the Alps with an army of 35,000 men and 37 elephants, but narrowly failed to take Rome.

In the treaty that followed a later defeat, Carthage lost all its possessions in Europe, its fleet except for ten ships, and with it control of the Mediterranean. And yet the city still prospered. Cato the Elder, a Roman ambassador to Carthage in 153 BC, was so awed by the city's grandeur that he was consumed with jealous rage. On returning to Rome, he would conclude every speech he made, on whatever subject, by declaring that 'Carthage must be destroyed'.

That destruction came at the end of the third Punic War (149–146 BC). The inhabitants of the ancient city held on with heroic tenacity against the Roman onslaught. Their last stand was made in the Temple of Eshmun. When the temple fell, the invading troops plundered and burned, levelling the city.

Scipio Aemilianus, the Roman general who presided over the destruction of Carthage, wept over the rubble of the ruined city. He was moved less by pity than by awe that so gigantic a power could be laid so low. 'This is a glorious moment,' he observed, 'and yet I am seized with fear and foreboding that some day the same fate will befall my own country.'

Pazyryk

The frozen tombs of the Altai

Civilizations are usually founded on urban settlements. But the horsemen of the Altai needed no fixed base. Their alternative, nomadic lifestyle led them to move with the seasons, creating a culture which flourished wherever they pitched their tents.

THE ALTAI MOUNTAINS OF SOUTHERN SIBERIA ARE A VAST MASSIF of jagged peaks and swooping valleys, thickly forested on the lower slopes in the north-west, yet semi-desert in the south-east. There are no fallen monuments or ruined city walls to break the landscape, but the mountains were once home to a nomadic race whose culture was influenced by both China and Achaemenid Persia (Iran). Only their frozen tombs – scattered through the extensive mountain system near the borders of Russia, China, and Mongolia – reveal the extraordinary vitality of their short-lived culture.

TREASURE IN THE STONES
Burial mounds – huge piles of stones known as kurgans – are the only signs of human presence in this area in ancient times. They dot the steppes of Asia, stretching as far west as the valley of the Danube. Those in the Altai have revealed some remarkable finds – at an altitude of 1,600m (5,250ft), ice has preserved their contents for more than 2,000 years.

In the early 20th century, Russian archaeologists began excavations at Pazyryk, high in the massif. Here, a group of five great kurgans had been discovered, surrounded by smaller mounds. After digging a shaft in one of the kurgans to allow access to its central chamber, the scientists entered a frozen world. As the ice melted, it revealed a tomb draped in brightly edged brown felt. All around lay scattered funeral objects – bright tapestries and clothing, luxurious animal furs, wooden furniture, and carved objects of bone and staghorn. North of the chamber, behind a partition of logs, lay the bodies of several horses. The manes were trimmed and bound, the tails plaited. Alongside them lay rich saddlecloths, leather cushions on wooden saddle bows, bits, bridles, and harness straps hung with vividly painted wooden ornaments embellished with gold leaf.

HORSEMAN OF THE ALTAI
On a felt wall hanging dating back 2,500 years, a flamboyant warrior rides a horse lavishly decked out with ornamental tack, trimmed mane and braided tail – just like those discovered in the Pazyryk caves.

It seemed that thieves had penetrated the kurgans shortly after the burial ceremonies. In one of the tombs, the embalmed bodies of a man and a woman had been lifted from the sarcophagus. Their hands and feet had been chopped off to retrieve valuable bracelets and anklets, their fingers amputated to free rings. The heads had been severed from the bodies so that necklaces could be removed easily. Aside from the desecration, by breaking into the graves the thieves had rendered an invaluable service to the archaeologists.

Autumn rains seeped into the tombs of Pazyryk through the tunnels dug by the grave-robbers. Year after year, the bitter steppeland winters froze the water in successive layers of ice. Screened from the summer sun by the stones above, the ice had never melted. The imprisoned riches had neither perished nor faded, and the bodies of the dead were frozen – preserved almost intact. Fabrics were as richly coloured as when they had been woven and velvety smooth. Carpets were still springy; furs were still silky soft. Textures had endured.

The people buried at Pazyryk were relations of the Scythians – a warlike tribe who made sporadic descents on the great civilizations to the east and west of the barren Asian steppes. These ferocious nomads made terrifying incursions into Persia during the 5th century BC. The Greek historian, Herodotus (c.484–425 BC), recorded some of their customs.

A FEARSOME REPUTATION

According to Herodotus, each Scythian warrior had to make at least one kill a year, or face disgrace. The skulls of slaughtered enemies were used as drinking cups, and their skins were tanned to make capes and cushions. Slaves were blinded so that they could not run away. The Scythians' peculiar savagery may have stemmed from their geographical position. Caught between the advanced civilizations of the Middle East and the warrior horsemen of the remote steppes, they had to be merciless in order to survive.

Herodotus also recorded that when a Scythian king died, his subjects embalmed his body and buried it in a square pit covered with stones. Interred with him were horses, personal treasures, and members of his royal household, strangled before burial.

FIERCE FIGHTERS A golden comb from a Scythian tomb bears a typical steppe scene of a warrior skirmish. Scythian art was influenced by the art of the Greeks settled in the Black Sea region.

Many of Herodotus's observations have been confirmed by the excavation of Scythian tombs on the western plains of Asia. But the Pazyryk kurgans reveal aspects of the nomads' life absent from the Scythian tombs. At Pazyryk, precious metals had been plundered, but a unique treasure trove of perishable accessories remained.

When Herodotus described a distant Scythian tribe known as the Argippeans, he may have been referring to the people of the Altai. The tribe occupies an important place in Scythian mythology. They inhabited a remote mountain region, and were known as the keepers of the gold. According to legend, it was they who first stole the precious metal from the guardianship of the griffins – the fabulous winged monsters often represented in Scythian art. In Turkish languages, 'Altai' means 'Country of Gold'.

The people of the Altai were nomads, driving their animals wherever good pasture was to be found. Animal herds were the lifeblood of the community. As long as the herds were fed and watered, the people had enough meat and milk, wool and leather. As soon as a pasture was exhausted the people had to move on. The whole tribe stacked their goods on horses and wagons in the same way as modern Asian nomads such as the Iranian Kashgai and the central Asian Kazakhs.

But the wanderings of the tribe did not follow a wholly random pattern. In the Altai, they were linked to seasonal change and to the ruggedness of the mountain terrain. In spring, the tribe sought grass along the river valleys. Summer was dry and cool – the mountain slopes were alive with plant life, and wild grains made delicious fodder for the herd.

But the season was short. As the weather grew colder, the tribe went into hibernation, living a semi-settled existence. They spent most of their time in circular tents made of felt, stretched over a framework of wooden slats. Dwellings like these, known as yurts, can still be seen throughout central Asia. They also made conical huts of felt and bark stretched over a light framework, which could be constructed against a tree.

DECORATIVE HOME COMFORTS

The nomads had little use for bulky furniture, favouring carpets and hides with cushions of felt, leather, or fur, stuffed with animal hair or grass. Carpets and hangings insulated against the cold, and offered ideal surfaces for decoration. The kurgans of Pazyryk yielded striking examples of native craftsmanship, including immense panels of felt decorated with coloured appliqué work.

Two outstanding furnishings indicate contact with distant civilizations. The first is a carpet of knotted wool, some 2m (6½ft) square, with a red background. Around the edges are geometrical motifs and griffins, a jungle of images through which pass several deer grazing in single file, and a procession of horsemen. The craftsmanship and decorative style suggest that the carpet had been imported from Iran.

The second item is a saddlecloth edged with red and blue felt and inlaid with leather studded with gold and tin. Six great lumps of yak hair hang from it, but the cloth itself is of delicate Chinese silk, with pheasants embroidered amid a swirling mass of multicoloured arabesques. Even in China, silk fabric of this quality was exceptional and found only in the trousseaux of court ladies. It is not impossible that this was the dowry of a Chinese princess. Perhaps she had been married off by a Chinese lord to one of the 'barbarians from the north' in an attempt to stem the raids of the warriors who threatened the peace of his realm – it was against their incursions that the Great Wall was built in the 3rd century BC.

These two pieces demonstrate that the people of the Altai were in some sort of contact with the great civilizations to the east and west of their mountain homeland. A trans-Asian route, a precursor of the Great Silk Road of the Middle Ages, was already being travelled by nomadic merchants. It spanned the vast distance between Persia and China, and the nomadic mountain people must have profited from it.

The few pieces of furniture discovered at Pazyryk are ingeniously adapted to the nomadic existence. There are several small, collapsible wooden tables, consisting of detachable trays resting on four legs, elaborately carved in the shape of cat-like creatures standing on their hind legs. When dismantled, the trays and legs could be stacked for easy transportation. The trays themselves are oval with a rim, and could be used as plates. Vessels such as clay pitchers and wooden bowls were also unearthed, along with a large number of leather containers. Many of these leather pouches, bags, flasks, bottles, and boxes are decorated with superb fur or leather appliqué work.

The men of the Altai spent most of their time on horseback, either supervising the herds or hunting. Riding with bow and arrow, they would defend their animals against attack by predators. The furs of wild animals were useful to the tribe, and could be traded with neighbouring peoples. Sable was the most highly prized fur, but squirrel, otter, panther, wild cat, and ermine were also greatly valued. Swans, wild geese, and grouse provided feathers and down.

DEFENCE AGAINST THE COLD

Men wore trousers of hide squeezed into felt leggings or tucked into boots made of soft leather. Shirts were made of raw hemp fringed with a braid of bright red wool. A kaftan, often made from a hide turned inside out, was worn on top.

Some kaftans were extremely luxurious. One garment found at Pazyryk was made of a velvety sable hide and decorated with finely stitched embroidery of the type seen on Afghan coats today. It was embellished with leather appliqué depicting a stag. The heads of griffins swarmed around the antlers, and the eyes were minuscule beads of gold.

Hats provided vital protection against the icy winds of the steppes. They were made of fur or felt, with ear flaps which could be worn raised or lowered, 'terminating in a point, and standing straight and stiff' in the words of Herodotus. Hats in this style are still worn by Asian nomads.

The exalted female occupants of the tombs were decked out as richly as the men. One woman's kaftan was made of squirrel

AT HOME ON THE STEPPES The modern nomads of central Asia still herd horses and live in yurts – felt tents with a wooden framework. The yurts are easy to pack and transport when looking for new pastures.

LAID OUT IN DEATH
The body lies in a coffin hewn out of a single tree trunk. Hangings cover the larch-log walls. The funeral ceremonies completed, stones and earth were heaped over the burial chamber, creating a telltale barrow or mound.

fur turned inside out, hemmed at the bottom with a wide band of pony skin and edged with otter fur. The sleeves were narrow and purely decorative. The kaftan was worn with a bodice of otter, squirrel, and sable, two pairs of fine felt stockings, and boots of red leather, elaborately patterned – even on the soles.

ANIMAL MAGIC

The grave-robbers of Pazyryk carried off much of its jewellery. But there was one kind of adornment that they did not consider valuable. The arms, legs, and torso of one man were covered with fantastic tattoos. He had pronounced mongoloid features. Though this was unusual at Pazyryk, where most were of a European type, there must have been a Mongol presence on the eastern fringes of the Altai. The man was about 60 years old and fairly stout. The tattoos had obviously been applied while he was young, for they were faded or distorted over the areas where he had gained weight.

An entire bestiary of weird and wonderful animals hugged the curves of his musculature: stags with antlers teeming with the heads of birds, and winged feline creatures with pointed teeth. A fish had been traced between ankle and knee, and four wild sheep ran up the inside of his leg. The head of a lion-griffin had been positioned exactly over his heart. The creature's curving back wound round the man's torso up to the shoulder blade, where the coiled whorl of the tail ended.

This 'Lionheart' had died in battle. His skull had been smashed and the scalp removed – scalping was referred to by Herodotus as a way of appropriating the enemy's vital force. To compensate for the deformity of the skull, before the burial the man's comrades had sewn on a wig. A false beard of horsehair, dyed jet black, had been fixed under his chin.

The practice of tattooing was, like scalping, referred to by ancient writers as one of the more extraordinary habits of the barbarian nomads. The Greeks associated the markings with the degrading stigmata used to brand slaves. But the wearers bore their embellishments with pride. Tattoos are still worn as signs of bravery and nobility by the Kyrgyz of central Asia.

The tattooist's art may have had practical uses, as well as an aesthetic and spiritual resonance. One man found at Pazyryk wore tattoo marks on his ankle and at key points along his spine. The points are well known in acupuncture, a practice widespread among the Asian peoples of his time.

The decoration on the skin, clothes, and household items of the people of the Altai reflects the fact that they lived in intimate contact with the animal world. The piercing eyes and beak of the eagle, the supple spine and sharp teeth of the wild cat, are rendered with expressive simplicity and accuracy. It is as though, by depicting an animal in art, its particular qualities were magically appropriated.

HOUSING THE DEAD

When death came to an important member of the tribe, the nomads exercised their skills in a different form of handiwork, creating burial mounds using rough wooden tools. Samples of these tools survive, including wedge-shaped wooden stakes, their ends hammered flat by mallet blows. The stakes must have been used to break up the ground before the digging began.

All the kurgans were built in roughly the same way, beginning with the construction of a rectangular pit, and inside it a chamber of larch logs to receive the body or bodies. It had a ceiling and plank floor and often double walls. The tomb was then ready for the funeral.

Little is known about the religion of the people of the Altai. Writing of the Scythians to the west, Herodotus noted that 'it was not their custom to raise cult statues, altars, or temples'. No places of worship have been found in the Altai. Since the nomads had no writings, there are no texts to shed light upon their beliefs.

Evidence of ritual practices has been found at Pazyryk – a leather bag containing fingernails and hair, which may relate to some obscure ceremony. There are other indications of practices similar to shamanism, widespread in Mongolia and Siberia.

The shaman was a priest, sorcerer, and healer, the mediator between the natural and supernatural worlds. To reach the spirit world, the shaman would don a stag's head or antlers and enter into an ecstatic trance induced by drugs and music.

LAST RITES

Shamans are likely to have presided over the burials at Pazyryk. From evidence at the site, some aspects of the funeral ceremonies can be reconstructed. They probably took place in the summer, the only time of year when the ground was not frozen. The bodies of the dead were embalmed, the muscle tissue removed through incisions in the skin and the cavities stuffed with grass. The incisions were then sewn up with sinews. The coffin containing the embalmed bodies, perhaps of the chieftain and his wife, was placed inside the larch-log chamber with the possessions that had been chosen to accompany them into the

afterlife: fine carpets and hangings, and vessels of food and drink. The resplendent horses were screened from the coffin area by a wooden partition.

The arrangement of the chamber seems to have been followed by a feast and a ritual fumigation using narcotics. Two of the Pazyryk tombs contained equipment for smoking hashish: small bronze cauldrons which held carbonized seeds of hemp and stones. A framework of sticks supported a miniature felt tent which would have retained the smoke for better inhalation.

Herodotus recorded how the Scythians performed fumigations after funerals, describing it as a 'vapour bath'. The details fit in remarkably well with the evidence that has been found at Pazyryk:

'On a framework of three sticks, meeting at the top, they stretch pieces of woollen cloth, taking care to get the joins as perfect as they can. Inside the little tent they put a dish with red-hot stones on it. Then they take some hemp seed, creep into the tent, and throw the seed onto the hot stones.

'At once it begins to smoke, giving off a vapour unsurpassed by any vapour bath one could find in Greece. The Scythians enjoy it so much they howl with pleasure . . .'

Music almost certainly contributed to the sacred ceremonies of death. Drums made of a membrane stretched across a horn body have been found in the tombs, and are similar to items that are still used in Tibet, Afghanistan, and Iran.

After the last rituals had been performed, the pit was covered with birch bark and twigs, followed by layers of larch logs. The earth dug out earlier was heaped on top, and covered with a pile of stones up to 4.5m (15ft) high. As the centuries passed and the nomads disappeared from the Altai, the stone mounds remained as the only visible testament to their civilization.

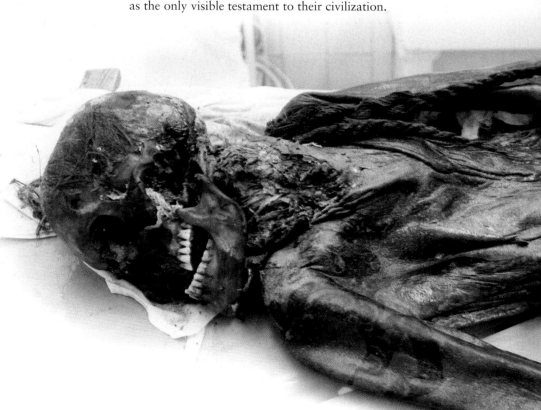

PORTABLE ART Tattoos of mythical beasts decorate the arms of a Pazyryk warrior (above) and the 'princess' (right), a body discovered recently in a frozen burial in the Pastures of Heaven, south-west of Pazyryk.

Preserved through time

Stone, metal, and pottery are almost indestructible, and are often found at ancient sites. But organic materials such as wood and clothing are subject to biological decay – a process which requires oxygen, moisture, and warmth. If one of these three conditions is removed, the material has a chance of survival.

Underwater treasures

Rivers and lakes inhibit the decay of organic materials because they lack oxygen – which is vital to the micro-organisms that cause decay. Europeans of the Iron Age and later regarded watery places as sacred, and left offerings in them of metalwork and even wooden boats. Many European lakes contain the remains of wooden villages once built on their margins.

Submerged coastal settlements and shipwrecks are damaged by ocean movements and the micro-organisms and corrosive salts in sea water, but once settled in silt, the chances of survival are high. The oldest surviving wreck is a Canaanite ship sunk at Kas, off Anatolia, in about 1350 BC.

Nature's way

In exceptional circumstances, organic remains have been preserved by chemicals. In the salt mines of early Celtic Europe, leather rucksacks and clothing used by the miners survived intact – the salt drew any moisture out of the objects. Tannic acid, which occurs naturally in plants, helps to preserve human bodies in environments such as bogs. It destroys bone but preserves the soft tissues by pushing water out of the skin and cementing its protein fibres together. The ancient Egyptians mummified bodies using natron, a dehydrating mineral gathered from the beds and shores of lakes.

Pockets of oxygen-free soil combined with chemicals were responsible for the survival of a series of wooden writing tablets bearing letters to Roman soldiers serving on Hadrian's Wall; these included one – perhaps from an anxious mother – about a parcel of warm underwear she had sent.

CELTIC FACES A pair of votive heads, carved from wood in the 1st century BC, were discovered underwater in a Celtic holy place at the source of the Seine in France.

A MOMENT IN TIME In the salt mines at Hallstatt in Austria, the chemical actions of salt have preserved not only leather objects such as the bag, complete with ties and stitching (left), but also the bodies of several miners.

BODY IN A BOG Tollund man (right), found in Jutland, Denmark, was at first thought to be a fairly recent murder victim, but analysis showed that he died more than 2,000 years ago. His stomach contained barley and wild seeds from his last meal.

Lost in the wetlands

Like lakes and rivers, bogs and marshes preserve organic remains by excluding oxygen. Wetlands are often acidic, which prevents the growth of bacteria. They dissolve bone and preserve skin. A number of wooden trackways survive in waterlogged sites in Europe, such as the Sweet Track in the Somerset Levels in England – the oldest road in the world, built in about 4000 BC. Wooden tools, basketry, and foods such as nuts, have been found near these tracks. But the best-known wetland finds are bog bodies – mainly Iron Age victims of human sacrifice. Often, the wound that caused their death is still visible.

Frozen in time

In the cold regions of Central Asia and the Arctic, temperatures are often too low for organic decay to take place. Spectacular finds have included whole woolly mammoths, frozen corpses clad in garments made of fur, feathers, and skins, and many artefacts made of wood and leather.

In the icy Taklimakan desert in Central Asia, abandoned wooden towns from the 1st millennium BC are still standing. The personal possessions of their inhabitants survive – felt garments, wooden musical instruments, mousetraps, and documents written on wooden slips and paper. They are evidence of the harsh life lived by the Chinese officials sent to man the desert outposts on the ancient Silk Road.

RELICS OF THE HORSEMEN Many tombs of the nomads of the Asian steppes were waterlogged in summer and frozen in winter. Their contents were preserved by low temperatures. The wood and leather horse harness (left) was discovered at Pazyryk.

HOT WORK The desert sands beyond the banks of the Nile in Egypt provided ideal conditions for the preservation of wooden objects, such as the model of a granary (left), placed inside a tomb at Beni Hassan in about 1800 BC.

GHOSTLY FIGURE Lava and red-hot debris from the eruption of Vesuvius in AD 79 destroyed the Roman towns of Pompeii and Herculaneum, but preserved the shape of the victims' bodies (right).

In the heat of the desert

The micro-organisms which cause decay operate most effectively in hot, moist environments, making humid rain forests a poor place to seek organic remains of the past. But when heat is combined with a lack of moisture, the resulting conditions are just right for preservation. Desert caves in the Mexican highlands have provided abundant archaeological material, such as desiccated plant remains, which sheds light on the early history of agriculture in the region. More direct evidence of early foodstuffs has been discovered in coprolites – dried faeces.

Hot deserts have also preserved objects made of wood, rope, reeds, and many other plant and animal materials. In south-west America, desert finds have included rope sandals and decoy ducks beautifully constructed out of reeds, duck skin, and feathers, used for catching wildfowl in about 1500 BC. Even human bodies can survive in these conditions. The corpses of Egyptians buried in desert sands before 3000 BC were perfectly preserved by desiccation – an effect that may have inspired the later practice of mummification.

Preserved by fire

Volcanic disasters have caused widespread loss of life throughout the course of history, but have also frozen moments in time. The volcanic debris that falls around organic material such as human bodies or wooden furniture eventually cools and solidifies. As the organic material decays, it leaves a void inside the debris. Plaster of paris or glass fibre can be poured into the voids to produce casts of vanished people or objects. The heat of volcanic ash and lava has also carbonized objects, such as loaves of bread found in ovens at Pompeii. Fire of any kind carbonizes grain, leaving clues about the staple foods of the past.

Olympia

Site of the Grecian Games

A lush valley on the Peloponnese peninsula provided the backdrop for the Grecian world's supreme festival: the Olympic Games. The Games were held in honour of a battle between two gods, yet they were marked by a nationwide vow of peace.

SINCE THE FOUR-YEARLY CYCLE OF THE MODERN OLYMPICS began in 1896, it has been disrupted by two world wars, terrorist outrage, and political boycott. The Games were revived as a forum for peaceful competition among the world's finest athletes. But the mood of international rivalry surrounding them reflects the tensions that lay behind their origins.

Ancient Greece never became unified as a nation; feuding between its city-states prevented any lasting political cohesion. And yet, once every four years in the month of July, internal warfare was formally suspended. A sacred truce was observed between the states, and for more than 1,000 years – from 776 BC to AD 393 – the Games remained the collective expression of a theme central to Greek civilization: the pursuit of excellence.

Today, the ruins of Olympia still stand in testimony to the glory of the ancient festival of sports. They lie in a fertile valley on the Peloponnese peninsula in southern Greece, nestled between two rivers – the Alpheus, and its tributary, the Cladeus.

A SITE CHOSEN BY THE GODS

Archaeological evidence indicates that Olympia was a place of worship in prehistoric times. Later, it became associated with festivities honouring Zeus, the greatest of the gods. According to legend, Zeus started the tradition of games at Olympia when he wrestled there with his father, fighting for kingship over the gods. Lesser deities then came to the same spot to test their strength. Here Apollo boxed against Ares, the god of war, and ran against Hermes, the messenger. Olympia became a place of divine contest, bounded by rules established by the mighty Hercules.

Olympic Games for mere mortals were established in 776 BC, in honour of a sacred truce made between the warring kings of the city-states of Elis and neighbouring Pisa. Foot races were held, and a man from Elis called Coroebus was the victor. Then, and afterwards, the names of the winning contestants were written down for posterity: the records of the Olympics provide the central chronology of ancient Greek history.

NO HOLDS BARRED While a political truce kept military conflict at bay, international rivalry found a new outlet in Olympic competition. Wrestling and boxing were major events, and a combination of the two known as the *pankration* (depicted here on a vase) was restrained by very few rules – almost any hold was permitted. At Olympia, winners joined the immortals, their likeness carved in stone among the statues of the gods.

The Games expanded over the centuries to include races on horseback and in chariots, jumping and throwing events, and several forms of unarmed combat. By the 5th century BC, the Games had become the supreme festival in ancient Greece, and a fixed programme of competitions had been agreed.

Despite the truce, the control of the Games continued to be a source of friction between Pisa and Elis. By about 700 BC their rivalry became so intense that the Greek states banded together to replace the local truce with a country-wide armistice, a tradition observed throughout the 1,000 years spanned by those early Olympics. Capital punishment was suspended and legal actions postponed. To fight a war during the Games or in the month leading up to them was sacrilege. Any violation of the truce was firmly punished.

PREPARING FOR THE CARNIVAL

The festival was supervised by the people of Elis, and required much preparation. Months beforehand, ambassadors called *spondophoroi* were despatched to the Greek cities and to colonies in Egypt and the Crimea to announce the opening day, and judges were chosen by lot from among the citizens of Elis. The judges, the *hellanodikai*, supervised the athletes' training and organized the events, as well as judging the results.

As soon as the opening day was announced, would-be competitors began training in their home towns. To establish their credentials, they would have to present themselves at Elis one month before the Games to endure a final few weeks of training – set exercises carried out under the watchful eyes of the *hellanodikai*, who wielded their authority by means of the rod.

Rigorous enquiries were made into each applicant's family history, and only free men and boys of pure Greek descent were allowed to compete. The rule was waived only when Rome affirmed her supremacy over the Greek world in the 2nd century BC; Roman citizens were then permitted to enter the Games. Women were not allowed to compete, with the exception of the chariot races, in which the owner of the winning team of horses, rather than the charioteer, was considered the victor. In this event, female owners could, and did, win.

While the athletes trained, vast numbers of pilgrims took to the roads, heading for the secluded valley in which the Games were held. The peace of Zeus guaranteed their safe conduct.

TRAINING GROUND From the end of the 3rd century BC, athletes honed their skills in the Palaestra, an annexe to the Olympic gymnasium. Its covered rooms and porticoes once surrounded a square sports arena.

A CLEANSING RITUAL Athletes spread olive oil over their limbs before each of their events. When the competition was over, the oil was removed from the skin using a curved bronze scraper known as a *strigil*.

Many travelled on foot, sleeping under the stars. The wealthy came on horseback or by chariot. Boatloads of visitors disembarked at the mouth of the Alpheus and followed the course of the sacred river up to Olympia's holy precincts. Acrobats, conjurers, and musicians swelled the throng. Barbarians, slaves, and young girls were admitted as spectators, but married women were excluded – they were forbidden to cross the Alpheus for the duration of the Games, which lasted for five days.

The first of the five days was given over to ceremony – for the offering of sacrifices and the swearing of the Olympic oath. The main sacrifice was carried out on the altar of Zeus Horkeios, or Zeus of the Oaths. Officials, athletes, and their families would assemble in the Bouleuterion, a building erected in the 6th century BC. Here, a wild boar was slaughtered before a statue of the god. Each competitor swore upon its limbs that he would not cheat, had no criminal record, and was entitled to compete under Olympic regulations. Those who broke the oath, or swore it falsely, were fined and banned for life from the Games.

The starting point of the modern Games is marked by the lighting of the ceremonial flame, brought to the host country from Olympia by a relay of runners. Little is known about the sequence of events in the ancient Games, but a fire ceremony took place at some point in the five-day cycle. It took the form of a solemn procession of purple-robed *hellanodikai* entering the stadium to the sound of trumpets, with the athletes following behind. The flame was lit on a sacrificial altar.

On the second day of the Olympics, spectators rose with the dawn to grab the best seats for the first events, congregating in groups according to their city of origin.

GLORY ... AND DANGER

The main competitions were chariot races, horse races, wrestling, boxing, the *pankration* (all-in wrestling), foot races, and the pentathlon. In all events except chariot-racing, the athletes performed naked – the Greeks revered the human form. There were no team sports. Each athlete appeared as an individual, though victory was a glory shared by his whole city.

Horse and chariot races took place in the hippodrome, an arena 706m (2,316ft) long to the south of the main stadium. Horse races began to a blast of trumpets, when the retaining rope was withdrawn. The length of the races is not known, but the jockeys rode bareback, with reins but no stirrups. A horse could win a race even if its rider had fallen. Such was the case with a mare named Aura, which threw her rider at the very beginning of the race, but completed the course ahead of all the others. Her Corinthian owner Pheidolas was declared the winner, and a statue of his mare was erected at Olympia.

The chariot-races were dangerous affairs. The charioteer drove his team of four horses – later, teams of two – with a whip. The course covered 12 circuits of the hippodrome – a distance of some 14km (more than 8½ miles) along a rutted track on unsprung vehicles – a very rough ride. Accidents were common, and it required incredible skill to negotiate at high speed the tight bends, the crashed chariots, and the bodies of fallen opponents. The field at the start might comprise 40 or 50 competitors; on one occasion, according to the poet Pindar, only a single chariot reached the finish.

TESTS OF SKILL AND STRENGTH

The wrestling events were contests of considerable skill. The aim was to throw the adversary three times to the ground so that his shoulders came into contact with the earth. As in modern judo, deft balance counted as much as brute strength.

Yet strength undoubtedly told. One of ancient Olympia's most famous wrestlers, Milo of Croton (in southern Italy), won the championship five times. He became famous for his exhibition feats, which included tying a cord round his forehead, inhaling deeply, and snapping the cord by the expansion of his veins. When the ageing wrestler finally lost during his sixth attempt on the championship, the crowd invaded the stadium and carried him round to tumultuous applause.

In boxing, the competitors' hands were bound in leather thongs which left their thumbs free. Boxing matches had no time limits – adversaries fought on until one raised his finger in defeat. They became a test of sheer endurance. If a fight dragged on, the judges might make the boxers lower their guards and swap blows undefended until one gave in – or collapsed.

Boxing and wrestling were combined in the most demanding of all the fighting events – the *pankration*. Every conceivable type of blow was allowed; the only tactics known to have been banned were biting or gouging an opponent's eyes out. This event was not for the squeamish. The raked ground was sprayed with water, and the bloodied competitors rolled around in the mud, wrenching, punching, and kicking.

The aim was to force one's opponent to admit defeat. Killing was frowned upon: death was a shameful way to terminate a contest of strength. When a pankratist called Arrhichion died in a stranglehold while executing a particularly telling grip on his

Gymnasium   Palaestra   Prytaneion   Temple of Hera

SACRED COMPETITION
Olympia's first temple, dedicated to Hera, was built in about 600 BC. The Temple of Zeus was built in the 5th century BC. Athletes took their oath in the Bouleuterion, then went to the Palaestra or gymnasium for training. The hippodrome and the stadium – which held 45,000 – led off the Portico of Echo, and the Leonidaion served as a luxury hotel for honoured visitors.

ALL-ROUND SKILL The pentathlon tested running, discus-throwing, long jumping and javelin throwing (above and below), and ended with a wrestling match between the highest scorers.

| Bouleuterion | Portico of Echo | Stadium | Hippodrome |

ON YOUR MARKS The toe-grooves on Olympia's stone starting line are just 18cm (7in) apart. The runners' stance was near upright, with one foot just slightly in front of the other.

opponent's toes, it was to the dead man that victory was awarded.

The foot races were run over three lengths: a sprint across the stadium, at a length of 192m (210yd); the *diaulos*, a double length of the stadium; and the *doliochos*, a test of endurance covering 24 lengths – just over 4.5km (nearly 3 miles). There was no marathon. This event was introduced in the modern Olympics to commemorate a legendary feat of 490 BC, when a runner, Pheidippides, is said to have run 35km (22 miles) from the battlefield of Marathon to Athens and died announcing the Greeks' victory over the Persian invaders.

The starting line of the original Olympic stadium still exists. It had room for 20 runners; qualifying heats were run before the finals of the two shorter-distance races. The starting blocks are rectangular stone slabs embedded in the ground, with parallel grooves to give the competitors a toe grip. The starting signal was given by a trumpet blast, or by a shout of '*Apite!*' ('Go!').

In addition to the three foot races, there was a fourth contest, the race-in-arms, run over a distance of 384m (420yd) – twice the length of the stadium – in which competitors wore the armour usually worn by Greek infantrymen or hoplites.

The most characteristically Greek of all the Olympic contests was the pentathlon. This was a multiple event, testing five skills: running, long jumping, discus throwing, javelin throwing, and wrestling. It encouraged all-round excellence, requiring strength and suppleness: the ideal of physical beauty in ancient Greece.

The discus was a circular stone or bronze plate. Those used in the Olympics have not survived, but other Greek examples vary, measuring between 15cm and 23cm (6in and 9in) across, and weighing up to 6.5kg (14lb).

An Olympic champion named Phaylus threw a discus 29m (95ft); the modern record stands at more than twice that – but today's discus weighs about 2kg (4½lb). It also seems that ancient athletes performed only one backward swing of the discus, bending and executing a three-quarter turn; modern throwers spin round two and a half times before releasing it.

When throwing the javelin, it is not clear whether the contestants threw for length or accuracy. The javelin itself was about 2m (6½ft) long. A looped thong, through which the index finger was passed, was attached to the shaft to give the javelin some extra thrust – in the same way that a sling extends the range of a hurled stone.

The long jump seems to have been practised from a standing start, accompanied by the music of flutes to aid the flow of the movement. The jumper held stones or lead weights in each hand and swung them to give greater distance to the leap.

POETRY AND PANEGYRICS

Away from the epic encounters in the stadium or hippodrome, there was also much to entertain the Olympic crowd. Feasting and carousing lasted long into the night. Pedlars sold wine and honey cakes, trinkets and amulets, and effigies of the deities. The multitude provided an audience for demagogues, and formal contests were organized for poets and orators. Many came to exploit their talents and look for new disciples.

The philosopher Plato (429–347 BC) spoke at Olympia, and Herodotus, the 5th-century BC historian, is said to have found fame giving readings of his *Histories* there. It was at Olympia in 380 BC that Isocrates presented his *Panegyrics*, proclaiming the need for peace and unity between the Greek peoples.

The last day of the festival was devoted to the proclamation of the winners and the distribution of the prizes. The immediate rewards were purely symbolic but the winners enjoyed immense glory. The crowd remained hushed while the name of a victor was read out, followed by the name of his father and city. He then received a crown of olive leaves, taken from a sacred olive tree which, according to tradition, had been planted by the hero Hercules himself.

When the ceremony was over, the Olympic champions would walk in a majestic

IN THE RING Wrestlers lock in a firm hold in a bas relief from around 500 BC. Greek wrestling made no allowances for weight and size differences, which some competitors could use to their advantage.

A VICTOR IS CROWNED There were no prizes for taking second or third place in the Greek Olympics – only the ultimate victor in each event received the accolade.

procession, accompanied by the *hellanodikai* and winning horses, into the Altis – a walled grove of sacred plane trees at the foot of Mount Kronos, said to have been consecrated by Hercules.

Special glory was reserved for *periodonikai*: competitors who were victorious not only in the Olympics, but in the full cycle of Greek athletic festivals. The Pythian Games brought crowns of laurel, the Isthmian Games crowns of pine needles, and the Nemean Games crowns of parsley. These symbolic rewards brought unimaginable prestige. Champions returning to their home state were given a thunderous reception. Some victors did not enter their native city through the gates; a breach was made in the walls to turn their arrival into a glorious spectacle.

RANKED AMONG THE GODS

Many victors returned year after year to the Games. Theogenes of Thasos, an unbeatable wrestler, participated in the games for 22 years in the 5th century BC, winning crown after crown. His reputation survived his death, and he received the ultimate accolade: he was declared a descendant of Hercules. From the beginning of the 4th century BC Theogenes was worshipped as a god.

The religious awe surrounding the champions is hardly surprising considering the strength of mythology in ancient Greece. The physical qualities of the athletes were a divine gift, and the Greeks believed that Zeus helped those who helped themselves – through sound and rigorous training. 'Never without effort comes that victory which is the reward of our exploits and the illumination of our life', sang Pindar.

Statues of the victors stood in the sanctuary alongside those of the gods. At least 200 such effigies once stood at Olympia. In 430 BC, the Athenian sculptor Phidias created a 15m (50ft) gold and ivory statue of Zeus on his throne for the god's temple. This giant effigy, set with precious stones, became one of the Seven Wonders of the World.

Champions returning to their home state ... did not enter their native city through the gates; a breach was made in the walls to turn their arrival into a glorious spectacle.

THE GAMES COME TO AN END

Celebrations in honour of Zeus and his champions continued for several days after the events, which were concluded by a banquet held for the athletes and guests of honour in the Prytaneion, or communal hall. Then the crowd would disperse. Tents and booths were packed up. The spectators, hawkers, and pedlars took to the roads, and peace would settle on the sacred precincts of Olympia.

After the Romans conquered Greece in the middle of the 2nd century BC, the fixed programme of the Games suffered occasional interference. In AD 65 the emperor Nero insisted that music and drama be included among the sporting contests. He entered the chariot race himself – using a team of ten horses. He crashed, but still demanded the olive crown of victory. The following year the emperor committed suicide, and this 211th Olympiad was struck from the records.

But such changes by the Roman overlords were rare. The Games continued until AD 393, when the devout Christian emperor Theodosius I suppressed them as a pagan abomination. Earthquakes in the 6th century AD brought floods which deposited almost 5m (16½ft) of alluvial mud over Olympia.

The site lay relatively undisturbed until major excavations began in 1875. Partly as a result of the excitement at the findings, an enthusiastic French sportsman, Baron Pierre de Coubertin, revived the Games as a showpiece for peaceful competition between nations. The 1896 Olympics included competitors from 13 countries. A century later, nearly 200 nations took part, a testimony to the spirit of international cooperation first created in ancient Greece.

Pataliputra

The largest jewel in India's crown

When Alexander the Great's army erupted out of Greece in the 4th century BC, the prospect of fighting the mighty forces of Pataliputra stopped it in its tracks. Today, little remains of the city's imperial majesty except a few eyewitness accounts.

BIHAR TODAY IS ONE OF THE POOREST STATES IN INDIA. It lies 800km (500 miles) south-east of New Delhi, the Indian capital, and is prone both to catastrophic droughts which turn its plains into choking dust bowls, and to monsoon floods which sweep down the Ganges valley, drowning crops and demolishing villages. Its capital, the town of Patna, famed for its rice, is described by modern Indian writers as the subcontinent's grubbiest town. Yet it is built on the site of a once-glittering city – the capital of the kingdom of Magadha, home of the Mauryan and later the Gupta dynasties, which controlled the Ganges valley and much of India from about 320 BC until AD 550. At its height the capital, Pataliputra, was one of the largest cities in the world.

TEMPLE RECORDS AND TRAVELLERS' TALES

The only remains of Pataliputra today are a few post-holes, fragments of wood, stone, and pottery, and chipped earthenware statuettes. If archaeology were the only source of information, much of the city's story would remain obscure, but scholars have used other sources to piece together how it looked.

The most comprehensive source is a book, *Indika*, by a Greek author, Megasthenes (*c.*350–*c.*290 BC), who spent many years as an ambassador to the court at Pataliputra. The original text of *Indika* has been lost, so the information, by other Greek authors who had read his work, is second-hand and sometimes conflicting. Nonetheless, the Greek authors' information is united in portraying a city of great prosperity.

According to these authors, Megasthenes described Pataliputra as 80 stadia long and 15 stadia wide – about 15km (9 1/2 miles) by 2.7km (1 3/4 miles). The whole city, he added, was encircled by a deep moat more than 180m (590ft) wide and a huge fortified wall more than 40km (25 miles) long, studded with 64 gates and 570 towers. The wall was built of timber erected in a double palisade, with earth packed in between. In the 1870s and 1920s, archaeologists found some of these timbers, preserved by waterlogging because of the high water table.

SACRED DOMES Little of Pataliputra remains but clues to the daily life of its people can be found in carvings on stupas – brick or stone domes containing Buddhist relics. Ashoka, emperor in the 3rd century BC, ordered the construction of some 84,000 stupas; the Great Stupa at Sanchi (top right) is the earliest.

SET IN STONE The gateways, or *toranas*, of the Great Stupa at Sanchi demonstrate the sophistication of the culture centred around Pataliputra. They are rich in iconography from both Buddhism and folk religion.

Other sources from which scholars have built up a picture of life in Pataliputra include stone carvings on religious monuments at the shrines of Sanchi and Bharhut in Madhya Pradesh state in central India; letters and essays left by Chinese travellers; and native Indian literature – particularly the *Arthasastra*, probably written by Kautilya, the Machiavellian advisor to the first Mauryan emperor, Chandragupta, who reigned from around 321 to 297 BC.

STRATEGIC POSSIBILITIES

Pataliputra had its origins in a village, Pataligrama, that existed on the site in the late 6th century BC. Its strategic location was appreciated in the 5th century BC by King Ajatashatru of Magadha – a ruler notorious for the murder of his father, King Bimbisara – and he built a fort there. His grandson, Udayin, made Pataliputra his capital. Later rulers strengthened Pataliputra's fortifications.

> *[The] figures for [Pataliputra's] fighting forces spoke for themselves: 200,000 men under arms, 20,000 cavalry, 2,000 chariots, and 3,000 war elephants.*

In 326 BC the troops of Alexander the Great were nibbling at the fringes of the subcontinent, subduing the fragmented kingdoms along the valley of the Indus river in present-day Pakistan. Alexander's spies had told him of the empire of Magadha that lay beyond. They brought figures for its fighting forces that spoke for themselves: 200,000 men under arms, 20,000 cavalry, 2,000 chariots, and 3,000 war elephants. This was a gigantic force, and only an enormously wealthy and well-organized state could have afforded it.

Alexander was ready to risk an invasion. But his war-weary, homesick men refused to go on, and he was obliged to turn back towards the west without giving battle. After he died in 323 BC, his far-flung empire broke apart as his generals set themselves up as rival rulers in different provinces.

In India, meanwhile, the Mauryan emperor, Chandragupta, had exploited the power vacuum left by Alexander's conquests and had seized control of the lands of the north-west, up to the Indus. By about 300 BC, the territories beyond the river were controlled by Seleucus I Nicator, one of Alexander's generals who now ruled an empire stretching from the Indus all the way back to the Mediterranean. Seleucus raised fresh troops in a bid to expand his realms into the Ganges valley, but the war elephants of

Magadha trampled bloody paths through his formations, and hordes of infantry overwhelmed the weary remainder. Seleucus's offensive turned into a humiliating retreat.

The Greeks never again threatened Magadha. But many of the hostages and envoys Seleucus had sent to the court at Pataliputra settled there, including artists, craftsmen, musicians, and soldiers. It was also Seleucus who sent Megasthenes as his ambassador to Pataliputra.

THE GROWTH OF AN URBAN CULTURE

The Mauryan dynasty, founded by Chandragupta, continued under his son, Bindusara, and grandson, the Buddhist emperor Ashoka. They and their descendants ruled the subcontinent from Afghanistan to Bengal (present-day Bangladesh) and south to Mysore until 185 BC.

Pataliputra was at its zenith under the Mauryans. Four main gates led through its high-toothed battlements on the north, east, west, and south sides. Wide avenues led from the gates to the city centre, their central gutters carrying waste water beyond the city walls.

The city was carved into 16 commercial sectors, each assigned to a different guild of craftsmen. The wealthy and the elite lived in brick mansions along the main avenues, near the palaces. Second-rank nobles and merchants lived behind the elite, and so on in bands. The poor lived just inside the city walls, in baked earth hovels.

People washed clothes and watered livestock in the canals which crisscrossed the city. There were inns, hospitals, and art galleries. Ashoka even provided veterinary centres. As a convert to Buddhism, he respected the sanctity of all living things. He is also thought to have ordered the first Buddhist monuments to

REGAL CREATURES Ashoka erected pillars at sites important in the life of the Buddha. The wheel on this pillar, erected at Sarnath, represents the Buddha's first sermon. The lions are symbols of royalty, linking Ashoka with Buddha.

be built at Sanchi, including the Great Stupa, or shrine – carved with pictures which show how life was lived at Pataliputra. The citizens belonged to many rival faiths, and Ashoka tried to develop a spirit of toleration. Respect, he decreed in one edict, was due not only to other people, but also to their beliefs: 'One should honour another man's sect, for by doing so one increases the influence of one's own sect and benefits that of the other man, while by doing otherwise one diminishes the influence of one's own sect and harms the other man's.'

To cater for the population's spiritual needs, great temples stood beside the public squares. Devotees of all the major religions of India had freedom of worship – Buddhists, Hindus, and Jains (members of a sect that broke away from traditional Hinduism in the 6th century BC). Even the Greek gods were tolerated in Pataliputra: the descendants of Greek soldiers were given the same freedom of worship.

LIVING IN LUXURY

The imperial palaces and their outbuildings sprawled across a huge walled compound at the heart of Pataliputra. Armed guards checked the identity of every visitor. Inside the main gate were the royal storehouses, where soldiers and officials collected their pay. Next came the almshouses, where, on fixed days of the year, the king would hand out gifts of food to the sick and the poor. Nearby, horses and elephants bedded down in the royal stables, close to tack rooms full of harnesses, saddles, carriages, gilded ceremonial coaches, and fearsome war chariots spread with tiger and lion skins.

On the edge of the palaces were public rooms: echoing halls supported by hundreds of carved and gilded pillars, decorated with silver birds and golden vines. The halls were used for royal audiences and banquets. Traces of one pillared hall survive in the form of 84 heaps of stone, lying in rows. Alongside, in a richly decorated gallery, the city's painters and sculptors celebrated the achievements of their royal master.

TERRACOTTA GODDESS Female figurines from the Mauryan period may represent mother goddesses or benign female spirits. They are characterized by large breasts and wide hips – symbolizing fertility.

Beyond the halls lay private apartments to which only senior nobles and officials had access. Inside the apartments, a royal arsenal held stores of bows and arrows, lances, swords, daggers, and shields, ready for times of war. The treasury, beside the king's personal rooms, housed a hoard of precious stones, incense, and bars of gold, silver, and iron. Guards patrolled it night and day, and from its contents, a team of jewellers created works of art.

THE ROYAL PAVILIONS

A series of pavilions scattered through the formal gardens contained the private rooms used by the royal family. The interiors were light and airy, and the rooms were sumptuously furnished with cane and wooden furniture, rich fabric hangings and animal skins. The royal residents could look out over gardens stocked with ornamental trees of every variety. Peacocks and tame gazelles wandered about between flowers, fountains, and fishponds.

Among the buildings in the gardens was one which did not have much of a view. This was the harem where the royal princesses and concubines lived, ruled by the reigning queen. Outside its walls, armed women, often dressed as men, stood guard. The princesses and concubines spent much of their time indoors, and most wore very few clothes when inside the harem – often only bracelets on their wrists and ankles and a jewel-studded belt. Occasionally they strolled through their own gardens, or accompanied one another on excursions into the city or to the river, escorted by their female guards.

On rare occasions, the entire court would parade through the city streets to attend a religious festival, or to watch the animal fights staged for the amusement of the people in arenas outside the city walls.

RIVER OF WEALTH

Pataliputra was a city that could afford luxury and extravagance on an almost unimaginable scale. Its wealth depended on trade, and it controlled the Ganges – the main freight route across the north of India. Along the city's northern walls, the fingers of dozens of wharves stretched into the great river. Boats shuttled between landing places and warehouses, unloading produce. Food was a common freight – the population of Pataliputra was too large to feed itself from the produce of its own lands alone. But cotton, stone, timber, and luxury goods also passed through the docks in enormous quantities. The population of the city grew as people were drawn in by its wealth, and new satellite towns sprang up nearby to house the excess.

The last Mauryan emperor, Brihadratha, proved to be weak and ineffective, and fell from power in 185 BC – a victim of internal unrest. The Shunga dynasty took power, and ruled for about 100 years, adding their own monuments to the growing collection at Sanchi. The city's fate over the next 400 years is unclear, but in about 320 AD, another family emerged to restore Pataliputra to its former glory – the Guptas – who, for a time, ruled most of India's east coast almost as far south as Madras, as well as the traditional territory of Magadha. It was to be Pataliputra's last flowering – when the Guptas fell, so did the city.

By the end of the 4th century, Pataliputra was grand enough to impress a traveller from the sophisticated culture of China. The writer Fa Xian visited the city during the reign of

Chandra Gupta II (*c.*380–*c.*415), and was lost in admiration. He wrote: 'The royal palace and the halls in the midst of the city, the wall and the gates with their inlaid sculpture work, seem to be the work of superhuman spirits.' A great Buddhist festival took place during Fa Xian's visit. 'On that day,' he relates, 'the monks and laity within the borders all come together. They have singers and skilful musicians; they pay their devotions with flowers and incense . . . All through the night they keep lamps burning, have skilful music, and present offerings.'

But when Xuan Zang, another Chinese traveller, visited the city in 637, he found heaps of rubble where its monasteries, temples, and shrines once stood. 'Once upon a time,' he wrote, 'these buildings could be counted in their hundreds. Now, only two or three of them are still standing. All that is left, to the north of where the palace was and near the Ganges, is a small town consisting of about 1,000 houses.' Some time between the 5th and 7th centuries, Pataliputra had been destroyed.

A MYSTERIOUS DISAPPEARANCE

What happened to the city? There are several theories. Its final destruction was probably caused by a catastrophic flood in the area in about 575. But it seems that a huge fire may have already played a major part in its collapse – archaeologists have found ash during excavations.

Geologists have speculated that the fire may have been started by an earthquake, because the city is near the edge of a tectonic plate that carries the Indian subcontinent. But the ashes may have been left by invaders. For more than a century, the Guptas and their neighbours were threatened by a tribe from

THE BIRTH OF MEDICINE IN ANCIENT INDIA

Ancient Hindus believed that medicinal knowledge – the 'science of life', or *ayurveda* – was a skill of divine origin. The *Vedas*, pre-Hindu texts of the 2nd millennium BC, discuss it in the form of hymns to the gods. But when doctors began to emerge from the ranks of Indian religious scholars in about 1000 BC, medical knowledge rapidly became accepted in its own right.

Doctors recognized four main types of treatment for the sick: sacred charts, or *nastras*; prayers to the gods; the juices of certain plants and animals; and drugs created by human ingenuity. By the 3rd century BC, this knowledge was being collected and passed on through schools. Under the Buddhist emperor Ashoka, plants were given prominence as a source of cures, and doctors began to prescribe a vegetarian diet as the basis of good health. By this time too, there were experts in diseases of the eye, the nose, and the ears, and others concentrating on diseases of the blood. This type of medicine – known as ayurvedic after its Hindu name – is still used in India. Many of its findings are being studied worldwide, in the hope that this ancient knowledge can throw new light on today's medical problems.

central Asia – the Hepthalites, or White Huns, who invaded northern India during the reign of Skanda Gupta (*c.*455–67). A retaliatory attack on the invaders in the early 6th century brought devastation to Pataliputra when the Huns sacked the city – perhaps they put it to the torch. By the middle of the 6th century, the Huns controlled most of the Guptas' territory.

Their mere presence north of the city would have greatly disrupted the flow of trade on which the empire's wealth was based. The resulting loss of financial power may have ignited social and political tensions among the empire's rulers, perhaps leading to fierce internal disputes among the different factions.

After the death of Skanda Gupta, several different lines of succession developed, which suggests that the royal family fell out over who should take power. If so, this magnificent city may have received its death-wound in the chaos of a civil war. Pataliputra may, in fact, have died by its own hand, leaving only shattered pottery and a few scorched stones in the dust to mark its passing.

ELEPHANT RIDERS Contemporary everyday scenes illustrate the life of the Buddha on a stupa erected at Bharhut by the Shungas. The carvings were commissioned by lay people hoping to gain religious merit.

Mount Li

An army on parade for 2,000 years

The ruthless but efficient king of Qin conquered all the rival Warring States to unite China, becoming its first emperor, Shi Huang Di. His empire surrounds him even in death, guarded by an army of nearly 7,500 terracotta warriors.

DRUNK WITH SUCCESS, REVELLING IN THEIR FREEDOM after years of oppression, the peasant soldiers of the rebel army attacked. The emperor's troops stood fast, their faces impassive as the rabble descended. Still they stood as the enemy soldiers, screaming abuse, stripped them of their weapons and set fire to the ground around them. The emperor's men had no choice. They were not made of flesh and blood.

As the fires raged, the colourful paint on their terracotta bodies began to disintegrate. The green, purple, blue, and red of their garments – colour schemes that identified the individual contingents – gradually took on the same shade of ashen grey.

Yet, despite the fire that stripped them of their colours, each of the pottery warriors remained unique, distinguished from his fellows by the arrangement of his hair and the finer details of his face. The range of different features bore witness to the ethnic diversity of a dominion that stretched from southern China to Mongolia – the empire of the Qin.

A TOMB FIT FOR AN EMPEROR

The rebels were looters, and the army they disturbed in 206 BC were the silent guardians of a tomb set in the plains around Mount Li, 40km (25 miles) east of the imperial capital at Xianyang, near present-day Xi'an.

Forty years earlier, in 246 BC, the new 13-year-old king of the state of Qin had commanded the construction of a funerary city to house his body after death. By the time he died in 210 BC, King Zheng had extended his power over a vast number of territories, and had proclaimed himself the first Emperor of China, Shi Huang Di.

His army accompanied him in death, moulded in terracotta and armed with real bows, spears, and *ge* – Chinese halberds. They were buried in three shallow pits, lined with timbers and floored with tiles. When the rebel army set fire to the pits, the timber chambers collapsed, imprisoning the warriors for more than 2,000 years. In March 1974, peasants digging wells in the Lintong district came upon fragments of the life-size terracotta figures. Archaeologists went on to discover the ancient pits.

ETERNAL SOLDIERS The army's cavalry wore short breastplates, rather than full armour, ready to fight on horseback to defend their ruler, founder of the Qin dynasty. They stood alongside thousands of infantry troops, their officers distinguished by elaborate armour and headwear. Teams of imperial charioteers stood in the wings, their horses primed for action. But when the offensive came, the empire was already on its knees.

SILENT SENTINELS Crossbowmen made up the front ranks in the largest funerary pit. Behind them stood other infantry armed with spears, and six chariots with their officers and horses.

The author of this extraordinary city of the dead, Zheng, ruler of Qin, was born in 259 BC into a period of great change. Qin was a feudal state in which a hereditary aristocracy wielded local power. Since the 8th century BC, neighbouring powers had been fighting over land and shifting their allegiances. These territories became known as the Warring States.

In the 4th century BC, an outstanding political theorist, Lord Shang, became chief minister of Qin. On his advice, the state was transformed into a bureaucracy in which officials were appointed by, and answerable to, the king. Shang was a leading exponent of Legalism, an ideology based on the belief that man is intrinsically selfish, and cannot be expected to respect his leaders and live in harmony without firm state coercion. The philosophy was put into practice through a strict code of laws and well-defined systems of reward and punishment.

LIVING UNDER STATE CONTROL

Agricultural productivity was rewarded and commerce encouraged by state regulation and standardized weights and measures. Peasants were freed of their serf status and their obligations to the now-abolished nobility. But in exchange they faced heavy taxation and were forced into hard unpaid labour on large-scale public works. Initially, these policies brought wealth and power, and when Zheng took the throne of Qin

THE SOLDIERS IN THEIR PITS
The emperor's funerary city covered 2km² (³/₄sq mile). The outer city contained official buildings such as the Sleeping Palace, where the tomb guards and attendants lived. The terracotta army lies buried in three pits outside the funerary city's boundaries to the east. The largest pit, Pit 1, holds 6,000 warriors. Pit 2 (shown in detail below) houses

1,400 soldiers, commanded by two generals (shown in red) and including cavalry (pink), infantry and charioteers (green), standing archers (yellow), kneeling archers (blue), and a reserve force of chariots (orange). Pit 3, the smallest, is the headquarters with a war chariot and 68 elite officers. A fourth pit was never completed, possibly because of the rebel attack of 206 BC, and is empty.

Cavalry

Infantry and charioteers

Standing archers

Kneeling archers

General

General

PIT 2

Unexcavated area

Reserve chariots

Pit 4

Pit 2

Pit 3

Pit 1

Terracotta army

Inner city

Outer city

Shi Huang Di's tomb

he continued his predecessors' policies. By 221 BC he had conquered and absorbed all the Warring States. From his capital at Xianyang, he set about the task of universally imposing the reforms that had made Qin such a success.

Looking back to China's past, he adopted an ancient title, 'Huang Di', or 'August Lord', and added the prefix 'Shi' ('First'). Shi Huang Di saw himself as China's first emperor, the founder of a new imperial line.

In a bid to unify the empire, he imposed many forms of standardization. A single axle width was set for wheeled transport, to ensure that ruts worn into the roads matched all vehicles. The numerous styles of Chinese script were consolidated into a single, standard version, encouraging the exchange of knowledge, and the various coinage systems were phased out in favour of a universal currency.

The emperor also created more than 6,000km (3,728 miles) of new roads across the empire, branching out from the imperial capital. Internal and foreign trade prospered, and foundations were laid for the flourishing networks that would later carry Chinese silk across Central Asia to the West.

THE GREAT WALL

Advanced Chinese civilization developed in the valleys of the central Huang He (Yellow River) and the River Wei, and from there spread east and north-east. This heartland in north China was both the starting point for the colonization of the south and the target of skirmishes and attacks.

Nomads from the steppe region to the north presented a perennial problem to the settled Chinese. They were mobile warriors who could swoop down, attack suddenly, and just as suddenly retreat into the hostile steppe terrain. They did not fight set-piece pitched battles in the time-honoured Chinese manner, but harried their foes from horseback, shooting arrows as they galloped away. The nomads had no permanent settlements which could be attacked and destroyed. Impossible to defeat, they had to be kept at bay.

In Zhou times, many northern states constructed defensive walls around their frontiers to keep out nomads and troops from rival states. Shi Huang Di undertook the mammoth task of joining stretches of these many

short walls into a single Great Wall defending the entire northern frontier of the Qin Empire. He put the task of construction in the hands of his leading general, Meng Tian.

The stonework of the wall which still stands today is largely the work of the later Ming dynasty (1368–1644). The original Qin wall was made of traditional tamped, or tightly packed, earth, sometimes mixed with reeds, branches, or stones, built up in layers inside wooden plank shuttering.

Meng Tian had an army of 300,000 men at his command, including soldiers to ward off attacks by nomads or other hostile groups. The rest were conscripts and convicts, thousands of whom lost their lives in pursuit of their task.

A FORMIDABLE BARRIER
The Great Wall stretches from the Yellow Sea to central Asia, across 2,400km (1,500 miles) from west to east. For most of its length, the wall is about 9m (30ft) high.

THE PRICE OF AGRICULTURAL REFORM

The peasants were the backbone of the Chinese state, and improving agricultural productivity was a major state concern. Shi Huang Di forcibly relocated large numbers of farming families from populous or troublesome regions into areas where he wished to promote agriculture and settlement.

Reliable water supplies were vital, and early in his reign Shi Huang Di commissioned the building of a 150km (93 miles) canal that would carry water from the Jing river, north-west of his capital, to the Luo river to the north-east. The completed canal irrigated 26,680km² (10,300sq miles) of land. A modified version of the watercourse is still in use today.

Rice was the main crop grown in ancient China, along with millet. Peasants also kept chickens, dogs,

UNIVERSAL CURRENCY The Qin's coins were pierced with a hole for carrying on a string, and embossed with symbols from the empire's newly standardized Chinese script.

and pigs, which provided them with eggs, meat for special occasions, and leather. Fish and wildfowl could be caught in the rivers and lakes and in the countryside.

Under Shi Huang Di, life for peasants was mostly prosperous, but a dark undercurrent ran beneath the strict policy of reform. The legal system, while impartial and efficient, was complex and bewildering to its subject peoples. Penalties for violation could be exceedingly harsh. Even minor offences attracted heavy fines or floggings – among these was the crime of dropping litter in the capital city. For more serious transgressions the punishments included the loss of a hand or foot, castration, forced labour, or execution.

Many of the public works on which the peasants toiled as conscript labourers ensured China's future prosperity, and built strong defences against foreign invasion. But at the time, removing the peasants from their land imposed an intolerable burden. It restricted food supplies, gradually bringing the country to the brink of economic disaster.

Shi Huang Di knew that his regime was harsh. In 213 BC, to protect himself from unfavourable comparisons with earlier rulers, he ordered the burning of any books that might inspire dissent, including not only political treatises and histories, but also poetry and other fine literature. Only practical manuals on agriculture, medicine, and divination were to be spared.

In the atmosphere of suspicion and fear that followed, Shi Huang Di came to distrust his scholars, and personally selected 460 of them for execution. They were buried alive. Indirectly, this barbarous act brought about the downfall of his dynasty, for his able eldest son, Prince Fu Su, ventured to oppose him, and was banished. When the emperor died, he was succeeded by his indolent and self-indulgent younger son Er-Shi.

LABOURING ON THE TOMB

And all this time, work had proceeded on the funerary city the emperor was creating for himself, with more than 700,000 labourers conscripted to this mammoth task alone. According to Chinese historian Sima Qian (c.145–85 BC), Shi Huang Di's tomb represented the Qin Empire in miniature. Through it ran shimmering trails of mercury symbolizing the Huang He (Yellow River) and the Chang Jiang (Yangtze), flowing into a silver ocean. The ceiling mimicked the heavens, recording the constellations of the night sky. When completed, a massive copper sarcophagus containing the emperor's body lay at its heart, surmounted by a tumulus 115m (377ft) high.

To guard against robbers, Shi Huang Di had ordered traps to be set, including crossbows ready to shoot anyone who entered the tomb. Nobody knows how effective these deterrents were, since the immense mound covering the burial chamber has not yet been excavated. The treasures described by Sima Qian, which include pine trees carved out of jade and birds crafted in silver and gold, may still be there, waiting to be discovered. The terracotta army, meanwhile, was buried about 1.6km (1 mile) away, drawn up in full battle order, ready to fight for the emperor in the afterlife as its flesh-and-blood counterpart had done during his

PATIENT ARTISTRY
The terracotta army was moulded from local clay. Parts such as heads and hands were made separately and joined together. A thin additional layer of clay, spread over the basic form, allowed the modelling of fine details.

CHINA AND ITS DYNASTIES

From an early date Chinese historians divided the history of their country into dynasties. This was not just a useful means of classification – it had a more fundamental basis. For the Chinese, history was not a development, but simply the maintenance of a traditional, heaven-ordained order.

The country flourished under virtuous emperors, who were blessed by heaven, but moral lapses on the part of an emperor would bring the displeasure of heaven on him and his country. The founder of a dynasty was always a capable and fortunate man leading China into a glorious age, but decline under incompetent rulers would lead to the dynasty's overthrow by a man chosen by heaven. Gaps between the periods listed below indicate times of division in which several dynasties ruled side by side.

1750–1027 BC	Shang dynasty
1027–249 BC	Zhou dynasty
221-206 BC	Qin dynasty
206 BC-AD 220	Han dynasty
AD 221-280	Time of the Three Kingdoms
AD 265-316	Western Jin dynasty
AD 317-419	Eastern Jin dynasty
AD 420-580	Time of the Six Dynasties
AD 581-618	Sui dynasty
AD 618-906	Tang dynasty
AD 907-960	Time of the Five Dynasties
AD 960-1279	Song dynasty
AD 1280-1367	Yuan dynasty
AD 1368-1644	Ming dynasty
AD 1644-1911	Qing dynasty

40-year reign. Each clay soldier is believed to have been modelled from life – none is the same. Their heads and torsos are hollow, but the legs are solid to carry the weight.

An unusual alloy was used to make their swords and spears – most of them looted by grave robbers. It is composed of 13 elements, including copper, tin, nickel, magnesium, and cobalt, and was treated with a preservative. This has proved so effective that even after 22 centuries the weapons have not corroded. When they were dug up, the blades of some of the surviving weapons were still sharp enough to slice through a hair.

PROVOKED INTO REBELLION

According to many historians, the revolt that destroyed the Qin Empire began when a group of peasants making their way to join the army as conscripts were delayed by heavy rain. Knowing that the penalty for their late arrival would be death, they chose instead to abscond. They became the nucleus of the rebel army that ransacked Shi Huang Di's tomb in 206 BC.

Shi Huang Di has been both admired and execrated by posterity. His shortcomings are obvious, yet he also worked tirelessly to unify the disparate lands under his control; he claimed that he never went to bed without completing a daily quota of 50kg (110lb) of documents. The imperial lineage he dreamed of founding extended to a mere three rulers – his father, himself, and his son Er-Shi. Nonetheless, it was Shi Huang Di who laid the foundations of the Chinese Empire that was to endure and prosper under the succeeding Han dynasty.

Delos

The birthplace of Apollo

Today, the sacred island of Delos in the Cyclades is almost deserted. But in the 2nd and 3rd centuries BC it was the linchpin of a multitude of trading routes, and became one of ancient Greece's busiest and most prosperous ports.

THE FIRST GLIMPSE THE TRAVELLER CAUGHT OF THE TINY ISLAND OF DELOS during its heyday would have been of a rugged mass of granite rising from the violet of the Aegean Sea. A long harbour stretched for more than half a mile in front of a large settlement at the north end of the island: a vast complex of docks and piers hugging the shoreline, with warehouses lining the quays. Behind the harbour the city spread in wild confusion towards the slopes of Mount Cynthus. With more than 20,000 people crammed into such a small area, Delos must have been one of the most densely populated places in the ancient world.

HOME OF THE GODS

Delos (now Dhílos) lies within the Cyclades, the 'encircling islands', scattered across the Aegean Sea south-east of mainland Greece. From about 3,000 BC a remarkable and enigmatic Bronze Age culture emerged on the islands – a culture notable for its elegant pottery and simple marble figurines. But the Cycladic culture had begun to lose its individual identity by the end of the Early Bronze Age, and was finally swamped by Minoan and Mycenaean cultures during the second millennium BC.

In Greek mythology, Delos had originally been a floating island. When Apollo's mother, Leto, was pregnant by Zeus, the earth was forbidden to offer her shelter, for she had angered the goddess Hera, the jealous wife of the great god. But Neptune took pity on the fugitive. He struck Delos with his trident, mooring it in place. Because the island had been floating at the time the ban was imposed on Leto, it was permitted to shelter her. In a cave nestled into the slopes of Mount Cynthus (now Cythos), Leto spent nine days and nights giving birth to the divine twins: Apollo – the symbol of youthful manly beauty – and his sister Artemis, the huntress.

These mythological connections gave the island an aura of sanctity. A geological fault in the mountain housed the oracle of Apollo, and the island boasted an altar to the god considered by some as one of the wonders of the world – a marvel to rank with the pyramids of Egypt and the Colossus of Rhodes.

A HERO TRIUMPHS Greek pottery was often decorated with scenes from everyday life or mythology. The 5th-century BC vase shows Theseus slaying the Minotaur, the legendary event celebrated by Delian dancers.

According to legend, the altar had been set up by Apollo himself when he was only four years old, and was made from the horns of goats killed on Mount Cynthus by Artemis. The temple lay in the heart of the island's huge religious complex – the hieron, hemmed in by the Sanctuary of Artemis, the Sanctuary of the Bulls, a colossal statue of Zeus, Apollo's father, and five small buildings used as treasuries.

Great festivals in honour of Apollo were held on the island at four-yearly intervals. The Delian games were held annually, when sacred envoys, or *theoroi*, were sent by the Athenians and the inhabitants of other islands in the Cyclades to offer sacrifices at the hieron. Every four years, the island was also the site of ceremonies and sacrifices in preparation for holy festivals.

Religious festivals made Delos famous throughout the Greek world. Ritual ceremonies included a dance that commemorated the Greek hero Theseus and his escape from the Cretan labyrinth after he had killed the half-man, half-bull Minotaur. Delian dancers followed a complicated pattern around an altar made of goats' or bulls' horns, imitating the circuitous route taken by Theseus out of the maze where the monster had lurked.

The impressive temples and sanctuaries attracted tourists and pilgrims from all over the ancient world who contributed to the island's economy. New settlers brought new gods, creating an eclectic mix of sacred buildings on the terraces of Mount Cynthus, including the Serapeion dedicated to Serapis, a Graeco-Egyptian god from Alexandria, and a temple of Isis – the Egyptian deity who, during the Hellenistic Age, became one of the leading goddesses of the Mediterranean world.

A STRATEGIC SITE

The inhabitants of Delos were originally a seafaring people and, before trade made them wealthy, fishing provided their main source of income. The island is also known to have abounded in game. Yet in the age of classical Greece, neither hunting nor agriculture was the chief means of livelihood among the common people. The inhabitants produced enough to feed only a quarter of the population. But the island's position was to shape it a new role as a trading centre. In the middle of the Aegean Sea, it stood at the crossroads of shipping routes between Greece, Asia Minor, Thrace, Crete, and the Levant.

The Cyclades archipelago includes more than 200 islands which formed a series of stepping-stones, allowing vessels to sail almost continuously within sight of land; Delos itself offered sheltered anchorage to ships sailing between Míkonos and Rinía. In the 5th century BC, under the leadership of Athens, Delos became the centre of the Delian League – a federation of more than 200 Aegean city-states and islands formed to maintain Greece's independence from Persia. This honour at first brought Delos prosperity, but in 454 BC the League's treasury was moved to Athens for greater security.

The island's greatest wealth was not to come until the 2nd century BC. Delos profited from the Roman conquest of parts of Greece. With the help of Athens, Rome defeated the Macedonian king, Perseus, in 166 BC – and gave Delos to her ally as a reward. The Romans also made the island a free port, to the disadvantage of Rhodes, which had sided with the Macedonians. From then on, merchants abandoned Rhodes and flocked to Delos.

Twenty years later, after the Roman destruction of Carthage and Corinth in 146 BC, Delos became a crossroads for trade routes from the East. Its role as a transit port for Roman trade between Italy and the eastern empire became still more important in 133 BC with the death of Attalus III, king of Pergamum in Asia Minor, who bequeathed his kingdom to Rome.

THE GROWTH OF TRADE

The Romans and southern Italians, mostly of Greek extraction, were the first to take advantage of the absence of customs duties. They established themselves next to the Sacred Lake, an enclosed pool of water north of the main quay. Here, towards the end of the 2nd century BC, they built an agora, or marketplace. This vast, four-sided square was surrounded by colonnaded, two-storey galleries, with elegant mosaics on their ground floors. Inside were the shops and offices of Italian traders and bankers.

HOMAGE TO APOLLO A line of regal stone lions look towards Apollo's birthplace on Mount Cynthus. They were erected in the 7th century BC, in the island's early days as a cult centre. Seven survive from an original ten.

THE DIVINE TWINS A decorative 5th-century BC water pot shows the virgin huntress Artemis, born on Delos, pouring a libation at the altar of her father Zeus while her twin brother Apollo plays a lyre.

All foreign traders and shipowners were grouped, according to their country of origin, under the protection of a number of Hellenized gods – various native gods who, as the influence of Greece spread, had been assimilated into the Greek culture. Phoenician merchants, for example, originally from Berytus (now Beirut), were known as Poseidoniasts. They had probably identified their own god Melqart with the Greek sea god Poseidon, whose festivals, the Poseideia, were held on Delos.

Delos soon became the main marketplace of the eastern Mediterranean. Sheltered by the other Cycladic islands, it was seen as a safe port, and goods of every sort were taken there and resold immediately, some of them hardly touching the quay. The Macedonians brought wood and pitch. The Peloponnesians and Ionians came to trade their wines, and the Phoenicians brought their purple-dyed cloth. The Greeks from Alexandria brought goods from as far away as India – gold, gems, ivory, spices, and strange animals. It is even possible that silk, transported at great expense from China, passed through the island's ports. But these products were, on the whole, exotic luxuries. What made the wheels of commerce turn were three main commodities: olive oil, cereals, and slaves.

It was at Delos that the price of olive oil from the various regions of the eastern Mediterranean was fixed. During the first half of the 2nd century, the price stuck at around 16 drachmas a metrete (39 litres/68 pints). But in the Italian markets, the price of oil was much higher, and rising steadily. As a result, importing it into Italy became a lucrative business.

The cereal market revolved around trading wheat and a type of grain known as olyra. Most of the corn came from Egypt, from Greek colonies on the Black Sea, and, before the destruction of Carthage, from North Africa. Judging from the honours that the Delians heaped upon Mithridates VI (120–63 BC), king of Pontus in Asia Minor, the Black Sea cities must have been important trading partners.

MYTHS IN MOSAIC The floors of affluent homes on Delos were carpeted with fantastical mosaics, such as the 2nd-century BC scene showing Dionysus riding a panther.

In the lively bustle of the quays and marketplaces of Delos, the busiest place of all was the slave market, where as many as 50,000 slaves were sold each day. Another effect of the destruction of Carthage and Corinth – themselves important marketplaces – was the rise of the slave trade in Delos. Not only did Delos inherit a large part of the custom built up by the two cities, its markets also sold large numbers of Carthaginian and Corinthian captives.

Delos also benefited from being close to Cilicia, a district in south-eastern Asia Minor. As the Seleucid dynasty – which ruled Cilicia from Antioch – crumbled, the region's sailors turned pirate. They arrived at the markets of Delos with bursting ships, ready to dispose of their plunder and their prisoners. So great was the demand for slave labour, especially among the Romans, that each ship's cargo of men, women, and children was hardly unloaded before it was sold to the highest bidder. The slaves were stripped and put on display on a platform. From their necks hung notices specifying their origins and abilities.

The dealer shouted to attract the attention of the customers before starting the bidding. If a large number of slaves was to be sold that day, they might be auctioned off in job lots. Sometimes the traders covered up their slaves' defects, or failed to mention diseases from which they were suffering. As a result, the Romans were forced to legislate against fraud.

Many men of means who had been captured and carried off by pirates quickly bought their freedom. They had to pay their ransom through the Temple of Apollo at Delphi – like Delos, Delphi was a major centre of Apollo worship – before being officially freed in a public ceremony which was performed in Delos's theatre at the foot of Mount Cynthus.

Thousands of slaves and freed slaves lived on the island. They were allowed to form associations and to hold banquets celebrating religious festivals. The associations were chaired by dignitaries who have left inscriptions dedicated to their gods in one of the markets near the harbour.

MAKING A HEALTHY PROFIT

Commercial traffic on such a scale involved enormous transfers of funds; consequently as the volume of trade increased it was accompanied by a banking boom to cope with the new demands. The result was a sophisticated system of loans and bills of exchange. The Greek financial world operated using an even greater variety of currencies than exist today – every kingdom and sovereign city produced its own. Moneychangers set up shop near the markets and ports. They worked at tables arranged out in the open, or in small shops.

When forecasting his profits, the Delian merchant, like any modern businessman, had to weigh up a number of factors: the initial price of the merchandise, the transport costs, and the exchange rates between different currencies. He would buy, for example, 3,300m³ (116,500cu ft) of wheat in Egypt for 25,000 drachmas, and load it on board ship. The journey from Egypt to Delos would cost him a further 5,000 or 6,000 drachmas. The going price for wheat in Delos in about 190 BC was 20 drachmas a cubic metre (35cu ft), so he could then resell his cargo for 66,000 drachmas.

Such attractive profit margins justified the high interest rates charged by the moneylenders. For the majority of loans, the going rate was 12 per cent, reduced to 10 with a guarantee. On some goods, such as iron or grain, the interest was charged in kind; but such loans were given only for a few months, and the penalty for late repayment could be up to half of the amount lent. Because of the risks involved in shipping, the interest rates for marine loans were also high – as much as 24 per cent in the province of Thebes in the 3rd and 2nd centuries BC.

LIFE OUTSIDE THE MARKETS

Delos was more than just a trading centre – it was home to tens of thousands of people. Thanks to the efforts of French archaeologists in the second half of the 19th century, many of its ancient buildings have been uncovered. These, more than the legends, evoke the life of the island and its inhabitants.

The quays, cluttered with bales and earthenware jars, ended in elegant colonnades, and beyond them, winding streets led towards Mount Cynthus. To the south-east, the streets converged on the theatre and the crowded residential quarter, where large, luxurious houses dwarfed miserable, single-room shacks.

Most of the houses were built of the island's granite and schist – a crystalline rock which splits easily. Marble from Delos and the neighbouring islands of Páros and Náxos was used in the construction of public buildings and the homes of the well-to-do. The houses of the affluent were two storeys high, with colonnaded balconies and rooms looking out onto a central courtyard surrounded by rows of columns. While the poor in their shacks had to make do with rough matting thrown onto a floor of beaten earth, the rich had floors of dazzling marble or mosaic, and walls brightly painted with trompe l'oeil scenes and frescoes similar to those at Pompeii.

Statues were often placed in the middle of reception rooms or in niches in the walls, a custom that had been introduced in the 4th century BC. In ancient Greece, the purpose of statues had been to honour the gods or commemorate champion athletes. They had been placed in sanctuaries and temples, along sacred ways leading to shrines, on the streets, and in city squares. But after Alexander the Great had established his empire throughout the Middle East, during the Hellenistic Age, foreign influences began to creep in. Artists started to sculpt mere mortals, and statues were used to decorate the interiors of wealthy homes. Art was becoming less sacred and more ornamental. In the home of Cleopatra, a wealthy Athenian who had settled on Delos, full-length statues of the owner and her husband have been found.

So many people were crowded onto this barren island that water must have been in short supply. There was a spring, a well, the Sacred Lake, and a few streams which ran dry as soon as spring came round. These were clearly not enough to supply the island's needs. To cope with the problem, a large number of rainwater cisterns were installed: privately in the courtyards of the large houses and publicly in the squares. It was to these that the women came to draw water.

Carrying pitchers on their heads or shoulders, they threaded their way through the incessant traffic of animals and people. The residential quarter resounded to the cries of small traders, who hawked their wares by the side of the street or in open stalls on the ground floor of houses.

Near the stalls were the workshops of the craftsmen: fullers, potters, ironsmiths, and goldsmiths. Most of their products were for local use, but some items, such as lamps, small terracotta ovens, and bowls decorated with relief work, were made for export. Some Delian

> *The residential quarter resounded to the cries of small traders, who hawked their wares by the side of the street or in open stalls on the ground floor of houses.*

products acquired a certain fame throughout the Greek world. Luxury goods, on the other hand – such as jewellery, ceramics, glassware, stone tableware, and furniture made from rare wood – were imported. They arrived from Athens, Corinth, the affluent cities of Asia Minor, and Alexandria – the city in Egypt named after the conqueror Alexander, which was fast becoming the new Athens of the Hellenistic world.

THE RUIN OF AN ISLAND

During the 1st century BC, the island's halcyon days came to an abrupt end. Protracted wars between Rome and Athens brought destruction in their wake; in 88 BC, while still at the height of its power, Delos was sacked by the army of Mithridates, the king whom they had honoured, during one of his wars against Rome. Trading alliances biased against the island quickly sapped its strength. Twenty years later, marauding pirates robbed Delos of its last vestiges of grandeur.

In 42 BC, Athens regained control of Delos, but by then the banking and commercial enterprises had disappeared. Pausanias, a Greek writer visiting the island in the 2nd century AD, described it in his *Guide to Greece* as being deserted except for a few Athenian officials. He commented: 'Were the temple guards withdrawn Delos would be uninhabited.'

Today the island is still almost uninhabited. And yet a complete city remains. Though in ruins, the temples, theatres, streets, spacious villas, and meaner residential quarters reveal every aspect of a once-great Graeco-Roman civilization.

FINDING FRESH WATER Public cisterns beneath the streets of Delos provided a ready supply of water, though most of the houses had their own roof cisterns to collect the rain.

Petra

Desert home of a trading empire

For nearly 500 years, the Nabataeans controlled one of the most important trade routes in the world. The remains of their capital – huge, elaborately sculptured facades – are hewn from the rose-red rock of a mountain stronghold.

THERE IS A CONCRETE HIGHWAY NEAR PETRA TODAY. It runs alongside the Esh Shara mountains, which surround the city like ramparts, on its way from Amman, the Jordanian capital, to the Gulf of Aqaba, a popular holiday area. The highway does not enter Petra – the only way into the city is along a sinister-looking defile through the mountains, known as the Siq.

As you enter the dark mouth of the Siq – on foot, or on a Bedouin pony – the 21st century vanishes with the sun at the first turn. Sandstone cliffs tower over both sides of the track, rising as high as 60m (200ft). The enclosed pathway twists for nearly 2km (1¼ miles). Now and again, opposing walls almost meet, and nothing but blackness can be seen against the glaring line of the desert sky.

The end of this dark valley opens out onto a terrace, where a rose-coloured city blooms in the arid landscape. The crystalline sandstone of its major buildings blazes red, orange, and darkest crimson, depending on the angle of the sun. As each day comes to a close, the facades flame higher as the dying light turns their bases into smoke, then charcoal, until all the buildings are in shadow. Last to fade, and first to catch the morning light, is the tallest peak, the 1,200m (3,937ft) mountain, Umm el-Biyara.

A GLISTENING JEWEL IN A DUSTY DESERT

Why was a city built here, in such a barren wasteland of rock and sand? It lay on what were, around the time of Christ, two of the ancient world's most important trade routes. The first route linked east and west – joining Arabia and the Persian Gulf with the Mediterranean. The second connected south and north – the Red Sea and the civilizations of Syria. Petra's desert fortress controlled the crossroads. The city also contained the region's main water supply, which became known as the Wadi Musa, or Valley of Moses. It is said to be fed by the stream that Moses made gush from a rock to quench the thirst of the Israelites after they fled across the Red Sea to escape the Egyptians. Merchants guiding loaded camels through the dry, empty landscape had no choice but to head for Petra.

A ROYAL TOMB The facade known as the Deir is thought to have been the mausoleum of the Nabataean king Rabbell II, who died in AD 106. After his death, the Romans annexed the desert kingdom. The following centuries saw Damascus (Dimashq) overtake Petra as a linchpin of major trading routes. The city's wood and mud buildings eventually crumbled away, leaving only these monumental carvings in the sandstone cliffs.

arrived to be sold to traders from the Red Sea and the Persian Gulf. For a time, Petra was so powerful that its people controlled territory as far away as modern Israel. In the early part of the 1st century AD they were masters even of Syria. When, as the Bible records, St Paul escaped from Damascus by being lowered down the city wall in a basket, it was Nabataean guards he was evading.

Ideas flowed along the trade routes, too: from a mixture of architectural and artistic traditions, the city devised its own cultural amalgam of East and West. Its also absorbed a broad range of military and technical knowledge. Its citizens became experts in conserving rainwater, capturing it as it ran off the bare stones of the mountains and guiding it into fields and cisterns, and damming the region's streams to save water for periods of drought. This enabled them to win enormous agricultural yields from the surrounding hostile terrain.

Petra's wealth, remoteness, and impregnability made it a formidable enemy, and the city was left to develop largely in peace. Even the Roman takeover in the 2nd century hardly affected the Nabataeans' individuality. The tomb of one of the city's Roman administrators, Sextus Florentinus, built in about AD 130, is Nabataean in style, with no Roman influences.

The people who built Petra are known to modern scholars as the Nabataeans. They emerged as nomads from the deserts of northern Arabia around 400 BC, and by about 300 BC, when they make their first appearance in recorded history, they had already begun to turn their settlement into a trading post.

Around that time, they demonstrated to the rest of the ancient world that they were not to be trifled with – not even by the conquering armies of Alexander the Great. After Alexander's death, one of his lieutenants, Antigonus, tried to add Petra to the portion of the empire he had inherited. One of Antigonus's generals did succeed in overrunning the city, but as the general's army straggled back across the desert laden with prisoners and plunder, the Nabataeans massacred almost the entire force. A second expedition under the command of Antigonus's son ended as disastrously as the first. Later, in the 1st century BC, the Roman general Mark Antony offered to conquer Petra for Cleopatra – but he made the same miscalculation as the Greeks. His forces, and hers, were destroyed.

TRADE ROUTES TO A MERCHANTS' PARADISE

According to the Greek geographer Strabo (63 BC–AD 21), Petra in its prime was the most important marketplace of the Eastern world. Arabian myrrh, frankincense, and spices moved up the trade routes from the city to the Mediterranean. Copper, iron, pottery, sculptures, and the purple-dyed cloth of the Phoenicians

DISCOVERING THE FORGOTTEN CITY

Only when other cities and newer, safer caravan routes weakened the Nabataean stranglehold on Middle Eastern trade did Petra become vulnerable to outsiders: first to the Roman emperor Trajan in the early 2nd century AD; then to Arab invaders; and finally to Christian crusaders, who built a castle above the city during the early years of the 12th century. After the Christians left, the city was forgotten beneath a shroud of sand for 700 years. It was discovered again only in 1812 by a daring Swiss explorer named Johann Ludwig Burckhardt.

Burckhardt was a colourful figure from a heroic age of exploration. Having taught himself Arabic and obtained a deep knowledge of the Koran, he explored North Africa and the Middle East in Arab disguise, using the assumed name of Sheikh

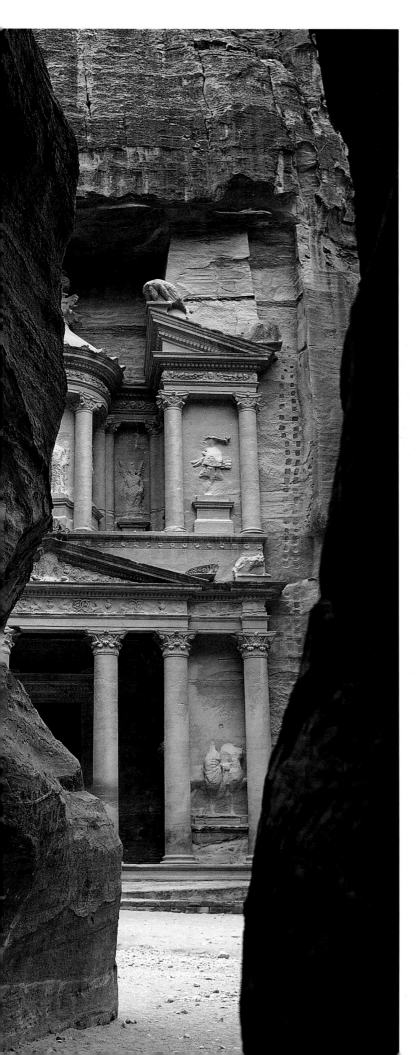

Ibrahim ibn Abdullah – a name he maintained throughout his travels, and under which he was buried. Posing as a faithful believer, he even entered the holy city of Mecca.

Burckhardt saw the monumental façades of Petra on his way from the Jordan Valley to Egypt, where he hoped to explore the sources of the Nile. He was struck with wonder, but a suspicious local guide forbade exploration, and he could only jot down surreptitious notes as his camel moved along.

Sketchy as they were, Burckhardt's notes lifted the veil of obscurity from the city, and Petra was more thoroughly explored in 1826 by an enthusiastic young Frenchman, Léon de Laborde. His magnificent illustrated study *Voyage de l'Arabie Pétrée* (*Journey in Petrean Arabia*), published in 1830, placed the unique desert spectacle clearly before Western eyes.

Laborde found evidence of a sophisticated, cosmopolitan culture. The Nabataeans had used their wealth to incorporate into their city elements of both Arab and Mediterranean culture. Their skill, for example, in designing and cutting huge areas of rock is reminiscent of the achievements of the pyramid-builders. But their architectural style, using broad pediments, ledges, and recesses, owed more to the elegance of Greece and Rome.

SUNLIGHT ON THE DEIR   After its rediscovery by Burckhardt, many 19th-century travellers visited Petra. Among them was David Roberts (1796–1864), whose lithographs record its ethereal beauty (above).

Evidence from ancient historians suggests that Petra was organized as a tribal monarchy, and one remarkably open and free for the period. Disputes were settled by customary laws and by arbitration. Women held an honoured position in society, there were no slaves, and nobody was exempt from work. At the pinnacle of society was the king, surrounded by a handful of ministers; they, too, did their share of work. The historians record that, on occasion, they would wait personally on their guests, observing the dignified code of desert hospitality.

A SANDSTONE TESTAMENT

The city that is visible today is incomplete. In Petra's heyday, the bowl of land within the mountains would have been cluttered with thousands of private houses, inns, stables, and warehouses. But most of these buildings would have been made of sun-baked mud and tree branches, and have long since been reduced to dust. All that remains are the ruins of the great central temple known as the Qasr el-Bint, and more than 500 façades hewn into the cliffs. The largest, measuring 46m (151ft) across and 42m (138ft) high, is known as El Deir, The Monastery, because early Christian hermits made it their home.

Behind some of the façades are a few bare, bleak chambers. The largest chamber is inside the Khazneh Firaoun, the Treasury of the Pharaohs. But even that is only a simple cube about 22m (72ft) across, with a smaller room on each side.

It seems that, despite their palatial appearance from outside, most of the carved cliffs were the homes of the dead, not the living. Archaeologists now believe that, although a few may have been shrines, the vast majority contained tombs. And since the Nabataeans sign-posted their entrances so unmistakably, the contents have long vanished.

ROYALTY AND RELIGION

Petra reached the peak of its wealth and beauty, archaeologists believe, between about 50 BC and AD 70. For much of that period, the Nabataean Empire was ruled by King Aretas IV, a monarch whose wisdom was so widely recognized that the Greeks gave him the nickname Philodemos – 'he who loves his people'. Under Aretas and his predecessors, the Nabataeans spoke Aramaic, the language used in commerce throughout the

ROCK-HEWN IDOLS
The Nabataeans carved conical or rectangular stone obelisks, often with stylized facial features, as images of their gods. Obelisks here on the high plateau of Jebel Madhbah are believed to represent the deities Dushares and Al Uzza.

Middle East, and the language spoken by Christ. The Nabataeans' supreme god, Dushares, symbolized fertility, and his consort, Al Uzza, was the goddess of water – the source of life in a desert kingdom.

As well as these major gods, the people adopted their own versions of numerous Eastern gods. Supporting these deities was a whole gallery of demi-gods derived from the city's kings and local heroes. Important religious ceremonies were held in the open air on the heights around the city. These 'high places', as scholars call them, were flat plateaus where altars were carved out of the mountain summit, some of which may have been covered with beaten gold. The best preserved of these open-air sanctuaries is known as the Zib Atouf. The peak towers above the inner mouth of the Siq, and the only way up to it is along a winding, narrow staircase, sharply cut from the rock.

Important religious ceremonies were held in the open air . . . altars were carved out of the mountain summit, some of which may have been covered with beaten gold.

FROM TRADING POST TO CHRISTIAN GARRISON

The rulers of Petra may well have thought that there could be no end to their prosperity. But under the unified rule of the Romans, an older and more economic trade route far to the north of Petra was reopened. This route, which was paved during the reign of the emperor Diocletian and is known to scholars as the Strata Diocletiana, ran north-east from the Syrian capital, Damascus (Dimashq), to the banks of the Euphrates. From there, traders could load their goods onto dhows and float them down the river to the Persian Gulf.

At the same time, overland caravans bringing incense from southern Arabia to Petra petered out as seaborne traffic took over, travelling through the Red Sea to India and beyond, controlled from Alexandria in Egypt. By the 3rd century Petra had been eclipsed by the main city on the Strata Diocletiana, Palmyra, about 160km (100 miles) from Damascus.

SACRIFICIAL STONES Thousands of Nabataeans would have gathered in Petra's open-air sanctuaries to watch priests perform religious rites, including animal sacrifices. It is still possible to see channels in the rocks where blood drained from the altars.

With the traders went the city's wealth and much of its population – labourers, soldiers, and camel-drivers. Inns closed, marketplaces shrank, and the farmers who fed the city let their outlying fields revert to dust.

From the 5th century, Petra became the home of Christian monks and hermits, and the Arab conquest in 636 did not halt its decline. When the seat of Arab power shifted in the 9th century from Damascus to Baghdad, the road past Petra became obsolete. Six hundred years later, Christian crusaders hardened by the battle for Jerusalem occupied the fallen city in the hope of controlling the route to the Red Sea. They built a fortress overlooking Petra.

The fortress is still there, in ruins; but the crusaders did not stay long. As the Saracens pushed the main armies back into Europe, the garrison at Petra retreated too. Only a scattering of subsistence farmers, goat herds, and desert nomads remained – and in time they moved in search of lusher pastures.

The ornaments that once decorated the city – sculptures, brightly painted frescoes and superb pottery – vanished, almost without exception … stripped or destroyed by looters, rubbed to powder by wind-borne sand, or bleached by the sun. Practically nothing remains, except the hand-carved rose-red rocks – all hidden beyond the dark throat of the Siq. The facades stand as a reminder of an oasis of civilization amid the desert waste.

Ancient trade routes

As early as 8000 BC, villages were trading with each other to obtain scarce resources. From these modest beginnings, by 2000 BC, ships from Mesopotamia, Egypt, and the Indus Valley had created the first overseas trade links. In the 7th and 6th centuries BC, coinage emerged in China and Anatolia, providing a flexible means of exchange. Soon a network of trade routes spread across the world.

LEAVING THE ISLAND
The first large cargo boats, 12m (39ft) long, sailed the Mediterranean in the 2nd millennium BC. A fresco found on Thera shows their elegant, curved shape.

A USEFUL INVENTION
A terracotta model from Mohenjo-Daro shows that the Indus civilizations used solid-wheeled carts to transport their goods to market.

COASTAL PATHWAYS
Goods were carried along the South American coast in reed boats. These vessels inspired the pottery of the Chimú people, based around the city of Chanchan.

Central American routes
Essential materials such as obsidian for tools were widely traded between the early cultures of Central America. Prestige materials included magnetite (iron ore) for making mirrors, and ritual objects such as bloodletting tools. Jade and turquoise were highly valued: expeditions to recover turquoise reached the south-west of present-day USA.

Andean routes
Early Andean cultures such as the Incas constructed roads on the coast and highland plateau along which foodstuffs, highland wool, and coastal cotton were carried. Valued materials were brought long distances: spondylus shells came from coastal Ecuador and lapis lazuli from the Atacama desert, far to the south.

Tin routes
In the 1st millennium BC, tin from Spain, Brittany, and Cornwall was traded within western Europe by the Celts. The Phoenicians linked into these trade networks via the Strait of Gibraltar, and the Greeks may have acquired tin by way of overland routes leading to the coast of Gaul. Tin was alloyed with copper to make bronze.

Amber routes
As early as 2000 BC, Greeks and native Europeans obtained supplies of amber from the Baltic. The trade lasted until late Roman times.

North African route
Greek and Roman towns were linked with Carthage and Egypt via the coast of North Africa, the source of its grain supplies.

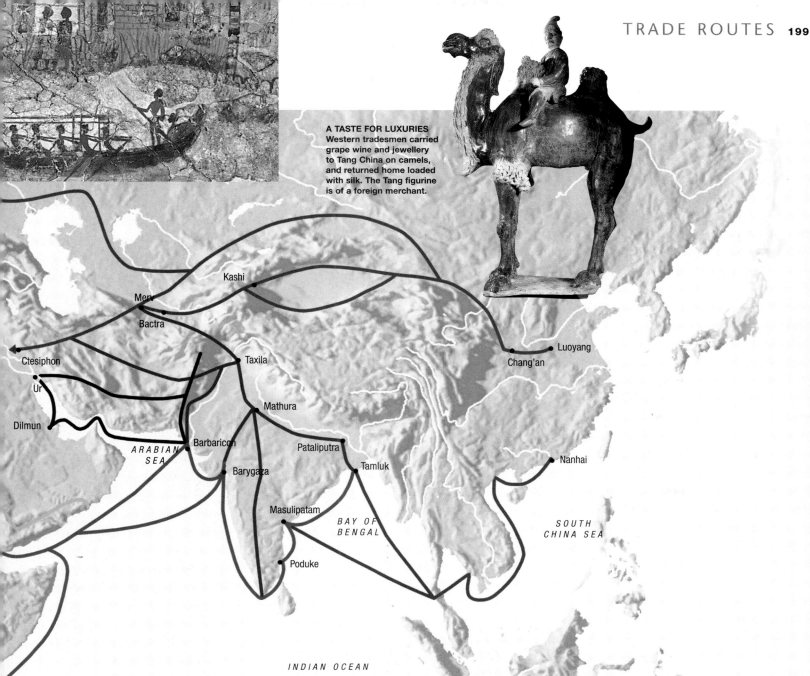

A TASTE FOR LUXURIES
Western tradesmen carried
grape wine and jewellery
to Tang China on camels,
and returned home loaded
with silk. The Tang figurine
is of a foreign merchant.

Kashi

Merv

Bactra

Ctesiphon

Taxila

Ur

Mathura

Dilmun

Luoyang

Chang'an

Barbaricon

*ARABIAN
SEA*

Pat␣aliputra

Nanhai

Barygaza

Tamluk

Masulipatam

*BAY OF
BENGAL*

*SOUTH
CHINA SEA*

Poduke

INDIAN OCEAN

Trans-Saharan routes
According to Herodotus, the
Garamantes – who dominated
part of Libya from 500 BC –
established a route across the
Sahara. Farther west, the
Carthaginians are thought to
have imported gold from
Senegal and Guinea across
Mauritania. In the 1st century
AD, trade expanded with
the regular use of camels for
transporting goods.

Nile routes
From the 3rd millennium BC,
Egypt traded with the Sudan.
The Nubian city and state of
Meroe (350 BC–AD 400) later
controlled trade along the
upper reaches of the Nile.

Incense routes
From the early 1st millennium
BC, traders transported incense
from southern Arabia overland
as far as Syria. But in the 1st
century AD, routes across the
Red Sea superseded the routes
overland, opening up the Horn
of Africa as a source of incense.

Indian Ocean routes
As early as the 1st century BC,
Greeks and Romans crossed
the Red Sea to acquire Eastern
spices from India and beyond.

Phoenician routes
In the 1st millennium BC,
traders from Phoenicia sailed
to Spain and the western
Mediterranean seeking silver
and other metals. Venturing
beyond the Pillars of Hercules
in the Strait of Gibraltar, they
may have reached as far south
as the Gulf of Guinea.

Silk Road
Silk, on which China held a
monopoly, was known in
Europe by the 6th century BC.
Chinese silk dealers traded at
markets in Turkistan from the
2nd century BC.

Spice routes
In the late centuries BC, Indian
traders travelled to South-east
Asia for metals and spices.
Han China and its successors
also traded with the emerging
states of South-east Asia.

Overland to India
Persian conquests in the
north-west in the 6th century
BC brought Indian trade routes
along the Indus and Ganges
into contact with routes leading
to western Europe and China.
By the 3rd century BC,
overland routes also linked
northern India with the south.

Sumerian traders' routes
Lapis lazuli, a semi-precious
stone highly prized by the
Egyptians and Sumerians,
was imported from Badakhshan
in north-east Afghanistan –
the only known source in
the ancient world – in the
4th and 3rd millennia BC.
By 2300 BC, seafarers from
the Indus region (known as
Meluhha to the Sumerians)
were trading through the
Persian Gulf with Dilmun
(Bahrain), Magan (Oman), and
Sumer. Sumer's exports
included fine woollen textiles,
pottery, and grain. Copper from
Magan was a major commodity.
Timber, ivory, and carnelian
were among Meluhha's exports.
The Meluhhans also gained
control of the lapis lazuli trade.

Qumran

A settlement near the Dead Sea

In the wastes of the Palestinian desert lies the monastery of an ancient Jewish sect. Its members hid cherished manuscripts in the caves surrounding the settlement to keep them from the destructive hands of the avenging forces of Rome.

EARLY IN 1947, A YOUNG BEDOUIN HERDSMAN seeking a stray lamb on the parched slopes west of the Dead Sea stumbled on a cave containing some ancient clay jars. His first thought was of treasure, and with two fellow tribesmen he explored the vessels for gold or jewels. The jars contained nothing but some ancient scrolls, carefully wrapped in timeworn linen cloth.

Without great hopes of reward, the shepherds collected a few of the best preserved manuscripts, which later found their way into the hands of a Bethlehem antique dealer. The scrolls were bought by an Orthodox monastery in Jerusalem. As scholars deciphered the writings, a fascinating story began to emerge – the story of a Jewish religious community whose ideas and traditions recalled those of the early Christians.

The Bedouins kept the source of the scrolls a secret, but in 1949 the cave was found by Brigadier Ashton of the Arab Legion. It lay about 13km (8 miles) south of Jericho. Nearby, the ruins of a small settlement had been discovered at Qumran. These were initially thought to be the remains of a Roman fort, but as the site at Qumran was excavated, archaeologists found pottery that matched fragments found in the caves: the two sites were contemporary.

As the picture became clearer, the documents from the caves – the first of several discoveries known collectively as the 'Dead Sea Scrolls' – became something of a sensation. These were authentic documents of the Holy Land, which had survived since the 1st century AD. Seven scrolls were virtually intact, with fragments of hundreds of others. They were the sacred texts of an ancient sect, hidden in the caves when their writers came under threat.

THE FORCES OF HELLENISM

The scrolls date the founding of the settlement at Qumran back to the 2nd century BC – a time of deep disturbance in ancient Palestine. The territory had become a province of the Seleucid Empire formed by the successors of Alexander the Great, and the culture and religion of Greece were beginning to penetrate the Holy Land. In 167 BC the Temple at Jerusalem became a centre for the worship of Zeus. To pious Jews, this was an abomination.

A SAFE HIDING PLACE Fragments of some 600 manuscripts have been recovered from 11 caves in the limestone hills around Qumran. They were the first of a series of similar documents recovered from sites in Judaea, and date from between the middle of the 3rd century BC and AD 68. They include Biblical writings representing the Old Testament, and previously unknown psalms, hymns, and sectarian tracts.

During these troubled times a particularly austere Jewish sect known as the Essenes had evolved. The Essenes' following probably numbered some 4,000 people, many of whom fled to desert retreats to avoid persecution. In 164 BC, the sect joined forces with a priestly family called the Maccabees in a revolt against the Seleucids. Their capital was liberated, but the Essenes were unhappy with the newly appointed High Priest, Jonathan Maccabee: they considered him an impious war leader unfit for holy office. Many of the sect's members returned to the desert.

The desert settlement at Qumran was founded in 150 BC. Interpretation of the site is still controversial, but most scholars now believe it to be a monastic community set up by the Essenes, though their name is not mentioned in the scrolls. Despite its unpromising location, the complex could also have been a farming estate producing dates, balsam, and wine, and gathering salt and asphalt (bitumen) from the Dead Sea. Coins discovered at the site suggest trading contacts with the outside world.

The settlement comprises a group of communal buildings overlooked by a watchtower. The buildings include a refectory where stacks of tableware have been found in an annexe, and a

WATER IN THE DESERT *Qumran was built on the edge of the Judaean wilderness, near a freshwater spring. Rainwater flowed along an aqueduct to the reservoirs, seen here above and to the left of the settlement*

long, rectangular room possibly used as a scriptorium. Stables, workshops, and storerooms have also been identified. The settlement's 200 inhabitants did not sleep inside the complex, but in tents, huts, and caves scattered around the site. At the end of their lives, they were buried in a nearby cemetery, where about 1,100 stone-covered tombs have been unearthed. Almost all of the skeletons that have been excavated are of adult men, confirming the impression given in the scrolls that the community was an all-male brotherhood.

WITNESSING THE MONASTIC LIFE

The Jewish historian Josephus (AD 37–*c*.100) once visited an Essene community, and described a typical day. After prayers before dawn, each member would set to a task in which he was skilled. An hour before noon, the community assembled and donned linen loincloths. They then washed with cold water to purify themselves before gathering in the refectory to eat. Grace was said before and after the simple meal, and they ate in silence. When it was over the sacred garments were put away, and work resumed until the evening meal. 'To people outside,' Josephus wrote, 'the silence within seems like some dread mystery; it stems from their permanent sobriety and the restriction of their food and drink to the bare necessities.'

Toil, indoors and out, probably occupied much of the brethren's time. Pottery workshops, a wine press, and a milling area have been found, and from the discovery of the bones of sheep, goats, and cattle, it seems that herds were tended, too.

SURVIVING THE AGES The dry conditions in the caves helped to preserve the scrolls. The cylindrical jars containing them were made in the workshops of Qumran.

Texts found among the cave scrolls give an insight into the structure of the Qumran community. All members had to be Israelites – descendants of citizens of the Kingdom of Judah. The sect was broken down into groups of ten men, each of which had to include one man well versed in Biblical Law whose authority was accepted by the others. The beliefs of the Essenes did not differ greatly from those of traditional Judaism, but the law was interpreted more rigorously at Qumran than elsewhere.

Overall authority was exercised by a Guardian, who oversaw all new admissions and established each candidate's moral aptitude. Potential members had to swear an oath to abide by the Law of Moses and the community's teaching. The first year was a trial period in which the candidate was allowed to keep his material possessions and was not admitted to certain sacred activities such as the solemn communal meal. In the second year he handed over his property and attended certain gatherings at the refectory, but many privileges and secrets were still withheld. After the third year, he was granted full membership.

The study of scriptural law was among the chief occupations at Qumran, and members of the community assembled nightly for reading and prayer. One of the common threads of their faith was a sense that the apocalypse was about to strike. The sect believed that God's vengeance would soon be unleashed on an unfaithful Israel, and that they alone would survive the Day of Judgment. They anticipated a 40-year struggle between the Sons of Light (the faithful few) and the Sons of Darkness (all others, both Jews and Gentiles), matched by a celestial war between the angelic and demonic hosts. God, it was thought, would finally intervene, guaranteeing eventual victory for the forces of righteousness.

Some of the Qumran scrolls envisage a Messiah ushering in the New Dawn; others allude to two or three Messiahs – the texts are obscure. And of course, while the brethren meditated on the impending events, a Messiah did indeed come to Israel.

In the initial flush of excitement generated by the discovery of the first Dead Sea Scrolls, theories were advanced connecting Christ directly with the Essene community.

The discoveries at Qumran have contributed hugely to our understanding of the setting in which the Christian Church was founded. There are parallels between the Essenes and the early Christians. Both groups saw themselves as communities of the elect, fulfilling scriptural prophecies, on the threshold of the Kingdom of God. But the Essenes dreamed of restoring temple worship to Jerusalem. Christ anticipated a new Jerusalem encompassing all mankind – it would require no sanctuary.

THE COMING OF ROME

Palestine fell under the direct rule of the Romans in 63 BC. In AD 66, Jewish resistance broke out in open warfare, and the following year Roman legions set out to crush the rebellion. It was in the face of the coming onslaught that the brethren of Qumran hurried to the caves to hide their sacred texts.

In AD 68, the settlement was destroyed by the Romans. Over the following few years, the Essenes were wiped out in a campaign of terror. The historian Josephus has left an account of the piety with which the faithful met their end: 'Though racked and twisted, burned and broken, subjected to every instrument of torture to make them blaspheme their law-giver or eat forbidden foods, they refused to yield. Not once did they cringe or shed a tear. Smiling through their agonies, and gently mocking their tormentors, they cheerfully offered up their souls, secure in the belief that they would receive them back again.'

Nimrud Dagh

A royal sanctuary in Anatolia

On a desolate peak in southern Turkey, giant statues gaze out across a remote mountain wilderness. Here, the dreams of an ancient king were inscribed in stone. And from here came a god who almost conquered the Roman Empire.

LONELY, BLEAK, AND REMOTE FROM MODERN HIGHWAYS, COMMAGENE is a place where man is dwarfed by the landscape. Bare mountains rise out of the arid terrain like vast sloping deserts. It is sparsely populated; a few scattered villages provide the only evidence of habitation in this harsh environment, near Turkey's border with Syria.

And yet, on one peak 2,000m (6,560ft) above sea level, a mysterious ruin suggests that the region was once heavily populated and powerful. A conical pyramid of crushed stones stands at the summit, and five colossal statues – the figure of a king among them – are ranged nearby. The giant effigies are flanked by lions and eagles hewn out of the rock. Below them are terraces littered with countless immense carved heads, and a vast altar where sacrificial fires once burned. The pyramid of stones housed the tomb of Antiochus I, ruler of Commagene in the 1st century BC. Nimrud Dagh (now Nemrut Dagi), the holy mountain, was his burial place, a testament to his dream of immortality.

FROM THE DUST OF A DYING EMPIRE

In ancient times, Commagene's bare landscape was less desolate than it is today. The waters of the upper Euphrates flowed between thickly forested slopes to the east, and its valley was a crossroads for major trade routes leading west into the Taurus Mountains. This great range was a vital source of silver, copper, and lead for the early civilizations of Mesopotamia.

The passes across the Taurus range were also strategically important to the imperial powers which swept across Asia Minor in later centuries. Commagene, like the whole of the subcontinent of Asia Minor, was overrun by two mighty empires. First came the Persians in the 6th century BC; then the Greeks under Alexander the Great in the 4th. These ancient superpowers shaped the development of the remote state.

A BLEND OF CULTURES
The giant heads represent gods who mingle the characteristics of both Greek and Persian deities, just as the statues themselves mix Greek features with Persian headdresses. They include the fearsome bearded figure of Zeus-Ahura Mazda (right) and Apollo-Helios-Hermes (left).

routes between the various sanctuaries. He stipulated that every month, the royal treasury was to finance two feast days: his birthday was to be remembered on the 10th of each month, and his coronation on the 16th.

Each feast day, a priest in traditional Persian robes was to adorn the effigies of the king with gold crowns consecrated to the worship of his ancestors. Offerings of incense and aromatic herbs were to be placed on the altars, and sacrifices were to be made.

The local citizens and military garrison were to be invited to banquets in honour of the deceased. An abundance of food should be provided, and wine served for as long as the guests remained within the sacred enclosure. A new caste of female musicians was to be created to perform at the banquets. Antiochus obviously foresaw that, over the years, priests might

As Alexander's realm disintegrated, Commagene emerged from obscurity. In about 80 BC the country detached itself from the decaying remnant of his empire and became a new kingdom. When imperial Rome began to annex territories in Asia Minor, Commagene kept its independence through the skilful diplomacy of its great monarch, Antiochus I (*c*.69–34 BC).

The blood of two mighty dynasties ran through the veins of the Commagenian king. On his father's side, Antiochus traced his ancestry to Darius, King of Kings, one of the greatest rulers of the Persian Empire. On his mother's side, he was descended from Alexander the Great.

The monumental effigies surrounding the tomb of Antiochus represent his gods and ancestors, and show both Greek and Persian influences. The statues are fashioned in Greek style, bear Greek features, and sometimes represent Greek deities. Yet the clothes and headgear are Persian.

The colossal scale of the conception is also in the Persian tradition. The statues range from 9m to 12m (29ft to 39ft) high; the heads alone are 2m (6½ft) tall. Such awesome proportions are alien to Greek statuary, in which sculptors valued harmonious ideals more highly than size.

Greek inscriptions composed by the king himself have survived to pass on the meaning of his monumental creation. The sanctuary, the king wrote, was erected in a high and holy place, close to the heavens and remote from the dwellings of men. The great sepulchre was built to preserve his remains throughout eternity. The effigies of the gods, and the 'heroic legion of my ancestors', bore witness to his pious devotion.

COMMEMORATING THE DEAD

Antiochus believed that in death he would take his place among the ranks of the gods. His own divinity was clearly a major preoccupation, and many lesser sanctuaries were built throughout Commagene. In each of them, the king is shown engraved in effigy on a great stone slab, extending his right hand towards a deity. The king made elaborate provisions for his worship after death, including the mapping out of processional

become selfish about the commemorative feasts, and perhaps hoard some of the provisions for themselves. Such a grudging attitude was expressly forbidden. Each of the priests could take a share appropriate to their status – but every person present must be allowed to enjoy the occasion 'without being spied on, eating and drinking to their hearts' content'.

'I HAVE BORNE WITNESS TO MY FAITH'

Other inscriptions unearthed at Nimrud Dagh are both pious in tone and generous in spirit. 'By the will of the gods', the king wrote, 'I have borne witness to my faith through this inscription. Its holy letters announce in humble language the great goodwill of the gods to our local people and to strangers, even to kings and princes, to free men and to slaves, to all human beings whatever their name or station.'

Antiochus laid down his instructions with clear confidence in the future. He had successfully steered his kingdom through a troubled period, and left a well-filled treasury. In addition, he had carried out some great public works in the royal city of

Arsameia lying in the valley below Nimrud Dagh. Here, a stone inscription glorifying the improvements has been found: 'In the city I have added new palace buildings and walls to improve its fortifications and its beauty. I have had the deep and remotely situated reservoirs replaced with conduits very close to the houses, supplied from most abundant springs.'

It is hard to imagine Arsameia as it must have been at the zenith of its power and glory. The site has been located near the modern, impoverished village of Kâhta, and the ruins of the

ETERNAL WATCHMEN At the foot of the man-made mound enclosing the king's tomb, the huge statues still gaze across courtyards laid out to the north, east, and west.

royal palace, Eski Kale (Old Castle), on the heights above the town, have been excavated. An impressive tumulus nearby has also been explored. The discovery of a column topped by an eagle earned the mound the name of Karakush, meaning 'the black bird'. An inscription indicates that the tomb once housed the bodies of three royal women.

TAKEN OVER BY ROME

Commagene's period of prosperity did not long outlive its king. The realm's independence was extinguished as soon as it stood in the way of Roman ambition. Although successive kings followed a pro-Roman policy, Commagene was conquered and annexed by Rome in AD 72, becoming part of the empire's province of Syria.

When the Romans first occupied the area, Nimrud Dagh was abandoned. It is likely that legionaries carried off – possibly by waterway – some of the immense and beautifully hewn stones. A Roman bridge was constructed nearby and dedicated by the XVIth Legion; perhaps their engineers were the culprits.

The real damage done at Commagene was the felling of its lush green forests. The resulting soil erosion laid much of the area to waste. The widespread deforestation can partly be explained by the Romans' need for timber to fuel their heating systems, but there is evidence that the hills were stripped for another purpose. The discovery of ancient furnaces and iron slag in the area suggests that iron was first forged in Commagene. This is supported by the fact that Roman soldiers worshipped Jupiter Dolichenus, god of military safety and success, who was said to come from the country 'where iron was born' – Doliche (now Dülük) in Commagene.

RELIGION AND RIVALRY

Although subjugated, Commagene had a pervasive influence on its conquerors. For it was from the little kingdom in Turkey that Mithras, the Persian god of sunlight, began his triumphant progress through the provinces of the empire.

The evolution of Mithraism can be traced back to the religion practised by the earliest Persian kings. They worshipped the universal supreme god, Ahura Mazda. Mithras emerged initially as a lesser deity. But in Commagene, he acquired a higher status. His cult survived the coming of the Greeks, and even borrowed aspects of their mythology.

CARVED CLIFFS South-west of Nimrud Dagh lie the ruins of Eski Kale. The cliffs below the royal residence are inscribed with reliefs and punctuated with rock-cut chamber tombs.

Mithraism was a solely masculine religion. All men and boys, free or enslaved, were accepted as initiates, but women were excluded. Disciples would assemble in underground chapels, or in grottoes, to perform sacred rites which are still shrouded in mystery.

Soon after the country's conquest by Rome, Mithraism spread along the trade routes, straight back to the heart of the empire. Merchants were keen disciples, for Mithraism exalted honest dealing in business. Slaves from Commagene were also devotees, because Mithras treated them as the equals of free men. But it was above all in the army that Mithraism took root. It soon became the favourite cult of the legions across the empire.

Mithraic altars generally bore a representation of the god wearing the conical Phrygian cap of the East. Key episodes in his mythology centred on his pursuit, capture, and sacrifice of a sacred bull. After the sacrifice, Mithras was believed to have ascended to heaven in the chariot of the sun. Altarpieces often depict the god sacrificing the bull, flanked by two torch-bearers.

Mithras was worshipped both as a god and a hero, a model to be followed according to a strict moral code. Like Christ, he was a redeemer. He offered immortality to his followers, and as in Christianity, his worship brought visions of a glorious heaven and a terrible hell. The two faiths proliferated throughout the Roman Empire side by side, hostile to one another, but sharing common elements. Both were accessible to the poor, which contributed to their mass appeal, but Mithraism's exclusion of women restricted the number of followers.

A MESSAGE FROM THE PAST

Although Mithraism had its devotees even among emperors, it did not become a lasting, official state religion as Christianity came to be. The Persian god was defeated by the crucified redeemer from Nazareth.

The obsession with Mithras would not have been fully understood by Antiochus I, for the god was only one among many in his sacred universe. This is evident from the king's own words, inscribed in stone, which offer an invitation and benediction to anyone who comes to view his monument: 'This stone tells in a gentle tone – Let all of those people who are moved by the spirit, who live a life that is without injustice, but full of zeal for saintly actions, look with confidence at the faces of the gods and follow in the happy footsteps of the blessed.'

GOD OF LIGHT The blood of the bull sacrificed by Mithras was believed to be a sacred substance from which all life sprang.

Pompeii

The resurrection of a city

Almost 2,000 years ago a provincial city in Italy was buried beneath a thick layer of volcanic ash. Hundreds of years later Pompeii was discovered – a miraculously preserved mausoleum which provides a vivid record of the life of a Roman city.

ON THE MORNING OF AUGUST 24, AD 79, carts and mules jostled their way through the streets of Pompeii. Pedlars hawked their wares from wayside stalls. Girls gossiped lazily at a corner fountain. In a wine shop, a customer had just put his money down on the counter for a drink. But the barmaid had no time to pick up the coins. For, suddenly, a terrifying noise ripped through the air.

Vesuvius (Vesuvio), the volcanic mountain which dominated the town, had erupted. Under pressure from the gases inside, the plug of lava that blocked the

opening of the volcano had burst, releasing a great mass of red-hot lava. Solidifying into balls of stone as it cooled, the lava rained down on the houses and blotted out the sun. By nightfall on August 25, Pompeii was buried beneath about 6m (20ft) of lava, dust and ashes. It happened too quickly for many of the inhabitants to escape. Asphyxiated by gases and crushed beneath tumbling buildings, they fell in the streets or met death in their homes and cellars. Before he died, one of them recalled the terrible fate that had befallen two Old Testament cities by scratching 'Sodom and Gomorrah!' on a whitewashed wall.

THE LAST NIGHT OF THE WORLD
Fortunately for us, the modern world has an eyewitness account of the fall of Pompeii. The two letters which the Roman writer Pliny the Younger sent to the historian Tacitus are exceptionally vivid. Pliny the Younger was staying with his uncle, Pliny the Elder, at Misenum, 30km (19 miles) from Pompeii. This is what he saw as he made his escape: 'Ashes were already falling,' he wrote, 'not as yet very thickly. I looked round: a dense black cloud was coming up behind us, spreading over the earth like a flood …

'Darkness fell, not the dark of a moonless or cloudy night, but as if the lamp had been put out in a closed room. You could hear the shrieks of women, the wailing of infants, and the shouting of men; some were calling their parents, others their children or their wives, trying to recognize them by their voices. People bewailed their own fate or that of their relatives, and there were some who prayed for death in their terror of dying.

DECORATIVE FEATURE A young girl's initiation into the mystic cult of the Greek god Dionysus is one of a series of wall paintings from the 1st century BC in the Villa of Mysteries. Many Pompeiians aspired to owning a luxurious home such as this one built on the outskirts of the city.

'Many besought the aid of the gods, but still more imagined there were no gods left, and that the Universe was plunged into eternal darkness for evermore.'

DEATH BY SUFFOCATION

At the time Pliny the Elder (a Roman administrator and himself a prolific writer) commanded the Roman fleet at Misenum. When the eruption first started, he went by boat to Stabiae to rescue a friend and get a closer view. After spending the night there, he 'decided to go down to the shore and investigate the possibility of any escape by sea,' wrote his nephew, 'but he found the waves wild and dangerous. A sheet was spread on

the ground for him to lie down, and he repeatedly asked for cold water to drink. Then the flames and smell of sulphur which gave warning of the approaching fire drove the others to take flight and roused him to stand up. He stood leaning on slaves and then suddenly collapsed, I imagine because the

HIGH AND DRY   The streets of Pompeii were paved in volcanic stone. In wet weather passers-by could use raised pavements linked by stepping-stone bridges.

CAST IN PLASTER In the 19th century, Giuseppe Fiorelli revealed the shapes of the city's lost residents by pouring plaster into the holes left in the hardened ash by their bodies.

dense fumes choked his breathing. When daylight returned two days after the last day he had seen, his body was found intact … still fully clothed and looking more like in sleep than death.'

UNCOVERING THE LOST CITY

Embalmed in lava, Pompeii remained undiscovered for nearly 1700 years. It was not until 1748 that Joaquín de Alcubierre, engineer to the King of Naples, chanced upon its business quarter. In order to inspect an old water tunnel, he sank pa shaft into the ground and unearthed a brilliant wall-painting. Next, he came upon the body of a Pompeiian clutching a fistful of gold. No one will ever know whether this man was a thief or was just trying to flee with money he had

saved over the years. Alcubierre went on excavating the site. It was another 100 years before the Italian archaeologist Giuseppe Fiorelli introduced the policy of moving forward slowly, house by house, to make sure that nothing was lost in the excavation. He also devised the technique of pouring plaster into the cavities left by the bodies, so that they reappeared as they were at the moment of death. As the city was disinterred, it seemed to come back to life.

(1) Via di Stabia

(14) Forum baths

(24) House of the Vettii

UNDER THE VOLCANO

Vesuvius, the cause of Pompeii's destruction, looms to the north of the city. Pompeii's chief north-south thoroughfare was the Via di Stabia (1), running between the Vesuvius Gate (2) and the Stabian Gate (3). Running east-west were the Via di Nola, from the Nola Gate (4) across to the west side of the city, and the Via dell'Abbondanza, between the Samus (5) and Marine (6) gates. The gate in the north-west corner of the walls (7) led to the neighbouring city of Herculaneum.

Pompeii's other main features included the Temple of Venus (8), the Temple of Apollo (9), the Basilica (10), the Temple of Jupiter (11), the Civil Forum (12), the Building of Eumachia (13), the Forum baths (14), the central baths (15), the Stabian baths (16), the Triangular Forum (17), the theatre (18), the gladiators' barracks (19), the Odeon (20), the *palaestra* (21), and the amphitheatre (22). Homes included the House of the Faun (23) and the House of the Vettii (24), both in the city's north-west sector.

used by both the Greeks who had settled on Italy's west coast and the Etruscans to the north. Its economy was based on the production of wine and oil and supplemented by a flourishing commerce in wool and woollen goods.

The coming of the Romans around 80 BC opened new vistas of economic enterprise. The neighbouring town of Puteoli (Pozzuoli) became Italy's principal port and Roman traders began to flood the eastern Mediterranean. Pompeii prospered not only as a market town and port, but also as an immensely popular resort. Every summer thousands of Romans flocked to the city to take advantage of its climate and its beautiful position in the Bay of Naples.

The pictures on the walls and sophisticated paintings, the bawdy graffiti and dignified inscriptions engraved in marble, all materialized before the eyes of the archaeologists. Even the streets still bear the track marks of carts.

SCENES OF EVERYDAY LIFE

A vivid picture of daily life began to emerge simply from the insults and proverbs scrawled on walls – ranging from 'Figulus loves Idaia,' to the more lyrical, 'You could as soon stop the winds from blowing and the waters from flowing as stop lovers from loving.' Election posters illustrated the vitality of political life in the city: 'Vote for Maurus Epidius Sabinus as administrator of justice. He is a respectable man, considered by trustworthy judges to be capable of defending the citizens.'

Every one of Pompeii's excavated buildings gives the historian an insight into the city's public and private life, yet surprisingly little is known about its early history. The uncovering of a Doric temple proved that the town existed in the 6th century BC and that it was subject to Greek influence. It was probably a settlement of the local Ausonian people, thriving as a free port

The orator Cicero was one of the many who acquired a holiday home in Pompeii. As the fashion caught on, the area became a playground for the rich.

Then, in AD 62, an earthquake struck. The drama is depicted in the bas-reliefs which a wealthy banker, Caecilius Jucundus, had sculpted in the hallway of his house. Buildings tilt, arches and monuments crash to the ground – all evoked with rude vigour. The banker probably commissioned the reliefs to give thanks to his household gods for his survival.

A CITY OF FINE BUILDINGS

Pompeii reacted to the ravages of this catastrophe with a frenzy of building that was proof of the city's prosperity. The art collection of a local politician, Julius Polybius, was found stored in one room of his house to keep it safe from the building work, still in progress when Vesuvius erupted 17 years later.

The largest public buildings stood in the south-west corner of the city, where the first settlers of Pompeii had made their homes. Here, clustered round the Civil Forum, stood the Temple of Apollo, the most ancient of all the buildings in Pompeii –

proved by the discovery of Greek pottery dating back to the early 6th century BC. Next door the Basilica, a combined market hall and law court, is the best preserved of the city's buildings. Thanks to graffiti on the walls, it can be dated to the 2nd century BC. Its main hall, surrounded by a colonnade, testifies to the commercial might of the city. At the end was a tribunal where justice was administered. Graffiti covers the walls. 'Lucius Istacidius,' wrote a citizen, 'who did not invite me to share his meal, is a barbarian!'

On the opposite side of the Forum stands the Building of Eumachia. Inscriptions inside describe how Eumachia, a public priestess, paid for the construction of the building and how she dedicated it to the 'Peace and Harmony of Augustus'.

The Macellum, or general market, stood at the north-east corner of the Forum. The rows of stalls which encircled the main building can still be seen, as can the remains of the various cereals and fruits that were being sold on the fateful August day in AD 79. A drain full of fish bones marks the position of a fish stall. Nearby stand the public baths of the Civil Forum.

A PASSION FOR ENTERTAINMENT

The second area of ancient public buildings clustered round the Triangular Forum, with Pompeii's public entertainment district spread out along its eastern side. The city's largest theatre could accommodate an audience of 5,000 in the open air. The Romans were passionate theatre-goers; its repertoire would have included classical drama, comic mime, and low burlesque, interspersed with clowning, dancing, and acrobatics. For lavish marine spectacles, the stage could be flooded with water, and in the heat of the Mediterranean summer a sprinkling device showered perfumed water on the audience.

The third area of public buildings consisted of the amphitheatre and the *palaestra*, or gymnasium. Providing free entertainment for the public was a passport to popularity and

political success. It was probably for this reason that one of Pompeii's two magistrates, Caius Quinctius Balbus, a rich landowner, financed its construction in about 80 BC.

Here, the Pompeiians would gather to watch entertainments which ranged from performances by clowns and pantomime artists to sports such as fencing and boxing. But what the crowds loved best was blood. A favourite spectacle included gladiatorial combats to the death between criminals and wild beasts. The different types of gladiators were often illustrated in the city. There was the *thrax*, who was armed with a short sword, shield, and visored helmet, and the *retarius*, who fought with net and trident. Champions enjoyed great popularity, and their praises were sung in the ubiquitous graffiti.

Of the public baths that have been uncovered, the Stabian baths contained a large *palaestra* for taking exercise, a swimming-pool, changing rooms, and chambers heated to varying temperatures. Alongside the baths stood the brothel.

A BUSTLING COMMERCIAL LIFE

Hard work went hand in hand with high living in Pompeii. One of the city's artisans had the motto 'to earn is joy' inscribed in mosaic in his house. And the vitality of the city's trade and commerce is reflected in the stalls which sprang up, often at house entrances. A fabrics shop, which an inscription tells us

THE BAKER'S TRADE A wall painting (above) shows customers at a bakery. Archaeologists unearthed a real-life bakery (left) complete with bread in the oven. The corn came from Egypt or Tunisia and was ground on millstones which were turned by men and animals.

belonged to a man called Verecundus, still has paintings that depict everyday scenes in the life of the workshop: the carders at their benches, the dyers sweating over boiling vats, and the owner proudly displaying the finished pieces of cloth.

Several bakeries survive. In one of them, a baker had slid 81 loaves into his oven minutes before the eruption. There is a laundry, which belonged to a certain Stefanus. Inside, a press, pestles, and basins have been found. Jars into which passers-by were encouraged to relieve themselves would have been left outside on the street. For urine was used as a washing agent on account of its alkaline properties.

One inn was identified when some jars were discovered with the address to which they had been dispatched: 'To Pompeii, near the Amphitheatre, to the inn-keeper Euximus.'

DESIGN FOR LIVING

In the typical Pompeiian house, the front door led into a small corridor running between two rooms – one on either side – that were usually used as shops. At the other end, the corridor opened onto a central courtyard, or atrium. The *tablinum*, or family meeting place, was at the far side of the atrium. In turn, this opened onto the garden.

The House of the Faun – so called because of its garden statue of a dancing faun – had a second atrium with rooms leading off it. It also had two gardens surrounded by columns. On the paving stones of one of the colonnades the skeleton of a woman was unearthed, probably overcome by poisonous fumes as she attempted to rescue her most precious jewels. Scattered over the floor are pieces of gold which would have made up the wealth of an average Pompeiian family.

For those who had the means, the ultimate status symbol was a villa built outside the town. The Villa of Mysteries stood slightly to the south of Pompeii. It is distinguished by a complete cycle of paintings on the walls which celebrate the mysteries of the cult of the god Dionysus. Here, as elsewhere, the inhabitants of the villa can be seen in their last tortured moments: a group of workmen asphyxiated in the cellars, a couple of women dashed to the ground amid the debris of the tumbling building, and the porter slumped across the couch in his dark cubbyhole.

One of the most striking features of Pompeiian houses is the sumptuousness of their decoration. They abound in marble and bronze sculptures, and precious plates and dishes. The sculptures were inspired by the art of the Greek world, and were to be found gracing the fountains, colonnades, and gardens of the villas. In 1978, the life-sized bronze statue of a young man was found in a house that had belonged to Julius Polybius. In the house of Menander, 118 silver dishes and plates

TAKING NOTES One of the most remarkable paintings to be found in Pompeii shows a woman holding a stylus and writing tablet, and a man with a book. It reflects the high level of literacy among the Romans.

. . . some jars were discovered with the address to which they had been dispatched: 'To Pompeii, near the Amphitheatre, to the inn-keeper Euximus.'

wrapped in pieces of wool and cloth were discovered stored in a large wooden chest, out of the way of the restoration works that were being carried out at the time.

Pompeii also had a large amount of mosaic decoration. In its early days this was a form of pavement art. Gradually, it came to be used to decorate walls and its designs became more elaborate. In some cases it took the shapes of animals or men out hunting, sailing, or participating in sports. There was a fashion for decorating the niches in which fountains were set with mosaic, using brightly coloured glass paste and gold leaf. So popular was mosaic as an art form that Pliny the Younger held it responsible for the decline of painting.

But of all the decoration to be found in the houses and streets of Pompeii, there is one piece of graffiti that must have the last word: 'I wonder, oh wall,' a wag has written, 'that under the weight of so much idle chat, you have not yet crumbled.'

From tents to palaces

The earliest humans sought shelter, to protect themselves and their families against attack and the extremes of climate. In satisfying these needs, they created ever more solid buildings, laying the foundations for modern community living. The many forms of habitation that developed reflected differences in climate, available materials, the culture of the area and the status of the owner.

SHELTER FROM THE ELEMENTS
Even in the depths of the Siberian winter, the tents were snug, their sides buried in the frozen earth and weighted down to prevent them tearing in the icy winds.

A tent of skin and bone

Stone Age men and women, though popularly seen as cave-dwellers, did in fact build shelters for themselves. The remains of a branch shelter 300,000 years old have been found at Terra Amata, near Nice in France. Much later, *Homo sapiens* moved north and east to hunt in areas bordering the great ice sheets. Some 15,000 years ago hunters in Siberia were using tent-like shelters made from animal skins, mammoth tusks and bones.

UNDER THE DOME
The inhabitants of the 'beehive' homes were farmers, hunters and herders belonging to a highly organised Neolithic society.

The 'beehives' of ancient Cyprus

Before 6000 BC, the inhabitants of the Cypriot village of Khirokitia, located on the slopes of a river valley near the island's south coast, built beehive-shaped houses. Each 'beehive' had a mudbrick dome resting on a round limestone base, probably the easiest shape to build using the locally available materials – similar structures have also been found, from the same period, on the Middle Eastern mainland. Inside, there was a hearth, benches, and often brick piers to support an upper floor. Some may also have had annexes to house farm animals. The courtyard outside had a well.

LIVING WITH COUSINS
The house accommodated an extended family. Each nuclear family within it had their own room; the long central chamber would have been a communal living room.

A family dwelling

In the small Mesopotamian village of Tell Madhhur, a fire some time in the 5th millennium BC spelt domestic catastrophe for the inhabitants of one house – but left a treasure trove for archaeologists. Its walls survived to 2m (6½ ft) high and everyday objects were left in the ruins where they had formerly been used. A long room with a hearth formed the centre of the house, with smaller rooms opening from it on either side. On one side, there were substantial rooms – a storeroom stocked with pottery jars and a kitchen. Between these, an earthen ramp gave access to the roof which would have provided additional working and sleeping space. The other rooms were used for a variety of domestic activities, such as sleeping, and making tools and clothing.

A solid house of wood and clay

As the Ice Age glaciers receded, farming communities were established across the continent of Europe, and houses were increasingly built to last. In the Mediterranean region and across Central Europe, they built rectangular houses, often with thatched roofs. One of these, dating from the 4th millennium BC, was excavated in the Danube Valley in present-day Bulgaria. In front of the house was an entrance room; behind a living room with an oven and a grindstone. As farmers moved deeper into temperate Europe, pitched roofs and overhanging eaves became important to cope with heavy rain and snow. Houses also began to include an area to stall animals in winter.

CLAY OR WATTLE
Clay was used to fill in the walls between wooden posts in the Danube Valley house. Elsewhere, builders used wattle, intertwined reeds or branches, which they then daubed with clay or mud.

In the shadow of the mounds

Cahokia was the largest town of the Mississippian culture of North America, lying across the Mississippi river from modern St Louis. It may have housed as many as 30,000 people in its heyday around AD 1050 to 1250. A substantial log palisade surrounded the central part of the town where the houses of the elite were built. These were constructed of timber poles and had high thatched roofs with a central opening through which smoke escaped from the hearth below. Each house was home to one family. Also located in the central compound were enormous terraced mounds in which the leaders of society were buried. Less important families lived outside the compound, their homes spread out on either side along a ridge above the Mississippi.

INTERIOR DESIGN
The Mississippians were fine craftsmen, and richer homes would have been adorned inside with pottery and objects of carved shell, stone and copper.

WITHIN AND WITHOUT
A walled yard separates the self-contained world of a small 8th-century AD Chinese palace from the wider world outside.

Within eastern walls

Chinese architecture embodies principles which have remained unchanged for centuries – wooden-framed buildings where it was the wooden uprights, rather than the walls, that supported the roof. This limited the height and width of the house, and dictated steeply sloping roofs and large overhangs. Chinese houses were designed to be self-contained worlds, each as precisely organised as the larger world outside, with the owner's status evident in the building's size. Set within a walled courtyard, rooms and porches provided a series of open and closed spaces.

Lugdunum

The little Rome of imperial Gaul

After the conquest of Gaul, Roman soldiers set up camp on a strategic site overlooking the Rhône. Within 20 years the military outpost was transformed into an imperial metropolis, which was to become the birthplace of two emperors of Rome.

BENEATH THE BUSTLING STREETS AND SQUARES of France's third-largest city the remains of an ancient capital rest quietly. When, just over 2,000 years ago, the Romans decided to build an outpost in Gaul – where Lyons stands today – little did they know that their town of Lugdunum would rapidly become a prosperous trading centre and a cradle of early Christianity. The remarkable success story of this 'little Rome' can be charted through the efforts of French archaeologists, who have pieced together the fragments of its layout and the remnants of its everyday life. France had been, for thousands of years, the home of prosperous agricultural peoples. When the Greeks and Romans first traded with the country, the area was known as Gaul, and its inhabitants were the Celts, who enjoyed a reputation as fearless warriors.

Julius Caesar embarked on the conquest of Gaul in 58 BC. One man with whom he shared the seven years of arduous campaigning was Lucius Munatius Plancus. As a reward for his tenacity, Caesar entrusted Plancus with the government of the area they had subjugated.

STRENGTH BY DIVISION

On March 15, 44 BC – the ides of March – Caesar was assassinated in Rome. After five years of dictatorship under the brilliant general, the Roman Republic was plunged into anarchy. Caesar's lieutenants, led by Mark Antony, joined forces in revolt against the assassins. But the Senate's overriding concern was to take power once more for itself. To put down the officers' rebellion it decided to keep the army, loyal to Caesar, in far-flung corners of the Roman provinces.

Plancus had only just eliminated the last pockets of resistance to Roman rule in Gaul when he was ordered, in 43 BC, to set up a permanent military colony. The Senate's idea was to keep him busy, and politically impotent, far from Rome. The site Plancus chose for his five legions – a steep hill near the junction of the rivers Rhône and Saône – was exactly the same one that Caesar had used for his headquarters 15 years earlier. Both men had been well aware of the site's strategic importance.

A LADY FROM GAUL
The woman in the bronze bust, from the reign of Emperor Commodus (AD 180-92), personifies the elegance of Lugdunum's aristocracy. The economic boom in the city in the 2nd century AD was the blessing of a period of peace in Rome's empire.

Most of the Roman cities in the western provinces were designed in the image of Rome itself. Where the lie of the land permitted, the city was given a strictly geometric layout, with streets forming a regular grid pattern. Lugdunum was no different. As the sun emerged from behind the distant Alps on Tuesday, October 9, 43 BC, Plancus caught it in the sights of his *groma* – an ancient form of surveyor's theodolite. He aligned the *decumanus*, the road which ran from west to east, with the point on the horizon where the sun had appeared; and then placed the *cardo*, the road which ran from north to south, at right-angles to it. On that autumn morning, as he ploughed the first ritual furrow, the military town of Lugdunum came into being.

With the words 'Colonia Copia Felix Munatia Lugdunum' – meaning 'Munatius's plentiful, happy colony of Lugdunum' – Plancus dedicated the settlement to the veterans of the Gallic wars. The town he built clambered in tiers up the hill of Fourvière – but he took care to respect the sanctuary which stood on its top. Here, the native Gauls worshipped the Celtic god who gave the town its name – Lug, the sorcerer, craftsman, warrior, and poet.

ALTAR OF UNITY Imperial coins minted at Lugdunum bore the imprint of the altar of Rome and Augustus – a symbol of the united provinces of Romanized Gaul.

Eventually a wall 1,300m (4,265ft) long enclosed the site. At the eastern end the colony nestled into the slopes of the hill. Laid out like a chessboard around the two main streets, it overlooked the ferrymen and craftsmen working on the river banks.

THE RISE TO PROMINENCE

For its first 20 years, Lugdunum was nothing more than a small market town. It was not until the reign of the emperor Augustus (24 BC–AD 14) that the town was transformed into a capital. Augustus was captivated by the beauty of the site, sandwiched between the Rhône and Saône which flow from the Alps to the Mediterranean. Like his great-uncle Caesar, he was also impressed by its strategic position. Lugdunum stood on the northern edge of Gallia Narbonensis – Rome's earliest western province – and bordered the lands of the independent tribes of Gaul. But what made the site particularly desirable was the potential of its roads and waterways.

A SPRAWLING CITY

By the mid-2nd century AD, the Island of the Canabae was well established as Lugdunum's commercial hub. The word *canabae* refers to the shops and stalls that usually sprouted outside the gates of Roman camps. Condate was the city's religious centre. Lugdunum's main features included: the original forum (1), the capitol (2), the imperial palace (3), the theatre (4), the Odeon (5), the new forum (6), the circus (7), the federal sanctuary of Rome and Augustus (8), and the amphitheatre of the Three Gauls (9). Five main roads led out of the city: to Narbonensis (10); to Aquitania (11); to the English Channel (12); to the Rhine (13); and across the Alps to Italy (14).

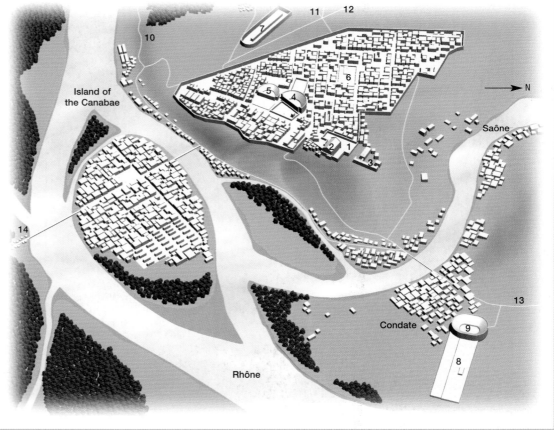

Island of the Canabae

Saône

Condate

Rhône

The city played a key part in Augustus's colonial policy. His intention was to push the Roman frontier north-west of the Alps, and to use the rivers Rhine and Rhône as his prime communication routes between the border zone and the heartlands of the empire. Roman towns on the sites of modern-day Arles, Orange, Valence, and Vienne already marked the course of the Rhône. Lugdunum completed this series.

In 27 BC Augustus divided Gaul into four provinces: Narbonensis (broadly, south-eastern France), Aquitania (western France, south of the Loire), Belgica (between the Seine and the Rhine), and Lugdunensis (between the Loire and the Seine). Gallia Narbonensis remained under the rule of the Roman Senate. The others – known collectively as the 'Three Gauls' or as Gallia Comata ('long-haired Gaul') – were controlled by a governor in Lugdunum who reported directly to the emperor. It was from Lugdunum that the 17 tribes of Aquitania, 18 tribes of Belgica, and 25 tribes of Lugdunensis were administered.

NEW BUILDING ON AN IMPERIAL SCALE

Augustus also made Lugdunum the centre of a network of military roads leading south to Narbonensis, north to what is now the English Channel, west to Aquitania, east to the Rhine, and across the Alps to Rome. As a result of its excellent communications by road and river, Lugdunum rapidly became an economic centre as well as an administrative capital.

Between 16 and 14 BC Augustus personally supervised new building work in the capital. Imposing new buildings and monuments sprang up all over the town: a vast forum, an imperial palace, and a temple which could be seen on its perch at the top of the hill of Fourvière from many miles around. It was here that Roman gods – Jupiter, Juno, and Minerva – were installed in place of the native Celtic god, Lug.

Augustus watched his capital grow rapidly. Soon, more water supplies were needed. To cope with the demand he constructed two aqueducts penetrating deep into the nearby mountains in quest of a daily total of nearly 14,000m^3 (494,500cu ft) of water.

CULTURAL UNITY – BY COMMAND

Augustus crowned these constructional achievements with a singular piece of audacity. Having transferred Lug's sanctuary from the hill of Fourvière to the southern slope of the hill of Croix-Rousse on the other bank of the river Saône, he replaced it with a sanctuary dedicated to Rome and himself. He wanted to impose a degree of cultural and political unity on Gaul by founding an imperial cult compatible with native tradition.

He persuaded members of the 60 tribes of the 'Three Gauls' to erect an altar on the site of the new sanctuary bearing the names of the tribes and a dedication to 'Romae et Augusto' (Rome and Augustus) – an image that was to become a symbol of Gallic unity. Augustus's stepson, Drusus, inaugurated the sanctuary on August 1, 12 BC. This particular day of the year had for centuries been the day on which the natives celebrated Lugnasad – a traditional Celtic festival which drew thousands of Gauls to the area. But from 12 BC onwards, delegates from each of the 60 Gallic tribes assembled on August 1 to mark a new festival – the feast of Rome and Augustus.

Over the next 200 years Roman emperors continued to shower privileges on the capital from which they hoped to control and administer Gaul. Tiberius, Caligula, Vitellius, and Hadrian all lived for a time in the imperial palace which Augustus had built, and two emperors – Claudius and Caracalla – were born there. In AD 19, during the reign of the emperor Tiberius (14–37), a great amphitheatre, designed for the

THE BUSTLE OF THE MARKET
Lugdunum's riverside streets were crowded with stalls, such as the one carved on a Roman funeral stele, selling local and imported wares. The city was also a trading centre for Burgundy wine.

entertainment of the delegates to a religious festival, was built next to Augustus's sanctuary. Thousands of gladiators, wild animals, and Christians, were to meet their end in this bloodstained arena which became famous in the 2nd century AD as the 'amphitheatre of the martyrs'.

Claudius (41–54) presented his native city with a new aqueduct, along with a new name – 'Colonia Copia Claudia Augusta Lugdunum' ('the plentiful colony of Claudius and Augustus') – and a fresh policy of assimilation. A bronze inscription found on the site of the town bears the text of a speech made by Claudius to the Roman Senate in 48 in which he upholds the right of the Gauls to be admitted to their ranks.

During the troubled reigns of the emperors Nero (54–68) and Vitellius (69), Lugdunum became an elegant place to live. Luxurious villas lined the streets of the upper town – the seat of the imperial bureaucracy – and the river quarters near the federal sanctuary. The commercial district, known as the Island of the Canabae (meaning 'the island of booths'), was transformed into a huge and bustling market.

A PERIOD OF OSTENTATION

Around 120, the emperor Hadrian (117–38) rebuilt much of Augustus's city. The dimensions of most of the main buildings were doubled. Hadrian also built the last of Lugdunum's four aqueducts, the aqueduct of Gier. This gigantic structure, which remains one of the masterpieces of its kind, channelled 24,000m^3 (847,560cu ft) of water a day from Mount Pilat, 75km (47 miles) away. By supplying water for the first time to

HADRIAN'S THEATRE Originally built under Augustus, around 17-15 BC, the theatre was greatly expanded in the 2nd century AD to provide seating for 11,000 people.

THE GODDESS FROM THE EAST

Before Christianity began to take hold in Lugdunum, it faced stiff competition from a religion introduced to the city by the powerful colony of Greeks from Asia Minor: the cult of the fertility goddess Cybele. Cybele won many followers among the Gauls. Devotees undertook the test of the *taurobolium*. After purification rites, which involved vigils, fasting, and flagellation, they were ritually anointed with the blood of a bull whose throat had been slit. A statue of the goddess stood inside her sanctuary at Lugdunum, the 'Campus Matris Deum' or 'Field of the Mother of the Gods' – a vast building covering an area of 4,252m² (45,768sq ft).

BOUNTIFUL MOTHER Only the head of the Lugdunum Cybele statue remains, wearing a calathos (fruit basket) fertility symbol, as in this complete statue from Spain.

the Sarra plateau to the north-west of the city, it enabled the upper part of Lugdunum to extend westwards, giving birth to a new residential quarter.

Under Hadrian and his successor, Antoninus Pius (138–61), villas sprouted everywhere. They were styled on the houses of the nobility in Rome – the ultimate in luxury, with central heating, elaborate mosaic floors, frescoes on the walls, and well-tended gardens. Their inhabitants were the *honestiores* – the city's top-level administrators and members of the upper class.

Pius continued the programme of public building, adding an Odeon – a building designed for concerts and public readings, which seated 3,000. Engineers lavished special care and expertise on the acoustics of this lovely auditorium, and on the glittering mosaic floor of the orchestra pit, which has now been restored.

A COSMOPOLITAN MELTING POT

By the 2nd century, Lugdunum had a population of about 50,000 – impressive for a rural country like Gaul, but tiny in comparison with imperial Rome's 1.2 million inhabitants. Apart from the noisy quarters where the boatmen and workers lived, the city was not densely populated. As the demand for new buildings grew, the city had expanded with ease around spacious gardens and public monuments.

Every day, people from far-flung corners of the Roman Empire rubbed shoulders with each other in the streets of Lugdunum: senior officials, Gallic craftsmen, legionaries from the Rhine, and traders from all over the Mediterranean. The city was, in fact, a perfect miniature of the Roman world in its heyday. Its squares and alleys were a cosmopolitan melting pot of colour and culture: pure Latins, Romanized Gauls, Celts, Greeks, and Asiatics.

The Greeks from Asia Minor soon made their mark. The first to arrive were those who held imperial office – freedmen who had often secured the best positions within the administration. They were followed by Greek traders who masterminded the city's biggest business enterprises. Soon they formed a colony of their own, making up 30 per cent of the population of Lugdunum.

As well as bringing a variety of goods and produce, other cultures also introduced new spiritual beliefs. Settlers from Antioch, Bithynia, Cappadocia, Pergamum, Pontus, and Smyrna brought their religions and their gods – including Mithras, Isis, Serapis, and Cybele.

In the long term, the most far-reaching of the new faiths was introduced by the Greek-speaking people who believed in the Gospel according to St John – Christianity – a creed which was still officially outlawed in the Roman Empire. Converts appeared among the aristocracy, the middle class, the freedmen, and the slaves. It penetrated every nook and cranny of the complicated structure of Roman society, and it encouraged the large-scale emancipation of slaves.

The Christian church of Lugdunum was well organized and influential enough to withstand even the brutal persecution which followed. One of the worst pogroms came in 177 under the emperor Marcus Aurelius (161–80). Many Christians suffered horrible deaths. One group, led by a woman called Blandina, were first mauled by savage beasts in the arena. Then their bodies were burnt and their ashes cast into the Rhône 'so that no vestige of them should remain on earth'. But the mark left by the martyrs was indelible; the rock on which the city's Christians had built their church stood firm.

BARBARIAN DESTRUCTION

A religion preaching salvation could not save the city from decline. During the 3rd century, trade slackened and decay set in. The emperor Diocletian (284–305) eventually stripped Lugdunum of its status as a capital.

When the first hordes of Germanic invaders – the Salian Franks – began to overrun parts of Gaul during the second half of the 3rd century, the end came quickly. The 'barbarians' took over with ease, depriving the city of its water supply by carrying off the lead pipes of the aqueducts. As a result, Lugdunum's inhabitants were forced to abandon the main parts of the city for less attractive quarters down by the river banks. It was not long before Condate, the district where most of the churches were clustered, suffered a similar fate.

Today, little remains of the old Roman capital in Gaul. Much was destroyed by the barbarians and most of the rest was buried beneath the large city which sprang up several centuries later. Hoards of coins are among the few artefacts that have been unearthed beneath the heart of modern Lyons. Hidden in panic and never recovered by their owners, they are a sad reminder of the death of a city governed by the 'Pax Romana' – the peace and stability guaranteed by the imperial might of Rome.

Hatra

A holy city in a hostile desert

The walls of Hatra once rose like a mirage from the parched landscape between the waters of the Tigris and the Euphrates. Lured by its promise, the most formidable fighting force in the ancient world was twice defeated at its gates.

AT THE HEIGHT OF ROME'S POWER, TWO OF ITS GREATEST RULERS suffered crushing defeats at the gates of a remote city that lay on the edge of the Mesopotamian desert. The emperor Trajan (AD 98–117) was vanquished in 117; Septimius Severus (AD 193–211) in 198. Both fell victim to the hostile desert, and to a people who had learnt how to survive in the harsh terrain.

Roman legionaries, parched and exhausted, were twice repulsed with a shower of blazing pitch and hails of deadly arrows delivered by elusive horsemen. The heavily fortified city of Hatra, stronghold of the Parthians, remained undefeated, to the greater glory of its god, Shamash, lord of the desert and its tribes.

RISING OUT OF THE WILDERNESS

Hatra lies west of Mosul (Al-Mawsil) and the upper Tigris in present-day Iraq. Water is scarce there. Farther to the west stretches the arid wilderness of the Mesopotamian desert, a dead zone incapable of supporting a community of any size. Excavations have revealed that Hatra's earliest settlers arrived in ancient times, perhaps to set up a staging post.

In the 4th century BC, the whole of Mesopotamia was conquered by Alexander the Great. After Alexander's death in 323 BC, one of his generals, Seleucus, gained control and founded the Seleucid dynasty. Under the Seleucids, an Arab-speaking people moved into the Hatra region, adding considerably to the existing population. But the city's metamorphosis into a prosperous religious centre was yet to come.

At the beginning of the 3rd century BC, much of the Middle East fell to the Parthians, a warrior tribe from the Asian steppes. From the heart of the Asian continent, roving tribes fanned out in a tide of conquest. One group, the Sarmatians, settled in southern Russia. Another, the Kushans, reached India. By 247 BC, Arsaces of Parthia (248–212 BC) had annexed most of the Seleucid provinces in western Asia, and established a Parthian Empire that was to last for nearly 400 years.

IN ALEXANDER'S WAKE
Corinthian columns echo classic Greek style in Hatra's temple of the Sun-god, Shamash. It is one of a group of buildings mostly from the 2nd and 1st centuries BC, many of which survive remarkably intact. The Greek influence was a legacy of the conquests of Alexander the Great.

THE GREAT SUN-GOD   Crowned in shining splendour, Shamash, god of the Sun, was Hatra's principal deity. The relief from Hatra was carved in the late 2nd century AD.

whose names and faces are known through the statues and inscriptions found at the site – but took on a new importance as the capital of the Parthian state of Araba.

It is uncertain whether the development of Hatra was brought about by the Parthians or their Arab subjects. But under Parthian rule, it became a holy city, dedicated to the cult of one of the supreme deities of the Middle East – Shamash, worshipped under many different names, and often known simply as 'Lord'.

FROM TENTS TO GREAT TEMPLES

Hatra grew into a centre for ceremony and pilgrimage. A new city was laid out on a vast scale, surrounded by two walls – an outer wall 8km (5 miles) long, and an almost circular inner wall more than 6km (about 4 miles) long. In the centre was an immense sacred enclosure, the *temenos*. This had its own wall, with towers and 12 gates. At the back of the enclosure stood the Great Temple of Shamash. Its main features – two vaulted halls – each had one side left open. These are known as *iwans*, similar to arcades, and are believed to have been an innovation of Parthian architecture – recalling in stone the tents of the Parthians' nomadic forebears. Although much of Hatra is Eastern in conception, many features, such as a temple with a double-colonnade near the gates of the *temenos*, are distinctly Greek in execution. Parthian civilization was a hybrid, a fact illustrated by its curious mixture of religious beliefs.

The Parthians were superb horsemen. Their favoured weapon was the short bow; they fired their arrows straight from the saddle. One of their tactics had such a devastating effect that its name has entered everyday speech. The parting shot – the conversational last word that leaves an opponent feeling crushed – was originally the Parthian shot: a volley of arrows unleashed by horsemen who were pretending to retreat, but suddenly turned in their saddles to shoot down their pursuers.

POWERFUL MASTERS OF RICH TRADE ROUTES

The Parthian Empire extended from the Caucasus to the Persian Gulf, and from the Euphrates to the frontiers of India. The domain embraced the centres of the ancient civilizations of Greece, Mesopotamia, and Persia. It commanded an emerging trade network linking Europe with the Far East: the Silk Road ran from the Mediterranean to China through Parthian territory. Great wealth flowed through the Middle East, and whoever was master of the trade routes was master of that wealth.

Like other nomadic invaders before them, the Parthians also came to enjoy the comforts of the settled communities they had overrun. Greek, Persian, and Mesopotamian traditions were assimilated. The barbarians were civilized by their subjects.

The Parthians never developed a strong central administration. Though ruled by a king, their domains were governed by a warrior aristocracy which allowed considerable freedom to its vassals. Hatra kept its own dynasty of Arab rulers – many of

A REGAL FIGURE   Senatruq I, a ruler of Hatra in the 2nd century AD, stands in the slightly rigid, eyes-front attitude of other statues found at the site. His baggy trousers reflect the Parthians' steppe ancestry.

THE SACRED PRECINCT

Excavations have uncovered the main features of the *temenos*, Hatra's religious enclosure. Archaeologists continue to reveal new finds, so the reconstruction is not definitive. The rectangular precinct, covering an area of some 435m (1,427ft) by 320m (1,050ft), was surrounded by a wall. Sizeable fragments of the wall's towers still survive. A forecourt was reached through a monumental gateway (1). The buildings on the left (2) were probably warehouses. A Greek-style temple (3) stood isolated at the back of the forecourt. Flanking it were two gateways giving access to the rear court or *peribolus* (4)

which housed the most sacred building, the great temple of the city (5), at first thought to have been a palace. Its frontage is more than 100m (328ft) long. Two huge *iwans* (6) – open-fronted halls – were flanked by smaller halls (7) with the same frontal arcades reproduced on a smaller scale. At the back was the inner shrine (8). Inscriptions found at the site indicate that it was the sanctuary of the god Shamash. Square in design, it contains a chamber which may have housed a statue of the god or, as some archaeologists believe, a sacred flame kept permanently alight in his honour.

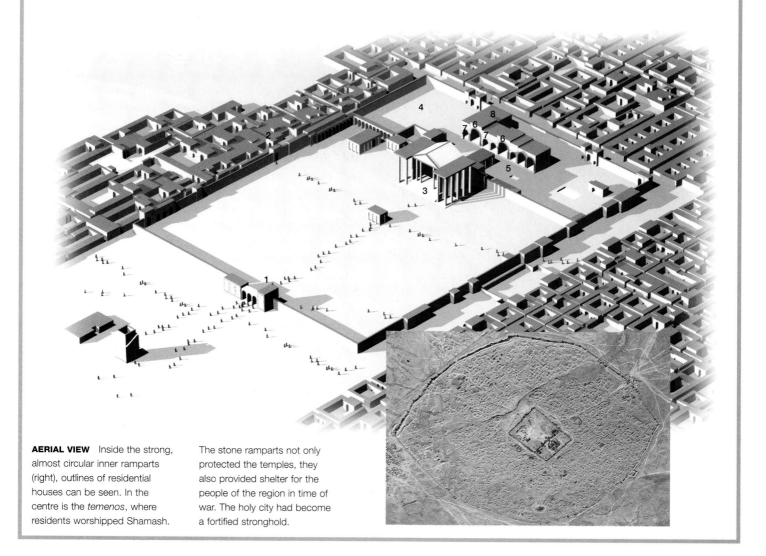

AERIAL VIEW Inside the strong, almost circular inner ramparts (right), outlines of residential houses can be seen. In the centre is the *temenos*, where residents worshipped Shamash.

The stone ramparts not only protected the temples, they also provided shelter for the people of the region in time of war. The holy city had become a fortified stronghold.

Some of the gods worshipped at Hatra were inspired by Arab or Babylonian cults, others by figures from Greek mythology. Shamash, the supreme godhead, may have been worshipped as a sacred flame kept permanently alight on an altar behind the Great Temple, similar to the customs of the Persian cults of fire-worship associated with Zoroaster.

A series of unusual sculptures has been unearthed at Hatra. Some are effigies of the gods, others portraits of worshippers. All the figures are depicted in the same attitude: face-on, staring straight ahead, solemn and impassive. Each is executed with an extraordinary realism. Every detail of their clothing has been carved with minute accuracy, from the footwear, headgear,

tunics, trousers, and weaponry down to the smallest pearls and gems adorning the fabric. Since excavations began early in the 20th century, dozens of similar figures have been discovered and more are still being brought to light. They provide a comprehensive costumed parade of ceremonial figures from the Parthian period. And their simple, face-on presentation is a forerunner to later Byzantine mosaics showing Christian saints in similar attitudes.

While the role of the Parthian holy city remained chiefly religious, its geographical position made the development of trade almost inevitable. The comings and goings of pilgrims and traders along the rivers and across the desert would in itself have created commericial opportunities Gradually, Hatra became a regular destination for desert caravans transporting goods. The sacred precinct, the *temenos*, was used as a marketplace. Halls were built against its walls, and were used as warehouses and shops. There was nothing unusual about this – temple complexes had often been used in the Middle East as centres for storing and selling goods.

The front of one enormous building uncovered at Hatra, thought to have been a temple, was supported by huge half-columns 3m (10ft) in diameter and more than 15m (50ft) high. The facade bore two reliefs, one showing a squatting camel, and the other a she-camel suckling her young. The glorification of this beast of burden is linked with the merchants who passed through the city. Camels had been introduced as pack animals during the first millennium BC, and became essential to the trade carried out across the huge expanse of desert.

LIFE IN THE CITY

Inside the city, people lived in flat-roofed dwellings, generally built around a central courtyard. The homes would be furnished with mats and rugs, and lit at night with small oil lamps.

Parthian society was male-dominated – a characteristic of Asian nomads, whose menfolk went off to hunt or tend the herds while the women remained in their tents. Women were forbidden to dine in the presence of their husbands. Much of their lives was spent shut away indoors, and when they did venture out, they covered their heads with a veil.

Other traditions from the nomadic past survived, including the Parthians' love of horses, and the care which owners lavished on their breeding. Hunting was another passion among the Parthian aristocracy, and walled parks were kept well stocked with game to keep them entertained. Parthian horsemen also enjoyed a

> As . . . the Romans broke ranks . . . , the archers swivelled in their saddles and fired a devastating volley of arrows into the Romans' exposed formations.

forerunner to the modern game of polo, which may have originated in a similar game still played by horsemen of the Asian steppes.

The Parthians left no great literary texts – their stories were passed down through an oral tradition. Heroic epics, once recited in the huts and tents pitched across the windswept plains of Asia, were retold inside the cities, passed down from generation to generation.

REPELLING ROMAN MIGHT

The Parthian Empire survived some 500 years, from the 3rd century BC to the 3rd century AD. The period coincided with the rise of Rome to the west, and the rival nations were often locked in combat. The Romans developed ambitions in Asia Minor under the Republic in the 1st century BC. They saw their mission, at least partly, as a crusade to reclaim Alexander's conquests for Western civilization. Rome was the aggressor, and its first major clash with Parthia ended in disaster.

In 54 BC, Marcus Licinius Crassus led a catastrophic expedition against the eastern neighbour. The next year, his army was routed at Carrhae (now Harran in south-eastern Turkey), and he was assassinated shortly afterwards. The Parthian victory stemmed from their brilliant deployment of cavalry. It was at Carrhae that the Romans first learnt the full effect of the Parthian shot as a tactic of warfare. The Parthians would first launch a charge by heavy lancers, and follow it with light, mounted archers. As they withdrew and the Romans broke ranks to pursue them, the archers swivelled in their saddles and fired a devastating volley of arrows into the Romans' exposed formations.

After Carrhae came recurrent clashes interspersed with periods of uneasy peace. The River Euphrates became the frontier and Mesopotamia one of the main flashpoints

WARRIOR KING A Sassanian royal relishes the thrill of the hunt, turning in his saddle as if to deliver a Parthian shot in the midst of a battle – a move calculated to take his prey by surprise.

SHAPUR THE CONQUEROR The Sassanian king Shapur I accepts the surrender of the Roman emperor Valerian in a relief from Naqsh-e Rostam. Shapur was responsible for the devastation of Hatra.

for conflict. Hatra's strategic position made it a tempting target for attack.

When Trajan and, later, Septimius Severus made their attempts to conquer the city during the 2nd century AD, their legionaries had first to cross hundreds of miles of desert waste, buffeted by strong winds and sandstorms, dragging their huge siege engines with them. Hatra must have appeared like a shimmering mirage, its splendid temple tops visible above the formidable double ring of walled ramparts. The city bore promise of immense plunder, but the task was daunting. Hatra had few gates and many defensive towers. The legionaries discovered that all the watering places had been drained to fill tanks set up inside the city.

Without warning, hordes of Parthian horsemen descended on the Romans from all sides in clouds of dust, let fly a vicious storm of arrows, and retreated as quickly as they had arrived.

The Romans used their siege engines to try to breach the walls. But no sooner was an assault launched than the defenders would bombard the legionaries with fiery missiles which could not be extinguished. Lumps of blazing pitch and naphtha stuck to men and machines, engulfing all in flames. Modern napalm is based on the same principle.

The emperor Trajan's health gave out soon after his failure at Hatra, and he died a few months later. Eighty-one years later, Septimius Severus was almost killed by a missile fired from inside the city's walls.

A CITY DISAPPEARS

In these short-term campaigns, the Parthians excelled. But the lack of a strong central administration made them vulnerable to sustained pressure. The long struggles with Rome gradually weakened their empire, while rivalries within the main dynasties undermined the authority of the throne.

But it was not Rome that destroyed Parthia. At the beginning of the 3rd century, the two rivals saw a common enemy emerge when the Sassanian dynasty, a Persian royal house, began a revolt against its Parthian masters. The Sassanians prided themselves on their true Persian ancestry, scorning the Parthians for their flexible government and hybrid

traditions – the very qualities that had contributed to Hatra's rise from a place of pilgrimage to a prosperous commercial city. By an odd twist of fate, the last kings of the holy city ended up in alliance with the Romans.

The Persian tide was not to be stemmed. In 240, Hatra was captured by the Sassanian king, Shapur I (240–72). According to legend, Shapur owed his victory to the treachery of the king of Hatra's daughter, who betrayed a secret talisman said to protect the city. Shapur had carried her off, intending to marry her. But he was so disgusted when he learnt of her disloyalty to her father that he had her put to death instead, by tying her to the tail of a wild horse which was then set free.

Hatra was pillaged and devastated. For many centuries the ruined site was visited only by nomads, and gradually the ruins themselves were overlaid with sand. Hatra became a lost city, a place alluded to by authors, its location unknown.

Then, in the 19th century, the British orientalist Sir Henry Rawlinson noticed the outline of some ruins which lay buried underneath the sand. Detailed research was carried out by German archaeologists between 1907 and 1911. In 1951 the Iraqi Department of Antiquities began further excavations, and since then, work on the site has been continuous.

The ruins are well preserved. Under Greek influence, Hatra's monuments were built of stone – much more durable than the mud brick usually used on Mesopotamian sites. In addition, the remoteness of the city ensured that it remained untouched. Stones still lie exactly where they fell in the days of the Sassanian conquerors. The Iraqi restorers may one day revive the entire city, and the full scale of this stronghold of the Parthian people – judged harshly by the historians as a civilization lacking in depth and achievement – will be revealed.

Sipán

Lords of gold and sacrifice

Material looted from ancient Peruvian graves gave tantalizing glimpses of the splendours of Moche craftsmanship. Its full glories were revealed in 1987, when an argument between tomb robbers led to the discovery of a previously untouched burial.

THE TREASURE HUNT BEGAN IN SOUTH AMERICA in the 16th century AD, when the Spaniards conquered the Inca and their neighbours. Their aim was to plunder precious artefacts, and they were prepared to go to any lengths to achieve it. In the city of Cerro Blanco, at the mouth of the Moche river in northern Peru, stood the vast Huaca del Sol (Pyramid of the Sun) – a sacred mound with huge potential for a rich haul. The Spaniards hatched a clever plan to reveal its secrets. They diverted the waters of the Moche towards the mound, washing away part of its outer wall. The sacred site gave up its silver and gold, crafted into works of art by a gifted civilization named after the river.

The Moche, whose culture laid the foundations for the later Chimú, who in turn influenced their Inca conquerors, lived in river valley settlements along the coast of northern Peru, between the 1st and the 8th century AD. Their realms comprised a number of related kingdoms, rather than a unified state. At the height of their power, the Moche occupied land covering some 35,750km² (13,803sq miles). East to west it spanned no more than 80km (50 miles) but stretched 550km (342 miles) from the Huarmey valley in the south to the Piura valley in the north. Between the two lay further treasure at Sipán, near present-day Chiclayo.

TOMB RAIDERS AT SIPÁN

It was here one night in February 1987 that a group of *huaqueros*, or tomb robbers, began digging into a sacred mound. They stumbled upon a fabulously rich burial. A series of mounds promised further treasures, but before the search could resume, the thieves fell out over the division of their finds, and one of the *huaqueros* gave his companions up to the police. The police called in Walter Alva, the director of the local archaeological museum in the town of Lambayeque.

Alva and his team investigated the chaotic remains of the looted tomb – with the help of armed guards to prevent further illicit plundering. The archaeologists set about painstakingly collecting clues to the nature of the burial and its rituals, unaware that the *huaca*, or sacred pyramid, was about to yield an amazing secret.

GILDED GLORY Cotton banners covered the body in the intact tomb at Sipán. The banners are decorated with gilded copper and figures, such as this, sewn onto the cotton fabric and adorned with metal triangles, discs, and turquoise bracelets. Fine line drawings on Moche pottery show warriors carrying similar banners. The Moche grew rich enough through agriculture to support a class of master craftsmen alongside its elite.

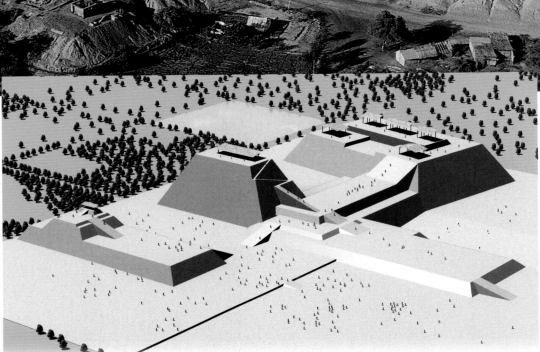

SACRED MOUNTAINS The *huacas* of Sipán were originally towering brick pyramids (right) that served both as shrines of sacrifice and as royal tombs. Interlocking platforms and ramps connected the three pyramids, each of which probably started as a simple platform to which successive levels were added. Today, huge mounds (above) are all that survive. The mound in which the intact burials were found is in the foreground.

Inside the plundered grave lay the skeleton of a man with a copper helmet and a shield. But beneath him were traces of decayed timbers – supports that formed the roof of another chamber below. This unexpected find led to the discovery of the most magnificent burial ever uncovered in the Americas.

FIGURES FROM THE RITUAL LANDSCAPE

Inside the wooden chamber they found cane coffins containing two men, a dog, and two women. In the centre of these lay another coffin made of wood, containing the body of the man for whom the tomb had been created. The man had died in his late 30s or early 40s – a good age for the period when he lived, around AD 250. He was a warrior lord, dressed in an elaborately woven white tunic and sandals of silver. In his right hand he held a gold sceptre, in his left a silver one.

Other gold and silver objects had been placed on or underneath the man's body, including a huge semicircular headdress, several helmets, and a series of decorated bells, which he had once worn at his waist. Out of the dust came gold and turquoise beaded pectorals, bracelets, and ear ornaments. Other funerary offerings included weapons, *Spondylus* (spiny oyster) shells, and fans with gold handles, some made of flamingo feathers. Archaeologists also found a series of cloth banners decorated with gilded copper.

As if this fabulous discovery were not enough, Alva's team subsequently uncovered two more richly furnished burials within the same mound. The second intact burial was of a similar date to the first, but was distinguished by a huge gold headdress in the form of an owl spreading its wings. The third had been buried several hundred years earlier, in a grave rather than a chamber, with a range of grave goods even more rich and elaborate than those in the tomb of the warrior lord.

One outstanding piece among the older lord's ornaments was a necklace of rattles. Each rattle consisted of a small gold hemisphere, about 8cm (3in) in diameter, containing three tiny gold balls. Above the hemisphere, a mesh of gold wires formed a spider's web, on which crouched a spider of beaten gold, its back decorated with a human face.

BUILDERS AND CRAFTSMEN

The sacred mounds of the Moche were constructed of adobe – bricks of sun-dried mud. The workers who built them were commoners, who paid their taxes in the form of labour. Labour gangs also constructed roads and canals for the transport of precious materials – turquoise and gold from the north and feathers from the forests to the east. Sea traders travelled far to the north to obtain *Spondylus* shells. These materials were wrought into the astonishing craftwork found

GOLDEN PRIEST The old lord in the third burial wore a nose ornament which stands just 11cm (4½in) high. This figure's owl headdress marks him as a priest, and he wears his own tiny, movable nose ornament.

DEATHLY COMPANY The warrior lord of Sipán lies in state, attended by sacrificed men. The women buried with him – perhaps concubines or relatives – had been dead for some time before being placed in the tomb.

WARRIOR LORD Mosaics of shell, gold, and turquoise decorate the ear ornaments found in the first tomb at Sipán. This minute gold figure wears the same nosepiece and headdress as one of the bodies in the tomb.

The Moche were not only skilled in metalwork; they were also fine potters. Huge collections of pots were placed in burials at Sipán and elsewhere in Moche territory – created to order as part of the funerary preparations.

Many Andean cultures illustrated aspects of daily life on their pottery, and the Moche brought this art form to its highest pinnacle. They decorated their pots with fine line drawings of subjects from everyday scenes, such as weaving and hunting.

On others processions of musicians play trumpets, bells, rattles, and panpipes. Some pots reveal the Moche's sea-going activities; the sea was a major source of food for them. Fishing boats made of tied reed bundles, complete with fishing lines, nets, fish, and fishermen, are a common theme.

A number of vessels were stamped with designs in relief. Others were created as three-dimensional sculptures, loosely based on the shape of a bottle or bowl.

inside the tombs. For the Moche were superb metallurgists. They mined and exported copper ores, as well as the goods created in their workshops. Traces of some of their workshops survive to the west, south, and east of Sipán. Some 15km (9 miles) farther up the valley, in later Moche times, a large town with substantial copper workshops emerged at Pampa Grande.

RITUAL AND SACRIFICE

Many Moche pots depict ritual scenes of sacrifice, funerary rites, and warfare. Some show battles fought in the desert regions between the river valley settlements. These encounters usually took the form of a series of single combats between warriors, in which the aim was not to maim or kill an opponent, but to stun him with a blow from a mace-topped warclub. The victor would then strip and bind the loser, and publicly parade him as his captive.

Ultimately, these captives of ritual warfare were sacrificed. In an important religious ceremony, their throats were cut by a priest, who caught the blood in a goblet. A second priest, wearing an owl headdress and attended by a priestess, offered the goblet to the ruler, who drank the blood. The bodies of the sacrificial victims were

GILDED TREASURES

Gold was the most highly valued metal. Gold-working had been a local industry in the upper valley for centuries before the development of the Moche culture. An alloy of gold and copper, known as *tumbaga*, was also popular among many Andean cultures.

The Moche finished objects made of this alloy with depletion gilding: they treated the surface of the objects with acid, which removed the surface copper and left a layer of pure gold in its place. To gild plain copper objects, they used a more sophisticated method. They immersed the objects in a solution of gold, water, minerals, and salts, which was then heated. A thin layer of gold formed on top of the copper. Further heating of the copper object bonded the gold to its surface.

AN OFFERING OF BLOOD Complex, three-dimensional pottery was made using moulds. It often depicted human sacrifice, carried out by a priest, a god, or an animal. Other pots show the sacrifice of deer.

POTTERY PIPER Musicians were a popular subject for moulded pots, and for drawings on plain vessels. Figures playing trumpets, rattles, and bells were found in the Sipán tombs.

then dismembered, and strings were tied around their heads and limbs so that they could be hung up as trophies.

Until recently, archaeologists studying these scenes suggested that they depicted mythological events involving deities. But the discoveries at Sipán tied them firmly to the real world. Severed hands and feet found near the Sipán mounds are evidence of sacrificial rites.

In many ritual scenes on pottery, sacrifices and offerings are shown taking place at sacred mounds. One common scene shows priests offering *Spondylus* shells to a supreme warrior priest seated within a pavilion on top of a *huaca*. The dress and accoutrements of the warrior priest in these scenes match those found with the body in the first tomb at Sipán – including his sceptre, headdress, weapons, and waist bells.

The man in the second tomb, with his owl headdress, wore the dress of the bird priest who presented the goblet of blood to his ruler. A female burial excavated more recently, at San José de Moro in the adjacent Jequetepeque valley, closely matches the figure of the attending priestess. The old lord in Sipan's third tomb was probably the warrior priest in an earlier guise, before the details of the ceremony had fully evolved.

THE SYMBOLISM OF THE MOUND

The sacred mounds of the Moche symbolized the mountains which played a vital role in South American religion. The Andes, as the source of essential natural resources, were revered by all the cultures who lived in the regions near to them. Rainfall was rare in the Moche region – and the rivers fed by the mountains were the only source of fresh water. The inhabitants of the valleys constructed sophisticated irrigation networks to take water to their fields.

The bodies of the sacrificial victims were then dismembered, and strings were tied around their heads and limbs so that they could be hung up as trophies.

Platforms were set among the fields for the officials who supervised agricultural work. It was agricultural labour and its produce that supported the hierarchy of nobles as well as the craftsmen who made metalwork and pottery.

At the apex of society was the supreme ruler, attired in death as the warrior lord. The sea also played a key role in Moche cosmology. Its significance is demonstrated by an artefact found in the burial of the old lord at Sipán – a golden crab with a human face and a pectoral in the shape of an octopus. The Humboldt current running through the south-eastern Pacific provides one of the richest harvests of marine food in the world, but the ocean also harbours fearsome powers of destruction. The devastating storms and upset weather patterns brought periodically by the El Niño phenomenon still spell ruin along the Pacific coast.

A FIGHT FOR SURVIVAL

Natural disasters – El Niño, earthquakes, volcanic eruptions, drought, and floods – were always part of South American life. But between AD 562 and 594, a period of severe drought brought enormous changes to the Moche realms. Ravaged by famine and disease, the population plummeted, and massive coastal dunes built up, driving the remaining population inland. The irrigation networks on which agriculture depended were disrupted and new systems had to be created.

Warfare, previously confined to ritual combat, developed into something more deadly – real aggression over natural resources. Fortifications sprang up, and communities hoarded produce to tide them over during difficult years. By AD 800, this fight for survival had fractured the territory of the Moche into numerous principalities, and the cultural unity once enjoyed by the river valley kingdoms became buried deep in the past with their glorious ancestors.

Constantinople

The city of the emperor Justinian

When Rome perished under barbarian fire and sword, a second imperial capital kept alive the glorious traditions of the fallen city. The new centre of power was Constantinople: luxurious, refined – and seething with poverty on an unimaginable scale.

MORE THAN A MILLION PEOPLE LIVED IN CONSTANTINOPLE (now Istanbul) in the 6th century AD. Its beauty was renowned far and wide. Suffused with the grey light of the Bosporus – the strait separating Europe and Asia – an undulating skyline of domes rose from a soft shimmering sea of pink brick.

Constantinople's churches, gardens and palaces, wondrous in their own right, housed some of the finest works of classical Greek statuary. Marbled walls flashed with iridescent mosaics. Despite undercurrents of suffering and depravity that accompanied its affluence, this city at the crossroads of the East and West was famed as a beacon of civilization – the heir of Rome and guardian of the Christian faith.

A STRATEGIC SITE

Its site is a promontory jutting out from the western shore of the Bosporus where the warm Aegean climate is tempered by cold moist winds blowing down across the Black Sea.

Greeks from Megara are said to have founded a settlement here around 668 BC. Their leader, Byzas, gave it its name – Byzantion, later Romanized to Byzantium. A deep-water inlet known as the 'Golden Horn' provided the site with a natural harbour, and gradually the city became a focal point for trade, handling timber and wheat supplies on their way to Greece from the steppes of southern Russia. Greek tradition took root, but it was the rise of imperial Rome that began the city's ascent to glory. In AD 196 Byzantium fell to the legions, and under Rome it developed into a metropolis.

By the 3rd century AD, storm clouds were gathering over the Roman Empire. Warrior tribes of Goths from the Black Sea region, and Franks and Alemanni from along the Rhine, threatened its western frontiers. By the early 4th century Rome was no longer secure, and the emperor Constantine (307–37) looked to Byzantium as an alternative capital. The city was sheltered geographically from the incursions of the Germanic barbarians, and could also act as a bastion against oriental tribes to the east.

The decision to make Byzantium an imperial capital was followed by a rapid and extensive building programme. A senate house, baths, a palace, and a forum were set up. The empire was scoured for splendid monuments, which were imported from Rome, Alexandria, Athens, and Ephesus in order to beautify the city. In 330 Constantine formally declared it the Roman Empire's second capital. Its provinces were also to be known as Byzantium, and the city itself took on an alternative name – Constantinople, city of Constantine – in honour of its benefactor.

Constantine managed to hold off the barbarian threat to Rome. But persistent onslaughts from tribes north of the Danube continued to plague his successors. Religious and ethnic divisions also began to split the eastern and western provinces. On the death of the pious Christian emperor Theodosius I in 395, the Roman Empire was formally split into two halves. The eastern capital, Constantinople, increased in prestige as the beleaguered western territories began to crumble in the face of constant invasions by Germanic tribes.

In 410, Rome fell to the Visigoths – invaders originally from the Balkans – and was sacked and burnt. Constantinople now became the main guardian of classical civilization, protector of the Greek and Roman heritage, and of the Christian faith. It was left to the emperor Justinian to fulfil the city's potential.

Justinian (527–65) is one of the most imposing and enigmatic figures in Roman history. A country boy from the Balkans, he was brought up in Constantinople by his childless uncle, the emperor Justin I. On his uncle's death he inherited the throne of Rome. Traces of his Slavonic roots remained with him – it was said that he spoke Greek with a barbarian accent. Yet this upstart was to become the last of the great Roman emperors.

ACHIEVEMENTS IN WAR AND PEACE

Justinian was a military leader of the highest rank. Brilliantly served by two generals, Belisarius and Narses, he held the eastern frontier of Byzantium against the Sassanian monarchs of Persia. More, he managed to claw back from the barbarian Goths and Vandals much of the territory that they had occupied in North Africa and Italy. The Byzantine Empire ruled by Justinian eventually included many of the territories which had made up the old Roman Empire: the Balkans, Asia Minor, Syria, Palestine, Egypt, and North Africa.

To his victories in war Justinian added achievements at home. He reconciled, at least temporarily, the warring factions in the Eastern and Western churches. Passionately concerned with the law, he drew together the strands of the existing Roman legal code into four major compilations: the Codex, Digest, Institutes, and Novellae. The Code of Civil Law, or Justinian Code as it is generally known, was the means by which Roman law was committed to posterity.

Justinian's wife, the empress Theodora, was no less impressive. The daughter of a humble bearkeeper at the Constantinople Hippodrome, she was endowed with remarkable beauty and an exceptional strength of will. In her youth she had been a popular actress and courtesan, achieving notoriety for evading a ban on total nudity in the circus by appearing on stage in nothing but a minuscule girdle. Justinian married her in 523, four years before he came to the throne.

Theodora seemed to wield considerable power, and with her background she was an easy target for gossip. Yet she exercised her authority with much common sense and political foresight. Her husband saw himself as God's

ALL GOD'S CHILDREN A mosaic from the Basilica of Aquileia in northern Italy depicts the diversity of fish in the sea – a symbol of the diversity of Christian believers in the Holy Empire of Justinian's dreams.

representative on Earth, and his state as an earthly model of the Kingdom of Heaven. Pursuing his dream, he spent many nights studying state files, hoping to become the 'perfect legislator'. As he walked the corridors of his palace, the shrewd, realistic Theodora was constantly at his side, moderating his wilder schemes.

Justinian was a man of astonishing energy; his citizens called him 'the emperor who never sleeps'. But the city he inherited presented a daunting challenge even to his titanic capabilities. Though created as the heir to Rome, the city had more in common with the old, densely populated Babels of the East – Alexandria, Antioch, Ephesus, Pergamum – bustling centres of business which survived while the cities of the Western Empire fell. It was overcrowded, and choked with squalor, misery, and disease. As the Roman Empire slowly crumbled in the west, the eastern capital attracted adventurers, from refugees and rebels to deserters and prisoners of war. Peasants from neighbouring areas flocked to the city in search of work.

BYZANTINE SAVIOUR Long after the fall of Rome, Constantinople held its position as a centre of Christianity. The spirit of the later age is reflected in this 11th-century mosaic of Christ from the cathedral of Hagia Sophia.

Justinian's mind, another solution was born: to build. He would quite simply expand his bustling city.

The scheme was, of course, partly intended to immortalize his own glory and that of his Lord. But there was more. Justinian saw in the vagrant multitude an immense pool of manpower. Harnessing the army of the unemployed, he organized the construction of schools, baths, theatres, palaces, gardens, harbours, aqueducts, monasteries, and especially churches.

PUTTING POVERTY TO WORK

Constantinople still prided itself on its Greek heritage. Greeks held the highest positions in society. They called themselves the *politikoi* – the people of the town, the 'Byzantines of Byzantium' – to distinguish themselves from the alien multitudes.

Among these multitudes were peoples of the Middle East – Syrians, Anatolians, and Jews. When Justinian reconquered Rome's western provinces, more visitors and immigrants arrived. Egyptians and Africans from Nubia and Ethiopia rubbed shoulders with fair-haired white giants from the north: Germans, and Viking traders and mercenaries who had come via Russia. Barbarians civilized by their settlement in Italy sent their children to Constantinople to study Christianity, literature, law, and philosophy.

But Constantinople also sheltered those with smaller ambitions. Squatters infested the marble porticoes of the city's great colonnades; in winter the authorities had to nail boards across the entrances to give the vagrants some protection against the cold. Justinian, devout Christian that he was, distributed bread and opened hostels, workhouses, orphanages, and leper hospitals. Theodora founded a house for repentant prostitutes. But charity could not rid the city of its plague of poverty. In

For Justinian, building became an obsession. Yet vagrancy could not be eliminated. In 539 the emperor was still ordering new public works, but was also applying increasingly strict surveillance: 'Natives', he decreed, 'who are sound in body and have no means of subsistence must be sent without delay to the organizers of public works, to the heads of bakeries, and to those who maintain the gardens and so on. If they refuse, they must be expelled from the city. The physically handicapped and the old shall be left in peace and looked after by the inhabitants who are willing to do so. The others shall be asked why they have come to Constantinople, to ensure that no idlers remain; and as soon as they have finished . . . they shall be asked to return home.'

The building programme did not get rid of unemployment, but it turned the city into the wonder of its age. The works of contemporary writers and excavations by archaeologists have created a comprehensive picture of the Byzantine capital.

MODELLED ON ROME

Constantinople borrowed much from the mother city. The public buildings were mostly Roman in style. As chance would have it, the city even included seven hills, like the original. It was also divided into 14 districts for the purposes of administration. Titles of office were borrowed from Roman tradition: magistrate, consul, and so on. There was even a senate house.

The Imperial District, sited at the tip of the peninsula, was the city's commercial, administrative, and ceremonial hub. The Sacred Palace, begun by Constantine and enlarged by Justinian, was built there amid beautiful gardens that descended in terraces

to the sea. It is now the site of the Blue Mosque, built by the Ottoman Sultan Ahmed I. Today, only a few mosaics remain from Justinian's palace, but it is known to have consisted of a complex of pavilions, with adjoining churches and barracks.

The Hippodrome, next door to the Sacred Palace and connected to it by galleries and staircases, was the venue for lavish spectacles and sporting events, with seating for perhaps 100,000 spectators. It had been restored by Constantine as a slightly scaled-down model of the Circus Maximus in Rome, and embellished by his successors. Near the Hippodrome, the Baths of Zeuxippos provided a fashionable backdrop for socializing.

DEDICATED TO HOLY WISDOM

Towering above the other buildings rose the gigantic dome of the cathedral of Hagia Sophia (Holy Wisdom), Justinian's supreme achievement and the masterpiece of all Byzantine architecture. To the historian Procopius, prefect of Constantinople at that time, the vast dome 33m (108ft) across seemed not to be supported by masonry at all, 'but rather to cover space as though it were suspended from the sky by a golden chain'. In fact the weight had been spread across the whole structure by the use of arches, semi-domes, vaulted aisles, and galleries. The basilica was all the more remarkable because of the speed of its construction – it was built by 10,000 workmen between AD 532 and 537.

The services held inside were of staggering magnificence. On ceremonial occasions the entire court would crowd into the sanctuary. Before them was a curtain embroidered with 500,000 pearls, veiling a massive gold altar inlaid with precious gems. The interior of the church was illuminated by thousands of candles; smoke rose from incense burners. Crimson-clad musicians accompanied huge male-voice choirs, and the curved surfaces of the dome produced extraordinary effects of resonance.

Much of the original ornamentation in the Hagia Sophia has disappeared, but several examples of Byzantine church decoration have survived elsewhere, such as in the Church of San Vitale in Ravenna. Exquisitely carved marble panels would have served as altar-pieces, walls and domes would have been inlaid

A NEW STYLE The basilicas of Constantinople blended Roman and Christian architectural styles in their long, galleried halls. A 6th-century mosaic from Ravenna shows the same influence in a secular building.

with coloured-glass mosaics. One characteristic feature of the Byzantine style was the bold presentation, in simple lines and flat colours, of sacred figures gazing upon the worshippers through wide and penetrating eyes – eyes deliberately enlarged to enhance the grandeur and mystery of the Christian faith.

In front of the Hagia Sophia, in the heart of the Imperial District, was the Augustaeon, an impressive forum or marketplace whose shady colonnades were the favourite meeting place of Byzantine high society. People gathered there to make their mark, to chat or argue, to parade in the latest fashions, and to watch the comings and goings of the imperial court.

The surrounding area was renowned for its luxury and beauty. There were countless bookshops, serving as meeting places for the city's aspirant intellectuals. Perfume shops were redolent with the whiff of scandal as well as scent, as gossips met to exchange rumours. Only the wealthiest could afford to live in the area: the land-owning aristocrats, for example, who lived in town palaces, away from their country estates.

MERCHANTS AND MAGNATES

These nobles were forbidden to engage in business. Commerce was the prerogative of an elite class of magnates who controlled the major businesses, trade, and administrative posts, and may also have lived around the Augustaeon. The imperial government shrewdly assembled these merchants in a single area in order to supervise them more easily.

Justinian himself had extensive commercial interests, especially in the manufacture of silk. Until the 6th century, the Chinese had monopolized silk manufacture. The fine silk thread had reached Constantinople along the ancient Silk Road from the East. How the thread was produced remained a mystery in

Europe. Justinian was determined to break the secret. Learning that the knowledge he required had reached the Persian Empire to the east of Byzantium, he persuaded two Persian monks to engage in some officially sponsored espionage. They returned to Constantinople with details of the technique and a few silkworm eggs hidden inside a bamboo. Justinian set up looms in the palace to manufacture the cloth: the entire European silk industry dates back to this beginning.

All luxury goods were a major source of wealth for Byzantium, and trade in them was concentrated along a short stretch of a great avenue called the Mese. This marble highway ran for some 8km (5 miles) from east to west. At its east end, in the Imperial District, it was lined with two-storey arcades, housing stalls and shops of every kind.

Prosperous goldsmiths and jewellers traded along the route between the Sacred Palace and the Forum of Constantine – a distance of about 600m (1,970ft). Money-changers plied their trade there too, often operating in the street itself, sitting at tables piled high with bags of gold and silver coins. The Forum of Constantine was the hub of the Byzantine business world. It was overlooked by the Senate and a splendid statue of the first Christian emperor perched at the top of a porphyry column.

From the Forum of Constantine, the Mese ran west to the Forum of Theodosius, dominated by a triumphal arch, and thence to the Amastrianum, the cattle market, and the Forum of Arcadius – thus connecting all the city's principal marketplaces. The highway then crossed what remained of Constantine's walls and passed through the Psamathia district. With every step away from the smart Imperial District, the shops became shabbier, the people poorer, the buildings more crowded.

ENTRY THROUGH THE GOLDEN GATE

At the west end was the city's most splendid entrance, the Golden Gate, set in a defensive wall built by the emperor Theodosius II (408–450) to protect the land side of the peninsula from a threatened attack by the Huns. From the Golden Gate a highway led, via Thessalonica (Thessaloniki), to the Adriatic coast. This route across northern Greece was trodden incessantly by merchants, travellers, and soldiers. Known as the Via Egnatia, or Western Road, it was one of the most famous highways of the ancient world.

Constantinople was built in terraces on the banked-up slopes of the peninsula's rocky backbone. The terraces were connected by a network of staircases and steep, narrow streets, climbing

RIVALRY AT THE HIPPODROME

In Constantinople, as in Rome, the public was passionately keen on contests and entertainments, which were held in the Hippodrome. Tens of thousands of people piled into the stadium, from the emperor himself to the lowliest dockland worker.

The Hippodrome was built during the reign of Septimius Severus at the end of the 2nd century AD, and was rebuilt by Constantine as a smaller copy of the Circus Maximus in Rome. It covered an area some 500m (1640ft) long and 118m (387ft) wide, and was later embellished by Theodosius and Justinian.

The main events were chariot races, which lasted all day. Four were held in the morning and four in the afternoon. The vehicles were four-horse chariots – quadrigas – and in each event four quadrigas raced seven times around the stadium. The chariots were drawn from the racing stables of the city's four political factions, and competed to defend their colours: blue, green, red, or white. Supporters wore coloured scarves to show their allegiance.

The opening ceremony of the games followed an ancient ritual. The emperor blessed the people three times, and was greeted with thunderous cheering and

RACING TO VICTORY The four-horse chariots known as quadrigas battle for supremacy at the Hippodrome. The scene was carved in ivory in the 5th century AD.

applause from the spectators. Then the choirs of the four factions sang hymns of victory. Finally, the emperor threw a mappa, or serviette, onto the sand of the arena, a signal for the doors of the chariot sheds to open and the contestants to drive on. Charioteers were often of humble birth, but victors, who were awarded the palm and crown by the emperor and town prefect, became celebrities. Between the chariot races, clowns, acrobats, musicians, and dancers entertained the crowd, and lavish animal hunts and fights were staged.

But the Hippodrome was much more than just a place of entertainment. Antagonism between rival supporters of the Blues and the Greens, the two major factions, caused constant trouble, and the building became a focus of civil unrest.

Games were staged regularly in the city until it fell to Frankish Crusaders on April 12, 1204. Diverted from their mission to the Holy Land by the prospect of plundering the Byzantine capital, the marauders sacked the town. The Hippodrome was pillaged. A single treasure may have survived: a bronze of four horses, once part of a quadriga, a copy of which now towers over the portal of Saint Mark's Cathedral in Venice – the original is kept inside the cathedral to protect it from air pollution.

Scholars still argue about where the statue came from; but some suggest that it once gleamed on top of the chariot sheds of Constantinople's stadium.

and swooping through the hills. Tenement blocks five or six storeys high were squeezed together, crammed full of tenants.

Self-contained communities developed within the slumland sprawl. Craftsmen grouped together in districts according to their trades: glassmakers, potters, metal-workers, armourers, and tailors.

The most crowded districts were those on the waterfront. Constantinople was, above all, a maritime centre, and the coastal districts of the Golden Horn to the north of the city, and Propontis to the south, were strung with harbours. In reclaiming much of the old Roman Empire, Justinian had made the Mediterranean a 'Roman sea', opening up markets for Byzantine goods along the coasts of North Africa and Italy as far west as the Strait of Gibraltar.

Great warships and cargo vessels vied for space with little caïques, the characteristic fishing vessels of the Aegean. The Golden Horn offered deep and well-sheltered moorings. Ships entered under full sail to unload their cargoes.

An immense class of dockland workers came into existence: sailors, carpenters, caulkers, sail-makers, and porters. They lived in dark alleys, blocked with carts and rank from the stench of fried fish – part of the staple diet of the people, eked out with bread, vegetables and fruit.

THE DAILY PAGEANT

For all the people, the street was their front parlour: the place where rich and poor spent most of the day. It was also the stage for a cavalcade of entertainers. Public speakers addressed the crowds from street corners. Jugglers, bearkeepers, and performing monkeys entertained passers-by.

The rich rode on horseback, for preference on white steeds richly decked out with elaborate saddlecloths and harnesses. They were escorted by liveried servants, usually armed with cudgels to beat a path through the multitude of pedestrians and the streams of asses, oxen, sheep, pigs, camels, and even elephants being driven through the streets to the market. The noblest figures in the empire were borne in gilded carriages drawn by teams of mules.

Though all people might be equal in the eyes of the Lord, social inequality on Earth had been pronounced inevitable – even in Justinian's perfect state – so the church leaders had condoned

THE ROYAL COURT Fine mosaics in the church of San Vitale, Ravenna, show Justinian and Theodora with their retinue in ceremonial dress.

AN ARCHITECTURAL TRIUMPH
The Hagia Sophia's dome, rebuilt after an earthquake in AD 558, was for centuries the largest in the world. It was the model for the dome of St Paul's Cathedral in London.

slavery. Now and then, shuffling columns of slaves became a feature of the street pageant, along with sinister processions of condemned felons. These prisoners faced death or, more commonly, mutilation; assassins or conspirators were slung onto the backs of donkeys and flogged mercilessly as they passed through the town.

For all the public display of vanity and squalor, religious feeling ran very deep in the people. That was the paradox of Constantinople. Heated theological discussions were as much a feature of street life as everyday haggling over prices.

One major controversy divided Byzantium in Justinian's time, centring on the person of Christ himself. The orthodox view in the church was that Christ embodied two natures, the human and the divine. A heretical group known as the Monophysites, however, held a different belief which had developed in Alexandria. They maintained that Christ's divine

PALACE OF WATER Justinian's pillared underground cisterns, built in 520, were still in use under Turkish rule a thousand years later.

It was the Byzantines, with their passion for argument about religious matters, who brought two Greek words into widespread use – 'orthodox' and 'heretic'.

The public disputes reflected the depth of religious feeling. Icons – wooden panels painted with religious motifs – were set up both in churches and in homes. Many people, the poor in particular, venerated them as sacred, even miraculous, objects. It became the practice to carry icons through the city in torchlight processions, for – like almost everything else – the solemn pageantry of religion was celebrated in the streets.

The power of the ecclesiastical leaders was subservient only to the dictates of the emperor. In the church councils which met to deliberate on key matters of doctrine, any final decision needed the approval of the supreme authority. To Constantinople and its emperor fell the destiny of shaping the world's first civilization embracing Christianity as a state religion.

GOVERNMENT BY SUPREME RULE

This cosmopolitan population was governed by a pyramid-like bureaucracy headed by the emperor. Like many bureaucracies, it was prone to corruption and inefficiency. Denied any democratic institution through which to air its grievances, the seething mob was always ready to show its resentment. With every bad harvest or increase in taxes, turbulent crowds filled the streets threatening insurrection. The population tended to align itself according to four broad groupings, or factions, known as the Blues, Greens, Reds, and Whites. Members wore distinguishing colours on their shoulders.

A VISIBLE HERITAGE The mixture of Islamic and European architectural styles in the ancient city of Constantinople provided a rich source of ideas for later Ottoman architects. Its influence can still be seen in the horizon of present-day Istanbul.

component was so overwhelming that it obliterated the human element. The Monophysites gained recruits at every social level in Constantinople, but especially among the poor.

One Byzantine chronicler wrote: 'This town is full of craftsmen and slaves who are all deep theologians and preach in the shops and in the streets. If you want a man to change some money for you, he will first teach you in what way the Son differs from the Father; and if you ask the price of bread, he will tell you by way of answer, that the Son is inferior to the Father; and if you want to know if your bath is ready, the bath attendant will reply that the Son was created from nothing . . .'

The factions were partly street gangs, partly political groups. In the time of Justinian, the Blues and Greens were dominant. The Greens represented the merchants, democratic in their political leanings and favouring Monophysite beliefs. The Blues were aristocratic and theologically orthodox. The enmity of the two groups set whole districts at each other's throats. The Hippodrome became a focus for the rivalry. At foot races athletes from the different factions competed against each other, backed by partisan support from the terraces. It was in this cauldron of political ferment that disorders erupted in January 532. In that month the imperial treasury was empty, and Justinian, whose military campaigns needed huge funds, decreed a further increase in taxes. It was the last straw.

Rebellion broke out at the Hippodrome. For once, the Greens and Blues united, channelling their outrage against the government. The two factions proclaimed a new emperor. Under the rallying cry of 'Nika!'('Victory!'), the rioters spilled into the streets, where they set fire to the Sacred Palace and several other buildings. Swarming into the wealthy districts, the uncontrollable mob pillaged the luxury shops along the Mese.

A BLOODY RESOLUTION

Justinian considered flight into Asia, but Theodora restored his courage, declaring that for herself, death was preferable to dishonour. 'If you wish to protract your life, O Emperor, flight is easy; there are your ships and there is the sea. But consider whether, if you escape into exile, you will not wish every day that you were dead. As for me, I hold with the ancient saying that the imperial purple is a glorious shroud.' Not for the first time, the bearkeeper's daughter showed herself more than worthy to share the throne of the Caesars.

His resolve now stiffened, the emperor set about dividing the rebels by reawakening the eternal animosity between the two main factions, corrupting their leaders with bribes, and making special overtures to the Blues. Meanwhile, 3,000 veteran loyal mercenaries under the command of General Belisarius marched on the mob through an inferno of flames and falling buildings. The rebellion was drowned in the blood of the people. On January 18, some 30,000 corpses littered the steps of the Hippodrome. The Imperial District had been devastated, but the Byzantine Empire was safe.

THE END OF AN EMPIRE

These insurrectionary tendencies were always least in evidence as soon as the spectre of invasion arose. Faced with the threat of conquest by barbarian horsemen from beyond its frontiers, Constantinople would rediscover its unity.

Several times the empire's boundary on the River Danube had been breached and alien hordes – including Asiatics, Avars, Slavs, and Bulgars – closed in on the city. The most serious invasion came in 558, when Asiatic Huns, the successors of Attila, camped under the city's very walls. The population was panic-stricken, but once again Belisarius, by now retired but ever faithful, came with his mercenaries to the empire's rescue. They succeeded in repelling the invaders.

On November 14, 565, Justinian died at the age of 82. His grandiose vision of a Holy Empire was already fading. In the last years of his reign, the Byzantine Empire was going bankrupt. Exhausted by public works and military expenditure, it was now facing a major war against the Sassanian kings of Persia – a war which Justinian had been unable to prevent.

The chaos and violence of the Dark Ages in Europe were drawing near, too – centuries which were to strip Constantinople of its provinces, leaving it as an isolated bastion of culture and learning in an alien universe.

It remained a bastion for more than 600 years after Justinian's death, until it was overrun and occupied by the Franks in 1204. Even after that it retained its imperial status for a time; its last emperor was not overthrown until 1453, when the city finally fell to the Turks.

By then, almost 900 years had passed since the death of Justinian. But the classical heritage was preserved and the Christian tradition protected. The philosophy of Plato and Aristotle, and the distinctive character of Byzantine religious art, were transmitted from the eastern metropolis to palaces and monasteries, shaping the culture of medieval Europe. The city had a particularly lasting influence on parts of Russia, Greece, and the Balkans. Its religious tradition, developed independently from Rome, survives today as the Orthodox Christian Church.

Constantinople was a crossroads in space and time. Here, Europe merged into Asia, the classical era into the Middle Ages. From its narrow promontory jutting into the Bosporus, the city witnessed the death of Western civilization, and its rebirth.

Chang'an

Heart of the Celestial Empire

Ambassadors, merchants, and scholars flocked from distant lands to see the dazzling Chinese capital of the Tang emperors. For 200 years, from AD 700 to 900, Chang'an enjoyed a reputation as one of the greatest cities of the world.

IMAGINE A CITY OF MORE THAN A MILLION INHABITANTS with streets laid out in a geometrical grid pattern. The commercial areas are carefully 'zoned' away from the residential districts. It is an affluent society. The shops are crammed with all kinds of luxury goods, the restaurants are exotic, and the women are highly fashion-conscious. Problems of juvenile delinquency worry the locals. Asked to place the city geographically and chronologically, many people might guess that it lay at the heart of a 21st-century Western nation. In fact, this description refers to a city that flourished in China (on the site of present-day Xi'an) nearly 1,400 years ago, when London was the small, tribal capital of the East Saxons, and Rome had been reduced to little more than a shantytown.

LINCHPIN OF A CELESTIAL EMPIRE

The city was Chang'an, founded by the first emperor of the Sui dynasty, Wendi of Sui (581–604), on the fertile plain of Guanzhong in north-west China.

The site he chose lay a little to the south-east of an old Han capital that had been sacked in AD 23. To the south rose the Qin mountains; to the north flowed the waters of the Huang He (Yellow River). The plain itself was threaded by the River Wei, whose waters irrigated its rich, sedimentary soil, and combined with a mild, pleasant climate to make it one of the great agricultural larders of ancient China.

The city, constructed in just nine months under the ruthless supervision of the architect Yuwen Kai, unfolded in three stages. First came the imperial palace, then the imperial city, and finally the outer city. It was originally named Daxing, or 'great prosperity', but within 50 years it had taken the name of Chang'an ('eternal peace'), and was the seat of the emperor Taizong (627–49) of the Tang dynasty.

Under the Tang, China enjoyed nearly 300 years of prosperity. It was the golden age in which men first printed books and paper money. The nation's armies penetrated Korea, northern India, Tibet, and Turkistan (in present-day Russia and Kazakhstan), and countries as distant as Persia (modern Iran) looked to the Celestial Empire of the east for protection. At the heart of the empire lay Chang'an.

SECRETS OF SILK Silk manufacture reached its peak under the Tang dynasty, when aristocrats and rich merchants in cities like Chang'an all wore silk clothes. Silk was also used for ink and colour paintings. This scroll depicts the sixth Tang emperor, Xuanzong (on the right), one of Chang'an's greatest patrons of the arts. He watches as his beloved concubine, Yang Guifei, scrambles into the saddle of her horse.

A WORLD IN MINIATURE

The ancient Chinese believed that the Earth was square, and the grid plan of Chang'an was intended to be a small-scale model of the world. The imperial palace was designed on the same principle: the emperors saw themselves as rulers of the world.

Chang'an was, in fact, three cities in one. The imperial palace (1), a town in itself, was built outside the main walls, to the north and north-east. The imperial city (2), the administrative district, was in the northern zone. This also contained the government-controlled Western (3) and Eastern (4) Markets. To the south lay the industrial and residential quarters (5). The massive defensive walls (6) surrounding Chang'an offered protection to its citizens in times of war. In addition, each district of the city was enclosed within its own system of walls, designed not so much to keep invaders out, as to keep the inhabitants confined in cases of civil insurrection.

The population level of each quarter was strictly controlled. If it rose too high, surplus numbers of citizens would be forced to leave their homes and settle in the country. Under the Tang dynasty, Chang'an's total population rose from 150,000 to 2 million.

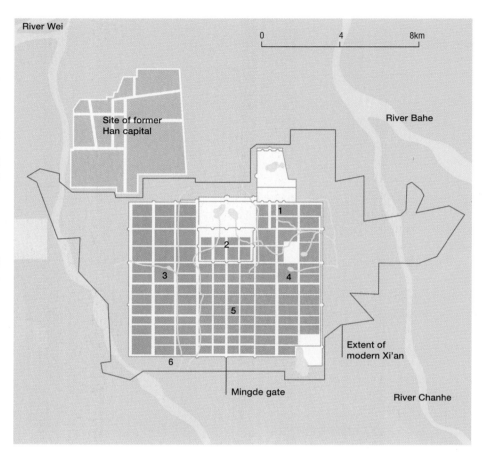

Wendi's city changed little during the Tang dynasty, though in 634 Taizong commissioned a sumptuous new palace as a retreat for his father, Gaozu (618–26), who had abdicated eight years earlier. The Yongan palace, or Palace of Lasting Health, did not live up to its name – Gaozu died before the work was completed. So Taizong changed its name to Daming, meaning 'great and luminous'. It consisted of about 30 separate buildings, with a gigantic throne room, the Hanyuandian, occupying the central area. In 662 the emperor Gaozong (650–83) completely refurbished the palace to reflect the increasing wealth of the city.

The findings of archaeologists, combined with historical records of ancient Chang'an, give a fairly clear picture of life in the Tang capital. The most immediately striking aspect of the city is its sheer size – 84km² (32sq miles). The palace complex alone was about 3km (2 miles) long and 1.5km (just under a mile) wide. The imperial city was the same length, but 229m (751ft) wider, and the outer city sprawled across an area about 10km (6 miles) long and 8km (5 miles) wide.

FACING THE CARDINAL POINT

The city's four outer walls were massive structures of rammed earth, up to 12m (39ft) thick. Just beyond the walls was a moat nearly 9m (29½ft) across and 4m (13ft) deep. Each of the walls was pierced by an enormous gateway. The largest and most important of these, the Mingde, or Gate of the Highest Virtue, was in the centre of the south wall. In ancient Chinese

architecture, south was the cardinal direction. Public buildings such as palaces and temples, and large private mansions, always faced south, with the principal entrance in the south façade. The Mingde was not a single entrance but a row of five openings, each 5m (16½ft) wide and more than 18m (60ft) high.

The whole of the outer city was designed on a grid plan. Eleven broad avenues ran from south to north, crossed by 14 lesser streets running east to west. The grid was divided into 108 districts containing government offices, temples and monasteries, the mansions of the nobility, two markets, and the houses of the common people.

The bulk of the city's traffic travelled along three main avenues running between the imperial palace

FOLLOWER OF FASHION A musician, one of many ceramic figures found in the Tang tombs near Chang'an, wears a Turkish hairstyle which was copied by Chang'an ladies with wigs up to 30cm (12in) high.

THE BODYGUARD Chang'an tombs often contained guardian figures, many of which took the form of a benevolent genie in a phoenix crest headdress. This 8th-century figure is trampling on an evil demon.

and the south gates, and along the main streets linking the east and west gates. Some idea of their scale can be gained by comparing them with modern counterparts – the grandest avenue in Chang'an measured 155m (509ft) across. The Mall in London, leading from Trafalgar Square to Buckingham Palace, is 80m (262ft) across; the Champs-Élysées in Paris is about the same. Like the walls, the roads were built of rammed earth, and they were lined with trees.

The city's districts varied in size, but their internal layout was as strictly systematic as that of the city itself. Each was enclosed by its own outer wall, and sub-divided into four sections, or blocks. Each block was divided into smaller sections by a grid of lanes and alleys. Houses facing the main roads had high, blank walls to protect the occupants from dust, prying eyes, and noise.

RULES AND REGULATIONS

The rigid organization behind the street-plan of Chang'an was reflected in the daily lives of its citizens. In many ways, Chang'an was governed as strictly as a monastery or a prison.

A curfew operated between sunset and sunrise. As night fell, drums were beaten in the streets to warn people to go into their houses. Total silence would then envelop the city. At dawn, the drums would beat again and the city would come back to life.

The commerce of the city was also subject to government control. Chang'an's two markets, the Eastern and the Western, each occupied an area roughly equivalent to two ordinary districts, and lay in the southern section of the imperial city. The eastern market, built near the mansions of nobles and highly placed officials, was quiet and free from crowds; the western market was crammed, clamorous and much more prosperous. Each market contained more than 200 colourful shops and

bazaars which opened directly onto the main streets. In the centre of each was the office of market administration, which operated, among a host of other regulations, a kind of commercial curfew. No trading was allowed until noon, at which hour the inevitable drums would beat, or after sunset, when a great bell was rung and all the shops closed.

SILK AND SEAFARING

The markets of Chang'an were more than a good example of enlightened planning, more even than a visible symbol of the wealth and acumen of the people. The high number of foreign traders, called *hu*, was a potent reminder that China had long since ceased to be a remote, introspective empire. Powerful and secure, she was now looking outwards: to Japan in the east, and as far as the shores of the Mediterranean Sea to the west.

The first Chinese adventurer to make contact with the Western world, Zhang Qian, lived during the Han dynasty. The epic journeys he undertook between 138 and 115 BC opened up an overland route leading from China into eastern Europe, via Persia – the route later known as the Silk Road.

Trade between East and West expanded rapidly during the early Christian era, largely because of the Romans' passion for silk. In Rome, silk was regarded as a fantastic luxury. The emperor Aurelian, who ruled from 270 to 275, declared that silk was literally worth its weight in gold, and tried to discourage its use. Silk manufacture remained a Chinese monopoly until the 5th century AD, when its secrets spread to Central Asia and Persia. Until then, the profits of Chinese spinners and their middlemen were enormous.

Gradually the Silk Road became a two-way thoroughfare as traders moved east, settled in China, and began importing luxuries from the west. One of the most prized imports on sale in the markets of Chang'an was wine made from grapes, rather than from rice or other grains. Zhang Qian had brought a handful of grape seeds back to China and successfully grown them, but the fruit was considered too rare and precious a delicacy to be turned into wine, and the Chinese continued to

A painting on silk (right), attributed to
the 12th-century emperor Huizong,
an accomplished artist, shows court
ladies spinning and beating the silk.
Below: An 8th-century glazed figure
depicts a camel with its foreign rider.
Merchants converged on Chang'an
from Arabia, Persia, Central Asia, and
Japan. Their covered wagons and
horse and camel caravans were
loaded with goods, which they traded
for the luxuries of China, notably silk.

drink alcohol based on rice
and cereals. The introduction
of grape-wine from the West
in about the 6th century
created a revolution in Chinese
drinking habits and made
considerable fortunes for
many of the *hu* merchants.

Another *hu* commodity
was jewellery. This trade was largely in the hands of
Persians, who had long been recognized in China as
master craftsmen. A large Persian community built up in
Chang'an. The Lizhuan and Buzheng districts near the
western market possessed grandiose Zoroastrian temples –
sanctuaries of the fire-worshipping cult founded by the
Persian seer Zoroaster.

RELIGIOUS CURIOSITY AND TOLERANCE

Although Tang China was bound by strict regulations, its
administration tolerated not only Zoroastrianism but also
Buddhism, Judaism, Islam, and even Christianity. During
Taizong's reign, one of the first Christian churches in China
was built in the Yining district of Chang'an – Da Qin
Significant (Da Qin being the Chinese name for the eastern,
Byzantine part of what had been the Roman Empire), dedicated
to Nestorianism.

Nestorius, a Syrian priest, was appointed Patriarch of
Constantinople in 428. He preached that the Virgin Mary had
been the mother merely of Jesus the man – in other words, that
it was wrong to think of her as the Mother of God. His ideas
were condemned by the Council of Ephesus in 431, and he was
deposed as exiled. But his faithful followers established a
powerful breakaway church based in Syria and Persia, and under
Taizong and his successors – notably Xuanzong (712–56) – the
Nestorians were encouraged to pursue their missionary work
throughout China. A tablet recording the introduction of
Nestorianism into China is preserved in the museum at Xi'ian.

The Tang emperors also fostered the development of
Buddhism. In 629, a monk named Xuanzang was sent to India
and Sri Lanka to seek a deeper understanding of the Buddhist

in other words, as their supreme ruler. The Dianzi's power was far more than ceremonial. Subject nations who acknowledged the Chinese emperor in this way were under an obligation to support him with their own armies.

In 648, when the Chinese envoy in Assam, India, was attacked by rebels, the armies of Tibet and Nepal were summoned to put down the insurrection. The emperors Suzong (756–62) and Daizong (763–79) later conscripted the Uighurs, a Turkish tribe, and the Arabs, to suppress uprisings. As a result of this policy, Chang'an became a diplomatic centre housing a number of foreign embassies, the largest of which was the Japanese, with a staff of more than 300.

Foreign students flocked to the city, eager to learn about the sophisticated Chinese administrative systems, and hoping to absorb the advanced culture of the Celestial Empire. A number of schools and universities were set up under the aegis of the national university, Guozi Jian.

INTO THE CULTURAL MELTING POT

Gradually Chinese ideas began to spread. The legal systems of Japan, Korea, Vietnam, Mongolia, and of the Kitan tribes in Manchuria, were all based on the Chinese model. The city of Kyoto in Japan, in former times the capital, was built on a grid pattern in imitation of Chang'an.

While the rest of the Eastern world borrowed ideas from Chang'an, the city's female population like to copy the fashions of Central Asian countries, which they saw worn by foreigners visiting or living in the city. Fashionable dress became a major preoccupation. In the early days of the Tang dynasty, hoods and capes were the mode. After 650, a combination of a hat and a veil, called *mili*, became all the rage. During the Kaiyuan period (713–41), the ladies of the court wore *hu* (foreign-style) hats without veils. Later they abandoned hats altogether for elaborate coiffures in a style made popular by the Uighurs.

Make-up became as vital as clothes: the ladies of Chang'an favoured stark white face powder, embellished with a little rouge and lipstick and painted eyebrows. Some women shaved their eyebrows, replacing them with painted lines higher up on the forehead, in a style similar to modern Japanese geisha girls.

faith. He returned to Chang'an in 645 with more than 600 volumes of sacred texts. Three years later, crown prince Li Zhi (later the emperor Gaozong) built a Buddhist temple in memory of his mother, the empress Wende, calling it the Temple of Maternal Grace. Gaozong ordered Xuanzang to live in the temple and devote himself to translating Buddhist scriptures into Chinese.

The number of manuscripts was so large that in 652, at the request of Xuanzang, a pagoda was built in the temple's inner courtyard to house them. This building – the Great Goose Pagoda – still exists in present-day Xi'an.

The religious tolerance of Chang'an ended with the reign of Wuzong (841–6), who banned the preaching of alien religions, tore down images of the Buddha, and expelled the Nestorians from China.

UNDER DIVINE RULE

Throughout the 7th, 8th, and 9th centuries, the power and prestige of the Tang emperors grew to great heights. In 630, at the beginning of his rule, Taizong received ambassadors from governments across the Eastern world. They had been instructed to acknowledge the emperor as the Dianzi, or 'Son of Heaven' –

SEEKING ENLIGHTENMENT A gilt bronze reliquary of the Tang period glorifies Buddha in the form of a miniature temple. The Tang dynasty established about a hundred Buddhist monasteries in Chang'an.

For both sexes, dress indicated social status. In a commoner's household the women wore red dresses; on farms they wore white skirts. Government officials of the fifth rank or above wore purple robes; those in the lower ranks wore red, blue, or green, depending on their seniority. Army officers wore embroidered suits; other military ranks wore yellow.

FEEDING THE CONSUMER SOCIETY

Chang'an was an affluent society. Trade made the city prosperous, but the real basis of its wealth was the landscape surrounding it – the natural resources of the Guanzhong plain. Every year at harvest time government granaries and private foodstores were filled to bursting with crops of rice, wheat, millet, and every other kind of produce. Like many affluent societies, Chang'an was also wasteful. There was such a glut of food in Chang'an that much of it rotted long before it could be consumed.

The city was famous for its gourmet restaurants and food shops. In one celebrated eating-house, special dishes were prepared for every one of the innumerable festivals in the Chinese calendar. It was the sort of society where a pastry cook could rise to great honour and wealth. The proprietor of the best pastry shop in Chang'an, having donated a large sum of money to the government, was given the title *Yuanwai*, a sort of minister without portfolio.

The Chinese of the Tang dynasty never drank wine before or during a meal, only after. Drinking sessions were as regulated as every other aspect of city life. They drank in rounds, each guest drinking his cup of wine in turn, with a 'wine judge' to oversee the proceedings. The penalty for failing to drain a cup of wine, thus delaying the next round of drinks, was sometimes a beating, but more often the offender was forced to drink more wine. An echo of this custom has survived into present-day traditions. In the various games the Chinese play round the dinner table, it is usually the loser who is given a glass of wine.

Tea-drinking became a craze in Gaozong's reign. After the publication of Lu Yu's *Book of Tea*, which appeared in three volumes between 674 and 676, it grew to be a national pastime.

A highly specialized method of preparing tea was invented by Chang Guan, the provincial governor of Jianzhou (present-day Fujian), between 785 and 805. The leaves were first steamed, then baked in an oven, and finally ground into a fine powder. Though powdered tea has long since disappeared in China, it is still used in the modern Japanese tea ceremony.

FESTIVALS AND FRIVOLITY

The year was filled with public holidays and festivals. Great ceremonies heralded the New Year and the Winter Solstice, during which the Tang emperors received homage from their imperial officials in the Hanyuandian, the huge throne-room of the Daming Palace. Other festivals revived the celebratory mood at various points throughout the year. On the 15th day of the first cycle of the Moon, the Lantern Festival lifted the curfew in Chang'an for three consecutive nights. For this celebration every house in the city was decorated with multicoloured lanterns.

The seventh day of the seventh moon brought the Festival of Love. On this night, according to folklore, a cowherd and a weaver-girl crossed the Milky Way on a bridge made of hovering magpies to meet and speak of love. A week later, on the 15th day, came the Ghost Festival, when people offered sacrifices to their ancestors.

One of the greatest festivals of all was that of the Full Moon, traditionally held on the 15th day of the eighth moon. This was a mid autumn celebration of all-night feasting and drinking, when the Moon was worshipped as a god.

Between the festivals, many of which are still celebrated in Chinese communities across the world, the citizens of Chang'an spent much of their spare time in search of entertainment. By far the most fashionable pastime in ancient Chang'an was gambling. A man who disliked gambling was considered eccentric – even antisocial. The most popular games were board games similar to modern backgammon.

The importance given to the pursuit of pleasure was inevitable in a society as prosperous as that of Chang'an. The emperor Xuanzong employed a troupe of 3,000 actors, dancers, and circus performers. As well as traditional Chinese drama, foreign plays and ballets were encouraged. Acrobats, tightrope walkers, sword-swallowers, fire-eaters, and jugglers found a ready audience. And, of course, there was sport.

Cockfighting had first been popularized in China during the era known as the Period of the Warring States, between 480 and 222 BC. By the Tang period it was being enjoyed by high and low alike. The emperor Xuanzong had a collection of several thousand fighting cocks, kept in the palace gardens, with 500 boys to train and feed them. Expertise in training fighting birds was one of the quickest ways to rise in royal society.

Another popular sport in Chang'an was polo – a game which originated in Persia and spread west to Constantinople and east to China, Japan, Korea, Tibet, and India.

At first the Chinese received their polo ponies as tributes from subject nations, and imported balls and mallets from the West. Later they replaced the Western balls – made of wool or felt encased in leather – with their own version, a wooden ball inside a leather skin, and they began breeding their own ponies.

Chang'an's most celebrated polo ground was in the Pear Garden of the imperial palace. Here, in 710, a match took place between the personal guards of the Tibetan ambassador and the Chinese emperor's own guards. The Tibetans won game after game. And Xuanzong – at the time a dashing young prince – watched with increasing dismay. At last he could stand it no longer. With three other princes he formed a small team and, much to the delight of the partisan Chinese crowd, gave the ten-man Tibetan team a resounding thrashing.

But this cultured, leisured society also had its fair share of problems. Hooliganism and various forms of youthful protest affected Chang'an as much as any other affluent society. A practice that deeply affronted the government and the establishment, and was associated in the minds of respectable people with villainy of the worst kind, was tattooing. But some young rebels evidently enjoyed the notoriety it attracted. One tattooed youth was nicknamed 'The Walking Anthology of Bo Zhuyi' because his body was entirely covered with pictures illustrating scenes from 30 of the best-loved verses of a well-known Tang poet.

A NEW CAPITAL FOR A NEW REGIME

In 904 the golden age of Chang'an came to an abrupt end. The last Tang emperor, Zhaozong (889–904), was deposed by the usurper Zhu Wen, who made the decision to move the imperial capital to his own residence, at Luoyang, farther to the east.

The Tang capital was almost totally demolished. Wooden beams and pillars were ripped from its houses and lashed together to make rafts. The city's wretched inhabitants were forced to float on these rafts down the Wei, into the Huang He, and on to Zhu Wen's new capital. Chinese literature records that the wailing and piteous lamentations of the displaced people could be heard for many weeks.

Two months after the forced evacuation of Chang'an, the local military governor, Han Jian, who was loyal to the new regime, tore down the walls of the outer city and of the palace city. The walls of the imperial city were left standing, however, and a new, much smaller city was founded on the site. This remained a key centre for the trade with Central Asia and Europe. During the Ming dynasty, this city was rebuilt extensively, creating the base of modern Xi'an.

Today, Xi'an contains few reminders of its predecessor's glory. The monuments, palaces, temples, and mansions have perished, yet much of the ancient capital's culture, and many of its customs and beliefs, have survived into the 21st century.

READY TO STRIKE   A Tang era pottery figure from a tomb captures the excitement of polo-playing. Polo was a source of employment for hundreds of riders and pony trainers.

Birth of technology

The first tools – rough-hewn stones more than 2 million years old, found at Hadar in Ethiopia – are the earliest evidence of humans. They were round stones dashed against a rock to produce a jagged edge that could be used to cut through tough animal hide or to hack up meat. It took the best part of another million years for

Flint hand axes from Swanscombe, England, c.1.5 million years ago.

Early mechanics

By 20,000 BC hunters were finding ways to propel projectiles more effectively than by simply throwing them. The harnessing of energy began with fire, probably 1.5 million years ago. Water was used for irrigation from around 5500 BC. Only much later – in the 1st millennium AD – were the forces of wind and water harnessed.

The first **boomerang** is made in Europe around 21,000 years ago. By a similar date, the **spearthrower** is developed to extend the range and power of spears and darts. Known in the Americas as the *atlatl*, it becomes widespread, used equally in hunting and in warfare. **Bows and arrows** appear around 16,000 years ago.

In Europe and Asia, asses and cattle are used for traction before 4500 BC. The first **cartwheels** are developed in Mesopotamia after 4500 BC. They are made of three shaped planks: two semicircles clamped to a solid hub with wood or copper struts. There are considerable advantages: an ox with a cart can transport three times the load it can bear on its back.

Pottery

Unbaked clay was first used to make figurines and line hearths and baskets. The secret of baking it to make it more durable was discovered about 13,000 years ago; because clay was cheap and easy to work, it was used to make bricks, lamps, troughs, and a range of practical and beautiful objects.

Baked clay is first used to make pots – strong, durable containers for cooking food and for storage – around 11,000 BC in Japan, possibly by 9000 BC in China, around 7500 BC in the Sahara but not until 7000 BC in the Middle East. These pots are generally built up in coils or formed around baskets.

Pottery-making begins in many more regions: around 6000 BC in South-east Asia and by 5000 BC in the borderlands of India and Iran. Chinese pottery-making is well established before 5000 BC. Finely made painted pottery in West Asia is fired in large domed kilns.

Pottery figurine from
Çatal Hüyük, 5400–5200 BC

Textiles

Weaving of cloth – for protection or status – is considerably older than urban civilization. Early yarns were made by rolling threads around the thigh, but by 6000 BC in Asia Minor the spindle was probably being used. The first looms were of two types – vertical, complete with tensioning weights, and horizontal.

The oldest surviving piece of **woven fabric** is a swatch of linen cloth found in Çatal Hüyük, Turkey. It dates from around 6000 BC, but the techniques that produced it were already old. The cloth is as finely woven as many modern fabrics and almost certainly made on a loom.

Spindle whorls and loom weights appear in many settlements across the Middle East and Europe. This reflects the widespread use of spindles and upright looms. **Flax** is widely grown for making **linen**, and other plant fibres are also used.

Before 4500 BC **sheep** begin to be kept for their **wool** in parts of the Middle East. Woollen textiles are later to become a major product and export of the Mesopotamian city states. **Cotton** begins to be cultivated in India around 4300 BC.

Metal-working

Metal – native (pure) copper and gold – was initially worked just like stone, by cold hammering. Metal was first used for jewellery and prestige objects, and only later for tools, replacing stone. Some types of stone, especially obsidian and jade, continued to be prized.

The oldest **metal artefacts**, small beads and pendants, are made in the Middle East before 8000 BC, using native copper which can be cold-hammered. Their makers seem to have been inspired by the metal's beauty rather than its practical potential. Smelted lead first appears around 7000 BC.

By 6000 BC, **smelted copper** is being used at Çatal Hüyük, Turkey. **Gold** is also worked in its pure native form, dug from the ground in nuggets or panned from streams. Gold is prized by societies across the globe, probably because it neither tarnishes nor corrodes and generally occurs in a pure form needing no smelting.

By 5000 BC **gold** and **copper** is being worked in much of the Middle East, including Mesopotamia, and in the Balkans. Copper ores containing arsenic or antimony are deliberately selected for their increased hardness. By 4300 BC copper is being cast in the Levant using the lost-wax technique.

Glassware and ornaments

From early times attractive and exotic materials were used to make personal ornaments. Man-made materials were also used, perhaps created as substitutes for natural materials that were hard to obtain. Some man-made substances, such as lacquer, acquired a high value of their own.

Settled communities in many regions acquire prestigious materials for making **ornaments and tools** – these include turquoise, spondylus shells, and obsidian. While the materials travel only short distances with each transaction, they may eventually arrive many hundreds of miles from their source.

Fine drills are used at Mehrgarh in the borderlands of India and Iran to perforate beads. The **bead-making** industry becomes particularly highly developed in India, but similar skills are displayed elsewhere.

By the end of the 5th millennium BC, efficient kilns, originally devised for pottery, are being used in Mesopotamia to fire a mixture of quartz sand, copper, and soda to make an attractive blue glassy substance known as **faience**.

Before 6000 BC

From 6000 BC

early humans to learn to make fire. In doing so, they also won some control of their destiny. Using fire for cooking, heating, light, and defence, they were able to move out of their African birthplace. By 300,000 years ago well-formed stone tools were being made. Around 10,000 years ago technological discoveries accelerated.

Farming developed in many regions, and a more settled way of life gave rise to a stream of inventions including metallurgy, spinning, pottery, and the wheel. Animals began to relieve their human masters of the burden of traction and transport.

Between 4500 and 4000 BC, **ploughs** come into use in the Middle East and Europe. **Wheel-making** spreads throughout the Middle East and into the steppes. The rims are often reinforced with metal. **Horses** are domesticated around 4000 BC on the European fringes of the steppe region; as a result people begin to explore the steppes and settle there.

From 3000 BC **levers** are used; they can be seen in Egyptian sculptures. Later, there is evidence in Egypt and Mesopotamia of more sophisticated principles with the *shaduf*, a bucket on a pole counterbalanced by weights used to raise water from a river.

In the Middle East lighter **spoked wheels** are developed, followed by **swivelling axles**, which make four-wheeled carts much easier to steer. Spoked wheels make it possible to develop light, manoeuvrable chariots which become formidable in war, from Africa and Europe to China, by 1200 BC.

The Archimedean screw, an efficient device for raising water, appears in Mesopotamia around 700 BC. At the start of the Christian era, the Romans refine the application of levers with pulleys. About the same time, Vitruvius, a Roman architect and engineer, describes the first **devices** using **natural energy, water and wind**.

In South America, pottery is being made in Amazonia and Colombia. The **potter's wheel** is developed in Mesopotamia around 3500 BC. The Chinese also develop the potter's wheel, around 3000 BC, and produce egg-shell thin pottery.

From around 2500 BC, **pottery** becomes more widespread in the Americas, appearing in Mesoamerica and the south-eastern USA and in the Andes by 2000 BC.

From 1600 BC, **glass** is used to **glaze** some pottery in the Middle East. Highly sophisticated polychrome pottery is made by successive Andean cultures, particularly the Nazca and Moche cultures. Often the vessels are moulded into the shapes of people, animals, and scenes.

Around 500 BC, the Nok culture in Nigeria starts producing beautifully modelled **terracotta** heads.

Around 3800 BC, fishing communities in coastal Peru weave mats from wild fibres and begin growing **cotton**. By 3500 BC cotton is also grown in Mesoamerica and used to make fishing nets and textiles. **Silk weaving** begins in China around 2700 BC. By 2500 BC woven cotton is made in the Indus Valley.

A form of horizontal loom suspended between a post and a backstrap around the weaver's waist is used in South America, where **textiles** of **cotton** and **alpaca wool** are being made by 2000 BC. They are highly prized and are considered as a principal form of wealth by Andean societies.

In West Asia, **tin** is being added to **copper** to make **bronze** by 3500 BC. By 3000 BC, bronze is being made in parts of Europe and in Egypt, the Middle East, India, China and South-east Asia. By 2000 BC, it is widespread.

Hammered gold helmet from Ur, *c*.2500 BC

The Hittites are probably the first to **work iron**, around 2000 BC. Iron is initially highly valued and changes hands as diplomatic gifts between kings. By 1000 BC iron-working is spreading through Europe and West Asia. It is independently developed in India, and is introduced into China. Around 500 BC ironworking begins in West Africa.

China is producing **lacquerware**, using the sap of the lacquer tree as a tough, waterproof paint on wooden vessels. One of the most highly prized materials in ancient China, lacquer is used for tableware, ornaments, and furniture.

The making of faience leads to the development of true **glass**, which the Mesopotamians and Egyptians use to produce beads from about 2500 BC. The Indus civilization excels in the production of shell, bone, and gemstone beads, creating perfect specimens both of microscopic beads and of beads of exceptional length.

Glass-making is perfected in Egypt during the 18th dynasty (1567–1320 BC). Small urns are made by plunging a clay mould into molten glass, then adding coloured glass threads. **Glass-blowing** appears during the 1st century BC. This enables vessels to be made larger and faster, and leads to a huge growth in glass-making during Roman times.

Phoenician glass vase, 5th century BC

From 4000 BC

From 2000 BC

Nara

A Japanese capital of Chinese culture

One of the most striking aspects of Japan's history has been its ability, at certain periods, to learn from foreigners. What happened at Nara, 13 centuries ago, was an example of the islanders' genius for adapting the traditions of other countries.

ACCORDING TO MYTH, THE ISLANDS OF JAPAN were divinely created, and the first Japanese were descended from the gods. In reality, their ancestors arrived from mainland Asia during the Palaeolithic period. Large numbers of immigrants also came from Korea in the 1st millennium BC, introducing rice cultivation and metallurgy. And it was from the mainland – China in particular – that Japan imported the beginnings of urban culture. Chinese Buddhism also took root in Japan, in the 6th century AD. The new religion came under the protection of Japan's emperors, supplementing the existing official religion known as Shinto, the Way of the Gods.

By the late 5th century the once fragmented nation, made up of small independent tribes, came under the rule of an imperial government established at the royal court of Asuka, today a small village 24km (15 miles) south of modern Nara. Major administrative reforms in the 7th century centralized authority under the emperor.

LEARNING FROM THE CHINESE

The glamour and richness of the civilization in China exercised a magnetic attraction on Japan's rulers. In AD 607 an imperial envoy, Ono no Imoko, was sent from Asuka to the Chinese court. He was granted an audience with the great Emperor Yangdi of China's brilliant Sui dynasty. At the imperial palace the Japanese envoy started the interview by announcing with confidence: 'The Emperor of the Land of the Rising Sun greets the Emperor of the Land of the Setting Sun.' To the Chinese – who thought of Japan as a semi-barbaric island – this opening was highly offensive. It must have taken some delicate diplomacy to smooth over the outrage, for in the end the mission was a success.

Over the years, many large delegations arrived from China in Japan. There were ambassadors with their secretaries and countless specialists, including doctors, monks, astrologers, soothsayers, sculptors, painters, carpenters, potters, and blacksmiths. The diversity of skills was immense. Many of the newcomers attached themselves to the Japanese court and became permanent residents.

A GILDED SAINT Nara became a leading light in the emergence of Buddhism in Japan. The new religion led to the establishment of a Daibutsu-den (Great Buddha Hall) in the city's temple complex, the Todaiji, in the 8th century. The hall contains a huge statue of Buddha, and other statues such as this figure of Kannon, the Japanese version of the Buddhist saint Avalokiteshvara.

THE WOODEN MONASTERY

The Horyuji monastery, built in 607 by order of Prince Shotoku, lies 18km (11 miles) south-east of Nara. The monastery was destroyed by fire and rebuilt in 690, and is the world's oldest surviving wooden monument. It served as a place of worship and as a school where Buddhist law was taught. The two main structures – a five-storey pagoda (1) and the main hall, or Kondo (2) – stand isolated in a large courtyard surrounded by a covered gallery (3). The main hall was destroyed by fire in 1949 but has since been restored. The interior walls are decorated with Buddhist frescoes dating back to the 8th century. A two-storey gateway, or Chumon (4), built in 610, leads into a great courtyard where ceremonial processions were held. Outside the covered gallery, annexes (5), built later, once housed a large library, and lodgings for the monks, students, and aristocratic visitors.

What Japan lacked was a capital city worthy of its growing splendour. There were no major urban centres, and the imperial court – first established at Asuka – had moved as each monarch constructed a new palace complex. The Emperor Temmu planned a splendid capital comparable to those of China, and his widow, the Empress Jito, oversaw its construction at Fujiwara, which became the capital in 694. But it was not until 710 that their vision was fully realized. Under the Empress Gemmyo, Nara was chosen as the permanent site for the imperial court.

CHEQUERBOARD CITY

The city, known at the time as Heijo-kyo, was laid out like a vast chequerboard in the style of the Tang capital, Chang'an, in China. The architecture was Chinese-inspired, from palaces and monasteries with tall pagodas to administrative offices and imposing mansions with stone paving, painted wooden pillars, and roofs with semi-translucent glazed tiles.

The power of the central government at Nara was open to challenge by provincial clan leaders. So in 712, to cement the authority of the throne, Empress Gemmyo (707–15) sponsored the writing of chronicles glorifying the myths of the imperial dynasty. The *Kojiki*, 'Records of Ancient Matters', were written using Chinese script to represent Japanese sounds. At the same time, monks and scholars were copying out Buddhist texts, and Japan developed its own style of exquisite calligraphy.

Manuscripts brought to Japan by Chinese monks and scholars included Buddhist, Confucian, and Daoist treatises, and works on astrology and fortune-telling such as the *Yi Jing* (*The Book of Changes*). Nara became a centre for Buddhist learning and worship. Japanese Buddhism mixed several different traditions, and came to be represented by six different sects founded in the capital. Each had its own monasteries and temples, and its own aristocratic patrons. The monks were recruited chiefly from the nobility, who fought constantly for influence at court. In a spirit of toleration, the new religion accommodated the spirits and gods of the Shinto cults.

In 735, a severe epidemic of smallpox struck down members of the imperial family. To appease the gods, the emperor Shomu (724–49) decided to build a huge gilded bronze effigy of the Buddha at Nara. The colossal statue, 15m (49ft) tall, can still be seen today – much restored, but intact. A vast hall was erected around the statue while work was still in progress, flanked to the east and west by two ten-storey pagodas. By 752, it had become part of a temple complex, known as the Todaiji. This was the pride of Nara, and it continued to be embellished for another ten years, during which time a Chinese monk and architect named Ganjin arrived at Nara with some of his disciples.

Ganjin founded a new school of architecture. He also attempted to bring Shintoism more firmly within the Buddhist fold, declaring that the native gods were earthly incarnations of Buddhist deities, and founded another school of Buddhism. In religion, as in all else, Japan displayed a remarkable ability to assimilate outside influence.

TREASURES AND TRIBUTES

Religion was not Nara's only concern. Among the city's notable buildings is the fabulous treasure house, the Shosoin – the world's oldest museum, built in 756 by the widow of the emperor Shomu. Its walls are constructed of horizontally stacked cross-sections of timber, which drain water, absorb moisture, and shrink to allow ventilation when the air is dry. The humidity of the interior remains constant all year round, and as a result the exhibits remain intact to this day.

The museum's 3,000 treasures provide a rich picture of court life during the 8th century. They include silks, brocades, inlaid furniture, mirrors, and ceramics, most of which were gifts offered by high officials to their sovereign. The emperor also stored tributes from travellers returning from China and Korea: medicinal plants, sacred manuscripts, technical treatises, Buddhist paintings, musical instruments, weapons, devotional objects, and numerous utensils. Goods from distant lands include a glass bowl of Persian origin, fabrics from Central Asia, and a marble bas-relief of Byzantine inspiration.

China's influence had changed life in Japan immensely – at least for the lords, courtiers, and religious leaders. But the peasant masses continued to live as they had done for centuries.

THE PRICE OF HIGH SOCIETY

Japan's many peasants, by their sweat, produced the wealth that supported the imperial court. Yet to the privileged citizens of sophisticated Nara they ranked no higher than animals. They wore clothes made of bark fibre, and their homes were simple mud huts. Their lives revolved around toiling in the fields, or breeding silkworms to produce finery for the elite. They were illiterate, and continued to worship their rural gods.

Because of this class distinction, ordinary people were almost completely ignored in the great works of Japanese literature of the time. They are mentioned only obliquely in the chronicles. The main change in their lives brought about by the foundation of Nara was a change for the worse.

> *Japan's many peasants . . . produced the wealth that supported the imperial court. Yet to the privileged citizens of sophisticated Nara they ranked no higher than animals.*

The taxes levied to finance building the capital weighed heavily on the poor. They paid the price for their country's prestige – partly in crops, and partly in labour.

At least they were not plagued by warfare. The Nara period was, on the whole, a peaceful age. It came to an end in about 794, as the monks of the capital's six main sects grew increasingly powerful. Peasants who could no longer bear the tax burden abandoned their fields. Finally, to escape the influence of the Buddhist priests, Emperor Kanmu established a new capital at Heiankyo (present-day Kyoto) – the 'Capital of Peace and Content'.

But the lessons learned at Nara were not forgotten. Japan had gathered all the elements necessary to produce a culture of its own, and at Heiankyo, a tradition of native Japanese architecture asserted itself. Chinese influence remained strong for the next 150 years, but the country was emerging from its formative era. By the 10th century, Japan's links with the mainland had been severed, its influences consolidated, and its high society had become one of the most sophisticated civilizations of all time.

THE VISIONARY Ganjin brought new ideas about architecture and religious practices to Nara, and laid out a garden of medicinal plants in the city. This statue of the Chinese monk was most probably made shortly after his death in 763.

Tikal

Temples in a tropical forest

For six centuries, the Maya preserved a civilization of astonishing sophistication in the jungles of Central America – then they vanished from history. The most impressive of their cities was Tikal, centre of one of their principal city-states.

NORTHERN GUATEMALA IS AN INHOSPITABLE PLACE. Its dense jungle is home to countless insects and poisonous snakes, and is drenched by at least 300cm (118in) of rain a year. Yet, in the 3rd century AD, it became the heartland of the Maya – a nation whose mathematicians invented zero centuries before the concept reached Europe from India, and whose astronomer-priests observed the heavens with an accuracy unmatched for more than 1,000 years.

At their peak, the Maya dominated an area of about 650km (404 miles) from east to west, and more than 17,000km (10,564 miles) from north to south. The region was the scene of constant warfare between rival city-states.

From Tikal – the largest city – Maya influence spread to the Caribbean and the Pacific, to Mexico and Honduras. After the city-states collapsed in the 9th century, Tikal lay strangled beneath the jungle until its rediscovery in 1848 by explorers working for the governor of Petén (the Guatemalan province in which the city now lies). Archaeologists later confirmed that the city was one of the Maya's main political and ceremonial centres.

HOLDING BACK THE JUNGLE

In about 800 BC, an ancient population settled on the site in wooden huts. They used local flint and obsidian from the Mexican highlands to make tools, and began trading goods and ideas with the larger cities of the Olmec people to the north-west and, later, with the people of Izapa in Mexico and Kaminaljuyu in southern Guatemala. Gradually, the settlement grew from a cluster of jungle villages into a major town, known to its inhabitants as Yax Mutal.

During the 1st and 2nd centuries AD, the torrid jungle proved too much for many neighbours of the Maya. The Olmec cities were abandoned, and the civilization of Izapa crumbled. But thanks to its people's agricultural skills, Tikal grew, and was a major ceremonial centre by AD 200. An acropolis of temples north of the main square marked the burials of its elite; to the south-west rose a pyramid known as the Lost World complex – probably an observatory. The city centre alone was home to between 40,000 and 45,000 people.

ROYAL CENOTAPH Tikal's main square is dominated by two great temples erected by one of Tikal's greatest rulers, Hasaw Chan K'awil. The smaller Temple II (right) was constructed in honour of his queen, but investigations have not revealed a burial inside the pyramid. Hasaw was buried beneath the 47m (154ft) high Temple I, surrounded by a treasury of vases, bone ornaments, and jade.

Labels on illustration: East market | Temple V | South acropolis | Central acropolis | East Plaza

THE JUNGLE CITY

By about 800, Tikal was the largest city in the Maya world. Flanking its Great Plaza, a temple complex known as the north acropolis rested on a platform covering almost 1ha (2½ acres). Dominating the plaza on its east and west sides were the great pyramids of Temple I and Temple II. Paved roads led out to the suburbs. The road fading out of view at the top right led to the city's tallest pyramid, Temple IV, 75m (246ft) in height.

ADDRESSING THE PEOPLE A high-ranking nobleman addresses an audience. The figure is a detail from the decoration of an earthenware vase, made in Tikal about AD 700.

In some ways, the jungle had worked in Tikal's favour. The forests teemed with wildlife which could be hunted for food. The river systems provided fish, and traders used the waterways to bring ocean produce to the city. Beneath the forests, the land was rich in raw materials such as flint, wood, and limestone. But the most important factor in the city's survival was maize. The earliest farmers had to cut down and burn off the jungle plants from an area before planting their crops. Each field was used for a few seasons, until the exhausted soil had to be abandoned. Later, the Maya developed more intensive cultivation, building hillside terraces and canal networks along the rivers.

When the city reached its peak between the 7th and 10th centuries, the metropolitan area of Tikal covered more than 62km² (24sq miles). The city centre, which has been excavated, covered 16km² (6sq miles). Within this central district, archaeologists have discovered more than 3,000

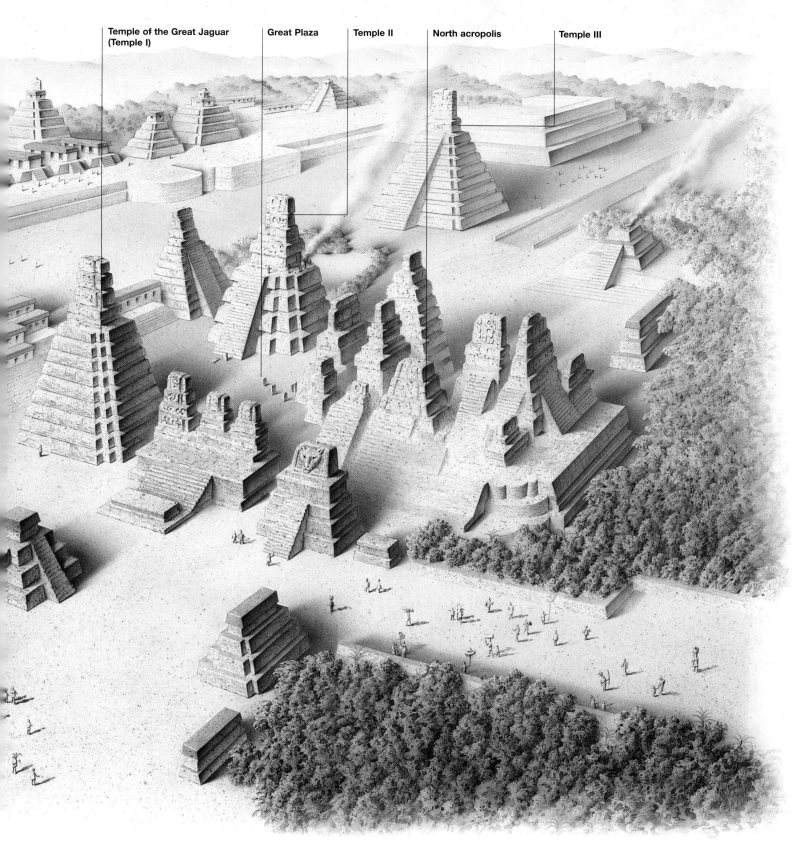

Temple of the Great Jaguar (Temple I)   Great Plaza   Temple II   North acropolis   Temple III

separate buildings – and another 10,000 hidden beneath them. Unlike modern builders, who demolish existing buildings before constructing new ones, the builders of Tikal simply added a new layer on top of and around the older structures.

The city was dominated by seven pairs of pyramids, each pair linked by a square containing a small hall and stelae (inscribed stone slabs). Each pair celebrated the passing of a *katun*, or 20 years. No other Maya city contained such constructions.

THE ARRIVAL OF A NEW DYNASTY

As Tikal grew in importance, so its trading links expanded. Fish and shellfish came from the Pacific and Caribbean coasts, as did stingray spines used for bloodletting. Jade for carving was brought from other parts of Guatemala, feathers from the jungle, salt and honey from northern Yucatán. Green obsidian for tools came 1200km (746 miles), from a place the Mexican Aztecs later revered as 'the city of the gods': Teotihuacán.

Teotihuacán lies 2,280m (7,480ft) above sea-level on a plateau to the north-east of present-day Mexico City. Its influence over much of the region was based mainly on its control of the trade in the glassy volcanic rock obsidian, and reached a peak in the century following AD 378. In that year a lord from Teotihuacán, Siyak K'ak (Fire Born), seized power in Tikal, and a Teotihuacán prince, Yax Nuun Ayiin (First Crocodile), was installed as ruler, founding a dynasty that introduced many elements of Teotihuacán culture to the Maya.

The most distinctive product of Teotihuacán's craftsmen was a cylindrical pottery vase with three slab-like legs and a cover. Vases of this type have been found in Tikal. New religious beliefs came with the new dynasty, too. The rain god of central Mexico, Tlaloc – with his fanged gaping mouth and his ringed, saucer eyes – is sometimes depicted on pottery found in Tikal.

For reasons that are still uncertain, by AD 650 Teotihuacán had begun to decline in importance. Within 50 years it was almost entirely abandoned, but Tikal had absorbed much of its culture, and continued to thrive for another two centuries.

> *. . . the gods made the Maya ancestors from a gruel of the sacred plant, maize. They were destroyed to make way for the present world – for men of flesh and blood.*

Historians have followed the fortunes of Tikal through Mayan records, carved onto the stelae unearthed from their urban centres. The inscriptions, which scholars have only recently begun to decipher, reveal details of the alliances and rivalries of the city-states.

WRITTEN IN STONE

Maya writing used pictographs and phonetic symbols. The first signs to be understood were mathematical, and usually appear in the form of dates. The Maya used what is known as the Long Count system, in which each date was recorded as the number of days since an earlier, fixed date. Many archaeologists believe that this fixed date corresponds to August 13, 3114 BC – a day which precedes the earliest settlements of the Maya tribes by about 1,000 years.

The date may relate to Maya legends about the origin of the world. The Maya believed that three worlds had been made and destroyed by the gods before their own world came into being. The first world contained men made from earth; the gods destroyed them because they were mindless. The men of the second world were made of wood; but they were soulless and unintelligent, and were drowned or devoured by demons. In the third world, the gods made the Maya ancestors from a gruel of the sacred plant, maize. They were destroyed to make way for the present world – for men of flesh and blood.

Using 3114 BC as a starting point simplifies the dating of the events of Maya history. At Tikal, all the engraved dates that have been found fall between AD 292 and 869.

Maya mathematicians mainly counted in multiples of 20. Each Maya year, or *tun*, contained 18 months of 20 days each, and another five 'unlucky days'. Years were grouped into *katun*, or 20-year periods; *baktun*, or 400-year periods; and so on up to the *alautun*, a period of more than 63 million modern years.

Until the deciphering of the stelae, the names and deeds of Tikal's rulers were surrounded by uncertainty. A puzzling gap of more than a century in the erection of stelae at Tikal, falling between 557 and 682, has now been explained. In 562, Caracol – a city subordinate to Tikal's arch-enemy, Calakmul – inflicted a defeat on Tikal. It was not until 672 that Tikal began to regain its former importance, and under the leadership of Hasaw Chan K'awil (Heavenly Standard Bearer), Calakmul was eventually defeated in 695. Hasaw guided Tikal to the peak of its power.

NOBLE RITUAL The ruling classes performed personal blood-letting to communicate with the spirits. An 8th-century lintel shows a Maya lady drawing a cord set with thorns through her tongue; her husband lights the scene with a torch.

SYMBOLIC FIGURES Maya writing used complex glyphs. The two large figures in the carving from Palenque represent the words 'zero' and 'day' – giving part of the birthdate of a king recorded in the Long Count system.

Maya rulers seem to have been regarded as demi-gods, or at least as high priests – the connection between the people and the warring gods and demons. Some divine figures were a complex mixture of benevolence and malevolence – many had four natures, corresponding to the cardinal points of the compass. At the centre were gods of the forces of nature, vegetation gods, and gods of the seasons – of time itself.

A DIVIDED CITY

The priest-kings were surrounded by an aristocratic elite whose power was based on their status within the religious hierarchy. When young, the children of these noble families had their heads bound between wooden boards so that they developed a high, flat, receding forehead – the mark of the nobility. Below the aristocrats came traders and craftsmen who supplied Tikal's specialist needs, and the bottom of the social scale was made up of the vast peasantry whose labour built and fed the city.

Few, if any, of the luxuries available to the nobles reached the peasants, and when the end came in the 9th century, thousands seem to have taken their chance to slip away, leaving the city to fate and the forest.

Archaeologists know, from the number of tombs and graves, that the population of Tikal declined sharply after about 830. By the end of the 9th century, it was a ghost town. The reasons for the collapse of the Maya civilization are still a mystery.

SERENE LORD In the 7th or 8th century, the jade pectoral ornament showing an unknown Maya king attended by a dwarf was taken to Teotihuacán, a city that greatly influenced Tikal in the 5th century.

Several factors may have been involved. Inter-city warfare intensified and many minor cities broke away from their overlords. Evidence from lake sediments suggests that the farmers exhausted the soil; a disastrous drought made matters worse. Excavated skeletons indicate that malnutrition and disease were widespread. Perhaps the peasantry, resentful of ever more ambitious building programmes, finally rose in revolt.

THE DEATH OF THE MAYA

The last great temple at Tikal, known as Temple III, was completed in 810. The last stela, known as stela II, bears the date 869. Across Maya territory, a trail of final dates records the death agonies of the great cities: Copan 830, Palenque 835, Tikal 869, Uxmal 909. Their end was not marked by fire or the clash of swords – it came with the gradual crumbling of priestly authority, a slow shrinking of the population, and an inexorable emptying of treasures.

At Tikal, the largest settlement of all, neglect gave the city's first and most implacable enemy a chance of victory. The lush, green jungle, which had waited for so long, slowly reclaimed its stolen territory.

Angkor

The Khmer jungle capital

The fabulous city of the Khmers, whose empire covered most of modern Cambodia and Thailand, was only rediscovered in 1860. While its temples still pay tribute to the gods and god-kings, they also tell of the daily life of the peasants whose labour created it.

TODAY'S KAMPUCHEANS TRACE THEIR ORIGINS BACK to a Hindu people, the Khmers. The Khmers ruled a large area of south-east Asia for some 500 years, until the early 15th century AD when the neighbouring Thais drove them from their home in what was then Cambodia. More than 400 years later, in January 1860, a French naturalist making his way along a vine-entangled track in the Kampuchean jungle caught sight of five conical towers rising above a canopy of trees. Henri Mouhot had stumbled upon a vast monument of this vanished civilization – the ruined city of Angkor, ancient capital of the Khmers.

HARNESSING THE LAND

The Khmer empire flourished between the 9th and 14th centuries across the whole of modern Kampuchea and parts of South Vietnam, Laos, and Thailand. Its founder, King Jayavarman II (*c.*770–850), chose a site for his capital near the Angkor plain – a vast tract of fertile land watered by tributaries of the Mekong river.

The city's people fed well all year round. Making the most of the brief monsoonal wet season, they used a complex system of reservoirs and canals to supply water to their rice paddies during periods of drought.

Jayavarman declared himself a god-king – a link between mankind and the spirits. He began a grand tradition of temple building that was to be kept alive by future Khmer rulers. The god-kings, most of whom were Hindus, marked their link with the divine by adorning their temples with statues of the principal gods made in their own likenesses. The duty of the god-king was to win the favour of the other gods for the benefit of his subjects. While the temples paid tribute to the generosity of these gods, who helped to swell the city's rice harvests, the sacred statues reminded worshippers of the power of their supreme ruler.

Each Khmer king, as well as adding to the irrigation network, tried to outshine his predecessor with the splendour of his temple. The most brilliant of all is Angkor Wat, built by Suryavarman II (1113–50). Like most of the Khmers' temples, Angkor Wat is a symbol of Mount Meru – in Hindu legend, the home of the gods.

A GLORIOUS RECORD The towers of the temple of Angkor Wat crown a huge terraced pyramid climbing toward the heavens, imitating the sacred Hindu mountain they represent. Angkor's temples were built to house the cremated remains of their founding kings. They record a procession of supreme rulers who took the Khmer empire to its height, then watched it crumble at the hands of a neighbouring people.

THE KHMERS AT LEISURE The walls of the Bayon temple in Angkor Thom are alive with scenes from daily life, capturing everything from modes of dress to pastimes such as chess.

Shortly after Angkor Wat's construction, the Khmer capital was sacked by the Chams from lower Annam (present-day Vietnam). Its people endured four years of submission, until the future Jayavarman VII (1181–*c*.1215) led a rebellion which drove out the hated invaders. They then embarked on an ambitious programme of construction, and rebuilt the royal capital.

Jayavarman VII's city is known as Angkor Thom. The square moat which surrounds it was once stocked with fierce crocodiles. Each side is more than 3km (about 2 miles) long and is reinforced by defensive walls 7m (23ft) high. The main thoroughfares align with the points of the compass, entering the city across the moat and through gateways large enough to allow the access of royal elephants. They meet in the centre of the capital, at the massive temple of the Bayon.

The walls could have contained the whole of ancient Rome, but most people lived in the suburbs outside. The walled area was almost exclusively a royal, religious, and administrative centre. Beyond the suburbs, villages were scattered along the canals – the arteries which carried water, the nation's lifeblood, to the paddy fields.

PICTURES OF THE PAST

In 1992, the ruins of Angkor became a world heritage site. Under the guidance of UNESCO, archaeologists began to investigate, preserve, and restore its unique monuments. The carvings on its stones have left many clues to the pattern of

WATCHING OVER ETERNITY
Serene faces carved into the towers of the Bayon temple mark a shift away from Hindu inspiration to Buddhism, a move which threatened the concept of the supreme god-king.

WATERS OF LIFE The entire Khmer capital covered 100km² (38sq miles). The network of irrigation channels and reservoirs surrounding the city reflected the importance of water to the Khmer people.

everyday life in ancient Kampuchea. Each peasant built his own house, following a design that remains unchanged to this day – a hut on stilts with a pitched roof, woven bamboo walls, and a planked floor. Inside, a single large room was divided by partitions. At night, the peasant tied his animals to the stilts and climbed inside the house using a crude wooden ladder, which he drew up behind him. Outside, piles of smouldering straw sent smoke wafting between the stilts to ward off insects.

The Khmer peasant usually produced enough from his well-irrigated plot to pay his taxes and feed his family. He fished, and reared cattle, water buffaloes, pigs, and fowl to barter for other goods in the local market. The women gathered cotton and kapok, kept silkworms, and wove the family's clothes. Though the peasants controlled their own land, the king remained the legal landowner. During the dry season, as part of their duty to their landlord, the peasants left their smallholdings to erect public monuments and build dams, working together for the good of all and for the glory of their leader.

TEMPLE MOUNTAIN The five central towers of Angkor Wat represented the five peaks of the sacred Hindu symbol, Mount Meru, a place said to separate Earth from Heaven.

In the bas-reliefs which decorate the Bayon temple built by Jayavarman VII, the Khmers recorded their day-to-day activities. The carvings show people bartering and hunting. Others prepare feasts, watch cockfights, or marvel at amazing acrobatic feats.

The bas-reliefs in the Bayon also depict vivid battle scenes commemorating the victory of the Khmers over the Chams, which tell something of the army that extended the power of the empire throughout southern Indo-China.

The king and his generals rode into battle on elephants trained for war. The animals were armed – sharp metal points were fitted to their tusks. On a platform on each elephant's back stood a fierce warrior brandishing a bow and arrow. The *carnac*, or driver, perched on the animal's neck. In battle, clashes between elephant-borne warriors often took the form of a duel. The winning warrior would leap on to his opponent's animal to press home his victory.

The king and his generals rode into battle on elephants trained for war. The animals were armed – sharp metal points were fitted to their tusks.

Lighted torches were waved to enrage other elephants, which were then used as battering-rams to break through enemy defences. They went into battle alongside sabre-rattling horsemen, riding without stirrups, and well-ordered ranks of infantry. After an initial exchange of arrows, the troops fell into hand-to-hand combat. When the battle ended, the wounded on both sides were usually killed to put them out of their misery.

Khmer soldiers seem to have worn only loincloths and leather jerkins. For protection they carried wooden shields. They attacked their enemies with lances, pikes, sabres, bows, knives, javelins, and sometimes ballistas – large catapults operated by teams of soldiers, which hurled rocks deep into the ranks of the opposing army.

EYE-WITNESS ACCOUNT

The most vivid account of Khmer society comes not from the bas-reliefs but from the writings of a Chinese diplomat. In 1296, Zhou Daguan was sent to Angkor by Kublai Khan's grandson and successor, Timur Khan. His impressions survive in his *Notes on the Customs of Cambodia*.

As a diplomat, Zhou Daguan observed the Khmer king at close quarters during royal audiences, and described the pomp and circumstance of the court: 'The king either wears a gold diadem on his head or simply wraps his hair in a garland of flowers that reminds me of jasmine … large pearls hang from his neck, and on his wrists, ankles, and arms he wears gold bracelets and rings set with tigers' eyes. He goes about barefoot, and the soles of his feet and the palms of his hands are stained red with sandalwood.

'When the king goes out, his escort is led by soldiers. Then come the standards, the flags, and the music, followed by his wives and concubines in palanquins, carts, and on horseback. Finally, the king arrives, standing on an elephant with a precious gold sword in his hand. Everyone who sees him has to prostrate himself and touch the ground with his forehead.'

In contrast to this splendour, Zhou Daguan paints a sorry picture of the prisoners of war or captured savages who were forced into slavery – they were a separate class with no privileges, 'bending the head while they are beaten, without daring to make the smallest movement …'

THE FALL OF THE GOD KING

Despite the blaze of royal splendour described by Zhou Daguan, Angkor's days were numbered. The reign of Jayavarman VII had turned out to be the city's final burst of temple and empire building. During the 300 years of construction, many changes in

GATEWAY OF THE GODS Statues and sculptured reliefs decorate the walls and doorways of Angkor Wat. The carvings are inspired by Hindu legend, particularly the Sanskrit epics *Mahabharata* and *Ramayana*.

architectural style had occurred. Towards the end, the buildings displayed a gradual move away from the Hindu cult of the god Siva.

The Khmers had come increasingly under the influence of a Buddhist sect which stressed austerity and self-denial. The old state religion headed by the supreme god-king may have faded out, the king's authority fading with it, bringing the close co-operation between sovereign and subjects to an end.

In the 15th century, when the armies of the neighbouring Thai kingdoms sacked the city, the Khmers moved to a new site near Phnom Penh. Angkor could not survive for long. The irrigation network on which the remaining peasants depended fell into disrepair, and gradually the jungle reclaimed its land. All that was left were creeper-infested ruins, and the memory of a unique culture living under the protection of a living god.

THE KHMER AT WAR A relief on the Bayon temple captures a moment of battle in the time of Jayavarman VIII (1243–95). The Khmer are beginning to overwhelm the hostile Cham.

Pagan

The city of temples

On a plain in central Myanmar (Burma), stone shrines mark the site of Pagan. They are dedicated to Buddhism – a creed that abhors violence. Many were built by slaves on the orders of a king who condoned the sacrificial murder of his own wife.

EARLY ONE MORNING IN THE YEAR AD 1044, VILLAGERS AND COURTIERS gather in front of a wooden palace in Myinkaba, northern Myanmar (now Burma). Their ruler, Sokka-te, still new to the throne, has been challenged to a duel by his half-brother Anawrahta. Sokka-te, confident of victory, accepts the challenge. Of the younger Anawrahta he says scornfully: 'His mother's milk is yet wet upon his lips.' Each of the brothers, armed with a lance, mounts a horse. They charge, thrusting and stabbing. Sokka-te shrieks and falls, transfixed by his brother's lance. Anawrahta is carried in triumph to the palace of his father.

So, according to a Burmese chronicle, began the reign of one of history's most unusual converts to Buddhism: a ferocious warlord who enslaved a nearby civilization in order to build a city that was devoted to Buddha, the prophet of gentleness.

THE SPIRITS SPEAK

When Anawrahta came to the throne he believed, like his people, in spirits: entities known as *nats* who determined human destiny by controlling the land and the forces of nature. Burmese chronicles record that a *nat* appeared to Anawrahta in a dream and commanded him to build monasteries and shrines, to dig wells and ponds, and to construct an irrigation system and grow rice for his people, all in penance for the death of his brother.

In obedience to the spirit's orders, Anawrahta chose a plain bordered by two rivers at Kyaukse, about 30km (18½ miles) south of the present-day city of Mandalay, and set to work. He collected forced labour from the nearby villages and hired irrigation experts from the Shan hill tribes of eastern Burma. For three years, tens of thousands of peasants toiled unceasingly in the steam-bath heat of the plain. They built dams, dug canals, and changed the course of the rivers as Anawrahta ruthlessly pursued his vision. In the course of the project, thousands died of tropical fevers and exhaustion.

PINNACLES OF FAITH
Scattered across a broad plain bordering the Irrawaddy river, towering stupas (bell domes) dominate Pagan's skyline. Each stupa, designed to hold saintly relics, crowns the elaborate halls of one of the city's Buddhist temples.

Finally, the mammoth undertaking was ready. As decreed by his people's grisly custom, Anawrahta would mark the occasion by offering human sacrifices, one for each dam. The victims, it was believed, would then become *nats*, the guardian spirits. Chronicles record that a wife of Anawrahta, sister of a Shan chief, offered herself as a single substitute sacrifice for all the dams. Her offer was accepted. She was ritually killed – possibly by having her throat cut – and her body was burnt on a huge pyre.

EVER-GROWING EMPIRE

The flooded paddy fields at Kyaukse became the economic powerhouse of Anawrahta's realm, producing food for the people and a torrent of wealth to swell the royal coffers. Gradually, more neighbouring chieftains came under Anawrahta's sway, and his territory spread north towards what are now the Indian and Chinese borders, east into Thailand, and west to the Bay of Bengal. At the same time, he expanded the town he had chosen as his capital: Pagan, on the banks of the Irrawaddy river.

The town needed work to turn it into a city. The native Burmese were poor architects and worse artists, but to the south lay a civilization, the Mons, living in a patchwork of city-states that had been a centre of culture for more than 1,000 years.

From this centre, in AD 1056, came a remarkable refugee: a Buddhist monk called Shin Arahan. Shin Arahan was a Mon who believed fervently in the traditional creed of his people: an ascetic variety of Buddhism called Theravada. His faith, however, had come under pressure in his homeland, both from other Buddhist sects and from the Hindu influence of India. The final insult came when the Mon leaders agreed to a number of compromises with Hindu beliefs. Shin Arahan, outraged by the changes, deserted his home and began his journey to Pagan.

Anawrahta was impressed by the power and passion of the monk. Within a year, the king was publicly converted to Buddhism, and had agreed to invade the Mon territories to help to re-establish the supremacy of Theravada Buddhism. With Shin Arahan at his side, the king marched south on one of the most important Mon cities – Thaton, on the coast of the Gulf of Martaban, east of Myanmar's present-day capital, Rangoon. When Thaton fell in 1057 after a three-month siege, the other Mon city-states submitted without a fight.

BUDDHISM SPREADS ACROSS ASIA

The doctrine of Buddhism – the belief that extinction of the self and its worldly desires leads to spiritual enlightenment – originated in the teachings of Siddhartha Gautama, a royal prince in northern India, in the 6th century BC. By 200 BC it had spread throughout India, and had been exported to Ceylon (now Sri Lanka) by the Indian Buddhist King Ashoka. In the next 200 years it went on to dominate the eastern part of what is now Afghanistan, and won numerous converts in central Asia, Burma, Kampuchea, and China. By AD 600 the new religion had reached as far as Japan.

Meanwhile, in its native India, Buddhism began to come into conflict with Hinduism and with Arab Muslims, who began to establish bases in what is now southern Pakistan in about 720. By the 12th century it had ceased to be a major religion in India. But its survival to modern times in South-east Asia, Japan, Nepal, Sri Lanka, and Tibet, has helped to create not only an Asia-wide religion, but also a recognisably Indian culture common to almost all Asian countries.

A LIVING SANCTUARY The huge Gawdawpalin Temple, built in the heart of Pagan in the 12th and 13th centuries, still attracts thousands of worshippers from all over Myanmar for ceremonies and festivals.

But the Burmese warlord
was no magnanimous
conqueror, despite his
conversion. When he
turned his victorious troops
north again for the 650km
(440 mile) journey back to Pagan, he took with him the
labour force that was to rebuild his capital: an army of slaves.
At least 30,000 Mon villagers made the long march north.
So did hundreds of monks and thousands of skilled artisans,
including stonemasons, potters, and architects.

As soon as he reached home, Anawrahta put his slaves to
work in the rice fields of Kyaukse and on the building sites of
Pagan. As the months of captivity stretched into years, a subtle
alchemy took place between the two peoples: the slaves began
to civilize their masters. The first inscription in Burmese –
written in Mon characters because the northerners had no
alphabet of their own – appeared at Pagan in 1058, a year
after the fall of Thaton. Later inscriptions on Pagan's temples,
detailing the costs of construction and the builders of each
shrine, make it clear that some of the skilled Mon workers were
being treated as free artisans.

Many workers chose to stay on in the north after they were
freed. Buddhist monks who had been forcibly imported seem to
have chosen likewise – attracted, possibly, by the king's support
of their faith, and by the challenge of missionary work among
the largely spirit-worshipping Burmese.

THE CONVERSION TO BUDDHISM

Shin Arahan, now a close adviser to Anawrahta, travelled the
growing kingdom, preaching, converting, planning new temples,
and setting up Buddhist monasteries and schools. Anawrahta
remained, for the most part at Pagan, directing the construction
of its pagodas, monasteries, and the cone-topped shrines known
as stupas. As the city grew in prestige, Buddhists, scholars, and
artisans flocked to it from India, Thailand, and even Sri Lanka.
Merchants followed the flow of people up the wide Irrawaddy
river, bringing trade and wealth.

By 1073–4, Pagan was so respected as a Buddhist centre that
when Sri Lanka's king, Vijaya Bahu, chose to revive Buddhism,
he turned to Anawrahta for help. The Burmese king sent monks
and in return, Vijaya Bahu gave him a replica of Sri Lanka's
holiest relic: a tooth reputed to be one of the Buddha's own.

After Anawrahta died in 1077, the building continued under his son, Sawlu (1077–84), and Sawlu's successor Kyanzittha (1084–1112). Kyanzittha was responsible for what is still one of the wonders of Pagan: the Ananda temple, a giant building detailed with gold and silver, decorated with statues and glazed terracotta plaques depicting Buddhist parables.

As Buddhism took hold in the Pagan Empire, it became the dream of thousands of Burmese to build their own shrine. Women took part in these religious and building activities on the same terms as men. Tribal customs and Buddhist doctrine guaranteed their freedom and equality. A white mantle of painted brick stupas and temples spread across the country.

SURVIVALS OF BARBARISM
But behind the devotion to Buddhism, echoes of barbarism remained – in the Burmese court, at least. Anawrahta himself had worshipped not only at the shrine of Buddha's tooth, but also at other altars built to appease the *nats*. At the start of work on the Ananda, Kyanzittha had a child buried alive to provide the building with a guardian spirit; this was not a Buddhist custom. He dedicated the temple in 1090 by ceremonially executing the architect who had designed it, so that its creator could not repeat or better the design elsewhere.

In the 13th century, the Pagan Empire ended as it had begun – in violence. Three main factors had pushed it to the brink of collapse. First, incessant border wars against outlying tribes drained the villages of men. Secondly, the obsession with building, and the granting of the best lands to monasteries and temples for their upkeep, deprived peasants of the space to grow crops. Thirdly, the land itself was becoming poorer with every building that went up. The bricks were made of fired clay, and over the years almost every tree in the region was felled to feed the kilns. The result was catastrophic erosion.

In the face of growing poverty and anarchy, traders began moving away from Pagan, taking with them the revenue that had been a vital source of the city's wealth. The end came during the reign of Narathihapate (1254–87). Ambassadors from the Mongol Chinese empire of Kublai Khan visited Pagan to demand tribute. Narathihapate, outraged at being given orders, had the envoys executed.

HEADING FOR DESTRUCTION
It was an absurd gesture. The deaths – and a subsequent Burmese raid on a frontier state that had submitted to China – provoked a punitive expedition by the Mongols. The Burmese chronicles proudly record that, in 1277, Narathihapate held back the invaders at Ngasaunggyan, about 560km (348 miles) north-east of Pagan. But they also admit that the Burmese war elephants eventually retreated before mounted Mongol archers.

Six years later, in 1283, the Mongol hordes attacked in earnest and defeated the Burmese at Kaungsin, about 440km (273 miles) north-east of the capital. The king and his court fled down the Irrawaddy, abandoning Pagan to the invaders.

Kublai Khan's officers were staggered by Pagan's magnificence. The Venetian explorer Marco Polo talked to the soldiers when they returned to China. He described the city they had seen. 'It was full of stone towers covered in gold and silver, with bells at the top, so that the wind made them ring,' he wrote. 'And truly these towers made one of the most beautiful landscapes in the world, for they were finished exquisitely, splendidly and at great expense.'

The beauty was not to last. Narathihapate tried to reclaim the throne of Pagan, but in 1287 the Mongols again invaded, and put the city to the torch. Looters stripped the temples of their gold and silver. But the buildings themselves survived, and have been tended by generations of devoted Buddhists ever since.

Ife

Africa's city of the gods

In the tropical rain forests of western Nigeria a great flourishing of art took place between the 12th and 14th centuries AD. Its legacy of superb clay and brass sculptures is testimony to a sophisticated culture ruled over by god-kings.

THERE IS AN EXPECTANT HUSH AS THE PRIEST briskly passes the ritual palm nuts from one hand to the other. He then recites one of 4096 ritual poems, or *odu*, that he has learnt by heart. The verses should provide a solution to the problems of those who have come to consult the oracle. Who should be made chief? Which of the various gods is behind the misfortunes caused by Eshu, the mischievous messenger of the gods? And what does the future hold in store?

From the streets comes the harsh blare of car horns, the roaring of taxis and cars, the rumble of lorries – all the clatter and din of a busy modern city. For this is Ife. Here – as perhaps nowhere else in Africa – the brash, bustling present co-exists with the magic and myth of the past.

BIRTHPLACE OF THE WORLD

Modern Ife, a university city with a population of well over 100,000 and an economy now based on cocoa farming, is built on land occupied by the Yoruba people of south-west Nigeria since at least the 8th century AD. From the 12th century it was the capital of a powerful kingdom and today it is still a religious capital for upward of 10 million Yorubas – the place where the gods first descended from the heavens to create the world.

In the West, Ife is famous for a different reason. Its name is associated with sculptures – in terracotta, stone and metal – that are among the greatest artistic creations ever produced in Africa, hauntingly beautiful human faces fashioned in a completely naturalistic style.

What sort of society was it that produced such high art? What was the purpose and significance of these superb sculptures?

The culture that produced them was not without its precedents in Africa. Iron technology, for example, was known south of the Sahara as early as the 5th century BC. Ironworking settlements, dating from that period, have been discovered at Taruga, about 500km (300 miles) from Ife in northern Nigeria. The people of the so-called Nok culture – after a village where the first discoveries were made – also produced some marvellously expressive terracotta figures which are generally regarded as ancestors of the much later Ife artefacts.

FACE OF DIGNITY Great men of state were often the subject of Ife's sculptors, whose life-size portrayals were immensely detailed. This terracotta head from the 12th–15th centuries even includes facial scars.

Historians know that black African states with organized administrations were flourishing around the Niger bend when Arab geographers began to take note of them in the 9th century AD. The Muslims imported slaves, ivory and gold from these shadowy kingdoms. But why Ife experienced its sudden explosion of artistic creativity is still a mystery.

The first scholars to study it were deeply impressed by the naturalism of its art and assumed that it must be derived from European culture. In fact, the city's artistic peak was between AD 1100 and 1500. The first European contact with the region was not until 1485, at Benin City, 180km (112 miles) to the south-east. By then, the art of Ife was in decline, suggesting that it must have been entirely African in inspiration and origin.

THE SCULPTOR AS MODEL-MAKER

The cast-metal sculptures are usually referred to as 'bronzes', although they are never actually made of bronze. The materials used are either pure copper or leaded brass (copper, zinc and lead). The method of casting was the *cire-perdue*, or 'lost wax' process. In this, the sculptor first makes a clay core, over which he lays wax. This he models to the desired shape. He then adds carefully placed rods of wax – to allow the metal to enter at a later stage. He coats the wax with a layer of very fine clay, over which he applies several more layers of coarser clay. Then he heats it until the wax runs away through the holes formed by the wax rods. This leaves an empty cavity into which he pours the molten metal. When the metal has cooled and solidified the clay mould is broken away, revealing a reproduction, exact in every detail, of the wax model.

The craftsmen of Ife probably obtained their raw materials indirectly from Europe, buying metal that had been traded in stages from the North African coast across the Sahara. Metal would have been costly, so it is no coincidence that the subject matter of the sculptures is royalty.

A CITY UPON A CITY

Archaeologically, Ife is a lost city, buried under a buzzing metropolis in which excavation is difficult. Even more importantly, fluctuations in humidity, soil conditions and the activities of termites soon break down organic materials, especially wood and bones.

Nonetheless, certain facts have been established about life in Ife. It was a fortified city, surrounded by earth banks and ditches. There were wooden gates where the main roads converged on the city, some of them made more secure by a narrow entrance with a second gateway beyond. Enemies could only pass through the first gate one at a time, making them vulnerable to attack. Sieges, then, must have been known at Ife.

The main occupation of its people, then as now, was farming – they grew yams, cassava, peppers, kola nuts, oil-palms. Within the city, people lived in family compounds containing a complex of mud buildings thatched with palm leaves. Rooms were windowless. The thatched roofs overhung the walls to form verandahs, supported on wooden columns. Cooking was done in the central courtyard, using a

round-bottomed stewing pot placed over three stones or a curved clay structure which served as a fireplace. Courtyards and passageways were paved using quartz pebbles or fragments of broken pottery set on edge in neat lines. Often, the road surfaces of modern Ife have been so worn by use that patches of these ancient pavements are revealed below. They provide an excellent non-slip surface to walk on in wet weather, and have even borne the weight of motor traffic without crumbling.

The royal palace of Ife has also survived, though most of it was rebuilt in the 20th century. Standing in the centre of the city, it had the same basic design as the houses of the common people, but on a grander scale. Until recently, it retained a large tract of open land, with an area of forest dotted with shrines and sacred groves.

LONG LIVE THE GOD-KING

During his lifetime, the king of Ife is still regarded as divine. When the kingdom was at its height, artists would sculpt a monarch's portrait in wax after his death, then cast it as a life-size brass or copper head. They were careful to fashion the head in such a way that it could carry the king's crown.

The metal head was then attached to a wooden 'body', which may have been no more than a simple framework to carry the head and robes. The crown was placed on the head; the frame was robed in royal costume, and the emblems of royal authority – a sceptre and a ram's horn filled with powerful magical materials – were placed in the hands. Then the entire figure was carried in solemn procession as a sign that, though the king himself was dead, the institution of monarchy went on. The king's statue was probably buried, but the bronze head was later placed in a shrine in the palace. Other statues in terracotta – of kings, queens and royal attendants – formed the centrepiece of permanent shrines at which the people would place offerings.

The sculptures reveal the fashions of the day. The king wore a hemmed skirt of woven material, reaching down to the ankles. Both kings and queens wore several sashes decorated with beaded tassels, either slung over the shoulder or knotted round the waist. Beaded neck-collars, anklets, and armlets completed the ensemble. They wore rings on their toes. Crowns bore a vertical crest in the centre, over the forehead. Both kings and queens wore on their chests a beaded badge of office, which may have been a symbol both of spiritual and of temporal authority.

Many of Ife's early kings are still worshipped as gods; other deities are the great spirits, such as the spirits of sky and earth, as well as more specific ones associated with natural features of the locality. Evidence of the ancient rites surrounding these deities can be found in the decoration of the pots used in present-day ceremonies.

Some depict drums characteristic of the ancient cults of Orishanla and Onile, the 'owner of the earth'. Others show ritual staffs from the Onile cult and the Osanyin cult (the medicine, or healing, cult) and cow-horns associated with

Oya, the goddess of the River Niger. Clearly, the religious festivals that still take place in sacred groves around the modern city of Ife have their roots in ancient practices.

The faces of the ancient god-kings of Ife, preserved in terracotta and finely cast metal, stare down the centuries, serene, proud, majestic – and silent. But the voice of ancient Ife can still be heard, above the roar of 21st-century traffic, in rituals and chants that hark back to the days that gave birth to an art that is an enduring monument to the spirit of Africa.

SUPREME SOVEREIGN A sculpture from the 13th century shows a king, or Ooni, of Ife. Monarchs at this time probably led more public lives than later kings and queens, who are often depicted wearing beaded fringes from their crowns to protect them from the people's gaze.

Pueblo Bonito

A settlement lost in the desert

For more than 300 years the Pueblo Indians of New Mexico wrung life from their harsh environment. Beneath the towering cliffs of Chaco Canyon they built their dwelling place – an apartment block of 700 rooms.

IN 1849 LIEUTENANT JAMES SIMPSON OF THE AMERICAN ARMY was a member of a punitive expedition sent to New Mexico against a group of Navajo Indians. One day he camped near the ruins of a massive dwelling – a cross between a primitive village and a modern high-rise apartment block.

Lieutenant Simpson later described the experience in a journal published in 1852: 'Two or three hundred yards down the canyon, we came across another old pueblo in ruins called Pueblo Bonito ... The circuit of its walls is about 1300ft. Its elevation shows that it has had at least four storeys of apartments.

'The number of rooms on the ground floor at present discernible is 139 ...

'Among the ruins are several rooms in a very good state of preservation, one of them being walled up with alternate beds of large and small stones, the regularity of the combination producing a very pleasing effect. The ceiling of this room is also more pleasant than any we have seen – the transverse beams being smaller and more numerous, and the longitudinal pieces which rest upon them only about an inch in diameter, and beautifully regular. The latter have somewhat the appearance of barked willow.

'The room has a doorway at each end and one at the side, each of them leading into adjacent apartments. The light is let in by a window, 2ft by 8in on the north side.'

VILLAGE IN THE SANDS

Simpson's discovery of this huge pile of terraced houses aroused a rush of interest, but it was another 50 years before serious excavations began. When, towards the end of the 19th century, American archaeologists started to explore Pueblo Bonito, they unearthed a village which in the 12th century AD may have housed 1200 people.

CANYON COMMUNITIES Between the 9th and 12th centuries AD the ancestors of today's Pueblo Indians built a vast communal dwelling at Pueblo Bonito (foreground) in New Mexico's Chaco Canyon. Roads crossed the landscape, linking similar settlements, but some ended abruptly. The network is thought to have had a ritual significance, possibly relating to the layout of the Pueblo cosmos.

THE 'PRETTY VILLAGE' OF THE ANASAZI

By about AD 1100 Pueblo Bonito was entering its heyday. With its back to a cliff, the city forms a huge D-shape. Its 700 rooms, built on five different levels, face south towards the river valley.

Life in Pueblo Bonito depended on agriculture and, therefore, on rainfall and irrigation systems. The Pueblo Indians stored the water – which cascaded down the cliffs after storms – in cisterns, and then distributed it to their nearby fields of maize, pumpkins, and beans through a network of channels.

Oldest part of Pueblo Bonito, built c.AD 850–950

Western plaza

Great kiva

PRAYING FOR RAIN

The constant need for water to irrigate their crops was an ever-present concern of the people of Pueblo Bonito. While they conserved all they could in cisterns, they also held secret rituals to pray for rain. These took place in large sacred, circular, underground chambers, known as *kivas*, built in the central courtyard. There were also smaller kivas (above) for family use. Thirty of these have been uncovered in the complex. Below: A decorative pot made by the women of the community. Skills were handed down from mother to daughter.

Eastern plaza | Other kivas | Building stone quarried from cliffs

Pueblo Bonito ('pretty village' in Spanish) is a remarkable monument to a North American Indian culture that flourished 500 years before Columbus set sail for the New World in the late 15th century. Its inhabitants were a Stone Age people who left no written record of their culture, but their story can be read from the shards of broken pottery they left behind.

THE NOMADS SETTLE DOWN

The civilizations of the south-western United States trace their origins to around 7000 BC. At this time, hunter-gatherers started to roam the dust bowl of the Great Basin, mostly in present-day Nevada and Utah. By about AD 100 the Anasazi, or 'Ancient Ones', had begun to develop a distinctive culture. As they became increasingly dependent on cultivated crops, such as maize and beans, they abandoned their nomadic lifestyle and built settlements of underground houses.

The Pueblo (village) period began in about AD 700, when houses began to be built above ground. Pueblo Bonito is just

PAINTED PITCHER
The decorative designs on pots made by the women of Pueblo Bonito are thought to have been inspired by the patterns on basketry. Colours were achieved using plant dyes.

one of 13 villages to be found in the Chaco Canyon in north-west New Mexico. At the foot of a cliff, the settlement has the outline of a huge semicircle with the straight side facing south towards the Chaco river. Its 700 rooms rise in terraces around the central courtyard like some great amphitheatre. Access to the pueblo was by ladder over the straight front side. The complex covers an area of 1.5ha (4 acres): it was the largest apartment block in the world until a bigger one was built in New York in 1882.

Pueblo Bonito's first stone was laid in about 850. The walls of the settlement were solidly built around a core of stone or adobe – mud bricks dried in the sun. They were faced with sandstone flags which fitted together so perfectly that it is difficult to insert the blade of a knife between them.

Religion and ritual were the common bonds of the people of each pueblo. The central courtyard of Pueblo Bonito had several large semi-subterranean ceremonial chambers, or *kivas*, for use by the community as a whole – the biggest is almost 20m (66ft) across. Each contains a brick bench which runs all the way round the room, surrounding a central hearth.

The inhabitants lived in rooms which measured about 5m by 4m (16ft by 13ft). Roofs consisted of two strong cross beams, supporting a series of wooden logs which were covered in matting made of willow bark and branches. The whole roof was then covered with adobe. The construction of the pueblo was a mammoth undertaking: the timbers had to be carried to the canyon from 80km (50 miles) away. The rooms at the bottom of the complex opened onto the central courtyard, but those at the top had no doors or windows and were reached by a ladder through a hole in the roof. They were probably used as granaries. Above them stretched the flat roofs on which the inhabitants worked. The building was insulated from extremes of hot and cold by the thickness of the walls. Floors were covered with willow-bark and the beds with furs.

The inhabitants depended on agriculture. They planted maize, beans, and pumpkins, and over the years they developed special irrigation techniques to cope with their dry, hot climate. Rainwater and cliff run-off was stored in cisterns and distributed by countless small channels which ran across the fields.

They would crush the daily ration of maize into flour using a flat millstone, or *metate*, and a stone pounder. Then they made small biscuits – like Mexican tortillas of today – which they baked on fires and stuffed with meat, beans, or nuts.

SKILLED POTTERS AND WEAVERS
The Pueblo Bonito Indians were an industrious people. Most of the daily work was done on the roofs of the settlement. The men were particularly skilled at weaving bags, belts and blankets on looms. The women made huge cotton ponchos and fashioned sandals from the leaves of the yucca plant.

Perhaps the most impressive legacy of the Pueblo Bonito Indians is their elaborate pottery. Unusual among ancient societies, all the potters seem to have been women. Bowls, pitchers and ladles were their speciality, and these were decorated with geometric patterns.

They made blankets from the feathers of the turkeys they kept, and from the parrots and macaws they imported from the south. Attracted by the people's skills, merchants travelled to Pueblo Bonito from the heartlands of Mexico to the

FAMILY INHERITANCE The pueblo known as White House is in the Canyon de Chelly. Property passed through the female line: when a man married he would go to live with his wife's family, or in a house she owned.

south to sell birds, and from the Pacific coast to sell seashells. In return, they took back sculpted ornaments. But the most highly prized treasures were the Indians' turquoise beads and mosaics. One necklace, found in an Anasazi tomb, was made of 2500 tiny turquoise beads, each one lovingly smoothed on sandstone tablets and drilled with a sharpened flint.

DROUGHT AND DECLINE
Rainfall was always a critical factor influencing settlement in the American south-west. Around 1130 a period of drought began that lasted 50 or so years. The people of Pueblo Bonito and Chaco Canyon began to move to other regions, such as Mesa Verde in Colorado. Another long period of drought in the 13th century finally set the seal on the Anasazi's decline. By the beginning of the 14th century, their great communal dwellings were abandoned. Their inhabitants settled on the more fertile plateaus where their descendants, Pueblo Indian tribes such as the Zunis and the Hopis, still live today. The original villages disappeared under a covering of sand and were consigned to centuries of oblivion.

Chanchan

A target of the Inca conquest

On the northern coast of Peru, a field of ruins stretches as far as the eye can see. This was Chanchan, capital of the Chimú, which fell to the Incas only decades before the Incas themselves perished under the swords of the Spanish conquistadores.

WHEN THE SPANIARDS DEFEATED THE INCAS in the 16th century, they inherited the remains of more than one civilization. Inca Peru, also an empire of conquest, embraced many different societies. But the Incas extinguished earlier traditions as mercilessly as the Spaniards were to crush their own, and many of the cultures that rose and fell in the Andes and its fringes are shrouded in mystery.

The first major culture to arise in Peru was that of the Chavin, around 1000 BC. Others followed: the Paracas of central Peru, who mummified their dead and wrapped them in magnificent fabrics; the Moche of the northern coast, who were great builders and goldsmiths. Farther south, the mysterious Nazca culture emerged around AD 500, leaving behind a fantastic network of designs – birds, spiders, and geometric figures – indelibly scored across the desolate southern plains.

By about AD 1000, the culture of the upland Tiwanaku people dominated much of Peru, which now enjoyed a rich cultural heritage. Among the civilizations that built on this heritage, none was more impressive than Chimor, the kingdom of the Chimú, ruled from the city of Chanchan.

THE LEGEND OF TAYCANAMO

A handful of legends collected by Spanish chroniclers have survived through the centuries to explain the origin of Chimor. The tales centre on the semi-mythical hero Taycanamo, founder of the Chimú royal dynasty. Taycanamo, so the stories say, arrived in the Moche valley on a raft as an envoy from a great lord beyond the seas. He brought with him a magical yellow powder – probably gold dust. He built a palace, learned the language, and was eventually recognized by the locals as their chief.

Taycanamo is said to have founded his dynasty in about 1300, but archaeology has shown that Chanchan, the Chimú capital, dates back to an earlier period. The site is thought to have been settled as far back as 800 BC, and monumental construction began in about AD 850. But it was not until the Taycanamon dynasty that the city became the wonder of its contemporaries.

CREATURES OF MYTH A pyramid complex just outside Chanchan, known as El Dragon, may have been used as a temple. The mud-brick walls of the complex are decorated with images of fabulous creatures. The designs were traced out on a thick facing of fresh clay, and the background cut away to create a well-defined relief. The rainbow-shaped motif on this section is a double-headed serpent.

RESTRICTED ACCESS The surviving mud-brick walls surrounding the ten compounds at Chanchan still reach a height of 9m (29½ft) in places. They were often decorated with friezes of marine motifs – here, unusually, the design depicts a small land creature.

GEOMETRIC STYLE The walls of palaces and other important buildings inside the ten citadels were often decorative in their construction, laid out in repeating patterns of diamonds and triangles, or in squares arranged in chequerboard-style designs.

Taycanamo's dynasty continued through nine more kings. His immediate successors conquered the whole of the Moche and six other valleys. But the empire reached its peak under the last monarch, Minchan-saman. In the mid-15th century, when the Incas were expanding southwards from their capital at Cuzco in the central highlands, Minchan-saman brought the valleys of the central coastlands within the fold of Chimor. The kingdom now stretched along 960km (596 miles) of coast, from Tumbes in the north to a point near present-day Lima.

Chanchan was even larger than Cuzco. It covered about 20km² (7¹/₂ sq miles), and supported 40,000 people. With its workshops, factories, warehouses, and temples, it was the hub of Chimú trade, religion, and administration. The heart of the city was dominated by ten great enclosures, with tapering walls ranging from 7.5m to 9m (24¹/₂ ft to 29¹/₂ ft) high. Each enclosure conformed to the same rectangular plan, with a single, narrow entrance in the north wall and an interior divided into three sections: north, central, and south.

The north and central sections contained living quarters, kitchens, audience chambers, courtyards, colonnades, storage areas, and water tanks. The southern sections often contained a mound or platform. When archaeologists excavated one of these mounds in 1969, they uncovered the remains of almost 100 young women. They had been sacrificed – perhaps by poison. In the centre, they found a T-shaped tomb and burial offerings.

A DYNASTY OF GREAT BUILDERS

What purpose did the enclosures serve? There were ten such structures, built one after another – and ten kings in the dynasty of Taycanamo. The generally accepted theory is that each king constructed an enclosure as his own royal residence. After death, it would have served as a shrine devoted to his worship, and his heir would then build his own complex.

The royal enclosures were built with a combination of clay and sun-dried mud bricks, as were the city's houses, storage areas, and colonnades, which were roofed with reeds, straw,

THE WEAVER'S ART

Weaving was one of the most remarkable expressions of the Peruvians' craftsmanship before the arrival of the conquistadores. Their finest technical achievements were produced on the south coast, home of the Paracas culture (500 BC–AD 100), whose weavers used up to 190 different colours of dye.

On the northern coast, the climate is more humid, and fabrics have tended to perish. But it is clear that the Chimú, though much later than the Paracas, never achieved the same perfection in textiles. In the few examples that have been found, the range of colours, for example, was more limited.

The main raw materials used by the Chimú were cotton and the wool of alpacas. Vegetable dyes were most commonly used to colour the thread; indigo made blue, for example. Animal dyes were less common. Elaborate weaving techniques produced gauzes, tapestries, and double fabrics. Embroidered or painted decorations were often

FIT FOR A KING Craftsmen of the Chimú used precious blue and yellow feathers to create the royal headdress. Their use of feathers from Amazonian birds reflects the diverse trading links of early Andean cultures.

applied in bands. Their motifs were the same as those used in ceramics, or in the relief-work friezes that adorn the walls of many of the buildings in Chanchan. Typical designs included abstract patterns and images of birds, fish, and human or mythical figures.

The Chimú also made glorious fabrics from the feathers of tropical birds, which were sewn to a cloth backing. The feathers were bartered from Indians living in the forest regions of the interior.

The Indians, too, prized the feathers highly, and used them to make ceremonial finery of their own. Because of their great value throughout South America, feather fabrics were extremely expensive and were reserved for kings and the ruling class.

and clay. Clay friezes of geometric motifs, animals, and various mythological monsters decorated the walls. The reliefs often depict sea-birds, fish, starfish, and crustaceans. Chanchan was close to the sea, and the ebb and swell of the Pacific must have been constantly in the minds of its inhabitants. The ocean was a divinity known as Ni, worshipped by casting offerings of maize and red ochre into the waves.

Around the outskirts of the citadels were humble dwellings made of cane. Two depressions at each end of the city appear to have been planted with gardens, and water was supplied to areas that needed it by a system of irrigation channels. A pyramid complex, probably a temple compound, stood just outside the city. This was not an innovation of Chimú society – flat-topped pyramids had existed in Peru as early as the 2nd millennium BC.

The Chimú were energetic builders, and established urban centres less grandiose than Chanchan in almost all of the valleys they ruled, including Tucume Viejo in the Leche valley and Pacatnamú in the Jequetepeque. They followed a tradition of urban construction established by earlier Andean civilizations, executing their work with greater skill, and on a larger scale.

A SOCIETY KEPT IN ITS PLACE

Only a powerful administration was capable of organizing such large building works. Some information has survived on the nature of Chimú government. The king was supreme, wielding absolute power. Known as the *Quie quic*, or Great Lord, he was like the Inca sovereign in claiming to be descended from the gods.

Below the king were the Chimú chieftains, known as *alaec*, and the members of the royal family. One myth states that the king and the nobility were descended from two stars, while the common people sprang from two others. The tale suggests that a strict class system existed, and that there was no possibility of movement between the classes. At the bottom of the social scale were the commoners,

LIFE ON THE OCEAN WAVE Chimú household pottery, such as the reed boat, was themed around scenes from everyday life. Many pots were mass-produced using moulds.

GAUNTLETS OF GOLD The purpose of the Chimú hands is unknown. In the mythology of the Chimú's Inca successors, gold was the life-giving 'sweat of the sun' and headdresses wrought in gold symbolize the sun.

who were referred to as *paraeng* and *yana*, generally taken to denote vassals and servants.

Agriculture was the main source of livelihood, on land owned mainly by the king and nobility. A few animals such as the dog and the Muscovy duck were raised for food. Fishing and hunting also supplemented the diet. The large-scale manufacture of craft goods also supported the economy, and trade was based on barter.

The centralized state supervised various public works. For example, a network of roads was built to link the kingdom's different regions. An irrigation system, begun by the Moche a few centuries earlier, was extended to reach some of the desolate spaces around the valleys, to secure abundant harvests.

THE POWER OF NATURE

Like other ancient peoples all over the world, the Chimú watched the movements of the heavenly bodies with fascination. Yet no divinity seems to have been worshipped as a supreme force. Legends refer to a variety of gods – notably the sea, the stars, the sun, and the moon goddess Si. Si was considered more powerful than the sun, because she was visible even during daylight hours.

While knowledge of the Chimú's beliefs remains sketchy, ample material survives to form a picture of their superlative craftsmanship. Their goods included figures identical to those on wall friezes in the capital. This suggests that a single model was used for multiple copies. Weavers worked on tapestries, embroidery, and ceremonial mantles made with feathers. Chimú potters specialized in a gleaming black ware – vessels cast in moulds and ingeniously embellished with human and animal figures. But it was in goldwork that the Chimú excelled. Chimú goldsmiths mastered the arts of soldering, chasing, and filigree work. Most goldwork was made from hammered

sheet metal, although some pieces were cast in moulds. The results were exquisitely shaped golden bowls and goblets, masks, breastplates, and jewellery. The Chimú goldsmiths were famed beyond the frontiers of their own state. When the Incas overran the Chimú kingdom, they took the most skilled craftsmen back with them.

UNDER ENEMY RULE

In about 1460, the Incas began to penetrate the northern regions of Peru. But Minchan-saman could offer only ineffective resistance, and Chimor was defeated and brought within the Inca domain.

The Chimú king was treated well, and his son, Chumun-caur, was appointed to govern the defeated kingdom. But between 1485 and 1490, the unity of the kingdom was destroyed – its ruler became merely a provincial chieftain of the Moche valley, with no power over the neighbouring territories.

The Incas went on to absorb Chimú achievements into their own empire, which extended beyond modern Peru to much of Ecuador and Bolivia, and parts of Chile and Argentina. Like Chimor, the Inca domain was rigidly centralized, with a system of roads and couriers running between the main centres. But now they carried the orders of the supreme Inca, the Child of the Sun.

After the disintegration of the Inca empire and its subjugation by the Spaniards, Chanchan – which was already partially abandoned – was sacked by the treasure-hungry conquistadores. The city fell into ruin, and the native goldwork was melted down in huge quantities and cast into ingots sold at the metal's market value.

Yet neither time nor conquest has completely obliterated Chimú civilization. The Incas disseminated Chimú culture over an area much larger than the original kingdom, and the Spanish chroniclers preserved their legends. And even in their fallen state, the regal ruins at Chanchan evoke the majesty of the Chimú rulers and the inventive energy of their people.

Tenochtitlán

A city surrounded by water

When the Spanish conquistadores arrived in the Valley of Mexico in 1519, they discovered an immense lake, bustling with boats. In the centre, on an island, stood a dazzling white city – the glorious capital of the Aztec Empire.

The winds that blew across the Gulf of Mexico to Cuba in the early years of the 16th century carried rumours that set men's blood racing: tales of vast cities, of pyramids bigger than those of Egypt, and of staggering hoards of gold, silver, and precious stones. Among the most eager listeners to these stories was Hernán Cortés, mayor of a small Cuban township. He secured command of an expedition to the mainland in search of gold, and on February 10, 1519, set sail from Cuba with 508 soldiers, 100 sailors, and 16 horses. They landed near the town of Tabasco where, after a couple of skirmishes that convinced the local Indians of the superiority of Spanish arms, they were showered with gifts.

Before long the Aztec emperor, Montezuma II, heard of the arrival of a splendid race of fair-skinned, bearded men. He believed that their appearance fulfilled an ancient prophecy: the promised return from across the sea of the god Quetzalcoatl – the priest-king who once led the ancient Toltecs of Central Mexico, and taught them how to plant crops and build temples.

CONQUER OR DIE

Montezuma sent messengers to the Spanish camp bearing dazzling gifts, including circles of gold and silver as big as cartwheels. But he feared for his position, and made it clear that he did not want the Spaniards in his capital. Cortés would not be put off. He discouraged any hesitancy among his men by sinking their ships, then set out for Montezuma's city. The journey was not easy; a series of fierce battles, notably at Tlaxcala, hindered his progress though he did manage to recruit many of the defeated peoples as auxiliary warriors.

Months later, on November 8, Cortés and his party scrambled down the slopes of the mountains that enclosed Lake Texcoco. They were confronted by an incredible sight. Sprawled across islands in the lake – and on the banks beyond – were numerous towns and villages. In the middle of the lake, served by causeways, rose a city as big as ancient Rome and as beautiful as Venice.

AN IMAGE OF DEATH Today, the site of Tenochtitlán is occupied by Mexico City, where many reminders of the Aztecs have been discovered, including this figure of their goddess of life and death, Coatlicue. Images of death, such as the skull and hands on the necklace worn by this figure, are a common theme. Coatlicue was believed to have given birth to Huitzilopochtli, the Aztecs' patron deity – a figure of blood and warfare.

Priests' quarters   Sacred ball court   Temple of Ehecatl, god of winds

BEHIND THE SACRED WALLS

The sacred precinct of monumental buildings at the heart of Tenochtitlán was dominated by the great double pyramid, the *teocalli*. Different deities, such as the gods of the night sky, fire, and maize, each had a temple in the holy city, which also contained the armouries, a music school, ritual baths, and hostels for noblemen who came to the city on pilgrimage.

One of Cortés's companions, Bernal Diaz del Castillo, describes the sight in his *True History of the Conquest of New Spain*, published in 1632: 'And when we saw all those cities and villages built in the water, and other great towns on dry land, we were astounded, and at that straight and level causeway going towards Mexico, we were amazed . . . some of the soldiers wondered if it were not a dream . . .'

In the distance stood another great city, Texcoco. But the scene was dominated by the central settlement, made up of dazzling white buildings, flower-filled terraces, proud palaces and temples, and huge pyramids. This was Montezuma's capital, Mexico-Tenochtitlán (as it was known to the Aztecs) – an American Venice connected to the mainland by three elevated causeways reaching across the waters of the lake.

To the explorers, the elaborate complex suggested a long established civilization. In fact, Aztec culture had reached its zenith only towards the end of the previous century.

VALLEY OF NATURAL RICHES

The Aztec capital had its beginnings, however, much further back in time. More than 10,000 years ago, settlers were attracted to the Valley of Mexico by its natural resources. The marshy shores of the lake of Texcoco were thick with reeds and alive with game. The stone arrow-heads of these early inhabitants have been found next to the skeletons of hunted mammoths.

Later, thick alluvial deposits around the lake proved ideal for early attempts at agriculture. Maize, beans, gourds, tomatoes, pimentos, oil-seeds, and the edible plant amaranth were first cultivated in the valley between 4000 and 3000 BC. Gradually, the area became dotted with villages. The Indians settled down as farmers, and began making pottery and weaving fabrics from cotton and cactus fibre. Pottery statuettes from this period show that social differences began to emerge. Some figures wear

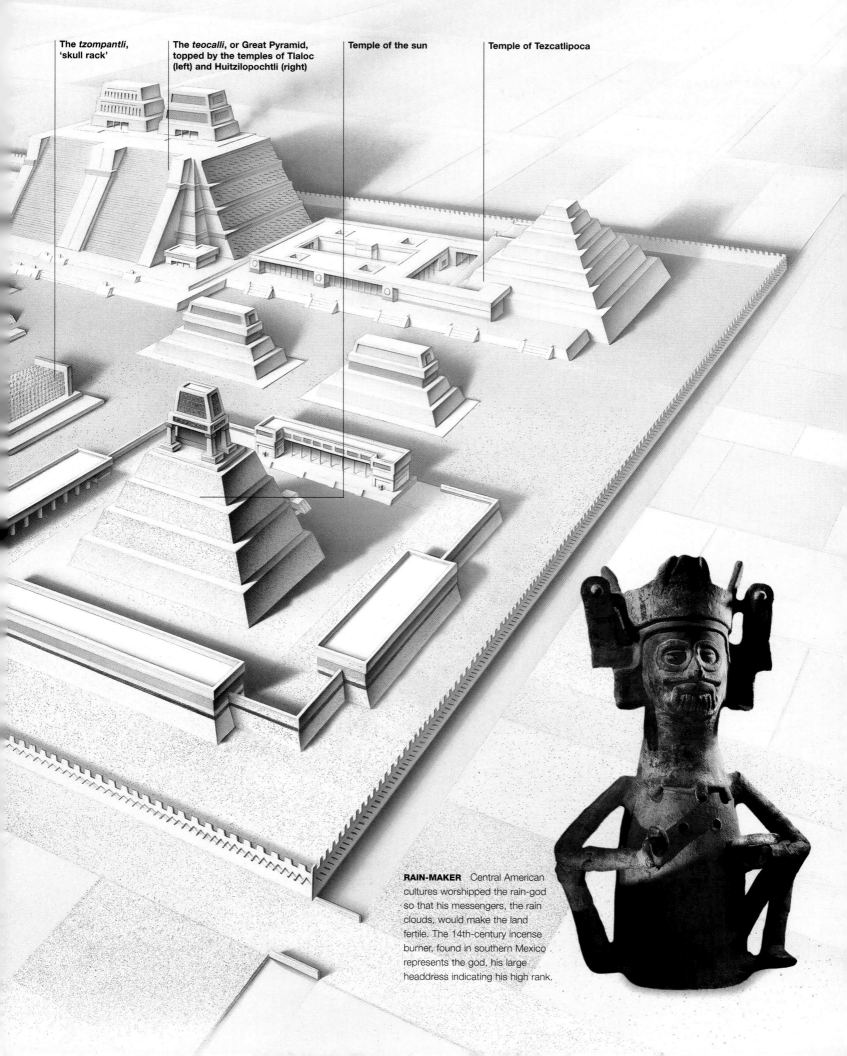

The *tzompantli*, 'skull rack'

The *teocalli*, or Great Pyramid, topped by the temples of Tlaloc (left) and Huitzilopochtli (right)

Temple of the sun

Temple of Tezcatlipoca

RAIN-MAKER Central American cultures worshipped the rain-god so that his messengers, the rain clouds, would make the land fertile. The 14th-century incense burner, found in southern Mexico represents the god, his large headdress indicating his high rank.

CITY ON A LAKE A stylised woodcut from Cortés's letters to the Emperor Charles V back in Europe shows the island shared by Tenochtitlán (lower part) and Tlatelolco (upper part). The size of the sacred precinct is exaggerated, and the size of the lake reduced.

turbans, and are bedecked with jewels – evidence of relative wealth; others depict people wearing masks, possibly medicine men. Female figures suggest the existence of a fertility cult.

In about 1000 BC, a tribe known as the Olmecs became prominent on the coastlands bordering the Gulf of Mexico. The Olmecs' influence spread far and wide. They were superb stone-carvers, and built the first monuments in the area – notably the pyramid of La Venta on the Gulf coast.

As the population increased, villages grew into small towns and primitive social structures gave way to a more complex order, probably dominated by priests. One monument known as the Cuicuilco 'pyramid' consists of a truncated cone surmounted by a platform containing a sanctuary. It was built on the south-western edge of the Valley of Mexico in about 300 BC and could not have been constructed without the co-ordinated effort of a population living within a sophisticated social framework.

THE RISE OF THE CITY-STATES

Mexico's first real city was situated in the northern part of the valley. Its name, Teotihuacán, means 'the great city where men became gods'. The city reached its peak in the 6th century AD, with a population of between 150,000 and 200,000, and the far-reaching influence of this religious and artistic metropolis touched even the Maya of distant Guatemala. Its grid-planned streets spread over 20km^2 (7^3/4 sq miles), and were dominated by the magnificent Pyramid of the Sun, which stood about 60m (197ft) high. An avenue lined with palaces and temples ran for nearly 2km (1^1/4 miles), north to south. Despite its magnificence, by the end of the 8th century Teotihuacán lay in ruins. It may have been invaded and destroyed by envious neighbours, aided by disaffected peasants – or perhaps by nomadic warrior tribes from the north.

In the 9th century, the Toltec capital, Tula, dominated the area. Wars and revolutions at the end of the 10th century led to the establishment of a militaristic

regime which practised human sacrifice on a monumental scale, and with unparalleled savagery. When Tula collapsed in 1168, the central plain was invaded by 'barbarians' who were absorbed into the Toltec tradition. In the years that followed, the city-states were in constant conflict. In about 1250, while 28 towns fought for control of Central Mexico, a small tribe from the north-west moved into the valley. They called themselves Mexica or Tenochca, but are better known as Aztecs, a name taken from the land of their origin, Aztlán.

WHERE THE EAGLE CRIES

One night, Huitzilopochtli, the god of war and the sun, appeared to the Aztec high priest, Quahcoatl, and commanded him: 'Go at once and find the cactus ('*tenochtli*') on which the eagle sits joyfully . . . That is where we shall settle, where we shall rule . . . where we shall conquer with our javelin and our shield. That is where our city Mexico-Tenochtitlán shall be, there where the eagle cries, opens its wings and eats, where the fish swims. There where the serpent is devoured.' As a result of the dream, the Aztecs began their search for a home.

After nearly a century of wandering, they penetrated the swamps around Texcoco and there saw an eagle landing on a cactus with a serpent in its beak, exactly as Quahcoatl had predicted. The cactus was on an island in the middle of a lake, and here the city of Mexico-Tenochtitlán was founded in 1325. The settlement, now known simply as Tenochtitlán, 'the place of the cactus', began as a shanty town of thatched mud huts. The inhabitants traded lake produce such as fish, salamanders and shrimps for timber to build homes. Progress was slow, but the Aztecs rose gradually to dominate their neighbours. They were skilled and ruthless fighters, and showed diplomatic skill in arranging dynastic marriages with established houses and alliances with other city-states.

Between the 14th and 16th centuries, an urban centre developed around two areas on the island: Tenochtitlán, which held the main religious and municipal buildings, and Tlatelolco to the north, which had been independent until 1473

> '*Go at once and find the cactus on which the eagle sits joyfully . . . That is where we shall settle, where we shall rule . . . where we shall conquer with our javelin and our shield.*'

LEARNING THE HARD WAY

Among the Aztecs, the children of ordinary people were schooled at 'houses of youth', where they were given a strictly practical training with an emphasis on military subjects. The children of the nobility attended monastic colleges where they were prepared for the priesthood, the civil service, or high command in the army. They studied the sacred books, history, religious rites, military and civil subjects – and good manners.

Ordinary children had more freedom at school than the young nobles, who were bound by strict rules. But both rich and poor could become victims of cruelty. The Codex Mendoza, a record of Aztec life made at the command of a Spanish Viceroy in the 1540s, depicts many facets of home education, including the punishments inflicted by fathers on their lazy or disobedient children. One father reprimands his young son by sticking thorns into his naked body; another chastises his son with a stick. One particularly unpleasant punishment involved holding the child over a fire on to which red peppers have been thrown to produce acrid fumes.

and had its own temple and market. What the Spaniards saw on their arrival was a 'greater Mexico' formed after the annexation of Tlatelolco. In a letter to Charles V of Spain, Cortés described the view: 'All the streets of the town are open from end to end, so that water flows right through them. All these openings, some of which are very wide, are spanned by bridges supported on strong beams . . . Most of the streets are taken up half by canal and half by quay'.

The simple, one-storey Aztec homes had windowless facades which gave onto the streets or canals, where an endless variety of small tradesmen hawked their wares. Each house had an interior courtyard where flowers and vegetables could be cultivated and a few turkeys raised. These courtyards also contained small, separate buildings which housed the *temazcalli*, or steam bath, still used in parts of Mexico. The usual building material was sun-baked bricks. Roofs were flat and supported on wooden beams.

The Aztec city had spread all over the islets and sandbanks. Houses were constructed on piles over the water and on the lake shore, and marshland was reclaimed with the construction of *chinampas* – fertile 'floating' gardens. By the beginning of the 16th century,

the city covered about 1,011ha (2,498 acres), and was divided into four main districts. To the north was Cuepopan, 'the place of the blossoming of flowers'; to the east Teopan, 'the temple'; to the south – near the swamps – Moyotlan, 'the region of mosquitoes'; and to the west Aztacalco, 'the place of herons'. The districts were divided into *calpoltin*, or 'groups of houses', the basic unit of Aztec society. Each calpoltin elected a leader who was assisted in decision-making by a council of elders.

There are no precise population figures for the Aztec capital. The Spaniards' estimates varied – from 60,000 homes to twice that number. An average of seven inhabitants to a house would suggest a figure somewhere between 420,000 and 840,000.

INSIDE THE HOLY ENCLOSURE

Excavations in present-day Mexico City have revealed the remains of the *teocalli* – a vast double pyramid set in the centre of Tenochtitlán, begun in the 14th century, which rose about 30m (98ft) from a base of about 100m by 80m (328ft by 262ft). A broad, double staircase with balustrades adorned by feathered serpents' heads led up to a platform on which two sanctuaries were situated: one dedicated to Tlaloc, the god of rain and abundant crops, and the other to Huitzilopochtli,

MARRIAGE VOWS A Mexican manuscript shows an 11th-century wedding. The bride's plaited headdress indicates her newly married state. Footprints between the couple represent future children.

the god of war and the sun, protector of the Aztec race. This monument towered over a cluster of temples, pyramids, and religious buildings enclosed within the *coatepantl*, or 'hedge of snakes' – a crenellated wall decorated with serpents' heads.

Inside the wall lay the sanctuaries of the other principal Central American gods: the feathered serpent Quetzalcoatl, god of the wind and the morning star; Tezcatlipoca, god of the night sky and protector of young warriors; and the mother goddess Cihuacoatl, the 'woman serpent'. The provincial Aztec gods were grouped in a temple known as the *coacalco*. The holy enclosure also contained the *calmecacs* – residential college monasteries in which austere priests dressed in black robes dispensed higher education to the youth of the aristocracy.

Here, too, were places of prayer and sacrifice, including the *tzompantli*, a rack on which the heads of recent human offerings were displayed. One of the companions of Cortés went to the trouble of counting the skulls: the final tally was 136,000.

The rack of skulls illustrates the taint of cruelty which ran like a dark thread through the fabric of Aztec society. Macabre sacrificial ceremonies featured in many of their festivals. In some rites, children were sacrificed; in others, priests danced in the flayed skins of adult victims.

HUNTING FOR HUMAN PREY

About 5,000 priests were attached to the temples in the capital – a ghoulish host who wore their hair long and clotted with blood, and whose dark mantles were edged with motifs of skulls and entrails. The plumed warriors who carved out the Aztec Empire were also engaged in the sacred task of sacrifice: warfare was inseparable from religion, and the Aztecs went to war to capture victims for blood sacrifice.

When the great *teocalli* was dedicated in 1487, Tenochtitlán's monarch lined up more than 20,000 prisoners of war and had them laid one by one across the sacrificial altar. Their hearts were cut out and displayed to the sun, then dropped into a vessel held by a reclining stone idol. The bodies of the victims were then cast down the temple stairway.

Such gruesome spectacles were thought to be essential to the stability of the universe, for in the spilling of blood the Aztecs attuned themselves to the mysterious rhythms of the cosmos – to the moving of the planets, the cycles of night and day, sun

RITUAL KNIFE The handle of a sacrificial knife depicts a warrior wearing an eagle helmet. It may commemorate the very warriors the knife was used to sacrifice as they winged their way to the heavens.

and rain. The prospect of a prolonged peace was disquieting to them; they believed that it might provoke a collapse of the world order. Stocking up the skull rack inside the sacred precinct was a guarantee against such a catastrophe.

PASTIMES OF THE RICH AND NOBLE

The sacred centre also contained courts for *ollama* – a cross between volleyball and the Basque game of pelota. Variations had been played in Central America since Olmec times. Among the Aztecs, only noblemen took part. The game was played on an I-shaped court with a stone ring sticking out, like an ear, on each side. Players had to pass a hard rubber ball through the ring using their elbows, hips, or legs. Huge sums were gambled on the games – one observer speaks of wagers including 'gold, turquoise, slaves, rich mantles, even cornfields and houses'.

Cortés played Montezuma at a board game in Tenochtitlán. The game resembled modern ludo, and was usually played using beans as counters. The object was to complete the course by returning to 'home'. Cortés played the game in grand style inside the emperor's palace, using gold pieces instead of beans.

The palace stood on the eastern side of the main square, its buildings grouped around courtyards and gardens. They included government offices of such size and splendour that the Spaniards were dumbstruck. Upper floors contained the apartments of the emperor and his most distinguished guests, and rooms below housed the Supreme Courts, the Grand Council, and the Public Treasury, piled high with exotic merchandise. Also on the ground floor were the accountants' offices, music rooms, and goldsmiths' workshops. The gardens were

GRUESOME MONUMENT The base of the *tzompantli* – the great stone rack on which the heads of the city's sacrificial victims were displayed – was decorated with serried ranks of macabre, sculpted skulls.

bright with flowers, and ducks and swans swam on huge artificial ponds. Cortés was impressed; he wrote to his sovereign to say that Montezuma's palace was so marvellous that there was 'nothing to equal it in Spain'.

THE REWARDS OF TRADE

The houses of the Aztec nobles were extremely luxurious as well. And the homes of the *pochteca*, or rich merchants, must also have been grand enough to satisfy the elite, for the wealthiest traders hosted opulent banquets and evenings of singing and dancing, to which the nobles were invited.

Three sources contributed to the prosperity of the Aztec capital: the local small traders who dealt in agricultural produce or craftwork; the rich merchants, who organized trading expeditions to and from other lands in Central America; and the tribute system, which ensured a constant flow of raw materials, fabrics, jade, and precious metals.

According to Cortés, many squares in Tenochtitlán held markets where these goods were traded. Eyewitnesses were unanimous in their admiration of the enormous market at Tlatelolco, north of the city. Every day, between 20,000 and 25,000 people crowded into the immense market square, which was surrounded by arcades and dominated by a pyramid. A larger market held every five days attracted about 50,000 people. The square was patrolled by supervisors who dealt with thefts or disputes. Three judges sat in a court at one end of the market, ready to pronounce judgment. The penalty for pilfering was death.

The Spaniards were awe-struck at the abundance of merchandise on offer. There were stalls selling foodstuffs: maize, beans, oil-seeds, pimentos, herbs, fruit, sweet potatoes, honey, salt, turkeys and small, hairless dogs bred for the table. Lake produce included shellfish and a protein-rich form of algae known as spirulina. Some stalls sold fabrics, clothing, shoes, jaguar and puma skins, and feathers. Others sold flint, obsidian, copper tools, ceramics, tobacco and pipes, wood, charcoal, and paper. There were barbers' shops, apothecaries, and food-stalls run by women.

Traders transported much of their merchandise by water. There were no wheeled vehicles for overland travel. The wheel was known in Mexico – some wheeled children's toys have been found – but it was not adapted for transport, perhaps because there were no draught animals. The conquistadores' horses caused considerable alarm among the Aztecs – one Indian described them as 'stags', noting with terror how they bellowed, sweated, and snorted: 'They make a loud noise when they run; they make a great clamour, as if stones were raining on the earth. The ground is pitted and scarred where they put down their hooves. It opens wherever their hooves touch it.'

A TIERED ADMINISTRATION

Every Central American Indian urban centre had a triple function: religious, economic, and administrative. The *euy calpixqui*, or town prefect, controlled the district authorities, who were responsible for street-cleaning. More than 1,000 people were needed to sweep and wash the streets, which were kept immaculate. Household refuse was normally buried or dumped in the marshes outside the town.

GOD OF THE WIND In records of the Aztec ritual calendar, deities such as Quetzalcoatl (left) were brought to life. Each god was associated with a particular day or period of time.

When Tenochtitlán was founded, all its drinking water was supplied by springs that gushed from the rocky soil – the briny lake water was undrinkable. But as the population grew, other sources had to be found. Aqueducts were built during the reigns of Montezuma I (1440–69) and Ahuitzotl (1486–1502) to transport water from outside the city precincts. As a lakeside city, Tenochtitlán was vulnerable to flooding during the rainy season. Montezuma I ordered the building of a dam 16km (10 miles) long to protect the city, but in 1499 great floods from the west caused serious damage.

In the historical manuscripts which record all of these exceptional events, there is no mention of any epidemics. The high levels of personal hygiene among the Aztec capital's inhabitants may account for their healthiness before the arrival of the Europeans.

THE PATTERN OF THE DAYS

The daily round in Tenochtitlán began at dawn. The courts, for example, started their sessions at sunrise. There were no clocks or chiming bells in ancient Mexico, but at the top of the city temples, from the places where the priests observed the sky, the raucous rattle of seashells along with the harsh beat of the *teponaztli* (wooden gongs) resounded at regular intervals to mark the rhythms of the day and night.

The day's meals consisted of a light snack in the morning, then a more substantial meal at midday, followed by a short siesta. People ate another light snack at dusk. The city was lit from sunset by torches of resinous wood, or sometimes by burning braziers set at the foot of the pyramids. Night-time rituals and dances took place in front of the palace, and banquets and evening entertainment continued until the dawn. Important meetings traditionally took place at night – a custom that persists in Mexico's Indian communities.

Throughout the night, the priest-astronomers followed the movements of the heavenly bodies, until the return of the sun. As well as the solar year of 365 days, the Aztecs used a calendar based on a 260-day cycle for religious purposes. Nobody knows for sure how the Aztec months corresponded to those of the modern Western calendar. But the rituals and festivities of each month are known. These spilled out all over the city; processions, dancing, singing, and real or simulated combat, all took place in the streets and squares. During the month of Panquetzaliztli (the feast of the flags), there was a procession for the god Paynal, companion to Huitzilopochtli. The month of Tlaxochimaco (the birth of flowers) was marked by flower parades, and that of Atemoztle (the fall of the waters) brought traditional battles in which young nobles, students of the *calmecacs* (schools for nobles), fought youths from the *telpochcalli* (the school for the sons of tradesmen).

Sometimes the emperor presided over the distribution of provisions to the townspeople; sometimes he took part in great dances with young warriors and courtesans. He also found time to present arms and shields to distinguished soldiers. Episodes such as the carnival of the month of Tititl (severe weather), and macabre dances such as that of the priests clothed in human skin during the month of Tlacaxipeuliiztli (bones of men), succeeded each other without interruption.

FROM SPLENDOUR TO RUINS

Tenochtitlán was a splendid city by any standards when the Spaniards first entered it. Yet within two years it had been obliterated from the face of the earth. What went wrong? For a while after the Spaniards arrived in Montezuma's capital, all went moderately well. A strange sort of understanding seemed to develop between Cortés and Montezuma, and for many months the Spaniards wandered freely through the capital, marvelling at its wonders.

But while Cortés was away from the capital, the Aztecs rose against the brutal actions of his deputy, Alvarado, and sparked an uprising. Cortés, on his return, forced Montezuma to speak to the people, and in doing so the emperor lost face – the magic surrounding the position of the god-king had been destroyed. Montezuma was stoned, and died a few days later. Cortés and his soldiers seized whatever gold and jewels they could lay their hands on and fled the city by night. Some of them were so overburdened with loot that they fell into the canals and were drowned. Even so, they had to leave more than they could take.

> *Tenochtitlán was a splendid city ... when the Spaniards first entered it. Yet within two years it had been obliterated from the face of the earth.*

The Spaniards and their allies travelled for six days, harassed every step of the way, until they reached the friendly territory of Tlaxcala, 50km (31 miles) away. There they halted.

Six months later, with the help of reinforcements from the coast and a large Tlaxcalan army, Cortés fought his way back to Tenochtitlán. He ordered the building of 13 small boats which were carried over the mountains for use on Lake Texcoco. When he reached the gates of the city, Cortés cut off much of its fresh water supplies. A bitter struggle followed. The boats played a successful role in the assault, but victory – and the end of the Aztec Empire – came only after Cortés demolished the city. Of the treasure that the Spaniards had left behind, there was no trace. Perhaps it now lies buried beneath Mexico City.

THE FACE OF A GOD
A human skull overlaid with a turquoise and lignite mosaic, represents Tezcatlipoca, a deity particularly associated with royalty.

Glossary

Words in UPPER CASE refer to other entries in the glossary.

accelerator mass spectrometer (AMS) A device used to identify and count particles of different atomic mass. It is used in CARBON DATING to measure the relative proportions of carbon 14 to carbon 12 and carbon 13 in a sample. Whereas conventional carbon dating using a geiger counter requires samples of *c*.1-5g in size, which may be hard to obtain, AMS needs samples of only 5-10mg.

Achaemenid Persian royal dynasty named after Achaemenes, an ancestor of Cyrus the Great (559–529 BC), the ruler who founded the Persian Empire. The last Achaemenid king, Darius III (335–330 BC), was overthrown by Alexander the Great.

agora The public square in Greek cities – equivalent to the Roman forum – where markets and meetings were held. Often the city's main temples and monuments were built around the agora.

Akkadian Empire The first Semitic empire founded by Sargon in SUMER in 2334 BC. The name comes from Sargon's capital: Akkad.

Alexander the Great Greek conqueror who destroyed the ACHAEMENID Empire of Persia, and founded the city of Alexandria in EGYPT. In 336 BC, at the age of 20, Alexander succeeded his father, Philip II, on the throne of the Greek kingdom of Macedonia; within two years he had forcibly united the warring Greek city-states. The battle of Granicus in 334 BC won him ASIA MINOR; the battle of Issus in 333 brought him Syria, Phoenicia and Egypt; and the battle of Gaugamela in 331 made him master of Persia. A mutiny in his army halted his eastward expansion in India and he returned to Babylon, where he died of fever in 323 BC, at the age of 32.

Anatolia See ASIA MINOR.

Aramaeans A Semitic people who for long wandered in the deserts of Syria and MESOPOTAMIA before founding minor states in Syria around 1000 BC. The most powerful of these was the kingdom of Damascus. In northern Syria, they set up small states known as Syro-Hittite states. Their language, Aramaic, is the language that Christ spoke. It was adopted everywhere in the Middle East, even after the Aramaean kingdoms themselves were conquered by the ASSYRIANS in the 8th century BC.

Asia Minor The Asian part of Turkey, on the peninsula between the Black Sea (to the north), the Mediterranean (to the south), and the Aegean (to the west). In the Middle BRONZE AGE, most of Asia Minor was occupied by the HITTITES. After their empire collapsed around 1180 BC, Asia Minor was overrun by neighbouring peoples. From the 6th century BC Asia Minor was dominated by the ACHAEMENID Empire; this was finally destroyed in 334–333 BC by ALEXANDER THE GREAT. Asia Minor later became part of the Roman Empire.

Assyrians The people of northern MESOPOTAMIA, whose homeland was centred on the city of Ashur. They enjoyed a brief period of expansion under Shamshi-Adad in the 18th century BC when their conquests included Mari. Defeating the MITANNI around 1350 BC, they became a major power controlling an area as far west as Carchemish but decline set in around 1100 BC. From 930 BC, they again began to expand, eventually establishing an empire that encompassed EGYPT, the Levant, Mesopotamia and ELAM. After the death of Assurbanipal the empire rapidly collapsed and Nineveh was sacked by the MEDES and Babylonians in 612 BC.

Aztecs An Indian tribe who probably came originally from northern Mexico. The Aztecs migrated south and in the 13th century AD they settled on the central Mexican plateau, then occupied by the TOLTECS and Mixtecs. In about 1345 they founded Tenochtitlán, the future Mexico City, on an island in Lake Texcoco.

Baal A major god in the Levant, son of El, the chief Phoenician deity. Baal was particularly associated with agriculture, thunder and rain. In his guise as Baal Hammon he was the supreme deity of the Carthaginians.

Babylonia The region of southern MESOPOTAMIA. The northern part of the region, with its capital at Babylon, rose to prominence under Hammurabi in the early 2nd millennium BC with the decline of its southern part, SUMER. Frequently in conflict with its neighbour, Assyria, Babylon gained the upper hand from 614 BC. The Neo-Babylonian Empire endured until conquered by Cyrus II of Persia in 539 BC.

ballgame Played throughout Mesoamerica, the ritual ballgame was already established in OLMEC times (early 1st millennium BC). It took various forms among the different cultures, but was generally played by two teams of well-protected players who had to manipulate the ball with their shoulders, elbows, or hips within a rectangular or I-shaped ballcourt with raised sides. In some versions, an outright win was achieved by propelling the ball through a ring in the centre of each of the side walls of the court. The game had a ritual significance and was often associated with human sacrifice: in some versions the entire losing team would be executed.

bodhisattva Buddhist equivalent of a Christian saint. In Buddhist belief, a bodhisattva is someone who has achieved true enlightenment but who denies himself the release of oblivion, or nirvana, in order to help other people find salvation.

bog bodies Well preserved human corpses periodically discovered in the bogs of northern Europe. The majority were sacrificed during the IRON AGE for religious reasons; often several means of execution had been used on a single individual. Many were sacrificed naked and their hands showed they had been exempt from manual labour.

Bronze Age The historical period characterized by the manufacture of bronze, an alloy of tin and copper, which revolutionized economic conditions and superseded the use of stone weapons and tools. Its onset occurred at different times in different areas but it was widely succeeded by an age in which iron was the dominant metal used for tools and weapons. Not all regions passed through a Bronze Age, since copper and tin ores were not universally available.

Canaanites Semitic inhabitants of Canaan, the biblical land of milk and honey to which Moses led the Israelites from EGYPT. The area covers much of present-day Israel, Lebanon and the coastal regions of Syria. The PHOENICIANS were a branch of the Canaanites.

carbon dating Carbon 14, the radioactive isotope of carbon, is absorbed by all living things but decays at a known rate after their death. Thus ancient organic material, such as wood and bone, can be directly dated by measuring the amount of carbon 14 (radiocarbon) that still remains, relative to the constant amount of the stable isotopes, carbon 12 and carbon 13. Carbon dating made it possible to date prehistoric material and thereby revolutionized our understanding of the past, for example revealing the long history of farming and the different times at which it developed in different regions of the world.

Celts A race of people recorded by classical authors as living in Europe north of the Mediterranean countries in the 6th century BC. The Celts probably came from central Europe. Their first migrations towards the west and Britain possibly date back to about 1000 BC. Their culture was an IRON AGE one. In the 7th–6th centuries BC they settled in the Basque regions of Spain and along the Atlantic coast of France. In the 3rd century BC, Celtic invaders ransacked Greece and others went on into ASIA MINOR, where they settled in Galatae, in the north-east.

Chaldaeans People from the southern portion of the Tigris-Euphrates valley (MESOPOTAMIA), but sometimes used loosely to refer to peoples from all BABYLONIA. In 612 BC, Nebuchadnezzar II, the Babylonian king, established the New Babylonian or Chaldaean Empire, famed for its luxury and splendour. It fell to Cyrus the Great, the Persian king, in 539 BC.

Chams A South-east Asian people, with an Indian culture, who lived in Kampuchea and Annam – part of present-day Vietnam – and who founded the kingdom of Champa in the 2nd century AD. It survived until the 15th century, when it was destroyed by the Vietnamese who invaded from the north. The Chams were then driven back into present-day Kampuchea and the delta of the Mekong river.

Chavín The first civilization in South America which flourished from 1200 to 200 BC. Its widespread and distinctive art style, displayed on pottery, textiles, sheet gold ornaments, and stone carvings, probably reflects shared religious beliefs. The temple complex at Chavín de Huantar, constructed around 800 BC, was a centre of pilgrimage. Its chief shrine, containing an image known as the Lanzon, was accessible only via a maze of passages, and a network of canals beneath this produced noises calculated to inspire awe in the worshipper.

cire perdue See LOST WAX.

cuneiform The name (literally, 'wedge-shaped') archaeologists give to the style of writing found on baked clay tablets in MESOPOTAMIA and throughout West Asia. This early script was developed by the Sumerians in about 3000 BC from an initial ideographic or pictorial script, and was further developed by the Akkadians and Babylonians. Scribes traced the characters on tablets of soft clay, using a small stylus with a triangular tip. The triangular impression left by the stylus gave the script its distinctive wedge-shaped appearance.

Dagon Semitic god, whose cult first appeared around 2500 BC. In Mari, where he was called 'king of the land', he was depicted as the supreme national god. His name appeared in the cults of the city of Ugarit, and he was an important figure in Phoenician legends.

Darius The name of three kings of Persia. Darius I (521–486 BC) reorganized the Persian Empire, which he extended into northern India. His expedition against Greece in 490 BC failed when the Athenians defeated his army at Marathon. The Persian Empire fell to Alexander the Great in the reign of Darius III (336–331 BC).

dendrochronology A method of dating by counting the annual growth rings in the trunks of trees. These vary in width from year to year, depending on environmental conditions at the time, and long sequences can be built up by overlapping the sequence of rings from a number of trees (living and dead) of different ages. Ancient trees and timbers used in creating long continuous tree-ring records include oaks preserved in northern European bogs and wood used in early buildings in the south-western USA. Computers are used to match wood found in archaeological contexts against the known tree-ring sequence in the region.

Dilmun A major trading partner of SUMER, identified as the island of Bahrein. Dilmun acted as a trade entrepot for goods from MAGAN and MELUHHA and produced pearls and dates for export. Good supplies of fresh water made it a natural port of call for ships travelling through the Persian Gulf. In Mesopotamian legend it was the home of Ziusudra (also known as Atraharsis or Ut-Napishtim), the survivor of the great Deluge, visited there by Gilgamesh.

Egypt The region of the Nile Delta was called Lower Egypt; Upper Egypt extended from about where Cairo is now situated south to the region of the modern Aswan High Dam. The two were separate kingdoms until they were united in about 3200 BC by a king called Menes. Menes was the first in a long line of kings whose names were preserved in temple records.

Elam The present-day region of Khuzistan on the Iran-Iraq border. The Elamite kingdom was one of the earliest civilizations to develop a written language. Elamite culture reached its peak between 1300 and 1100 BC when the Elamites conquered and sacked the glittering city of Babylon. But Elam later declined in power, becoming part of the Persian kingdom of Anshan in the 7th century BC.

Essenes One of four ancient religious sects of the Jews, along with the Sadducees, the Pharisees, and the Zealots. The Essenes – whose name means 'pious ones' – lived in strictly regulated communities, fasting and praying in the pursuit of holiness, much like early Christian monks. The sect is thought to have had one of its major monasteries at Qumran on the shores of the Dead Sea, where the first of the Dead Sea Scrolls were found in 1947.

Gaul The region inhabited in Roman times by the CELTIC Galli, roughly the area of modern France.

geophysical survey A battery of devices are used by archaeologists to locate buried features and objects by measuring variations in the electrical resistance or magnetism of the soil. Buried ditches and pits show up as areas of low electrical resistance, whereas high readings indicate buried walls, floors, and roads. Conversely, buried structures register as areas of low magnetism whereas pits and ditches containing organic material have higher magnetic susceptibility than the surrounding soil. In recent decades, sonar devices have also come into use. Some devices detect remains such as shipwrecks on the seabed; others can produce a picture of what lies within marine sediments.

Global Positioning System (GPS) A method of determining the exact position of a point on the Earth's surface by reference to the position of satellites orbiting the Earth, using special instruments. The technique has proved invaluable in underwater excavation and reconnaissance where poor visibility, water movement, and weather can all seriously hamper conventional methods of recording a position.

Gupta An Indian dynasty founded by Chandra Gupta II in AD 320. Initially ruling a small kingdom in the Ganges valley, the Guptas extended their empire into central India; it fell to the invading HUNS in the 5th and 6th century. The period of Gupta rule was regarded as India's Golden Age, when the arts and sciences flourished and Hinduism underwent a revival.

Han In 206 BC an adventurer called Han Gaozu overthrew the last Qin emperor and founded the Han dynasty, one of the most brilliant in Chinese history. It reached its zenith with the reign of Wudi (141–87 BC), who greatly extended the empire's lands and founded the Chinese civil service, or Mandarinate. Apart from the reign of a usurper, Wang Mang, in AD 8–23, the dynasty controlled China until AD 220 when it was overthrown by people from central Asia.

Hannibal Carthaginian general. A member of the prominent Barca family and son of the general Hamilcar, Hannibal (247–182 BC) was, from an early age, committed to pursuing the conflict between Carthage and Rome. Between 221 and 219 he took control of Spain and in 218 made his famous crossing of the Alps to attack the Romans from the north. After many successes, he was recalled to North Africa in 203 to face a Roman army under Scipio, who defeated him. He ended his life in exile in ANATOLIA.

Hellenistic The term used to describe Greek civilization at the time when it was partly influenced by Middle Eastern cultures. This influence was a result of the conquests of ALEXANDER THE GREAT, who brought EGYPT and large parts of Asia under the control of Greece. The Hellenistic period lasted from the 3rd to the 1st century BC.

hieroglyphs Originally the signs used in Egyptian religious writing. The word comes from two Greek terms meaning 'sacred carving', and has now come to mean the signs in any type of ideographic or pictorial script.

Hittites An Indo-European people who settled in ASIA MINOR around 2000 BC. In the 18th century BC, the Hittites established an empire in central Anatolia in Turkey, which reached its peak in the 14th and 13th centuries. Their civilization was destroyed by the SEA PEOPLES at the beginning of the 12th century BC.

huaca Peruvian name for a sacred place or object, now particularly applied to the huge brick-built burial mounds and temple platforms of the MOCHE and other Andean civilizations. Organized looters of ancient sites, whose attentions are directed particularly towards such mounds, are known as *huaqueros*.

Huari A militaristic Andean empire which flourished in AD 600–1000, named after its capital city. It was contemporary with TIWANAKU, and possibly closely linked with it.

Huns A people originally from Central Asia. One branch spread into Europe in the 5th century AD and settled in the plains of Pannonia – part of present-day Hungary. From there, they harassed other regions of Europe. A devastating coalition of Huns and other barbarian groups under the powerful leadership of Attila the Hun collapsed in 453 after his death. In the 5th century AD another branch, the White, or Hepthalite, Huns, settled in the north of what is now Afghanistan, and from that base conquered the Indus valley and part of India.

Hurrians A nation that established itself in north-western MESOPOTAMIA some time before 2000 BC. Around 1500 BC, the Mitanni tribe, probably from the Caucasus, brought new class structures to the Hurrians, including a tradition of glorifying warriors. Together they founded a new kingdom. In the 15th century BC they fought a series of wars against the HITTITES and Egyptians. The Hurrians disappeared from history in the 13th century BC under attacks from the Hittites and ASSYRIANS.

iceman A remarkably preserved frozen body discovered by hikers in the Alps in 1991, and nicknamed Otzi. He was dressed in a leather cap, coat, loincloth, leggings, and shoes, covered by a cape of grass or reeds. With him were a wooden bow and arrows, a backpack of fur on a wooden frame, several containers made of birch bark, a flint knife and a copper axe with a wooden handle. CARBON DATING of his body, the tools made of organic material and the grass with which he had stuffed his shoes to keep out the cold revealed that he had lived around 3300 BC. Much interesting information about the period has been discovered from analysis of his body, clothing, and equipment. The latest twist in the story is the discovery that he was the victim not of the weather but of an enemy.

Inanna See ISHTAR

Inca A word describing both the sovereign of the Inca Empire and its people. The home of the Incas was the Cuzco region in Peru and the area around Lake Titicaca, where their civilization was established around the 12th century AD. In the second half of the 15th century the Inca Empire extended rapidly along most of the length of the Andes, from the north of Chile to the Equator. It collapsed in AD 1532 after the arrival of Spanish conquistadores under Francisco Pizarro.

Iron Age Iron was first widely used in the Middle East towards the end of the 2nd millennium BC. From there, it spread rapidly into Europe, generally replacing bronze for tools and weapons by the 6th century BC. By 1000 BC, iron-working was developing over much of India and by 500 BC had begun in West Africa. Around 650 BC, iron-working was introduced into China, where casting rapidly developed.

Ishtar Principal female deity of the Akkadians, Babylonians and ASSYRIANS. From about 2500 BC she appeared as the protector of Sargon, founder of the Akkadian Empire. Originally she was the goddess of the planet later known as Venus, the daughter of the moon god Sin, and sister of the sun god SHAMASH. She was the goddess of love and fertility and was known to the Sumerians as Inanna.

Isis Egyptian goddess, wife of OSIRIS and the mother of Horus. She was regarded as a mother-goddess, the source of life. In Roman times, her cult quickly spread across the empire. Scores of temples were built in her honour, and her initiates believed that they would have eternal life.

jade A general name given to several types of exceptionally hard and attractive stone, including nephrite and jadeite. It was highly prized by many cultures, including the Chinese, the Maori, and the peoples of Mesoamerica and West Asia, for making ornaments and prestige weapons.

Jupiter Supreme god of the Romans, equivalent to the Greeks' Zeus, and also known as Jove. He was the god of the heavens and also the universal father. His principal shrine, which he shared with his wife Juno and their daughter Minerva, goddess of wisdom, was on the summit of the Capitol, one of the seven hills of Rome.

Kas Earliest known shipwreck. The ship, probably from a Canaanite home port, was wrecked off the Anatolian coast near Kas (Uluburun) around 1350 BC. Its destination may have been a Mycenaean town. Its main cargo was copper from Cyprus; other valuable items included tin ingots, for alloying with the copper to make bronze, blue glass ingots and terebinth, an aromatic resin used by the Mycenaeans in making perfume. The wreck also held the personal property of the crew; these included a Canaanite goddess figurine.

Kassites A people probably of Caucasian origin who settled in the Zagros mountains, in the west of Iran, some time after 2000 BC. About 1595 BC, after a raid by the HITTITES on Babylon, the Kassites took advantage of the disorder to establish a dynasty in BABYLONIA. They were overthrown in 1157 BC by the people of ELAM.

Khmers The people of Kampuchea (formerly Cambodia). Between the 1st and 6th centuries AD they formed two states – Chenla and Funan – but the two kingdoms were later united under Chenla. After a period of disorder, Jayavarman II (AD 790–835) restored unity and set up what was to become the Khmer Empire. The empire disappeared under the onslaughts of the Thais in the 15th century.

kiva A circular underground room in a Pueblo Indian village, used both as a shrine and for councils.

kurgan A stone-lined tomb in a burial mound or TUMULUS. Kurgans are found in southern Siberia and across the steppes of Russia. Many are attributed to the SCYTHIANS.

Kushans A branch of the Yuezhi nomads who settled in present-day Afghanistan after being driven out of the eastern steppes in 165 BC. The Kushan Empire, established in the 1st century AD, included parts of Afghanistan and much of northern India. The empire reached its peak in the 2nd century AD under the Buddhist emperor Kanishka.

lapis lazuli An intensely blue stone which in the ancient world came only from mines near Badakhshan in Afghanistan. It was widely used, especially by Mesopotamian and Egyptian goldsmiths.

lost wax A method of casting objects in copper or bronze. Wax was modelled into the desired shape, then coated in clay. The clay mould was fired and the wax ran out. The molten metal was poured into the clay mould, taking on the shape of the original wax model. The mould was broken to remove the object.

Magadha One of the 16 Mahajanapadas (great states) in northern India in the 6th century BC, Magadha commanded a strategically important position in the Ganges valley and was rich in agricultural land, forests and minerals. From the late 6th century it grew at the expense of its neighbours, through warfare, diplomacy, and dynastic marriages. The MAURYAN dynasty brought it to its peak in the 4th–3rd century BC, when the empire covered most of the subcontinent.

Magan One of the three foreign lands with which SUMER traded through the Persian Gulf in the 3rd millennium BC. Magan has now been identified as the Oman peninsula, an area rich in copper ore. Magan may also have included the Makran coastal region opposite Oman at the mouth of the Gulf.

magnetite A form of iron ore widely traded in Mesoamerica and used to make mirrors which were valued prestige objects, probably with a ritual significance.

Marduk Principal god of the Babylonians, son of Enki, and patron deity of the city of Babylon. His rise to pre-eminence in the pantheon mirrored the rise of Babylon as principal city of Babylonia from the 18th century BC. The great shrine Esagil in Babylon was dedicated to Marduk, as was the ziggurat now known as the 'Tower of Babel'.

Massilia A colony established by the Greek city of Phocaea around 600 BC, near the mouth of the river Rhone where Marseille now stands. It was a major centre for trade between the Mediterranean world and the chiefdoms of Celtic Europe in the 6th and 5th centuries BC, exchanging Greek wine and luxury goods for metal ore and other raw materials and for slaves.

Mauryan Dynasty founded by Chandragupta who established the first great Índian empire around 321 BC. The dynasty ended in 185 BC with the reign of Brihadratha, assassinated by one of his officers.

Medes Indo-European people who settled in northern and western Iran. The Medes set up their capital in about 1000 BC at Ecbatana, modern Hamadan, south-west of Tehran. Allied with the CHALDAEANS, they took Nineveh in 612 BC, destroyed the Assyrian Empire and established an empire covering part of Iran, northern MESOPOTAMIA and eastern Anatolia in Turkey. Their ruler, Astyages (585–550 BC), was overthrown by his vassal Cyrus, who founded the ACHAEMENID Empire of Persia. The new sovereigns adopted the Medes' court ceremonial, and the Medes were deemed equals of the Persians in social rank.

Meluhha A trading partner known from Sumerian texts, now identified as the Indus civilization.

Mesolithic The period between the PALAEOLITHIC and NEOLITHIC eras of the Stone Age in some parts of the world. It is characterized by the appearance of small flint cutting tools. Mesolithic cultures were hunter-gatherers.

Mesopotamia The name applied rather generally to the area of south-west Asia between the Armenian mountains in the north, the Persian Gulf in the south, the plateau of Iran in the east, and the Syrian Desert in the west, closely corresponding to modern Iraq. The more specific area is that between the Tigris and the Euphrates rivers: the name is derived from the Greek, and means 'between the rivers'.

Middle Kingdom A period of Egyptian history from the 11th to the 13th Dynasty (c.2040–c.1670 BC).

Mitanni See HURRIANS.

Mithra Persian sun god, also worshipped in India. In Iran, Mithra was the god of oaths and truth, and judge of the dead. Later, he became popular among soldiers as an unconquerable warrior, the slayer of a mythological bull whose blood was thought to be the source of life on Earth. In this form, as a god of fertility, under the name of Mithras, his cult became widespread in the Roman Empire, particularly among the troops.

Moche Pre-Columbian culture of the Moche valley in Peru, also known as the Mochica. It developed between the 1st and 8th centuries AD and was the first great civilization in the northern part of Peru.

Montezuma European version of the name of Motecuhzoma II, king of the AZTECS, who died during the Spanish occupation of Tenochtitlán in 1519-21 and who had become ruler in 1502.

Nanna Sumerian-Akkadian god of the moon, and the city god of Ur.

Nazca A culture on the Andean coast which flourished between 200 BC and AD 600. Its people are best known for the enigmatic Nazca Lines, huge designs of animals, birds, and geometric shapes laid out in the Nazca desert. They also produced superb pottery, whose designs closely match those of the Nazca Lines.

Neolithic Name of the age during which the domestication of livestock, settled agriculture, carpentry, weaving, and pottery appeared. The period, whose name comes from Greek words meaning 'new stone', came after the PALAEOLITHIC, or Old Stone Age, or in some areas after the MESOLITHIC or Middle Stone Age. It began in the Middle East between about 8000 and 7000 BC and at different times elsewhere.

New Kingdom Period of Egyptian history covering the 18th, 19th, and 20th dynasties. It started in about 1567 BC with the expulsion of the Hyksos, and ended in 1085 when the high priest of Amun, Herihor, took power in Thebes. At the peak of the period, the Egyptian Empire extended from the Euphrates river to what is now the Sudan.

obsidian Volcanic glass, highly prized in the ancient world for its attractive translucent appearance and for the exceptional sharpness of tools made from it.

Old Kingdom The second stage in the unification of EGYPT (following the Early Dynastic period). The period of the Old Kingdom covers the 3rd, 4th, 5th, and 6th dynasties, and extends from about 2686 to 2181 BC. This was the time when the great pyramids were built at Giza, near Memphis, then the centre of the Egyptian Empire.

Olmec The first culture of Mexico to establish a highly developed civilization, around 1200 BC. It was based on the Caribbean coast of southern Mexico, but extended to the Pacific. It laid the foundations of all later civilizations of Mesoamerica but was in decline by 300 BC.

Osiris Egyptian god, husband of ISIS, one of the important deities in HELLENISTIC times, and father of Horus.

Palaeolithic The Old Stone Age, the earliest period of human history. The Palaeolithic era began in Africa around 5 million years ago. It entered a new epoch over 2 million years ago, with the appearance of the first shaped pebbles, and ended around 10,000 years ago with the final retreat of the last glaciation and the development in some regions of settled agriculture. Modern humans (Homo sapiens) evolved in Africa by about 120,000 years ago and are believed by most scholars to have subsequently spread to Asia, Australia, and Europe. Around 40,000 years ago many revolutionary new developments took place: modern humans had virtually replaced all other species of human; they had fully developed spoken language, made sophisticated stone tools and practised many of the activities which we associate with being human, such as burial and art.

papyrus Fibrous plant originally from the marshes of the Nile Delta. Pieces from the inside of the plant's stems were glued together to form paper-like sheets which were used throughout the ancient world. The earliest examples date from 3300 BC.

Paracas Culture which flourished in the late centuries BC on the Peruvian coast. It is particularly noted for its fine textiles, used to wrap the bodies of the dead.

Parthians A people who settled to the east of the Caspian Sea in the 3rd century BC. One of their princes, Arsaces, established a kingdom there and founded the Arsacid dynasty. Arsaces and his successors conquered most of Iran and captured MESOPOTAMIA from the SELEUCID kings of Syria. The Parthian kingdom was overthrown by the Sassanians about AD 225.

Phoenicians Semitic people who were related to the CANAANITES. In the 1st millennium BC, the Phoenicians established a trading empire throughout the Mediterranean from their cities of Tyre, Sidon, and Byblos. They also founded colonies in Africa and explored the Atlantic.

prehistory The period of the human past for which no written records exist.

protohistory The history of civilizations which had no writing (or whose writing has not yet been deciphered) but which are known from the written documents of contemporary cultures.

Qin One of the Chinese Warring States of the ZHOU period. It gradually gained ascendancy over the others, and finally united China under the short-lived but highly influential Qin dynasty, which lasted from 221 to 206 BC.

Ra Egyptian sun god. He was thought to cross the sky in his boat during the day, and cross the underworld at night. According to Egyptian legend, he was the father of all the gods, the ruler of gods and men. Under the 5th Dynasty, the pharaohs took the title Son of Ra.

radiometric dating techniques Many dating techniques (of which CARBON DATING is the best known) rely on the decay of radioactive elements or isotopes, such as uranium and potassium-40. Generally, they are used to date deposits in (or between) which the fossils and stone tools of our early ancestors are preserved. Others are more widely applicable; for instance, fission-track dating can date volcanic rocks up to 2.5 billion years old, and also glass and pottery glazes that are 2000 years old.

Scythians Nomadic people from central Asia, who are first noted in the 13th century BC in southern Russia. In the 7th century they pillaged part of Assyria and Iran. In the 5th century, the Greek historian Herodotus reported them in the Danube region. They disappeared about the time of the birth of Christ when they were absorbed by the Sarmatians, people from the Caucasus and southern Russia.

seal A stamp of authority or identity, particularly in MESOPOTAMIA. Seals were being used in West Asia from around 7000 BC to mark designs on textiles and as a stamp of identity impressed on the clay used to fasten containers. By the 3rd millennium BC, several types of seal existed. The people of DILMUN used flat seals,

shaped like buttons, with engraving on one face. The people of the Indus civilization used rectangular steatite seals engraved with a design, usually of an animal, and a short inscription. Cylinder seals, the size of a finger, were made from various stones and carved with designs and writing. They were used in Mesopotamia between 4000 and 3000 BC and later in Syria, ASIA MINOR, and Iran.

Sea Peoples Collective term for sea-borne raiders and settlers who upset the balance of power in the Middle East around 1200 BC. Their identity and origins are uncertain, but their encroachments into other lands occurred over a very large area. They were probably involved in the destruction of the HITTITE Empire, and invaded eastern Anatolia, Syria, Palestine, and Cyprus. Their assaults also contributed to the decline of the Egyptian Empire.

Seleucid A dynasty of Greek Macedonian origin, the Seleucids ruled Syria and part of western Asia. Seleucus Nicator, one of Alexander the Great's generals, founded the dynasty in 312 BC. It ended in 63 BC, when the Roman general Pompey made Syria a Roman province.

Semitic languages A family of languages spoken in much of the Middle East and in north-east Africa. Their speakers are known as Semitic peoples. There were three branches; the eastern one was Akkadian; the southern covered Arabia and Ethiopia and now includes Arabic; while the north-western branch included Amorite, Canaanite, Ugaritic, Phoenician, Hebrew, and Aramaic.

Seven Wonders of the World The seven structures considered to be the most awe-inspiring in the ancient world. They were mentioned in an epigram by the poet Antipater, who lived in Alexandria in the mid-2nd century BC, but it is believed that the list was compiled much earlier. Although the list varies among later writers, it generally consists of the Pyramids of EGYPT, the Hanging Gardens of Babylon, the Statue of Zeus at Olympia, the Temple of Artemis at Ephesus in ASIA MINOR, the Colossus of Rhodes in Greece, the Mausoleum of Halicarnassus in Asia Minor, and the Pharos (or lighthouse) of Alexandria.

Shamash The MESOPOTAMIAN god of the sun and of justice.

Shang The first historical dynasty of Chinese kings. According to tradition, they succeeded the legendary Xia around 1700 BC and were deposed by the ZHOU in 1027 BC. They repeatedly shifted their capital city; of those known from tradition, the capitals at Zheng Zhou and Anyang have been identified and excavated. Writing on oracle bones was developed under the Shang, and bronze casting reached great technological and artistic heights.

Shiva One of the three great Hindu gods of India, along with Brahma and Vishnu. Shiva, represented with three faces, constitutes the union of these deities into one whole. In Hindu belief, Shiva is both the creator and the destroyer of all life. He also embodies the reproductive power of nature, symbolized by his attributes, the sacred lingam, or phallus, and the bull Nandi. Shiva is often shown with four arms and he is represented dancing the tandava, a cosmic dance which expresses the cycle of life and death. It is likely that the worship goes back at least to the time of the Indus civilization.

Silk Road A series of trade routes skirting the Taklimakan Desert of Central Asia and passing through a number of oasis towns. These ran from China to join longer established routes to the west. Silk was the main commodity carried from east to west. The Chinese developed the Silk Road after Zhang Xian, an emissary of the HAN emperor Wudi, returned from a pioneering expedition to the west with news of the riches to be found there.

small find An object found in an excavation or survey that is of sufficient significance to merit an individual record. This includes noting its find spot within an excavation in three dimensions. It contrasts with the treatment of ordinary finds, whose context is recorded as a particular layer, structure, or feature.

spondylus shell A shell with an attractive pink interior, spondylus have been valued both as whole shells and as a material for making ornaments and jewellery. They were widely traded by cultures in the Old and New World alike.

stele An inscribed monolith, often erected to record the deeds of kings or other major events within a state.

Stone Age See MESOLITHIC, PALAEOLITHIC and NEOLITHIC.

stratigraphy In archaeological usage, the superimposed layers that have accumulated in succession on an archaeological site and which provide a relative chronology for activities there. These layers are crosscut by features like pits, graves and ditches that are dug into them. Layers are interrupted or separated horizontally by standing features (structures) such as walls.

stupa Buddhist monument or shrine, originally a mound containing the ashes of the venerated holy men. Typically it consists of a dome set on a square base with a pole and umbrellas (often in the form of a spire) rising from it. In Buddhist belief the dome symbolizes the upturned begging bowl of a monk, while the pole represents the World Axis and the umbrellas are a symbol of royalty, denoting honoured status. The larger stupas in India are reputed to contain some of the ashes of the Buddha.

Sumer The southernmost part of MESOPOTAMIA. The Sumerians' civilization dominated Mesopotamia from around 5000 BC. It produced the oldest-known script and the world's first cities by 3000 BC. Around 2334 BC, Sargon of Akkad, to the north of Sumer, united southern Mesopotamia, but Sumer regained control under the 3rd dynasty of Ur in 2113 BC. Sumer lost its dominant position around 2000 BC when Ur was sacked by the Elamites and the region was beginning to suffer environmental decline; by 1800 BC, the centre of power had shifted north to Babylon.

thermoluminescence (T-L) A dating technique that has the great advantage that it can be used to date pottery, the material most commonly found in archaeological contexts of the past 10,000 years. Radiation from commonly occurring radioactive elements strips electrons from atoms in the minerals included in the pottery. When a sample of the pottery is heated, these pop back into place, emitting light whose intensity is proportional to the age of the pottery. Related techniques involving trapped electrons include optical luminescence dating, used on sedimentary deposits, and electron spin resonance dating (ESR), which can date tooth enamel.

Tiwanaku South American city, centre of a state closely allied to HUARI, which flourished around AD 600–1000. Situated on the southern shore of Lake Titicaca, Tiwanaku was a major religious centre with temples, plazas, and a monumental arch known as the Gateway of the Sun. It also boasted many fine sculptures.

Toltecs Indian people which settled in the northern part of Mexico between the 10th and 12th centuries AD. They established an empire in central Mexico.

tumulus An artificial mound, usually one covering a tomb. The word comes from the Latin for a hill.

Yorubas People of south-western Nigeria. They established the Ife culture, which flourished about the 12th to 15th centuries AD.

Zhou Early Chinese royal dynasty which deposed the SHANG in 1027 BC. The dynasty, while remaining nominally the rulers of northern China, gradually lost control and the country disintegrated into a collection of warring states, from among which the QIN emerged to unify China in 221 BC.

ziggurat Multistorey temple tower of ancient MESOPOTAMIA. Shrines to the gods were built on their summits. Although the architectural form had been evolving for many centuries, the first true ziggurats were constructed by Ur-Nammu, first king of the 3rd dynasty of Ur, around 2100 BC.

Index

Page numbers in **bold** refer to main entries, those in *italics* to captions and/or illustrations only.

Acknowledgments

The position of photographs and illustrations on each page is indicated by letters: T=top; B=bottom; L=left; R=right.

Cover: Magnum Photos/Bruno Barbey, T; Bridgeman Art Library, B; Musée du Louvre, ML; Oriental Museum, Durham University, R.

1-2 The Art Archive/Dagli Orti. **3** AKG/ National Archaeological Museum, Athens. **4** Michael Holford/British Museum,T; Bridgeman Art Library/ Musée du Louvre, M; © Walter Alva/ Bruning Museum, B. **5** AKG/Mossul Museum, T; British Museum, M; AKG/ Erich Lessing, B. **10** SPL/James King-Holmes,T; Network/Rapho/Xavier Desmier, M; Michael Freeman, B. **11** Frank Spooner/Gamma, L; Werner Forman Archive/Idemitsu Museum of Arts, Tokyo, R; Martin Woodward, B. **12** Matthew White, T; National Geographic Image Collection/Kenneth Garrett, L, B. **13** National Geographic Image Collection/Kristof Emory, T; Jonathan Blair, M. **14** Lorraine Harrison. **15** James Mellaart. **16-17** National Geographic Image Collection/Nathan Benn. **18** Martin Woodward. **19** Matthew White, T; The Art Archive/ Dagli Orti, B. **20-21** Colin Woodman/ Mountain High (map); AKG/Museo Archeologico, Tarquinia, T. **20** The Art Archive/Mireille Vautier, B. **21** The Art Archive/Dagli Orti, B; Werner Forman Archive, TR. **22** Lorraine Harrison. **23** Bridgeman Art Library. **24** AKG/Erich Lessing/Musée du Louvre, L; Réunion des Musées Nationaux/Gerard Blot, M. **25** C.M. Dixon. **26** Network/Georg Gerster, T; Matthew White, B. **27** Robert Harding/Jennifer Fry. **28** Bridgeman Art Library, T; The Art Archive, B. **29** Bridgeman Art Library, T; AKG/Erich Lessing, B. **30** Lorraine Harrison. **31** BPK/Alfredo Dagli Orti. **32** The Art Archive. **33** Michael Holford, T; Werner Forman, B. **34-35** Trip/D. Harding. **35** Matthew White, T. **36** Robert Harding/Nigel Francis, T; Werner Forman Archive, B. **37** Scala. **38** The Art Archive. **38-39** Werner Forman Archive. **39** C.M. Dixon. **40** Lorraine Harrison. **41** Scala. **42** The Art Archive/Dagli Orti. **43** The Art Archive, T; AKG, B. **44** Matthew White. **45** Robert Harding. **46** AKG/ National Museum, Damascus. **47** The Art Archive/Dagli Orti/Aleppo Museum, Syria, T; Scala/Musée du Louvre, B. **48** Lorraine Harrison. **49** The Art Archive/Dagli Orti/National Museum, Karachi. **50-52** Robert Harding. **53** The Art Archive/Dagli Orti/ National Museum, Karachi; Bridgeman Art Library/National Museum of India. **54-55** Colin Woodman/Mountain High (map). **54** AKG, T; Martin Woodward, ML; David Lyons, MR. Matthew White, BL. **55** Robert Harding, TR; Hillprecht Collection/Friedrich Schiller University, Jena; Robert Harding, BR; AKG, BL. **56** Lorraine Harrison. **57** Michael Holford/British Museum. **58** Michael Holford/British Museum, T; Bridgeman Art Library/British Museum, B. **59** Bridgeman Art Library/British Museum, B. **60-61** Michael Holford/ British Museum. **62** Network/Georg Gerster. **62-63** Matthew White. **64** Bridgeman Art Library/Musée du Louvre. **65** British Museum. **66** Lorraine Harrison. **67** Trip/B. Turner. **68** Michael Holford. **68-69** Matthew White. **70** AKG/National Archaeological Museum, Athens. **71** Hutchison Library/Bernard Regent. **72** AKG/Archaeological Museum, Heraklion. **73** AKG/National Archaeological Museum, Athens, T; C.M. Dixon, B. **74** AKG/Archaeological Museum, Heraklion. **75** Bridgeman Art Library/Ashmolean Museum, Oxford. **76** Lorraine Harrison. **77** Sonia Halliday. **78** AKG/National Archaeological Museum, Athens. **79** Sonia Halliday. **80** Matthew White. **81** Robert Harding. **82** Michael Holford/British Museum. **83** C.M. Dixon. **84** Institute of Nautical Archaeology. **85** BPK/Archaeological Museum, Heraklion. **86** Lorraine Harrison. **87** AKG/Erich Lessing. **88** The Art Archive/Dagli Orti. **89** Network/Georg Gerster. **90** Institute of Nautical Archaeology, TL; C.M. Dixon, B. **91** The Art Archive, Dagli Orti. **92** Réunion des Musées Nationaux, TR; Michael Holford, ML; SPL/Brian Brake, BL; Werner Forman Archive, BR. **93** Michael Holford/British Museum, TR; The Art Archive/National Museum, Karachi/Dagli Orti, TL; The Art Archive, MR. Robert Harding, B. **94** Lorraine Harrison. **95** The Art Archive/Egyptian Museum, Cairo/Dagli Orti. **96** The Art Archive/Dagli Orti/Musée du Louvre. **97** Werner Forman/The Egyptian Museum, Cairo, T; Magnum Photos/ Ferdinando Scianna, B. **98-99** Michael Holford/British Museum. **100** The Art Archive/Dagli Orti. **101** AKG/Erich Lessing, T; Michael Holford/Ashmolean Museum, Oxford, B. **102** Matthew White, T; AKG/François Guenet, B. **103** AKG/Erich Lessing. **104** Lorraine Harrison. **105** Robert Harding. **106** The Art Archive. **107** Robert Harding/Robert Frerck/Odyssey. **106-107** Hutchison Library. **108** The Art Archive/Dagli Orti/Hittite Museum, Ankara. **109** The Art Archive/Dagli Orti/Hittite Museum, Ankara, T; Robert Harding/Robert Frerck/Odyssey, B. **110** Lorraine Harrison. **111** The Art Archive/Dagli Orti/Musée Cernuschi, Paris. **112** The Art Archive. **113** Robert Harding/Tom Ang, T; Werner Forman Archive/British Library, B. **114** Lorraine Harrison. **115** Michael Holford/British Museum. **116** Network/Georg Gerster. **117** Michael Holford/British Museum, B; The Art Archive/British Museum/Dagli Orti, T. **118** Michael Holford/British Museum. **119** British Museum. **120-122** Michael Holford/British Museum. **123** Werner Forman Archive/British Museum, TL; Matthew White, TR; Robert Harding, MR; Michael Holford/British Museum, BM, TR. **124** Lorraine Harrison. **125** BPK/Klaus Goken. **126** BPK/ Jurgen Liepe, T; AKG/Erich Lessing, B. **127** Network/Georg Gerster. **128** Bridgeman Art Library/Musée du Louvre, T; Michael Holford, B. **129** Bridgeman Art Library/Ashmolean Museum, Oxford. **130** Lorraine Harrison. **131-132** Scala. **133** AKG. **134** Scala. **135** The Art Archive/Dagli Orti/Archaeological Museum, Florence, T; C.M. Dixon/British Museum, B. **136** AKG/Archaeological Museum, Tarquinia, T; Michael Holford, B. **137** AKG/Musée du Louvre. **138** Lorraine Harrison. **139** Otto Braasch. **140** Matthew White. **141** AKG/Erich Lessing/Musée Departemental de l'Oise. **142** The Art Archive/ Archaeological Museum, Chatillon-sur-Seine. **143** AKG/Wurttembergisches Landesmuseum, Stuttgart. **144** Lorraine Harrison. **145** Hutchison Library/Isabella Tree. **146** Trip/Eric Smith. **147** Trip/Eric Smith, T; Trip/M. Good, B. **148** Trip/A. Gasson, T; Trip/TH-Foto Werburg, B. **150** Lorraine Harrison. **151** The Art Archive/Dagli Orti. **152-153** Sonia Halliday. **153** AKG/Erich Lessing. **154** AKG/Vatican Museums. **155** AKG/Erich Lessing. **156-157** Michael Holford. **160** The Art Archive/Hermitage Museum, St Petersburg. **161** Trip/David Pluth. **163** C.M. Dixon, L; Corbis/ Sygma, R. **164** AKG/Erich Lessing, TR; ML; SPL/Silkeborg Museum, Denmark/ Munoz-Yague, B. **164-165** DigitalVision (artworks). **165** C.M. Dixon, TR, MR; Michael Holford, L. **166** Lorraine Harrison. **167** Michael Holford/British Museum. **168** Sonia Halliday. **169** AKG/Erich Lessing. **170-171** Pavel Kostal. **171** Michael Holford/British Museum. **172** BPK, T; AKG/Erich Lessing/National Archaeological Museum, Athens, B. **173** Michael Holford/British Museum. **174** Lorraine Harrison. **175** Christine Osborne Pictures/J. Worker. **176** Trip/Dinodia. **177** AKG/Jean-Louis Nou. **178** Bridgeman Art Library/Prince of Wales Museum, Bombay. **179** AKG/Irmgard Wagner. **180** Lorraine Harrison. **181** The Art Archive/Dagli Orti. **182-183** National Geographic Society/ O. Louis Mazzatenta. **184** Network/ Georg Gerster, T; British Museum, B. **185** Trip/T. Bognar. **186** Lorraine Harrison. **187** Trip/T. Bognar. **188** Michael Holford/British Museum. **188-189** Hutchison Library. **189** AKG/ Erich Lessing. **190** Bridgeman Art Library. **191** Hutchison Library. **192** Lorraine Harrison. **193** Robert Harding/ P. Hawkins. **194** Sonia Halliday/Jane Taylor. **195** Robert Harding, L; Bridgeman Art Library/Lithograph of El Deir, Petra, after David Roberts, engraved by Louis Haghe, 1839. **196** Sonia Halliday/Jane Taylor. **197** Trip/M.Good. **198** The Art Archive/ Archaeological Museum, Lima, B; Robert Harding/Karachi Museum, R. **198-199** AKG. **199** Werner Forman Archive. **200** Lorraine Harrison. **201-202** Zev Radovan. **203** Zev Radovan, L; AKG/Louvre Museum, R. **204** Lorraine Harrison. **205** Sonia Halliday/Jane Taylor. **206-207** Robert Harding. **208** Trip/A. Blomfield. **209** Michael Holford/British Museum. **210** Lorraine Harrison. **211** BPK. **212-213** Scala. **213** C.M. Dixon. **214-215** Pavel Kostal. **214** Scala. **215** AKG/Erich Lessing, L; C.M. Dixon, R. **216** AKG/Erich Lessing. **217** C.M. Dixon, T; The Art Archive/Dagli Orti, B. **218** The Art Archive. **219** Scala. **220-221** Matthew White. **222** Lorraine Harrison. **223** Réunion des Musées Nationaux. **224** British Museum, T; Matthew White, B. **225** AKG/Musée de la Civilisation Gallo-Romaine. **226** AKG/Erich Lessing, T; Musée de la Civilisation Gallo-Romaine/Christian Thoc, B. **227** AKG. **228** Lorraine Harrison. **229** Christine Osborne Pictures. **230** AKG. **231** Network/Georg Gerster. **232-233** The Art Archive. **234** Lorraine Harrison. **235** © Walter Alva/Bruning Museum. **236** National Geographic Image Collection/Bill Ballenberg, T; Hutchison Library/Titus Moser, B. **237** © Walter Alva/Bruning Museum. **238** Matthew White, T; Werner Forman Archive/Museum fur Volkerkunde, Berlin, B. **239** Hutchison Library/H.R. Dorig. **240** Lorraine Harrison. **241** Sonia Halliday/University Library, Turkey. **242** The Art Archive/ Dagli Orti. **243-244** AKG/Erich Lessing. **245** Scala. **246** Robert Harding/Adam Woolfitt. **247** AKG, T; The Art Archive/ Dagli Orti, M. **248** Hutchison Library/ Tony Souter. **248-249** Trip/A Ghazzal. **250** Lorraine Harrison. **251** The Art Archive/Freer Gallery of Art, Washington. **252** Matthew White, T; Werner Forman Archive/Idemitsu Museum of Arts, Tokyo, B. **253** Werner Forman Archive/Eskenazi Ltd, London. **254** Werner Forman Archive/Christian Deydier, London. **254-255** Museum of Fine Arts, Boston, Special Chinese and Japanese Fund. **255** Werner Forman Archive/Yamato Bunkaken, Nara, Japan. **256** The Art Archive. **257** Werner Forman Archive/Sotheby's, London. **258** Michael Holford/British Museum, T; The Art Archive/Dagli Orti, M. **259** Michael Holford, L; AKG/Erich Lessing, R. **260** Lorraine Harrison. **261** Trip/C. Rennie. **262** Matthew White, T; Michael Holford, M. **263** Todai-ji Temple, Nara. **264** Lorraine Harrison. **265** Robert Harding/Doug Traverso. **266** The Art Archive/Dagli Orti. **266-267** Pavel Kostal. **268** Werner Forman Archive/British Museum. **269** The Art Archive/Dagli Orti, T; Michael Holford/British Museum, B. **270** Lorraine Harrison. **271** Michael Freeman. **272** Michael Freeman. **272-273** Robert Harding/Gavin Hellier, B; Michael Freeman,T. **274** Michael Freeman. **275** Network/Rapho/Louis Frederic, T. Network/Rapho/Christian Sappa, B. **276** Lorraine Harrison. **277** Hutchison Library/Jeremy Horner. **278** Michael Freeman. **278-279** Robert Harding/James Strachan. **280** Robert Harding. **280-281** Michael Freeman. **282** Lorraine Harrison. **283** Werner Forman Archive/Museum fur Volkerkunde, Berlin. **284** Werner Forman Archive/National Commission for Museums and Monuments, Lagos, T; Frank Willett, B. **285** Werner Forman Archive/British Museum. **286** Lorraine Harrison. **287** National Geographic Society/David Hiser. **288-289** Pavel Kostal. **289** Michael Freeman, T; Werner Forman Archive/Maxwell Museum of Anthropology, B. **290** Trip/M. Barlow, T; Werner Forman Archive/Maxwell Museum of Anthropology, B. **291** Trip/M. Barlow. **292** Lorraine Harrison. **293** The Art Archive/Dagli Orti. **294-295** Hutchison Library/T. Moser. **296** Scala, T; The Art Archive/Mireille Vautier/Archaeological Museum, Lima, B. **297** The Art Archive/Dagli Orti/ Museo del Oro, Lima. **298** Lorraine Harrison. **299** Michael Holford/ Anthropological Museum, Mexico City. **300-301** Pavel Kostal. **301** Werner Forman Archive/Philip Goldman, London. **302** AKG. **303** Werner Forman Archive/Museum fur Volkerkunde, Vienna. **304** Scala. **305** National Geographic Image Collection/Victor R. Boswell, T; Magnum Photos/Alex Webb, B. **306** AKG/Bibliothèque Nationale, Paris. **307** Werner Forman Archive/British Museum.

The publishers are grateful to the following for their kind permission to quote passages from the publication below:

Penguin Books Ltd from *The Letters of the Younger Pliny*, translated by Betty Radice, 1963.

Acknowledgments

Vanished Civilizations was published by the Reader's Digest Association Limited, London

First edition Copyright © 2002 The Reader's Digest Association Limited, 11 Westferry Circus, Canary Wharf, London E14 4HE

We are committed to both the quality of our products and the service we provide to our customers. We value your comments, so please feel free to contact us on 08705 113366 or via our web site at:
www.readersdigest.co.uk

If you have any comments about the content of our books, you can email us at:
gbeditorial@readersdigest.co.uk

Copyright © 2002 Reader's Digest Association Far East Limited Philippines copyright © 2002 Reader's Digest Association Far East Limited

Vanished Civilizations was edited and produced by Toucan Books Ltd, London, for the Reader's Digest Association Limited, London

Consultant
Dr Jane McIntosh

Managing editor
Andrew Kerr-Jarrett
Editor
Alison Bravington

Picture researcher
Wendy Brown
Proofreader
Ken Vickery
Indexer
Laura Hicks

Design
Bradbury and Williams

For Reader's Digest, London

Project editor
Rachel Warren Chadd
Art editor
Joanna Walker

Reader's Digest, General Books, London

Editorial director
Cortina Butler
Art director
Nick Clark
Executive editor
Julian Browne
Publishing projects manager
Alastair Holmes
Development editor
Ruth Binney
Picture resource manager
Martin Smith
Style editor
Ron Pankhurst

Book production manager
Fiona McIntosh
Pre-press accounts manager
Penny Grose
Production controller
Nikola Hughes

Origination
Colour Systems Ltd

Printing and binding
Mateu Cromo, Spain

ISBN 0 276 42658 4
BOOK CODE 400-115-01
CONCEPT CODE FR0323/G